# Restorative Justice and Practices in New Zealand

## Towards a Restorative Society

Edited by

**Gabrielle Maxwell and James H. Liu**

Institute of Policy Studies

WIPF & STOCK · Eugene, Oregon

Wipf and Stock Publishers
199 W 8th Ave, Suite 3
Eugene, OR 97401

Restorative Justice and Practices in New Zealand
Towards a Restorative Society
By Maxwell, Gabrielle M. and Liu, James H.
Copyright©2007 by Maxwell, Gabrielle M.
ISBN 13: 978-1-60899-905-7
Publication date 8/3/2010
Previously published by Institute of Policy Studies, 2007

# Contents

| | |
|---|---|
| List of Tables | v |
| List of Figures | v |
| List of Case Studies | v |
| Foreword | vii |
| Acknowledgements | ix |
| Contributors | xi |

**Part One: Restorative Justice in the New Zealand Context**

| | | |
|---|---|---|
| Introduction to Part One | | 3 |
| 1 | The Defining Features of a Restorative Justice Approach to Conflict – *Gabrielle Maxwell* | 5 |
| 2 | Social and Historical Contexts for Restorative and Retributive Justice: Te Ao Pō – Te Ao Mārama (Worlds of Dark and Light) – *James H. Liu* | 29 |

**Part Two: Restorative Practice in the Criminal Justice System**

| | | |
|---|---|---|
| Introduction to Part Two | | 43 |
| 3 | The Youth Justice System in New Zealand: Restorative Justice Delivered through the Family Group Conference – *Gabrielle Maxwell* | 45 |
| 4 | Restorative Justice in the Youth Court: A Square Peg in a Round Hole? – *Andrew J. Becroft and Rhonda Thompson* | 69 |
| 5 | Restorative Justice for Adult Offenders: Practice in New Zealand Today – *F. W. M. McElrea* | 95 |
| 6 | Diversionary Policing of Young People in New Zealand: A Restorative Approach – *Gabrielle Maxwell* | 111 |
| 7 | Restorative Policing – *Howard Broad* | 125 |
| 8 | Resolving Conflict and Restoring Relationships: Experiments in Community Justice within a New Zealand Faith-Based Prison – *Kim Workman* | 139 |

Contents

**Part Three: Restorative Practices in Civil Society**

Introduction to Part Three — 165

9 Restorative Justice in the Civil Jurisdiction – *David Hurley* — 167

10 Restorative Practices in Schools: Far-Reaching Implications – *Wendy Drewery* — 199

11 Restorative Practices in Education: The Experiences of a Group of New Zealand Schools – *Sean Buckley* — 215

12 Negotiating History: Crown Apologies in Historical Treaty of Waitangi Settlements – *Maureen Hickey* — 221

13 Saying Sorry Effectively: Government Apologies for Historical Wrongs – *Nicola White* — 235

**Part Four: Reflections on Restorative Justice**

Introduction to Part Four — 263

14 Restorative Justice Serving the Need for Justice – *A. J. W. Taylor* — 265

15 Reflections on a Social Psychology of Justice: Implications for Restorative Justice Practices – *James H. Liu and Katja Hanke* — 275

16 Justifying Restorative Justice – *Karen Baehler* — 289

**Part Five: Conclusion**

Introduction to Part Five — 303

17 Can a Restorative Approach Heal and Restore? – *Gabrielle Maxwell and James H. Liu* — 305

18 Reflections on the Spirit of Justice – *Christopher D. Marshall* — 311

19 Towards a Restorative Society – *Jonathan Boston* — 321

**References** — 327

# Tables

| | | |
|---|---|---|
| 1.1 | Key differences between conventional and restorative justice | 13 |
| 6.1 | Police responses to youth offending: comparison of police national data and research data, 1990 and 1999 | 114 |
| 6.2 | Reoffending for a sample off cases dealt with by the police in 1998 and followed up after 18 months | 116 |
| 6.3 | Nature of police diversionary plans | 117 |

# Figures

| | | |
|---|---|---|
| 3.1 | What happens at a family group conference | 55 |
| 3.2 | Rate of youth offender (aged 10–16 years) appearances per 10,000 distinct cases in the Youth Court, 1987–2001 | 59 |
| 3.3 | Number of young people receiving custodial sentences as a result of a conviction and sentence in the District Court or High Court, 1987–2001 | 59 |
| 11.1 | Shared case study values and beliefs | 216 |
| 11.2 | Shared case study elements | 217 |
| 11.3 | Shared case study benchmarks | 218 |
| 17.1 | Conclusions from the New Zealand experience | 307 |

# Case Studies

| | | |
|---|---|---|
| 9.1: | Agreement can provide unique outcomes | 174 |
| 9.2: | Outcomes from mediation may be more satisfying than those from litigation | 175 |
| 9.3: | Disputant's desired outcome is often not money | 178 |
| 9.4: | Addressing the emotional impact of conflict | 180 |
| 9.5: | 'What do you want to achieve from this process?' | 181 |
| 9.6: | (Mis)communication | 188 |

# Restorative Justice Classics Series Foreword

The phrase "restorative justice" was unknown before the 1970s. Forty years later restorative justice is a vast international movement: nearly a million pages on the Internet refer to it; Google Scholar lists 16,600 books and essays on restorative justice; many states around the world have written it into law; and more important, hundreds of thousands of people and communities have had their fear and shame transformed by encounters with and efforts of those practicing restorative justice.

Along the way, while having intentions to repair harm, restorative justice initiatives have also added to harm. The growth of this mass movement is not without missteps and failures, some very painful. If this movement is to be advanced wisely into the future, its advocates need to remember both fruitful attempts and painful ones.

The Restorative Justice Classics Series is an attempt to help create foundations and share memories for those interested in restorative justice. In a movement that grows and changes so incredibly fast and in so many diverse places, this book series creates space for cultivating restorative justice memory. Amidst the frenzy of work, growth, and missteps, this book series represents a commitment to bring back into print those restorative justice books and articles that could be considered classic. The label "classic" is used here loosely to refer to books that have shaped the restorative justice movement and whose writing continues to be worth remembering, worth sharing, and worth reconsidering amidst the changing scene. In most cases there is still a need for the content and thus a continuing demand for the books.

Books are chosen in this series because they will be of special ongoing value to practitioners and scholars of restorative justice. Wipf and Stock Publishers, at the instigation of Series Editor Ted Lewis, has set up the series in such a way that the books will stay in print and remain available. Anyone wanting to understand the origins, history, diverse practices, and spirit of restorative justice will find the series particularly helpful.

Jarem Sawatsky, Series Consultant
Canadian Mennonite University
Winnipeg, Manitoba
April 2009

*To see a complete listing of books in this series, go to www.wipfandstock.com and click on "Advanced Search" to locate the Restorative Justice Classics Series in the series box. Recommendations for further reprints in this series can be directed to Ted Lewis, Series Editor, at tedlewis@wipfandstock.com or can be made by calling 541-344-1528.*

# Foreword

I am delighted to provide a brief foreword to this book, which takes its title from an excellent conference, *Towards a Restorative Society*, that was organised in October 2005 in Wellington by the Institute of Policy Studies. The book is, of course, about restorative justice, but it takes a wider lens on what is happening in the movement than is usually taken by those like myself who have an interest in criminal justice systems.

The conference provided an opportunity for people across quite different parts of New Zealand society to contribute to a discussion about the movements in New Zealand and elsewhere intended to achieve a gentler and more inclusive society.

The restorative initiatives described in the papers begin with the restorative conferences found in the criminal justice system that have for the most part derived their inspiration from the success of the youth justice system and its family group conferences. The book then goes on to describe restorative initiatives with a much wider scope both in the justice system (policing and prisons) and in a variety of other areas where disputes need to be resolved. Perhaps the broadest of these are the restorative approaches involving all the affected parties that have been developed for resolving historic injustices.

The results of this collaboration across disciplines, functions and activities throughout this country can be seen in this excellent book, which picks up the excitement and the stimulation of the conference itself.

Some of the material is practical and operational, some is academic and thoughtful, and some is philosophical and analytical, but all chapters share a common theme: the promotion, practically and theoretically, of a movement that is exciting and dynamic, and that utilises ancient ways of participating that are still relevant to a modern liberal democratic society. All the examples described here contribute to the development of inclusive, restorative and positive ways of resolving the diversity of tensions that arise every day in a changing world where a variety of people from many backgrounds and with a diversity of values are learning to live together within a civil society.

I commend those who had the vision to hold this conference, those who funded it and those who have taken the time and had the energy to collect together these valuable contributions in the hope of assisting us all to live in a society that is truly respecting of all parts of its diversity.

Judge David Carruthers
Chairman, New Zealand Parole Board

## Acknowledgements

The editors wish to acknowledge all those who were responsible for arranging and taking part in the conference *Towards a Restorative Society* that was organised by the Institute of Policy Studies at Victoria University of Wellington in October 2005. Many of the chapters in this volume were first presented at that conference.

The conference enabled people to participate in an investigation of the ideas that have sprung from the emergence of the 'restorative justice' movement. This is a unique and diverse social movement centred on ideas of fostering more inclusive, 'just' and restorative societies both here in New Zealand and around the world. It is a movement that has already demonstrated its ability to provide the necessary momentum to change our society and to build positive human relationships in several sectors of society.

A hundred people from governmental agencies, law, academia and the non-government sector and other interested individuals gathered to share information on their involvement in restorative initiatives in New Zealand. Many of the papers from the conference have been revised for inclusion in this book. In addition, the enthusiasm, ideas, experiences and support of those who attended the conference have added immeasurably to our thinking.

Key people who contributed to the conference, but whose work is not directly represented here, include Dr Andrew Ladley, Professor Jonathan Boston, Barbara Gillespie, Jessie Williams, Rod Alley, Judge Phil Recordon, Judge David Carruthers, Professor James Ritchie, Steve Christian, Judge Carrie Wainwright and Dr Warwick Tie. Some of their original contributions are available on the Institute of Policy Studies website (http://ips.ac.nz).

Sponsorship for the conference was provided by the Department of Corrections, Ministry of Health, Ministry of Justice, Victoria Foundation and National Bank.

Those who have subsequently played a key role in the preparation of this book have been Jonathan Boston, without whose active encouragement and efforts on our behalf nothing would have happened; Maureen Revell, the administrator at the Institute of Policy Studies, who is always patient and extremely helpful; Belinda Hill, the copy editor; Sean Buckley and Jessie Williams, who have been an unfailing source of support in numerous ways; and the Ministry of Justice, Ministry of Social Development and 'G' Trust, which provided financial support to assist with the costs of publication. The Centre for Applied Cross-Cultural Research also provided critical intellectual and social support for the preparation of the book that was essential to its completion.

# Contributors

**Dr Karen Baehler** is a Senior Lecturer in public policy at the School of Government, Victoria University of Wellington, and an Adjunct Senior Lecturer at the Australia and New Zealand School of Government. Before joining Victoria University, Karen worked for 10 years in the Washington, DC, think-tank sector. In addition to conducting academic research on New Zealand's liberal egalitarian traditions and their impact on public policy, she is co-authoring a textbook on policy analysis and advising in Australasia. She holds a doctorate in policy sciences from the University of Maryland. Contact Karen at karen.baehler@vuw.ac.nz.

**His Honour Judge Andrew Becroft** was appointed Principal Youth Court Judge of New Zealand in June 2001. Andrew was born in Kuala Lumpur, Malaysia, and obtained his law degree at the University of Auckland in 1981. He practised in Auckland, where he assisted with the establishment of the Mangere Community Law Centre and worked as a criminal barrister in South Auckland until his appointment to the District Court in Wanganui in 1996. Andrew is a former council member of the Auckland District Law Society and New Zealand Law Society. He is a current editor of *Transport Law* (LexisNexis) and the patron of the New Zealand Speak Easy Association, which assists people with various forms of speech impediment. Andrew is also President of the New Zealand Tertiary Students Christian Fellowship and is a strong advocate of youth issues. Contact Andrew at Chief Judges Chambers, PO Box 10167, Wellington.

**Professor Jonathan Boston** is Professor of Public Policy and Deputy Director of the Institute of Policy Studies in the School of Government, Victoria University of Wellington. Jonathan is the author or editor of 20 books on various matters relating to New Zealand politics, public policy and public management. From 1995 to 2002, he was a member of the New Zealand Political Change Project, which explored the behavioural, institutional and policy implications of mixed-member proportional representation. During 2000 and 2001, he served as a member of the Tertiary Education Advisory Commission and, between 2002 and 2005, he helped to design, implement and evaluate the Performance-Based Research Fund in the tertiary education sector, working mainly for the Tertiary Education Commission. Contact Jonathan at jonathan.boston@vuw.ac.nz.

Contributors

**Commissioner Howard Broad** has been the Commissioner of Police since April 2006. Before his appointment, he was Assistant Commissioner responsible for planning, performance and deployment, held a secondment to the United Kingdom Home Office, and was District Commander for the Auckland City Police District. In his career, Howard has had a wide range of operational challenges, including the investigation of serious crime, governance over a busy metropolitan police district for 5 years, and protection of visiting heads of state, including the President of the United States during *APEC 99*. He has a strong developmental focus and has been involved in improving police operational practice, intelligence, planning, responses to diversity, and executive management processes. Howard holds the Diploma in New Zealand Policing and Bachelor of Laws from Victoria University of Wellington. He is a barrister and solicitor of the High Court of New Zealand. In 2002, Howard was the inaugural winner of the International Law Enforcement Award by the Society for the Policing of Cyberspace (Canada) for his work in developing a national multi-agency Internet Safety Programme. Contact Howard through the New Zealand Police (http://www.police.govt.nz).

**Sean Buckley** is a graduate in political science and international relations from Victoria University of Wellington. Since 2005, Sean has been involved in research projects at Victoria University's Institute of Policy Studies. In particular, Sean has worked closely with Dr Gabrielle Maxwell in the field of restorative justice. In 2007, Sean and Gabrielle co-authored *Respectful Schools* (Office of the Children's Commissioner/Institute of Policy Studies), a summary report on the use of restorative practices in education. Sean is involved in a restorative justice youth diversion pilot in the Kingdom of Tonga. He looks to continue focusing on the use of restorative justice as a conflict resolution tool within the Pacific region. Contact Sean at sean.buckley@vuw.ac.nz.

**Judge David Carruthers** has had a distinguished career as a District Court Judge, holding Family Court and Youth Court warrants. He piloted, in the Porirua Youth Court, an early example of a restorative approach to young offenders. More recently, he has been Principal Youth Court Judge and then Chief District Court Judge, before 'retiring' to his current position as Chair of the New Zealand Parole Board. His championship of restorative justice and his example of how to apply these principles in a court have been major factors in its effective use among the judiciary in New Zealand, and have influenced approaches in overseas countries where he has been invited to describe our system. Contact David through the New Zealand Parole Board.

# Contributors

**Dr Wendy Drewery** is an Associate Professor in the Department of Human Development and Counselling at the University of Waikato, where she teaches human development and developmental psychology. She was a member of the team that produced the first formal process for restorative conferencing in New Zealand schools, and continues to promote the development of restorative practices in schools through research, publishing and support of professionals in the field. Her research interests are in the process of respectful conversations (including classroom and disciplinary interactions in schools) and issues facing young adults. With Lise Bird Claiborne from Victoria University of Wellington she is co-author of the lifespan development text *Human Development in Aotearoa* (2004, McGraw-Hill). Contact Wendy at w.drewery@waikato.ac or through the School of Education, University of Waikato, Private Bag 3105, Hamilton.

**Katja Hanke** is a PhD candidate in the School of Psychology, Victoria University of Wellington, and is part of the postgraduate network affiliated with the Centre for Applied Cross-Cultural Research. Katja obtained a Diploma in Psychology (equivalent to a Master of Science) at Georg-August-University of Göttingen in Germany. Her main research interests are inter-group forgiveness, peace psychology and research methods. Contact Katja at katja.hanke@vuw.ac.nz.

**Maureen Hickey** is Senior Historian at the Office of Treaty Settlements, which negotiates and implements historical Treaty of Waitangi claims settlements on behalf of the Crown. In the past 7 years, she has been involved in negotiations of Crown apologies and other aspects of redress with iwi in the eastern Bay of Plenty, central North Island, Muriwhenua and the Chatham Islands. Before that, Maureen worked on the interdisciplinary Caversham Project at the University of Otago. She is a co-author (with Erik Olssen) of *Class and Occupation: The New Zealand reality* (2005, Otago University Press). Contact Maureen at maureen.hickey@justice.govt.nz.

**David Hurley** LLM, AAMINZ was a lawyer in general practice for 25 years before becoming a member of the Employment Tribunal in 1991, handling both mediations and adjudications. Under the Employment Relations Act 2000, David was appointed as a mediator. His combined experience in this field and other areas of dispute exceeds 2,500 cases. He has presented papers and published articles on mediation, and has held office in voluntary organisations, including the Outward Bound Trust of New Zealand, J. R. McKenzie Trust and

Mary Potter Hospice. He has been President of the Wellington District Law Society and has served on several law society subcommittees, including acting as inaugural co-ordinator of both the Wellington Duty Solicitor Scheme and Visiting Solicitor Scheme to Prisons. David has contributed to community law centres and the Access to Law Committee (for the Department of Justice). Contact David at david.hurley@dol.govt.nz.

**Dr James Hou-fu Liu** is Associate Professor of Psychology at Victoria University of Wellington and Deputy Director of the university's Centre for Applied Cross Cultural Research. James was born in Taiwan and grew up in the United States. He completed a doctorate in social psychology in 1992 at the University of California, and has been at Victoria University since 1994. His research specialties are in cross-cultural psychology and inter-group relations and social identity. James has more than 80 academic publications, and his edited volumes include *New Zealand Identities: Departures and destinations* (2005, Victoria University Press) and *Progress in Asian Social Psychology* vols 2 and 6. He was Secretary General of the Asian Association of Social Psychology, and is editor-elect of the *Asian Journal of Social Psychology*. A naturalised citizen of two countries, James describes himself as a 'Chinese–American–New Zealander'. Contact James at james.liu@vuw.ac.nz.

**Dr Christopher Marshall** is the St John's Associate Professor of Christian Theology in the Religious Studies Department at Victoria University of Wellington. He has been involved in the practice of restorative justice in New Zealand for many years, and in 2004 received the International Community Justice Award in London for his contribution to restorative justice practice and thought. Chris has also published extensively on the topic, and has a particular interest in developing the religious and theological dimensions of restorative justice theory. Among his many publications is the award-winning book *Beyond Retribution: A New Testament vision for justice, crime and punishment* (2001, Eerdmans). Contact Chris at chris.marshall@vuw.ac.nz.

**Judge F. W. M. (Fred) McElrea** has been a District Court judge since 1988, and in that time has held warrants for the Youth Court (1990–2001) and Environment Court (2001–2007). He was co-author of *Butterworths District Court Practice (Civil)* (1996–2004), and has lectured in civil and criminal procedure at the University of Auckland. Fred has written and spoken in several countries on the subject of restorative justice. His interest in that topic derives from his academic background (MA (first class honours in philosophy), LLB

(Otago), LLM (London), Dip. Crim. (Cambridge)) and his practical experience as a lawyer and judge. Since 1993, he has been closely involved in the development of restorative justice procedures for adults, culminating in the Sentencing Act 2002. With former Chief Judge David Carruthers, Fred was instrumental in establishing the Restorative Justice Centre at Auckland University of Technology in 2006. He is Deputy Chair of the Governance Board of the Restorative Justice Centre. Contact Fred at judge.mcelrea@justice.govt.nz.

**Dr Gabrielle Maxwell** is a research associate at the Institute of Policy Studies, Victoria University of Wellington. Before she retired, she was Director of the Crime and Justice Research Centre, having spent most of her working life as an academic in psychology and then criminology. As a social psychologist, Gabrielle's major work was in the field of relationships. In recent years, her primary research interests and most of her publications have focused on youth justice, restorative justice, and violence in families and towards children. This work has resulted in her international reputation in restorative justice. Contact Gabrielle at g.maxwell@paradise.net.nz or through Victoria University of Wellington, PO Box 600, Wellington.

**A. J. W. (Tony) Taylor**, after service in the Royal Navy in World War Two, trained as a probation officer in London, before emigrating to New Zealand and training as a prison psychologist. Later Tony moved into academia and retained contact with the outside world through his work with people in Antarctic isolation and Volunteer Service Abroad, and by liaising with those working in hospital psychiatry as well as disaster studies. Now an emeritus professor, he has recently revived his interest in crime, delinquency and a concern for victims. His focus remains firmly interdisciplinary and applied. In 1994, he was awarded a Docteur Honoris Causa by the University of Reims, and in 2003 he was made a Companion of the Royal Society of New Zealand. Tony serves on the editorial panels of journals in the trauma field, and, in 2006, was invited to the advisory board of the new International Organisations for Victims Assistance. He has well over 250 publications, the latest of which is the book he edited entitled *Justice as a Basic Human Need* (2006, Nova Science). Contact Tony at tony.taylor@vuw.ac.nz or phone +64 4 902 3651.

**Rhonda Thompson** BBS, LLB(Hons) was the Principal Youth Court Judge's research counsel at the time of writing chapter 4, and is now a legal adviser for the New Zealand Police. There, she continues to be involved in youth justice

Contributors

issues. Rhonda is writing her Master of Laws dissertation on an aspect of child offending. Contact Rhonda at rhondat@clear.net.nz.

**Nicola White** prepared the original version of chapter 13 while she was Senior Research Fellow at the Institute of Policy Studies in the School of Government, Victoria University of Wellington. Before coming to the university, Nicola worked in a range of legal and policy roles in central government, including as an adviser in the Cabinet Office and Policy Advisory Group of the Department of the Prime Minister and Cabinet. Her chapter draws on reconciliation initiatives in which she was involved while working in those roles, as well as on her general research interest in constitutional relationships, public law and administration, and the Treaty of Waitangi. Nicola left the university at the end of 2006 to take up the role of Assistant Auditor-General, Legal, at the Office of the Auditor-General. Contact Nicola through that office, phone +64 4 917 1500 or fax +64 4 917 1545.

**Kim Workman** (Ngati Kahungunu ki Wairarapa) is a retired public servant, whose career spans roles in the New Zealand Police, Office of the Ombudsman, State Services Commission, Department of Maori Affairs and Ministry of Health. He was head of the Prison Service from 1989 to 1993. In 2000, Kim was appointed National Director of Prison Fellowship of New Zealand, which has become a significant provider in the criminal justice sector and is responsible for establishing the first faith-based prison unit in the British Commonwealth. In 2005, Kim was the joint recipient (with Jackie Katounas) of the International Prize for Restorative Justice. He was made a Companion of the Queens Service Order in 2007. Contact Kim at director@pfnz.org.nz or phone +64 4 570 1252.

# Part One

# Restorative Justice in the New Zealand Context

## Introduction to Part One

The first part of this book provides a background to the discussion that follows of how restorative justice and restorative practices have developed in New Zealand over the past 18 years.

Chapter 1 by Gabrielle Maxwell sets the scene by describing restorative justice and how it contrasts with the conventional justice system with which we are all familiar. The contrast resides not only in the principles and objectives that underlie justice processes, but also in the responses of those who are engaged in the process as offenders or victims and as members of the wider community of people who are affected by crime and its aftermath. This chapter then describes the psychological factors that underpin the practice of restorative justice and potentially provide a benchmark for successful processes.

However, any restorative justice process exists within a wider societal context. And there are light and dark elements in all societies. In chapter 2, James Liu explores the tensions between the desire for revenge and the desire for building inclusive societies. He places this exploration in the context of New Zealand society; a society full of contradictory elements. He examines the tension that results between the desire for accountability and retribution and the desire for healing, forgiveness and the restoration of harmony when there has been a breach of the social contract. Continual calls for naming, blaming and shaming offenders and the growing emphasis on incarceration reflect the extent to which people feel unsafe in a society becoming increasingly culturally diverse and economically stressful. This pattern conflicts with the alternative ethic presented in this book that stresses non-violence, respect for others and building communities of care that can support and reintegrate people who have offended.

# 1

# The Defining Features of a Restorative Justice Approach to Conflict

*Gabrielle Maxwell*

## Introduction

The world around us, and New Zealand too, is changing. Increasingly we see evidence of a heightened fearfulness. Security cameras, border checks, armed police, the identification and public labelling of offenders, and the increased surveillance at all levels are evident here as well as abroad. When misfortune occurs the media demand instant action to identify any offenders or negligent public officials who can be shamed, blamed and punished. Personal and community safety has come to mean increased vigilance in identifying threats, labelling possible miscreants, and blocking or containing troubles by various forms of exclusion from the social group.

These trends are at variance with a concern for civil liberties, human rights, social inclusion and a compassionate response to the least fortunate in our society. Traditionally in New Zealand, these values have been accepted by governments of both the right and the left, but, increasingly, a tougher rhetoric that calls for more and more restrictive and exclusionary measures in the interest of public safety is being heard. Human rights, although recognised in law, are often seen as an impediment to ensuring public safety. Education is under pressure to teach the basics rather than focus on building communities that protect, support and nurture their students. The teachings of Christian churches are no longer effective in providing leadership in relation to a positive ethic. The multicultural and pluralistic society that is New Zealand today offers many different ways of viewing essential questions of human values.

A focus on restorative justice is an approach to conflict that draws attention to these fundamental issues of values. It also focuses attention on the negative consequences of the increasing reliance in New Zealand on responses to offending that emphasise penalties and custodial sentences as approaches to offending; responses that are not only costly but have not proven their effectiveness either in protecting the public or deterring potential offenders. The rhetoric of shame, blame and punishment provides a competing rhetoric that represents the 'dark' side of society discussed in chapter 2. Proponents of this view argue that crime rates can best be reduced, public safety ensured and victims vindicated if we stridently denounce offenders and enforce stringent penalties.

The second part of the book describes in detail the ways in which restorative justice approaches have emerged within the criminal justice system in New Zealand: in relation to youth justice, in the adult criminal courts, in the work of the police and in prisons. In New Zealand, since the late 1980s, penal practices have increasingly emphasised longer sentences, more stringent prison conditions and the use of imprisonment for a wider range of offences. The result has been one of the highest rates of imprisonment in the Western world, prisons that are increasingly characterised by wire fences, intensive surveillance and more limited contact between inmates and the outside world.

By analogy, a focus on restorative justice draws attention to responses to conflict and injustice in other areas of society (see chapters 9–12). It challenges us to examine the evidence for and against alternative approaches to crime and conflict (see, for example, the issues raised in chapters 14 and 15). It also draws attention to the more universal ideas and values that have recur throughout the history of ideas (see chapter 16).

This chapter sets out the challenge to conventional criminal justice and advances the case for restorative justice. It contrasts the salient characteristics and values of the two systems and how these impact on processes and outcomes. The first section of the chapter describes the restorative justice model, contrasts it with conventional justice systems and identifies some of the arguments for and against both models. The second section describes some of the basic psychological values that underpin some of the restorative justice practices that are proving successful.

## The restorative justice model

The core aims of restorative justice are to repair the damage created by criminal offending and restore the balance of relationships within the society. In practice, this can be achieved by the participation of all parties affected by the offending in a process that aims to ensure that wrongdoing is acknowledged and harm is repaired. The aim is also to create conditions that can lead to the (re)integration of all within the social group. Such an approach is seen as necessary if hurts are to be healed and wrongdoing forgiven. At a more practical level, restorative justice focuses on processes and practices that are more likely to build and restore rather than to stigmatise and punish. A fuller account of the meaning of restorative justice is presented by Johnstone and Van Ness (2007b, chapter 1).

Other key references include Morris and Young (2000), Van Ness and Strong (1997) and Zehr (1990).

The analysis presented here contrasts a restorative justice system, such as is developing in New Zealand today, with the conventional criminal justice system that has characterised our past and that of the rest of the Western world (Maxwell and Morris, 2006; Morris and Young, 2000). Table 1.1 (on p. 13) sets out the principal differences between a restorative justice model and a conventional criminal justice model at each stage of the justice process. However, before discussing this figure it is important to describe the contrasting values, processes and outcomes that characterise the two models.

## *Contrasting values*

The conventional criminal justice system emphasises the centrality of state authority and gives primacy to the interests of the state. For these reasons, it uses a formal court system where detached and impersonal professionals representing the state make decisions using formal processes. The first step is to determine individual culpability by a trial process (except in cases where a guilty plea is entered). The second step is the sentencing process, which involves the court in determining an appropriate penalty for the individual or individuals found guilty. At the same time, fairness, in the sense of equality before the law and consistency in practice, is seen as being afforded to defendants by giving priority to their legal rights. There is a strong focus on punishment as a method of both denouncing criminal actions and exacting payment for them.

However, the state assumes only a limited role in the care of its citizens. Court decisions take little responsibility for the offenders' behaviour either in the past or in the future. The existence of a relatively small range of rehabilitative services does little to soften this fundamental abnegation of state responsibility for improving the behaviour of those who have offended. Moreover, the system has been criticised as monocultural in its values, standards and understanding of the factors underlying criminal actions (Department of Justice, 1986).

Restorative justice, on the other hand, puts the interests of those most affected – victims, offenders and their 'communities of care'[1] – at the centre of

---

1  It can be argued that many of those identified as 'offenders', and at times even those identified as 'victims, do not have 'communities of care'; that is, no one can be found who cares about them and can support them in need. In such cases it is often necessary to develop ways of rebuilding such communities (chapter 8 provides examples of this).

its concern. Their participation is seen as the key ingredient of a fair and just process. The state may be an interested party but it no longer has a monopoly over decision making. Communities are seen as having a collective interest and responsibility for the decisions and outcomes. The emphasis is thus on identifying communities that can provide support and are willing to become involved in finding ways to respond to the offending and its consequences, and take responsibility in assisting the reintegration of victims and offenders.

Restorative justice is also expected to protect human rights and take account of the inevitable disadvantages of those offenders who lack knowledge, skills and support when they are called on to be accountable before the law. And, finally, restorative justice encourages cultural connectedness and sensitivity rather than cultural dominance of a majority group. In practice, this points to the necessity for a strong society to be able to cater to the needs of the multiplicity of cultural groups within it. These values are given expression by ensuring that the parties themselves are able to shape the types of processes that are used and the nature of the outcomes that can be arrived at. The essence of restorative justice is the building and rebuilding of connections between offenders, victims and communities rather than labelling those who are 'guilty' and excluding them from the rest of society.

## *Contrasting processes*

The public rituals of the conventional criminal justice system are formal and complex. The language is highly specialised and often incomprehensible to anyone who is not a legal professional. Thus, it is judges, lawyers, police officers and court staff who are the principal players in the court process. Court staff manage the setting, lawyers shape the dialogue and judges make the key decisions. The setting itself indicates the relative importance of the participants. All of this ritual, of course, does have a purpose and meaning. It signifies how we as a society regard crime and criminals, and it also expresses and signifies the authority of the state. At the same time, the victims and offenders stand outside these arrangements both literally in terms of the way they are fenced off from the centre stage and practically by their limited ability to participate in and even to comprehend what is happening.

Restorative justice is, in contrast, a relatively informal and less public process. Those who are most affected by an offence – the victims, offenders and 'communities of care' – come together and, with the aid of a facilitator, resolve how to deal with the offence, its consequences and its implications for the future. The procedures followed and the venue chosen can be agreed by the parties themselves, and this allows for a cultural flexibility in the way decisions are arrived at. The role of the state is now changed to one that is less central to the drama: it provides for restorative justice options by setting the framework within which restorative justice will operate, enabling appropriate processes to be established, providing for the implementation of the outcomes arrived at in this way, and monitoring the quality of the outcomes achieved. But unlike the ritualised conventional process, the script of restorative justice is more often spontaneous and novel; emotion is at the centre of the action and those most affected by the offending are the key players.

With the introduction of restorative processes and values, the role of other key players changes. Chapters 4–7 describe how, in New Zealand over recent years, changes have occurred in the courts and in police practice.

## *Contrasting outcomes*

Within the conventional criminal justice system, outcomes tend to be punitive. Their aim is to reassert the values underpinning criminal law by denouncing the offence and the offender, and thus deterring others. In this way, they are seen as acting in the interests of public safety. The use of incarceration to remove the most dangerous offenders from society serves as a benchmark against which most sentences are determined. Outcomes with a rehabilitative or reparative focus are, of course, possible, but they are usually an optional, rather than crucial, part of the primary sanction that is benchmarked against the magnitude of the offence.

The aims of restorative justice processes, on the other hand, are primarily to hold offenders accountable for their offending in meaningful ways and to try to make amends to victims at least in a symbolic sense and, where possible, in a real sense too. Thus, restorative justice outcomes are more likely to focus on apologies, reparation or community work as ways of restoring the property stolen or compensating for the injuries endured. A prison sentence may be agreed to as necessary to protect society but need not be the benchmark against which the sufficiency of the response to victims or other parties is judged. While outcomes that protect society and signify the gravity of the offending are not excluded within a restorative justice system, they have now become secondary to the tasks of repairing harm and restoring the balance and harmony within the community in ways that respond to the needs of those most harmed by what has happened. Thus, restorative processes can lead to an acknowledgment of the collective responsibility of people other than the individual offender in allowing a situation to develop where an offence has occurred, and may involve actions that will make people feel safer or bring people together to protect those at risk rather than simply respond with sanctions directed at an individual offender.

One of the principal hopes of restorative justice is that reconciliation between the offender and victim will occur and the offender can be forgiven. Indeed, there are countless examples of tears and embraces at the end of restorative meetings. Yet, this is not always possible – victims may remain angry or bitter, offenders may remain unmoved and untouched, and communities may continue to reject those who are seen to have been responsible for the trouble. However, there is no doubt that reconciliation can take place between victims and offenders, and offenders can be forgiven by those affected by their behaviour. Overall, the principal objective of restorative outcomes is to reintegrate victims and offenders into their respective communities.

### *Contrasting victims' experiences*

In the conventional criminal justice system, when there is a trial, the victim may be called on to give evidence, but, at the same time, this makes them liable to be cross-examined, a process that many experience as abusive. On the other hand, when there is a 'guilty' plea, the effects of offences on victims are communicated to the court, if at all, through a victim impact statement presented by the prosecutor in written form. Consequently, victims, particularly of serious offences, frequently feel alienated from the process; they receive little to aid their healing, and may end up harbouring grievances and feeling that the process has not been fair (in Lind and Tyler's (1988) terms, there has been a lack of procedural justice). In other words, some of the key psychological needs outlined in chapter 15 may not have been met.

Restorative justice aims to offer victims the opportunity to meet with their offender, express their concerns and be part of the process of decision making. Victims' attendance at restorative justice meetings is, of course, voluntary. Generally, however, research shows that some victims want to meet their offender and their presence (or the presence of someone else who can represent their views) is central to the restorative justice process (Strang, 2002). In this way, victims can tell their story, describe their feelings and the consequences of the offending for them, and express their views on how the offender can assist to repair the harm that has been caused. These are typically powerful occasions far removed from the typical courtroom scene and they can create a situation that touches the emotions of the offenders as well as the others who are present. Being present at restorative meetings offers victims further potential benefits: some of their emotional needs may be met; for example, they may be provided with the opportunity for some healing, for some understanding of what happened and why, and for some closure. Successful restorative justice

## The Defining Features of a Restorative Justice Approach to Conflict

processes put victims, as well as offenders and the community of care, at the heart of what happens.

### *Contrasting offenders' experiences*

By and large, offenders and victims in many ways have similar experiences of conventional criminal justice processes. Pre-trial and trial procedures do not engage them. As a result, offenders rarely participate; they are generally expected to communicate with the court through their lawyer; and they are discouraged from direct dialogue with the victim. As those who represent or work with offenders in the court process know only too well, they thus feel alienated from the process; they frequently have at best only a vague idea of what has happened to them; and they are not held accountable in meaningful ways. Overall, they remain fundamentally untouched by both processes and outcomes.

Restorative justice processes require not just the presence of the offender, but their inclusion. They are expected to participate directly in the process, to speak about their offending and matters associated with it, to interact with the victim, to express their remorse about what has occurred, to apologise for what they have done, and to contribute to decisions about eventual outcomes. From all this, the offender is expected to have a better understanding of their offending and its consequences, to become accountable for the offending in ways they understand and to contribute to repairing the harm they have caused. The presence of the victim also means that their justifications for offending – 'she could afford it', 'he is insured', 'those people aren't like us' and so on – can be challenged. The restorative process, therefore, is able to touch – and perhaps change – the hearts and minds of offenders (and, coincidentally, of victims) and become the beginning of a new way of life.

### *Contrasting effectiveness*

Effectiveness cannot readily be contrasted on the same terms in the two models because the primary objectives of the conventional criminal justice system and restorative justice are so different. However, research on restorative processes compared with conventional processes indicates that reoffending is certainly no more likely and often less likely, and both offenders and victims are more likely to express satisfaction with outcomes under restorative justice. Both victims and offenders see the outcomes from restorative processes as fair, and more often report being able to put matters behind them than in the conventional justice system (Maxwell et al., 2004a; Maxwell and Morris, 1993; Strang, 2002).

Also, although the rhetoric of the conventional criminal justice system emphasises the protection of the public, particularly the use of imprisonment for that purpose, it pursues that objective in a haphazard and often completely misconceived way. The conventional criminal justice system does provide some protection of the public, but there is no reason to believe restorative justice, which would, of course, retain the option of imprisonment, is incapable of doing so at least as well. Nor is there compelling evidence to indicate the conventional system deters the most likely groups of potential offenders: those who are already to some degree disengaged from conventional values and norms.

## *Summarising the differences between restorative and conventional justice*

It is now appropriate to turn to Table 1.1, which summarises the main differences between restorative and conventional criminal justice, and relates these to the stages of the justice process.

The first necessary step in any justice process and indeed in the resolution of any conflict is the investigative process. This step determines what happened, its effects on others and the alleged responsibility of the various parties. In restorative justice, the same concerns are characterised by an increased emphasis on the impact of the events on those most affected, including the direct victims, the wider community and the offenders themselves. There can also be a concern for a wider exploration of the factors that provide the context for understanding the offences that are the focus of the investigation.

The next step is that of determining responsibility. Restorative justice shifts the process at this point from an impersonal judgement of a 'dispassionate' court in a ritual setting to an informal process in a setting where those directly involved come together to discuss what happened and express their views directly to one another, often with all the emotion that may be felt but also with the possibility of a real understanding developing among all parties about what the events have meant for everyone. In many cases in the New Zealand system, it is only if this process fails to result in shared agreement about responsibility, that it becomes necessary for a court hearing to determine sentencing.

The different setting also promotes and enables a detailed discussion of how best to repair harm and reintegrate those who have been alienated. Responses to the crime focus on deciding how to repair the harm that has been caused and developing plans for the reintegration into, rather than exclusion from, the community of those at risk of becoming alienated from the community by the events around the offending and its aftermath. In other words, restorative justice emphasises *making amends*.

**Table 1.1:** Key differences between conventional and restorative justice

| Stage of the justice process | Conventional justice | Restorative justice |
|---|---|---|
| *Investigation*<br>Identifying those likely to be responsible<br>Gathering evidence<br>Assessing the impact on victims<br>Assessing needs and risks | Investigation occurs in all cases reported to the police.<br><br>The police investigate only cases reported to them. | Investigation occurs in all cases reported to the police.<br><br>Restorative justice may be initiated by the parties involved in cases not reported to the police |
| *Determination of responsibility*<br>Who is responsible?<br>Do they accept responsibility?<br>What is the extent of culpability? | If there is no guilty plea, a court trial determines guilt.<br><br>If there is a guilty plea, a conviction is registered and the sentence reflects decisions on culpability. | Parties are involved in a participatory process to determine responsibility and consider what needs to be repaired. |
| *Repair of harm*<br>Degree of damage<br>Options for repair<br>Extent to which damage and repair are the responsibility of offender and supporters<br>Extent to which repair can be met within the community | Legislation determines the options for repair, punishment and the measures to ensure public safety.<br><br>The court makes and enforces orders (eg, for reparation, fines, community sentences or custody). | Greater emphasis is placed on repair and reintegration.<br><br>Participants most affected make the decisions about repair and are responsible for carrying out the agreed actions. |
| *Reintegration of offender and victim*<br>Role of state<br>Role of offender<br>Role of community<br>Role of family and friends | The state may make the decisions and provide services to reintegrate the offender. These services are often limited and decisions are often dominated by concerns for public safety.<br><br>The state relies on post-release reporting (probation), and offenders, families and the community have limited involvement in developing and managing reintegration plans. | The emphasis is on reintegration plans, involving community services and support.<br><br>Those most affected by the offending decide how to reintegrate the offender and victim, with the involvement of, and heavy reliance on, family, friends and community, as well as the offender's initiative and the state's support.<br><br>Public safety is seen as better managed by wrap-around support than by ongoing surveillance. |

If the court later becomes involved in making decisions about outcomes, it can do so with a set of agreed recommendations from those most affected, or at least with a clearer understanding of their views. In jurisdictions, like New Zealand, where restorative processes precede any hearing by a formal court, the role of that court is usually changed dramatically to one of considering legal issues and setting up orders to support the implementation of agreements usually already reached between the parties.

The final stage of the conventional justice process is making arrangements for the return to the community of those who have offended. Conventionally, this often occurs after a custodial sentence has been completed, and at this point, parole is often used to monitor the parolee in order to ensure the ongoing safety of the public and to put in place a plan for reintegration that relies mainly on professional services. Restorative approaches that attempt to actively rebuild communities of care are relatively rare, although one is described in chapter 7. This system relies on people in the local area providing wraparound support for all aspects of the return to society for as along as is needed.

On first consideration, most people respond warily to the idea of returning to a justice system where there is a potential for confrontation and perhaps explosive outcomes. The control by courts and police of processes of decision making and sentencing has been the main method of guarding against kangaroo courts and vigilante justice. On the other hand, there are risks attached to the current commitment by governments to conventional criminal justice processes, which place at the forefront of their considerations issues of public safety and ensuring that the punishment fits the crime: penal populations continue to grow with no increase in community safety, at considerable cost, and with little likelihood of reducing reoffending, while victims' concerns remain unmet.

Restorative justice is continuing to grow in a piecemeal way and there is considerable popular and community support for it. Increasingly, it is becoming accepted within New Zealand as a central part of both the youth and the adult justice systems. And, unlike the conventional system, it provides a greater opportunity to restore both victims and offenders to a sense of worth and wellbeing. The experiments documented in this book show that most of the fears about dangerous outcomes from restorative approaches are unwarranted, if the processes are set up in ways that protect both the interests and rights of the parties and the interests of the state in ensuring public safety.

In promoting restorative processes and outcomes, I am not suggesting that jurisdictions should abandon the use of courts or prisons. Restorative justice does not deal with issues of guilt or innocence when these are contested; this remains the task of judges and jurors; nor does it remove imprisonment as a possible sanction when parties to the restorative justice process determine that it is necessary in the interests of public safety. And, of course, at least in some examples of restorative justice, courts will have to be used when offenders fail to agree to a plan or to complete the plan agreed to through restorative processes. What restorative justice offers us, however, is a new set of values and priorities for future practice that can help rebuild the lives of individuals, families and communities affected by offending.

Along with many others in the restorative justice movement, I do not believe that these characteristics belong only in the justice sphere. They can be used to benchmark the effectiveness of any set of practices and any institution that deals with people where there can be conflict and the need to reintegrate a social group. Hence, this book focuses not simply on restorative justice in the criminal justice system, but on the growing development of restorative practice and values in many aspects of life in New Zealand today.

## *Criticisms of restorative justice*

Inevitably, faced with the relatively simple arguments presented above, there will be doubt about the ability of restorative justice to deliver what it proposes and concerns about its failure to provide the protections to society that the conventional justice system has evolved to deal with.

If restorative justice is to depend on communities of care, where can these communities be found in our highly mobile and fragmented modern urban societies? How can restorative justice respond to the inequalities of power and wealth between victims and offenders, within families, and between men and women? What about issues of social justice and the inevitable disadvantage of the poor faced with the power of the state that is vested in police and courts? Where is the protection for the rights of individuals in a process that is informal and not closed to public scrutiny? How can a multicultural society with multiple norms and values bring together parties from different groups in a process that all will see as fair and appropriate without the guidance of a strong central state? How can the core principles of equity and proportionality in sentencing be achieved with people arriving independently at their own solutions? Surely, these processes will work only in minor matters or for first offenders, and more serious matters and repeat offenders will need to be dealt with in more conventional ways. Does this not lead to opportunities for vigilantism and arbitrariness – features that led states to develop formal systems in the first place? Is not a lot of this talk of emotion too amorphous? Surely, the core realities of fairness and public protection are the key issues that a justice system must focus on?

All of these are important questions. However, the answers do not lie in theory, but in an examination of restorative processes in practice. In this book, we present many examples of restorative practices that have emerged in New Zealand since the 1990s. Whenever possible we have asked the authors to describe not only what happens but also to reflect on the advantages and disadvantages of these practices compared with those of the more conventional responses that reflect the conventional justice system described here. In the final part of this book (chapters 17–19), we return to the questions raised here and provide some answers.

## Core ingredients of a successful restorative outcome

In the second part of this chapter, I tease out how my understanding of restorative theory has grown by researching justice and educational processes.[2] In my work, I have attempted to define benchmarks against which the success of a restorative justice process can be assessed. What are the outcomes by which we can judge results?

Reoffending seems an obvious benchmark but it proves to be a problematic concept. Reoffending is not always detected, or it may be a response to new factors in the person's life or to other problems that have never been previously identified or responded to. Even when there is an agreement with which all concur, this may not be a guarantee against future offending: the process of restoration is not one that can be achieved quickly, if at all. It is not easy to acquire new and different skills for managing relationships and finding a place in society, and the marks of trauma are sometimes beyond healing. And there can be other real gains from the restorative process for families and victims that are not measured by an assessment of the reoffending.

### *Belonging: the goal of the journey*

Howard Zehr (2002) has suggested that the ultimate goal of restorative justice for victims and offenders cannot be defined in terms of appropriate punishment but rather in terms of the acceptance of responsibility, the restoration of meaning and the return of respect. In this paper he builds his analysis around the metaphor of a journey to belonging. The notion of a journey is important: it underscores the fact that a process is involved that occurs over time and does not involve a quick and simple solution.

---

2  See Maxwell (2005), Maxwell et al. (2004a) and Maxwell and Morris (2006).

'Belonging' is a concept that is part of the vocabulary of the psychologist as well as the vocabulary of the restorative justice theoretician. For the social psychologist, 'belonging' can be seen as the ultimately successful goal for any individual: the concept encompasses notions of having a place in the social structure, having good relationships with others, being engaged in activity where one can experience success, and experiencing a sense of personal wellbeing. Such conceptualisations resonate with psychologists' conceptions of the mature and happy person. Chapter 16 discusses the importance of justice and belonging in Maslow's (1954) theory of human needs. Allport in 1960 published a series of lectures examining the centrality of belonging as the goal of human striving. These themes recur in the writings of modern students of psychological wellbeing and happiness as Argyle (2002) and criminologists examining the options for reintegration such as Ward and Maruna (2007).

A feeling of belonging is a basic human need. People are social creatures. In part, this is about the necessity of the group for survival, but there is more to the need for the society of others that is important. The psychological support and affirmation of those to whom one is close is critical to a sense of psychological wellbeing – to human happiness. Most often this comes primarily from kin – for Māori, the essence of whanaungatanga, the sense of belonging, is defined through the connectedness of kinship links (Williams, 2004). But belonging is not just about having a connection to the social group of family and friends, it also about having a recognised place in wider society and the affirmation of self that this brings with it, especially when facing an external threat.

The involvement in the justice process, therefore, of the people to whom one feels most connected, the 'community of care' as it has been described (Morris and Maxwell, 2001), is part of this 'belonging'. But often potential communities of care are weak or fractured or have become disengaged from a concern for those involved in the offending. Thus, effective justice outcomes need not only to *involve* but also to *build* these communities and find ways of strengthening the relationships within them.

## *Overview of key concepts*

The question, however, remains of what are the effective strategies and processes in situations of conflict for enabling a return to belonging. What then are the elements that can provide a practical way of achieving 'a journey to belonging'?

In the research I have been involved with, we have needed to face the very real challenge of identifying ways of both defining and measuring some of the key psychological factors that are involved, such as healing, remorse, forgiveness, fairness and empowerment, in ways that meet conventional criteria for reliability and validity. Too, we have had to find ways of testing the extent to which these factors are linked to achieving life outcomes that involve a reintegration into the community. In this chapter it is not possible to describe the methodology that we have developed for achieving these goals; suffice it say that large samples, complex statistical analyses and studies of different samples over time have been necessary in order to reach convincing conclusions.[3]

The psychological factors discussed here are:
- respect: the antithesis of shaming;
- fairness and equity (in relation to process, voice, participation and agreement);
- effective relationships that give support, affirmation and identity;
- responsibility and repair;
- empowerment; and
- reintegration, forgiveness and healing.

However, the views of participants and the facts that are recorded in the official records are only windows that provide a partial understanding of how a restorative criminal justice system works and, in particular, the psychological processes that are involved in the youth justice 'family group conference', which was the first example of a restorative process in New Zealand. Here, I attempt to build on the data we have collected and the more general psychological literature to describe the psychological factors that underpin the family group conference process and its success or otherwise in achieving its goals of repairing harm to those affected by the offending and reintegrating the offenders in the wider society. Much of the research is based on the responses of young people who have offended, but I am confident the same factors are equally important for the victims, the families and the communities who are also affected by the offending. And the same principles are likely to apply to achieving effective outcomes for all parties in the justice system or in any other institution in society from prisons to schools to workplaces and to families.

---

3   The research that we have conducted provides an understanding of the relative effectiveness of various options for managing youth justice (Maxwell and Morris, 1993, 1999; Maxwell et al., 2004a; Maxwell and Paulin, 2004). Through quantitative and qualitative analysis of records of the conference process and outcomes, and from the responses of the young people and other participants, it has been possible to identify several factors likely to result in outcomes that satisfy participants, are associated with a reduction in the probability of reoffending, and are associated with an increase in the probability of positive life outcomes for the young people (Maxwell et al., 2004a).

## Effective and ineffective aspects of the social context

### Respect: the antithesis of shaming

A feeling of being respected is important to everyone and in all contexts – even when one has acted wrongly. The consequences of not feeling respected can lead to both verbal and physical attacks on others. A common justification for aggression in the school playground is that I was 'dissed' (Buckley and Maxwell, 2007). Alternatively, disrespect can lead to a feeling of shame. Emotional abuse has often been seen as a form of bullying and certainly has the same psychological impact. But regardless of the consequences of not feeling respected, the emergence of the term 'dissed' in teen language is an affirmation of the right of all people including children to be treated with respect, to be allowed to stand tall and to be spoken to with courtesy.

Respect also emerges from discussions about what it is that can go wrong in relationships between different groups. Racism, sexism or any other distinctive treatment that disadvantages another group is fundamentally not just about abuse or differential outcomes, but about differential treatment in day-to-day situations. The converse is to be treated with respect, to be addressed in a language you can understand, to be greeted, to be listened to, to be involved, to be consulted, and to be validated as a person.

The frequency of the use of violence in response to being shamed provides evidence of the negative impact of shaming, and the righteous indignation when the aggressor is called to account indicates the extent to which physical retaliation is so often seen as justified. Shame is an emotion where the negative effects are more complex and often less easily recognised than with other emotions such as fear and anger (Braithwaite, 1989; Maxwell and Morris, 2002b). At the same time, shame is often part of a group of feelings that make up remorse (Harris, 1999). To feel shame is often a consequence of feeling empathy with the victim and part of wanting to repair the harm that has been done. It is a by-product of the offender accepting that harm has been done to another person and accepting responsibility for causing that harm.

The extent to which shame is a complex emotion and one that can have enormously negative effects is described in the writings of Tangney and her associates (Tangney, 1991; Tangney and Dearing, 2002). It can lead to the disengagement of the person shamed from the process of attempting to repair harm can and prevent that person from hearing what others are saying and responding to and identifying with their perspective. Thus at the same time as being a by-product of empathy and the acceptance of responsibility, it can also be a barrier to these outcomes.

Shame can be generated internally by the self: 'to be shamed' is a response to the recognition that one's own actions are not ones that are valued positively by oneself or by others whose opinion one values. But shame can also be generated by others: 'to shame' a person can be the intended consequence of acts of disapproval and rejection. At times, claims have been made in the popular press for the efficacy of shame as a method of changing behaviour, leading to proposals for responding to offending by blaming, labelling and treating the offender as despicable. However, in the psychological literature there is now strong evidence to suggest that such actions are not effective ways of changing behaviour. They may make those who are angry about the offending feel better, but they do not have constructive effects on the person who is being shamed. This is because intense shame is incompatible with a belief in oneself as a worthwhile person: one who is well regarded by others, accepted as a member of the social group and able to achieve positive life goals.

A consensus exists among psychologists and criminologists who have examined the impact of shame in depth that the avoidance of 'stigmatic shaming' is highly desirable. Several cite graphic examples of the pain of those feeling intense shame and the effect this can have in generating anti-social, dangerous and violent behaviour towards oneself or others. Tangney (1991) has referred to shame as "the ugly emotion". Olthoff (2000) concluded that "inducing shame in an offender could lead to a desire to avoid being in such a situation again but [it is] potentially risky in that it could evoke further negative and anti-social behaviour". Miller (1996, p. 151) describes shame as the "bedrock of much psychopathology". More simply, Braithwaite (1989, p. 12) refers to shaming as "a dangerous game". In our research (Maxwell et al., 2004a; Maxwell and Morris, 1999b), we have consistently identified feelings of being shamed as an independent predictor of negative outcomes and reoffending. The manner in which police and others respond to a young person who has offended is hence an important contributing factor to whether they will eventually feel a sense of remorse or react against those who call on the offender to account for their deeds. Restorative justice aims for the respectful treatment of all parties concerned, including the offender, throughout the justice proceedings.

Māori (along with other Polynesian peoples) have a concept of whakamā that is seen as closely related to wairua (spiritual identity) and waiora (health). When one feels whakamā, one is deeply ashamed, unable to look at others and unable to participate in the life of the group. At the extreme end of the spectrum, a person feeling whakamā may run away, become enraged, hurt others or hurt themselves or even, literally, die of shame (Metge, 1986).

## Fairness and equity

A sense of fairness is a basic determinant of human behaviour. Its importance is demonstrated early in life by the responses of young children to issues of sharing. Some of these issues in relation to parents and children are teased out in recent research on fairness and forgiveness in families in New Zealand (Evans et al., 2007). When it comes to the question of deciding whether the outcome of any situation involving the division of rewards will be acceptable and satisfying to all parties, it is whether the agreement is seen as fair that is the critical issue.

Fairness is not a simple concept, however (see chapter 15). Lind and Tyler (1988) for example, distinguish 'distributive justice' from 'procedural justice'. 'Distributive justice' is about the perceived equity of any repayment that is made to the amount of damage that was done: goods that are stolen are returned, damage that is done to property is repaired, or money that was stolen is repaid. In more complex situations where an exact repayment is not possible, reparation may be arranged or work may be carried out for an organisation nominated by the victim. Further, when there is emotional harm involved, this may mean that the amount of money or time involved in the repair may need to be more than equal to the amount of damage originally inflicted for the arrangement to be regarded as equitable. However, the resources and the perceptions of the two parties can be very different: for a very poor offender, a payment of several thousand dollars seems not only impossible but also disproportionate in relation to the amount of harm suffered by a very wealthy victim. Alternatively, there is often no possible repayment for the loss of a loved one or the permanent harm that can be caused by violence. There also comes a point when financial and community work arrangements can begin to seem more like punishment than an equitable response to a harm that has been done.

'Procedural justice' refers to the extent to which the process of making decisions about culpability for and responses to crime is fair. Relevant questions include such issues as whether the investigation was thorough and carried out without prejudice, whether all the affected parties were informed of their rights and appropriately involved in the decision making, and so on. Liu and Hanke discuss these issues further in chapter 15.

These two major distinctions about aspects of justice appear to be important universally, and they underpin much of what has been built into the traditional criminal justice system to ensure its fairness. However, the parties involved, can have quite different views. Simple equitable repayments, even when accompanied by genuine remorse, sincere apologies and good resolutions can be seen as falling far short of adequate in providing justice. From the perspective of victims, a punitive response may be seen as the only one that will be equitable –

for them, the degree of suffering of the offender needs to be of at least an equivalent level to their own and that of their family.

Furthermore, for some, including at times the representatives of the state, fairness in process and equity in penalties are not the only yardsticks of a just outcome. A belief in the importance of deterrence, both as method of changing the particular offender's potential future behaviour and in having an exemplary effect on society at large, is also a factor that can affect people's judgement of a just solution. And other mitigating and aggravating factors that relate to the offender and their personal circumstances are generally recognised by courts as relevant to sentencing.

Finally, experience with restorative justice meetings that involve all those directly affected produces yet another perspective. Agreements that are reached in this way often vary considerably even when the nature of the offending and the characteristics of the offenders seem similar. The personal views and values of the individuals involved can have a major effect on decisions. One victim may want the offender to experience vicariously what they went through; for example, in one case the relatives of a severely injured victim of a car accident asked the offender to spend several weeks voluntarily working in an accident and emergency ward. In other cases, the victim wants to be reassured that the offender will not reoffend, so is concerned to make sure that plans are developed that will lead the offender to a more constructive future. In other words, what is seen as restoring the balance and harmony within the social group can be very particular to the time, place and people involved.

### *Effective relationships that give support, affirmation and identity*

The fairness of the process and the respectfulness of the way one is responded to are two important preconditions for making it possible for offenders to take responsibility for their actions. But by themselves, these two factors are not necessarily sufficient. The support and acceptance of one's family and friends is also part of what makes it possible for an offender to take responsibility. It is having close relationships with others that is an important correlate of positive life outcomes and not reoffending (Maxwell et al., 2004a). Related concepts for Māori are whanaungatanga (being part of a wider kinship group), being the recipient of awhi (loving support) and ngaki (the nurturing that one gives a young person as they grow) (Williams, 2004).

There are two aspects to this when a decision is being made about a response to one's offending. First, if the people you care about most are present and continue to accept you, then your sense of shame and worthlessness is minimised, which in turn makes it possible for you to feel remorse, admit wrongdoing and attempt to repair the harm done. Second, the involvement of family and friends in the decision is also an incentive for you to accept responsibility and repair the harm in order to regain the respect and love of those who are most important to you.

But it is not only the respect and support of family in the decision-making process that is important to the young person. The attitude of the professionals who are present at a restorative conference is also important. If the young person who has offended is treated as a person worthy of respect and as a person with positive qualities and achievements as well as someone capable of making mistakes, then the possibility of remorse, taking responsibility and making repair is enhanced. And the alternative of the young person rejecting a society whose representatives disdain them is avoided.

After any justice process concludes, close relationships, support and acceptance continue to be key factors in preventing a person's reoffending. Thus, the justice process itself will be more effective if it builds plans that identify and engage people in the life of the person who has offended and who can continue to provide support and guidance in the future.

*Responsibility and repair*

With respect to emotional harm, money or time is not usually seen as the preferred currency for repair. For the offender to listen and acknowledge the hurts of the victim is the first step, taking responsibility for what they did is the second. However, genuine repentance, heartfelt apologies and a determination not to offend again are often the most valued currency for contributing to healing for the victim (Strang, 2002). For the victim, these are usually seen as the important responses to the emotional harm that has been done.

But this depends on the perceived genuineness of the responses. Genuineness is not easy to judge. Young offenders who are slow to respond, speak little, fail to look the victim in the eye, or smile and giggle with embarrassment are likely to be judged as uninvolved and unresponsive. Apologies that are mumbled quickly or written clumsily may be discounted. Victims may even see the gaucheness of embarrassment and youth as signs of disrespect and denial of any real responsibility for the harm. They may feel further insulted and enraged, even though most of these behaviours signal the shame felt by the young person about what they have done and/or their simply not knowing how to respond adequately.

After the restorative process there can be further effects on the victim that are not necessarily the responsibility of the young person. Unfortunately, it is often the case that apologies, financial reparation and information about the completion of tasks are not transmitted quickly and effectively to the victim. In a few cases, this may be because the offender does not have the ability to write an apology (or the victim may disbelieve the apology because it is awkwardly expressed); help and support are needed in many cases. In other cases, systems for collecting money, letters and information and passing them on to the victim may be inadequate. Such problems are likely to affect the victims' views of the extent of the genuineness of apologies and remorse so that their opinions may have little relationship with the offender's views.

The New Zealand system of restorative conferencing requires young people to acknowledge their responsibility for offending before the conference can proceed (see chapters 3–5). Thus, we have no direct research evidence on the importance of taking responsibility for one's offence being a critical first step in the process of achieving positive outcomes. One study, however, compared a sample of people in the adult justice system who had had a conference with a sample who had not (Maxwell et al., 1999). Outcomes were significantly better for the sample who had had a conference and who all formally accepted responsibility for their offending and were involved in plans that included measures to repair the harm they had caused. However, this could be due to other differences related to having or not having a restorative conference. Nevertheless, I feel confident that taking responsibility must be a first step, both logically and psychologically, to repairing the harm for the healing of both offenders and victims.

In our youth justice research (Maxwell et al., 2004a) offenders had to accept responsibility as a pre-condition for the conference, but there were, nevertheless, differences in the extent to which the offenders felt they could repair the harm they had caused. Multivariate analyses, which separated out the importance of individual factors independently of other variables, showed that feeling able to repair the harm was a significant and important predictor of an offender's adult life outcomes. In other words, walking away from the conference feeling that harm has been repaired is, at least in this study, definitely related to finding a place in the world in the 2–3 years following – potentially a critical step on a successful journey to belonging.

*Empowerment*

Being in control of one's life and destiny is also a basic need. It is closely related to the sense of self-worth. A person is also more likely to take responsibility for their actions and make amends for what they have done if they feel that their actions are important and can affect their future. Furthermore, psychological research has demonstrated that those who participate fully in the decisions that are taken about them are more likely to take responsibility for what has happened, agree to actions that will involve a constructive response to a problem, and follow through on any undertakings that are made about future actions (Page and Czuba, 1999; Rappaport, 1981, 1984). This is true equally of nations, of organisations and of individuals who have the responsibility for making plans for action. It is true both of those who are building for the future and those who are repairing the damage of the past. (Chapters 12 and 13 reflect on these issues.)

The first step to empowerment is through an offender's participation in all aspects of the justice process. Participation puts an offender in a situation where they are expected to acknowledge and accept responsibility for their actions and to consider how to make amends and repair the harm they have done. At the same time, participation can lead to empowerment: the active handing back to the offender of the responsibility for both what has happened in the past and what will happen in the future.

Psychologically, most offenders see that accepting an active part in the justice process and taking responsibility for their actions are more difficult than allowing an impersonal justice resolution to take its course. Often this is the case even when punishment is a likely outcome. Participation means accepting the blame that is attached to the offending and admitting one's failure. It means experiencing the emotions of shame and guilt. Active engagement raises doubts about one's worthiness to be a valued and loved member of one's own group.

Active engagement in decisions about one's future is also likely to result in constructive outcomes. Research has shown that decisions about the future taken voluntarily and made by the person most affected are more likely to result in the fulfilment of agreements than when outcomes are mandated or decided by others (Page and Czuba, 1999; Rappaport, 1981, 1984). Later chapters in this book (especially chapters 8–11) support these findings.

*Forgiveness, reintegration and healing*
The final aspect of enabling belonging lies in the opportunity for reintegration. Finding ways in which the person can build a future as a full and valued member of the wider society is essential to enabling them to find pro-social outlets for their energies. Assisting them to overcome past difficulties and achieve their goals is also a practical demonstration of faith in the person's ability to realise their positive potential. In practice, this means identifying the specific needs for rehabilitation and reintegration and finding ways to meet them through programmes, services and ongoing support for as long as it is necessary. Constructive theory and models around developing 'good lives' have

been described by Ward and Maruna (2007) among others and is an essential feature of the processes described in chapter 8.

Forgiveness is a complex concept. Inside a Christian reference frame, it has been regarded as a virtuous and charitable response to harm. But for some it also suggests not only a wiping of the slate and a new start, but a positive affirmation of the person who has done the harm – perhaps an unrealistic and even undesirable response to offending. A realistic goal of the justice system is to enable a fresh start for the young person unmarked by continuing reminders of past delinquencies and continuing doubts about their capacity for achieving positive life goals. Operation Jericho (described in chapter 8) is another example of how forgiveness within a religious framework and, more generally, a fresh start can be given a very real meaning for those released from prison.

Despite these examples, it is unrealistic to attempt to make the achievement of healing and forgiveness a benchmark of success or a formal goal of process. On the other hand, the result of processes that are empowering, outcomes that are fair, and genuine remorse that is unequivocally expressed by the offender and accepted by those present, particularly the victim, can result in a genuine reconciliation that is accompanied by a sense of healing and forgiveness. In these circumstances all parties have been able to agree that the outcomes are equitable, put the past behind them, have their fears and anxieties about the future allayed, and envisage a positive future. For the victim, this is likely to mean being able to feel safe, that they have contributed constructively to preventing future reoffending, and that they have had some recompense for the harm that was done to them. For family and friends, this means having confidence in making a commitment to providing ongoing support. For the professionals, this means being able to meet their targets of achieving a response to offences that involve keeping offenders within the community and away from lengthy court processes or custodial solutions whenever possible, and ensuring that targets of accountability, repair and reintegration are achieved through a process that was timely and participatory. For the person who has offended, it is important they feel they have repaired the harm they have done, decided not to reoffend and had their reintegrative needs met.

Psychologically, the key feelings for both offenders and victims are ones of acceptance and self-worth and these in turn can make possible a healing of hurts and forgiveness for harm that has been done to others. (Some of these issues are dealt with on a broader level in chapter 14.)

However, it is important to recognise that there are inevitably limits on what can be changed. It is unlikely, and indeed, inappropriate, that what has happened will be forgotten. Victims may take a long time to feel safe again and a new caution is likely to enter into their behaviour. Offenders may have a continuing sense of vulnerability and possibly less self-confidence. Like most human experience, even when there is a successful resolution there are likely to be lasting effects, but those effects can be both positive and negative for everyone who has been involved.

### *Summary of ingredients of a successful restorative outcome*

Evidence on best practice in youth justice shows that there are key factors that can be assessed by asking questions of those involved, particularly of the person who has offended, that are associated with positive life outcomes and reduced reoffending. These have been summarised in previous presentations and publications (Maxwell, 2005; Maxwell et al., 2004a). On the basis of the evidence derived from the views of participants and observations of family group conferences it is possible to construct an analysis of the psychology underpinning the responses of the participants in the family group conference. In this chapter, the focus has been primarily on the young person who has offended but a similar analysis can be made with respect to the family and victims.

The key constructs that are important to building the sense of belonging are being treated with respect and fairness, being supported, being able to participate and empowered by being making decisions, taking responsibility for and repairing the harm that has been done, and being reintegrated within the wider social group. The analysis emphasises the importance of maximising the responsiveness of the justice processes to all of these human needs, and minimising the feelings of shame, exclusion and abandonment. This can best be achieved through an emphasis on enabling those who have done wrong (and, as relevant, their families, supporters and victims) to be informed, participate, exercise control over what happens, be treated with respect, take responsibility and repair harm, feel remorse, be forgiven, and have their identity affirmed through a recognition of the cultures to which they belong. Stigmatic shaming needs be avoided and outcomes need to be fair and equitable.

These best practice lessons can be learnt and developed by building on the experiences of people who are experienced in facilitating restorative justice conferences. These lessons can be put into effect by developing facilitators' skills and abilities, affirming their strengths, and supporting them in their development and the assessment of their practice. It is as important for restorative justice facilitators as it is for other participants in the restorative conference to be treated with respect, affirmed, empowered, treated fairly and recognised for their role in enabling the achievement of the central goals of repairing harm, empowering others and reintegrating offenders into the wider community. Moreover, they should be given the reward, respect and standing appropriate to the value of their work, which is certainly as important, in my view, as that of the professionals in the formal court system.

## Conclusion

A good state will be one that builds systems that are based on respect, that aim to restore dignity, meaning and a sense of belonging and fairness to the lives of those in need. Much that is being done today in New Zealand bears these hallmarks. This book is about sharing examples from New Zealand and providing an opportunity to reflect on the strengths, weaknesses and commonalities among these examples. It is an opportunity to critique our theory and conceptualisation, to compare our practices and to look to how we can continue to learn from one another. It is also a first step in a process of developing a common language that may assist us all to gain a higher profile for the common values and core elements of innovative programmes.

On the other hand, there are real dangers in trivialising the difficulties in resolving conflicts; nor is it appropriate to suggest that introducing a restorative justice approach is merely a matter of choosing from a list of optional additions to the justice system. Justice is best served and outcomes are most constructive when all aspects of the justice process are fair, consistent and respectful of all the participants affected by the events and do all that is possible to assist them to rebuild their lives within the wider society without undue risk to others.

# 2

# Social and Historical Contexts for Restorative and Retributive Justice: Te Ao Pō – Te Ao Mārama (Worlds of Dark and Light)

*James H. Liu*[*]

## Crime and violence in history

The ideas of crime and punishment, of harm-doing and retribution, are as old as human society (Boehm, 1999), but not older than the ideas of damage and restitution, harm-doing and making amends. Retributive justice and restorative justice are the yin and the yang, the dark and the light of conflict resolution that are deeply woven into the fabric of human society everywhere, though they have been called by many and various names.

A system of criminal justice punishing wrongdoers is one of the most basic elements of civilisation; yet codes of criminal justice can function only in the context of a wider range of mechanisms in society that prevent conflict from escalating to the point where officials are called to provide resolution. In traditional Chinese civilisation, for example, there was no court of law to deal with civil disputes. These were handled by business associations and communities (Fitzgerald, 1964, pp. 38–40). To encounter an official in court was to brook danger, as China's criminal codes of law were draconian, officials could be despotic, and winning cases was politically complex. A whole raft of mechanisms evolved to handle civil disputes outside the purview of the state, involving mediation, restitution, apology and shaming by civic- or community-based collectives. To this day, Chinese prefer to avoid courts of law as far possible, preferring mediation and other less formal means of dispute resolution to formal adjudication by the state (Leung, 1988).

---

[*] The title of this chapter was inspired by Professor James Ritchie's talk 'Te ao po – te ao marama: New Zealand character: the light side and the dark' given at *Towards a Restorative Society* 10 and 11 October 2005, Wellington.

Pacific peoples also have significant civil and restorative traditions for resolving disputes that are described by Consedine (1999) and Maxwell and Hayes (2006).

Closer to home, Māori societies lacked the formal bureaucratic mechanisms associated with modern states, and had little capacity for incarcerating wrongdoers. In place of law there was tapu, often translated as sacredness, but concretely involving religious proscriptions or sanctions against doing certain things that maintained a similar function to Western concepts of law. Like other tribal societies, a more informal, but no less powerful, set of mechanisms evolved to dispense justice and settle disputes, involving criticism, ridicule or gossip, mediation by prestigious people or the community as a whole, and payment of restitution (for example, in the form of muru, a collective plundering of the offender and often their family's possessions) (see Best, 1952; Consedine, 1999). The concept of utu, which may be loosely understood as balancing the scales, was central to Māori methods of dispute resolution. As in many other tribal societies, efforts were made to restore damaged relationships, for if the scales could not be balanced, then death or exile was the only other option.

In forager and tribal societies, all justice short of death or exile is by necessity restorative, as there is neither material surplus nor the moral intention to incarcerate wrongdoers. Avoidance is difficult given the intimate scale of community life. Most wrongdoing could be handled by the moral power of the community; Boehm (1999, p. 214) notes that strongest community sanctions are often directed at males who most powerfully resist the will of the majority:

> active sanctioning merely involves offering criticism, engaging in ridicule, or establishing some social distance. Most social control is accomplished in this way, and the psychological stress is likely to be far greater for the deviant than for those who exert the pressure.

As Best (1952, p. 97) puts it:

> We are quite unable to conceive of the force of public opinion in a communistic society; it has a crushing effect on the recalcitrant. In the Maori community the powers of public opinion were remarkable, and had no small effect in the preservation of law and order.

We should not overestimate the power of moral community, however. Keeley (1996), in one of the most comprehensive and controversial reviews of violence through history, reports that the homicide rate among the Kung San, the famously peaceful Bushmen of the Kalahari Desert was "from 1920 to 1955 ... four times that of the United States and twenty to eighty times that of major industrial nations during the 1950s and 1960s" (p. 29). While some scholars have criticised these figures for underestimating violent deaths due to warfare in modern states, Keeley's rejoinder is to compare rates of warfare in nation states from 1800 to 1945 to an ethnographic sample of non-state societies. For the states, there was about a war every generation, whereas for non-state societies, there were "65% at war continuously; 77% at war once every five years" (p. 33). Ethnographic accounts of Māori and Polynesian societies are no exception to this rule. In all these accounts, it is male on male violence, or male on female violence for infidelity, or retaliation thereafter that predominates.

As a method of last resort, non-state peoples were perfectly prepared to use homicidal violence, and they may have used it at rates that far exceeded the rates of even the most violent of contemporary states per capita. Indeed, Johnson and Earle (2000) in their magisterial volume on the evolution of human societies include conflict reduction as one of the important social processes driving the transition of tribal societies to larger and more authoritarian chiefdoms, and chiefdoms into still larger and even more hierarchically organised states (see especially, chapter 12). Because it was personal, violence in pre-state societies always had the potential to spiral into vendetta, where families exacted vengeance against families, and tribes against tribes (see Boehm (1999) for detailed ethnographic accounts). Furthermore, the notion of equality before law was noticeably lacking in most pre-state and pre-modern societies; typically, elites were subject to a different standard than commoners.

## Limitations of restorative justice

The legal system in modern states is the latest in a long series of human inventions designed to prevent blood feuds when restorative justice fails, by depersonalising conflict through submission to a higher authority. One of the clearest limits on restorative justice is the case of homicide. A life taken cannot be restored, so impersonal systems of justice are often required to prevent a cycle of retaliation. Furthermore, in New Zealand there has been stronger and more sustained public support for restorative justice involving youth compared to adult offenders, reflecting the perception that youth offending is more a product of a poor social environment rather than hardened inclinations (see Watt, 2003). The essence of restorative justice is preventative, to re-socialise rather than to punish, to hate the sin not the sinner, but there were clear limits to the amount of deviance that non-state peoples were prepared to tolerate.

A second limitation to restorative justice is that in more complex and multi-segmented societies, moral community is neither so powerful nor as all-encompassing. In larger communities, each person is not morally obligated to treat others fairly, for they are not necessarily bound together by a community of people who will work to ensure justice and to restore relationships when wrongs are done. This necessitates a role by some more impersonal mechanism of dispute resolution like the courts of law. Legal systems in Western societies drew heavily on Roman conceptions that concentrated power in the state (Zehr, 1990). English common law and rational enlightenment thinking expanded the role of civil justice, in part to contain the power of despotic rulers and officials by putting them under the law as well. The concept of the law standing objectively above relationships, to be administered impersonally and rationally by officials, is a cultural innovation of immense value (Liu and Liu, 2003). It follows the apparently unstoppable historical movement towards ever larger and more complex societies. But in the field of criminal justice, the efficiency of impersonal mechanisms for administering justice reached their limits following World War Two.

Reviewing historical data, Braithwaite (1989, p. 49) argues that the increase in crime in most Western societies following World War Two is a product of the collapse of moral community (he devotes particular attention to Victorian England (pp. 111–118)) and the rise of the modern bureaucratic state. In his account, formal mechanisms of law administered by Western post-war states have displaced communities from their traditional role of imposing more heartfelt penalties on wrongdoers through such procedures as compelling an offender to face their peers, feel ashamed, acknowledge harm-doing, make restitution and be reintegrated into society. He contrasts this to the remarkably low rates of both crime and incarceration in post-war Japan. He claims this is a result of Japanese society adopting a "family model writ large", writing that "the fact that convicted American offenders are more than twenty times [likely] to be incarcerated as convicted Japanese offenders says something about the respective commitments of these societies to outcasting versus reintegration" (p. 63).

Braithwaite (1989, pp. 44–50) uses robust empirical findings in criminology to argue for a need to restore the balance between the light and dark and put more power back into communities, so they can administer restorative justice: crime is committed disproportionately by males, 15–25-year-olds, unmarried people, people living in large cities, people who have high residential mobility, and people at the bottom of the class structure (in terms of wealth, employment or ethnicity). Braithwaite further elaborates the features of youth offenders: they dislike school, have low educational aspirations and outcomes, have low occupational aspirations, and are less attached to their parents than are non-offenders. In summary, these are people with low attachment to others and to the community. Hence, reintegrative shame (as opposed to stigmatising shame)

directed at changing offensive behaviour without rejecting the person as a whole serves as a far better deterrent of crime than severe punishments (p. 81) because:
- deterrent effects of such shame are mediated through continuing relationships, so reintegrative shaming builds up rather than breaks down a person's attachments to others;
- reintegrative shaming leads to cognition that a particular type of crime is unthinkable, or morally wrong; and
- a combination of reintegrative shaming and then repentance increases the symbolic power of the community, and empowers the community to push its members towards having a conscience.

In Braithwaite's model, most offending needs to be dealt with on a personal or relational level by the community so that correct behaviour can be internalised. Such a process of reintegrative shaming is distinguished by Braithwaite from the destructive consequences of stigmatic shaming that blames, labels and excoriates the offender. Stigmatic shaming does little to change behaviour while having the potential to further destroy the fragile bonds of the offender with others in society (for further discussion, see Maxwell and Morris, 2002b). Justice is seen as a work in progress directed towards socially integrating members of society, particularly young males. As incarceration cannot do this, it should be reserved only for the most severe of offences and more incorrigible offenders.

Strang (2002) takes a victim of crime perspective that further strengthens the case for restorative justice. She summarises the literature (p. 2) by stating that victims want:
- a less formal process where their views count;
- more information about the processing and outcome of their cases;
- more participation in their cases;
- to be treated respectfully and fairly;
- material restoration; and
- emotional restoration, especially an apology.

Her empirical work shows that such practices as family conferences produce lower expectations of repeat offending, increased feelings of self-respect, confidence and dignity, and more forgiveness relative to baseline and to a comparison group of cases using formal court proceedings. Some of these benefits are reduced for victims of violent offending.

## Implications of the new global economy and greater ethnic diversity

The need for more community-based, restorative justice practices became ever more apparent in the 1970s, following the dismantling of comprehensive systems of welfare and full employment that had prevailed in the 'golden era' of post-war Keynesian economics where health, education, employment and a social safety net seemed within reach of most, if not all, citizens in the developed Western economies (Hobsbawm, 1994).

In New Zealand, Māori, who predominantly earned their livings through traditional means of working the land, migrated to centres of industry en masse to partake of the economic bounty after the war. Pasifika were recruited from their island homes to work in booming factories in New Zealand. By the 1960s, New Zealand was one of the wealthiest and most crime-free societies in the world. This happy state of affairs was not to last long. The combination of a stagnating economy with inflation began in the 1970s, spurred by increasing oil prices. This led Great Britain and the United States to liberalise their economies in the 1980s, allowing market forces to dictate macroeconomics rather than central planning (Yergin and Stanislaw, 1998). New Zealand followed in their footsteps (Kelsey, 1995).

There was a light and a dark side to these reforms. On the positive side, both Great Britain and the United States revived their flagging economies of the 1970s, and became drivers of a new wave of economic growth hinged on the unfettered ability of capital and corporations to exploit markets and labour wherever in the world it was most efficient to do so (Yergin and Stanislaw, 1998). Similarly, New Zealand's economy rebounded after market-based restructuring replaced central planning. Goods and services unimaginable in the post-war era became commonplace to those able to afford them. The downside to this was structural unemployment, and the creation of a permanent underclass who formerly earned money by the sweat of their brows but became unable to compete with cheaper labour that could be sourced anywhere in the world (Kelsey, 1995). Formerly cohesive rural communities, especially Māori communities, were devastated, and a new demographic of the urban dispossessed emerged (Hobsbawm, 1994).

Discourses emerged to justify inequality and poverty that would never have been accepted during the post-war era. All Western nations, but especially the English-speaking nations that embraced Ronald Reagan and Margaret Thatcher's 'neo-liberalism', saw income inequality within their populations increase substantially from 1980 to the present (Bhalla, 2002; Firebaugh, 2003), and with inequality came a greater fear of crime. Crime, and incarceration, was mainly directed at those unable (or unwilling) to succeed economically, which in all states is underpinned by social class (Braithwaite, 1989). By the 1990s, these were straining the prison capacities of all the countries that had embraced the 'invisible hand' of the free market; the United States under Bill Clinton even privatised prisons, making this into a profit-making enterprise for 'commercial providers of incarceration living'.

Currently, the United States incarcerates more of its citizens per capita than any other country in the world by a wide margin, but New Zealand is second among member nations of the Organisation for Economic Co-operation and Development, holding 179 people in prison per 100,000 of population in 2004. New Zealand's per capita prison population in 2004 was more than double that of Scandinavian countries in the same year, and more than triple what it was in New Zealand in 1950 (for fact sheets and sources for these statistics, see the Howard League for Penal Reform website, http://www.howardleague.co.nz).

A major characteristic of the new global economy is the interchangeability of its components; both labour and capital in theory are free to go wherever work is and profit can be made (Yergin and Stanislaw, 1998). Money, not traditional or hereditary standing, becomes the primary determinant of status. Such an economic system is not conducive to maintaining cohesive moral communities capable of effective informal sanctions against the anti-social tendencies of its members. In many economically efficient societies, communities and the state are paying for the hidden costs of a lack of social cohesion. This has led some theorists to speak of a 'third way', integrating market forces with social responsibilities, and factoring in the costs to civil society of market reforms (see Giddens, 2000).

The other major factor requiring the administration of restorative justice was the increasing ethnic diversity within Western societies, particularly, English-speaking societies. Civil society and civil methods of settling disputes work best within cohesive communities, where people share similar values, are connected with one another through various associations, and are motivated to maintain their standing within a community of peers (Putnam, 2000). Such civil society became increasingly challenged, from within, by indigenous minorities, such as New Zealand Māori, and long-standing ethnic minorities, like African-Americans, who became less willing to accept subordinate status and more willing to assert alternative value systems. From without, economic prosperity beckoned to new migrants, Asians and Mexicans and Jamaicans who left their homes for New Zealand, America and Great Britain, and brought with them their own languages, customs and values (Ward et al., 2001).

In such a context, traditional mechanisms for handling civil disputes, which often implicitly involve shared values and social relations, became increasingly inadequate. The increasing vibrancy and efficiency of the social fabric made it more difficult to sustain communities and identities that cross-cut and maintained civil society amidst diversity. The sovereign individual and their immediate family remained intact, but a broader sense of attachment to place and a willingness to make sacrifices for others within the community and the national umbrella suffered. Previously unspoken social contracts between members of society sharing cultural values have a greater need to be articulated in the context of ethnic diversity (see chapter 10). By practising restorative justice, the state and its institutions step into this breach to restore and transform relationships where damage has been done, or to foster new relationships or articulate new values.

In English-speaking societies, the welfare state peaked in the 1970s and has steadily decreased since then (Yergin and Stanislaw, 1998). Globalisation, stratification and ethnic diversity have all increased. These are neither good nor bad in and of themselves, but are part and parcel of a social fabric where greater wealth is concentrated in the hands of economic and political elites, but where the promise of equality and freedom, both real and imagined, still abounds.

## Role of a restorative justice approach

Restorative justice can be read in the broadest sense as trying to increase and strengthen the scope of civil society as far as possible by changing the practices of state institutions in such a way as to put more power in the hands of its citizenry. It does this by increasing the participation of citizens through such institutions as family group conferences, where the family takes an active role in disciplining youth offenders, or where the family and school work together to develop a programme to counter anti-social tendencies among school-age children.

A restorative justice approach acknowledges that the communities affected by anti-social behaviour often are the least well resourced to deal with them, so it brings in the mechanisms of the state to strengthen an otherwise fragile set of relationships, and tenuous or non-existent respect. Its mission is educational, relational, restorative and transformative. By diverting resources to building fences and safety nets at the top of a cliff, before a person falls off, it reduces the need for ambulances and cages at the bottom of the cliff, after a person has fallen.

Restorative justice practices cannot ameliorate the darkness produced by the lack of opportunity and deprivation of inequality. They can offer an alternative path from youthful anti-social tendencies and youth offending to increased punitiveness. Rather than repay offending with punishment, it demands that offending be repaid with respect for the victim, and restoration of the standing of the victim and the offender through such processes as apology and restitution. Restorative justice practices cannot prevent police officers from bearing the brunt of society's failures to properly socialise its members – police must have some of the most justifiable negative stereotypes of people in the world – but it can provide them with an expanded repertoire of ways to deal with offending. About 75% of youth offending in New Zealand is now handled by diversionary plans or family group conferences rather than a court of law where formal charges are pressed. Restorative justice practices will not turn a poor student with no academic motivation into a great student, but they can teach the student that they are valued within their community for their potential – that they are worth the time invested in them to keep them in school and learning rather than being excluded or stood down. In short, restorative justice is not a panacea for the broader social and economic practices of society. Given its lack of an economic or political programme, it falls short of offering a vision for a restorative society. But it points a way forward by illuminating some of contrasts between the dark and light sides of Anglo-settler societies, especially in New Zealand where many present-day difficulties in the criminal justice system date back to a colonial legacy of injustices.

## Biculturalism and restorative justice

Māori, the indigenous people of New Zealand, form 16% of the total population, and about 50% of the prison population. The status of Māori as an economic underclass in New Zealand is the dark side to the light they exert as symbolic partners to the Crown in the only state in the world whose sovereignty rests on a 160-year-old treaty with indigenous people.

The signing of the Treaty of Waitangi in 1840 as a covenant between Māori and the Crown was followed immediately by a half century or so of sometimes dodgy land purchases by settlers that led to intermittent warfare, and the subjugation of Māori within a British settler nation (Belich, 1986). Beginning in the 1990s, a succession of New Zealand governments representing both the right and left have apologised for illegal land grabs and other actions of the colonial era and offered restitution for these injustices (see Graham, 1997).

Currently, a 'bicultural' model where a relationship between Māori and the Crown stands at the heart of New Zealand statehood stands as one viable model for New Zealand identity (Liu, 2005). It is driven by Māori and other New Zealanders' aspirations to create a more inclusive society, and positive distinctiveness that 'loyal colony of Britain' can no longer provide. The restorative justice movement finds fertile grounds among Māori and other New Zealanders for whom the history of the nation is bound in a long struggle to obtain justice and inclusion. The basic strategy of restorative justice to transfer power from the state into local communities and the use of reintegrative shaming and other strategies to restore relationships among community members and empower the community resonates with Māori traditions and aspirations (Consedine, 1999; Hall, 1996).

Ironically, but in accord with Braithwaite's (1989) theory, the cultural renaissance of Māori has been coupled with a rise in the number of Māori in prison. Until the middle of the twentieth century (post–World War Two), Māori lived in rural areas where iwi (tribe), hapū (sub-tribe) and whānau (extended family) managed disputes and administered justice through the traditional power of prestigious leaders backed by the social cohesiveness of a moral community. As Māori moved into the cities, these traditional forms of conflict resolution lost power. This was relatively painless as long as there was economic prosperity and full employment in the cities, but with the collapse of Keynesian economics, many Māori became part of an urban underclass.

The Howard League for Penal Reform (1999) cites justice statistics from the Department of Statistics that show Māori forming 4% of the prison population in the 1920s, 15% by 1940, and then "[b]etween 1950–1990 there was a sevenfold increase in the number of Maori sent to prison – about four times the comparable non-Maori increase". Current figures show Māori at 16% of the national population and about 50% of the prison population. This has led numerous activists and political leaders to offer alternative means of treating young, usually male, offenders within Māori communities (including using pan-tribal marae, see the Te Awhina Community Panel Diversion Scheme described by Maxwell and Morris (1999a)), rather than through the criminal justice system.

Māori have in recent years been at the forefront of advocacy for a return to traditional community-based processes, particularly the use of restorative justice, through such seminal figures as Pita Sharples, and using such concepts as whānau meetings and iwi processes to resolve conflict. Māori have been and continue to be advocates of restorative justice practices, even if they have often had doubts about the ability of restorative justice approaches that are part of the traditional justice system to be effective in responding to Māori and delivering culturally appropriate processes (see Consedine, 1999; Hall, 1996; Ministerial Advisory Committee, 1988). Hall's (1996) recommendations to the Ministry of Justice provide a concise summary of Māori aspirations for a new system of justice that gives Māori a stake in the system by offering them control of the decision-making process. Control includes such features as identifying communities to which Māori belong and where their offending must be dealt with, and recognising the validity of community-based processes for conflict resolution and the value of resourcing them properly.

## Conclusion

In conclusion, restorative justice promises to balance the scales that have tipped too far towards state power and formal procedures of criminal justice in contemporary societies. It puts power back into the hands of the community, and makes offenders answer to their moral community rather than simply being punished through impersonal mechanisms that ascertain guilt and administer penalties. All human beings, including criminal offenders, respond to some moral community whose standards they have internalised and to whom they are answerable. In contemporary multi-ethnic and globally oriented societies, these communities are often restricted to segments of the whole, based on ethnic and civil associations. The principles of restorative justice direct the state to empower lower-level community organisations with mechanisms that make offenders answerable to them in a personal way that involves remorse and re-integrative shaming rather than incarceration. They are part of global efforts such as Giddens' (2000) concept of the third way and Putnam's (2000) idea of social capital to restore communities to their rightful place as part of the civil society from which the state derives its authority.

The role of the state in providing the ultimate sanctioning body that administers justice in an impersonal way, and the role of smaller, more cohesive moral communities that socialise their members to be answerable to other members of the community through more personal and heartfelt mechanisms are the yin (dark) and yang (light) of any healthy functioning system of justice. The centuries-long rise in the power of the state has resulted in a weakening of moral communities that have traditionally been far more effective in dealing with all but the most serious of offences and offenders. The restorative justice movement faces globalisation squarely by empowering local communities to be interconnected with the power of the state, but to take responsibility for disciplining their members to become parts of a whole rather than isolated from it.

# Part Two

# Restorative Practice in the Criminal Justice System

# Introduction to Part Two

The principles and practice of restorative justice were given their first modern expression in New Zealand in the legislation for the new youth justice system introduced in 1989. Gabrielle Maxwell in the first chapter in this part (chapter 3) describes the antecedents of the system, its principles and objectives, and the key processes through which these are given effect. She then reviews the research on the system that provides information about the extent to which the system achieves its objectives and offers an analysis of best practice in relation to the key processes, particularly the family group conference. In chapter 4, Andrew Becroft and Rhonda Thompson go on to examine the unique role of the Youth Court in New Zealand, which operates under a unique set of restorative principles yet with many of the traditional practices and expectations of a Westminster system courtroom.

Restorative justice has also found a place within the adult criminal justice system. In chapter 5, Fred McElrea describes some of the many models of providing restorative justice for adults that developed in different communities throughout New Zealand during the 1990s. This chapter describes the legislative amendments in 2002 that have enabled the outcomes of restorative justice conferences to have a place in the adult court system, and the subsequent development of court-operated pilot projects for those appearing before the District Courts in selected areas.

Police practice too, has been touched by the development of the ideas of restorative justice. Gabrielle Maxwell in chapter 6 and Howard Broad in chapter 7 and describe police practice in relation to youth justice and throughout the police service generally. Transferring concepts and practices that are restorative to prison management and to post-release reintegration have been even more challenging tasks – yet here too important progress has been made and in chapter 8 Kim Workman describes these.

In all these developments, the key concepts are the *participation* of those most directly affected by the offending in decisions about what should be done by way of restoration; the importance of offenders *acknowledging responsibility* for their actions and becoming involved in *repairing the harm* they have done; and the importance, wherever possible, of supporting offenders in ways that enable their *reintegration* within society.

# 3

# The Youth Justice System in New Zealand: Restorative Justice Delivered through the Family Group Conference

*Gabrielle Maxwell*

## Introduction

The principles and objectives set out in the Children, Young Persons, and Their Families Act 1989 are central to the operations of all aspects of the youth justice system including the Youth Court itself. This chapter describes how this Act with its innovative goals came into being. It then focuses on how the more serious offenders are dealt with through family group conferences and in the Youth Court and describes the outcomes of research on the experiences of these young people.[1]

Although the police act as gatekeepers in the youth justice system in New Zealand and take responsibility for the warnings and alternative diversionary actions that are used to deal with 75% of young offenders (chapter 6 deals with their role), it is through the family group conference that the many of the most innovative of these key goals are achieved. Research followed up the outcomes over 3 years recorded in the files for 1,003 young people aged 16 years who had had family group conferences in 1998 (Maxwell et al., 2004b). Five hundred and twenty of these young people were interviewed in late 2001 or early 2002. Observational data and interviews were collected from another 115 cases over the same period. Findings are presented on the extent to which restorative goals have been implemented. Critical factors predicting outcomes are identified, and the implications of these for policy and practice are discussed.

The research demonstrates that the family group conference, together with the impact of the Youth Court when this is also involved, does affect critical

---

[1] The research reported here was funded from a variety of government agencies involved with children, young people and justice, for the most part coordinated and managed through the Ministry of Social Development. Also involved in carrying out these studies were Allison Morris, Venezia Kingi, Jeremy Robertson, Chris Cunningham, among others. Sections of the text have been adapted from previous articles (including Maxwell, 2004a, 2004b).

outcomes for young people: both in terms of reducing offending and increasing the probability of other positive life outcomes. Restorative practices that include empowerment, the repair of harm and reintegrative outcomes make a positive difference, while the extent of a young person's embeddedness in the criminal justice system, severe and retributive outcomes, and stigmatic shaming have negative effects.[2] There are also important findings for crime prevention that suggest the need to focus on support for families, the importance of educational qualifications, and the need for the state to respond effectively when children first come to the attention of the welfare and youth justice systems. Proposals are made for standards against which practice can be assessed.

This chapter describes the factors leading to the development of the unique provisions contained in the Children, Young Persons, and Their Families Act 1989. It then examines the findings of the research on the effectiveness of the system in meeting the Act's objectives, the factors associated with successful outcomes, and the implications of the research for policy and best practice.

## New Zealand origins

The family group conference was the result of a variety of factors that converged in the New Zealand of the 1980s: concern for children's rights; new approaches to effective family therapy; research demonstrating the negative impact of institutionalisation on children; inadequacies in the approach taken in the 1984 legislation to young offenders; the failure of the criminal justice system to take account of issues for victims; experimentation with new models of service provision and approaches to youth offending in the courts; and concerns raised by Māori about the injustices that had been involved in the removal of children from their families.

---

2  Doolan (2003) has raised questions about the extent to which the New Zealand system, in particular, the family group conference, is an example of restorative justice. He suggests that while empowering the victim could be restorative, he doubts this is the case for families, and sees the focus on victims being secondary to the focus on offenders. Johnstone and Van Ness (2007a, p. 10) refer to the empowering potential of restorative encounters, and the psychological literature on empowerment suggests that increased control of decision making can be beneficial for all those involved (Page and Czuba, 1999; Rappaport, 1984). Johnstone and Van Ness (pp. 10ff) make it clear in their handbook that various conceptions of restorative justice place different emphases on the various participants, and, clearly, various authors throughout the handbook recognise family group conferences as a key process for delivering restorative justice.

The ongoing discussion of children's rights both within New Zealand and internationally was another important factor. These were the years when the processes of consultation that led to the United Nations Convention on the Rights of the Child 1989 were occurring throughout the world. Among the issues being debated, which were eventually incorporated in the convention, were: the right of the child to be part of a family; the right of the child to have a voice in decisions affecting them; and the responsibility of the state for ensuring children receive the support and help that is needed for them to develop their full potential.

In New Zealand, not only were the rights being talked about, but so too were the processes for better protecting these rights, including the possibility of establishing a commissioner for children who could monitor the state's actions in relation to children and advocate for children's rights and improvements to the provisions for family support (Renouf et al., 1989). Family involvement was increasingly being seen as central to effective counselling services for children: Family therapy emerged as a new and more effective model for working with children and their families. At the same time, the empowerment of those most affected by conflict and abuse was being recognised in the psychological literature as a crucial part of effective recovery and reintegration (Rappaport, 1981, 1984).

Internationally, research was also demonstrating how ineffective state care had been in helping children grow and learn. New studies indicated that 'children's homes' had often deprived children of a sense of identity that could only come from growing up in a family-like setting. The research also showed that children who spent significant parts of their childhoods in institutions failed to develop the life skills they needed to cope constructively with the world. Instead, they acquired new skills and friends among others who had also learned to respond to difficult and hurtful situations with anger, violence and anti-social behaviour (Doolan, 1988; Dowden and Andrews, 1999).

In New Zealand, both experience and research had identified deficiencies with the Children's Boards set up in 1974 to respond to young offenders; in particular, their reliance on custodial care and their 'net-widening' approach to youth offending (that is, the effect of their actions in increasing the frequency and severity of penalties for relatively minor offending by young people) (Morris and Young, 1987).

These were also the years when the omission of victims from any significant role in justice processes was being questioned. The representation of victims' views in the justice system and opportunities for redress were being called for.

In New Zealand, the Victims of Offences Act 1987 was introduced, providing for victim support groups and victim impact statements.[3]

The above concerns were all part of an ongoing international debate. In New Zealand an even more immediate and important concern was being voiced by Māori. In 1985, the Minister of Social Welfare set up a ministerial advisory committee "to advise ... on the most appropriate means to achieve ... an approach which would meet the needs of Maori in policy, planning and service delivery in the Department of Social Welfare" (Ministerial Advisory Committee, 1988, p. 5). This committee was headed by John Rangihau, a senior social worker and Māori leader. The committee travelled widely, listening to the concerns of Māori throughout the country. Its report commented at length on history, legal perspectives, racism and biculturalism. One of the report's substantial concerns was that both law and practice in delivering services for children had locked out Māori families and communities from the care of their children (p. 29). Several recommendations were aimed at removing young people from institutions and responding to them within their own communities (recommendations 6–10, pp. 11–13). Appendix II to the report (pp. 74–76) elaborated on the relevant legal perspectives that were of concern in relation to the existing Children and Young Persons Act 1974.

Against this background it is hardly surprising when, in the same year, new draft legislation (the Children and Young Persons Bill 1986) saw Māori throughout the country voicing their anger at the prospect of legislation that still included many proposals already identified as having caused problems in the past. New proposals for strengthening the role of experts in decision making about the care of children were challenged as denying the rightful role of whānau, hapū and iwi (family, clan and tribe) to decide about the care of their own tamariki (children) and rangatahi (young people). The 1986 bill was seen as even more likely to continue to remove Māori children from their families, whānau, hapū, iwi and communities. In these years, Māori whānau and hapū meetings were advocated by commentators, including Moana Jackson[4] (1988, pp. 186–194) and social work staff at the Lower Hutt District Office of the Department of Social Welfare (1989), who piloted the first family group conferences, as the only appropriate model for Māori when decisions were to be taken about children.

Meanwhile, processes based on Māori customary practice and family and community involvement in decisions were set up in different parts of the

---

3  Subsequent legislation (the Victims' Rights Act 2002) has extended these provisions.
4  At that time employed in the Department of Justice.

country to resolve historical grievances relating to sexual abuse, as well as to reach decisions about children. New Youth Court models were piloted. Judge Mick Brown (who later became the first Principal Youth Court Judge) ran a pilot in Waitakere of a new model of a Youth Court that showed a respect for Māori views and aimed to shift power from the court to the community, using, at times, marae-based court hearings (see Brown and McElrea, 1993). Judge David Carruthers (who later became the second Principal Youth Court Judge) operated a similar pilot in Porirua that relied heavily on volunteer community advisers to the court and input from family members in reaching its decisions (Watt, 2003).

In September 1987, the new Minister of Social Welfare, Michael Cullen, asked the Department of Social Welfare to establish a working party to report to him on how the 1986 bill could be made simpler, made more culturally sensitive and use resources for services rather than relying on a costly infrastructure. The working party included Māori and Pacific staff, and held hui (consultation meetings) throughout the country and received oral and written submissions from Māori and Pacific peoples (Renouf et al., 1989).

The working party also adopted many of the proposals developed in a report written by Mike Doolan after a study tour to the United Kingdom and United States. Doolan (1988) proposed the family group conference as a new diversionary process that could allow Māori ownership of the process, empower those affected by the offending to make decisions, and emphasise responses to offending that would involve accountability and reintegration. The dramatically changed new version of the bill was returned to parliament in May 1989, rapidly passed through its second and third readings, and came into effect on 1 November as the Children, Young Persons, and Their Families Act 1989.

## Children, Young Persons, and Their Families Act 1989: a new philosophy and a new system

### Principles and objects

The youth justice system in New Zealand is set out in the Children, Young Persons, and Their Families Act 1989. (Unless otherwise stated, all legislative references in this chapter are to this Act.) The goals and values underpinning the system are explicitly described in the Act's objects and principles (sections 4, 5 and 208). These, together with specific ensuing sections, emphasise several established values relating to welfare, justice and the protection of rights.

- *Protection of rights* (section 208(h)): Children and young people must be informed of their rights, including that they are not required to make a statement (sections 215–220); strict and limited conditions govern police powers of arrest (section 214); a parent or nominated person is required to be present any at interview (sections 221–226); parents are to be fully informed (section 8), especially when a young person is taken into custody (sections 229–232); children and young people are entitled to legal representation (sections 227–228); and children and young people must be fully informed of their rights and the legal processes in a language and a manner that they can understand (section 10).

- *Welfare*: Rehabilitative options and support for families should be provided (section 4(a)), children cannot normally be prosecuted in the Youth Court until they reach the age of 14 years (section 272), and time-frames for resolving matters must be appropriate to their age (section 5(f)).
- *Justice:* Diversion from courts and custody is to be preferred, as are the least restrictive sanctions (sections 208(a) and (f)(ii) and 209). The emphasis is on accountability (section 4(f)) and a separation of welfare and justice matters (section 208(b)).

At the time the Act was implemented, the philosophy of restorative justice had not yet been clearly articulated; nor had its distinctive practices been fully theorised as principles. However, when the practices are related to principles, it is clear that the Act also emphasises the newer and restorative values of the participation and empowerment of children and families, repair of harm and reintegration of offenders into society.

- *Participation and empowerment:* Whenever possible, the child or young person's family is expected to participate in making decisions (section 5(a)) or at least to be consulted or involved in some other way (section 5(d) and (e)) and for consideration to be given to the wishes of the child or young person (section 208(d)). These provisions, along with the requirements that families, young people and victims be consulted about the family group conference process (section 250) and invited to the family group conference (sections 251 and 253), have their views ascertained (section 254), and, if present, to be part of the decision making (sections 260, 263 and 264), all provide for participation and involvement in family group conference decisions. Section 11 specifically requires court and counsel to encourage and assist the young person to participate in any court proceedings. Sections 9, 10 and 205 also are designed to ensure young people and their families are informed about and understand the decisions that are taken.
- *Repair:* Young offenders are expected to be accountable for what they have done and are encouraged to take responsibility for their behaviour (section 4(f)(i)) and have regard to the interests of any victims of that

offending (section 208(g)). While there is no specific wording in the Act that requires young people to become involved in making amends for their actions, in practice the most common outcomes of the family group conference process in response to these principles are apologies and agreements to undertake actions, which are seen as going some way to make up for the harm that has been done (Maxwell and Morris, 1993; Maxwell et al., 2004b).

- *Reintegration:* Section 4(f)(ii) specifically requires that young people involved in offences "are dealt with in a way that acknowledges their needs and that will give them the opportunity to develop in responsible, beneficial, and socially acceptable ways". Specific principles in section 208 spell out clearly that the intention is that these measures will involve the placement of children or young people with family or whānau and in the community whenever possible, take the least restrictive form possible, and provide support to family and whānau that will foster their ability to deal with their own children and young people.

## Key processes

The new youth justice system adopted six new processes that are key to achieving the goals outlined above.

### Police warnings

Police warnings, either informal verbal warnings or more formal written warnings, are sent to the young person and their family to indicate the inappropriateness of the offending behaviour and to warn of the consequences of future offending (sections 209–213).[5] About 44% of young offenders are dealt with in this way (Maxwell et al., 2002; Maxwell and Paulin, 2004; chapter 6 in this book).

### Police youth diversion

Police youth diversion (or, as it is sometimes referred to, 'alternative action') is used for about a third of all children and young people who come to the notice of the police (Maxwell et al., 2002). This involves a police Youth Aid officer developing a plan with the young person and their family (sometimes in consultation with the victim), which can include actions intended to repair harm and to prevent further offending (for example, by referring the young person

---

5   There is provision for a formal police caution, but in practice this is not used.

and/or their family to suitable services or negotiating about schooling problems). (Chapter 6 describes this process more fully.)

*Family group conferences*
Family group conferences are at the heart of the new system for the more serious offenders (sections 247–266). The police refer about 8% of those who offend to such conferences directly and the Youth Court refers the 17% who are formally charged for a family group conference before any decision is made about the court's response (Maxwell et al., 2004b).

Family group conferences have been described fully elsewhere (Maxwell et al., 2004b; Maxwell and Morris, 1993). However, they are intended to provide an opportunity to those most affected by the offending (the young person, their family and the victim) to play a full part in the process of discussing possible outcomes and reaching a consensus about recommendations and plans for repairing harm and preventing future reoffending.

*Youth Court*
The Youth Court is required to manage matters in ways that enhance the understanding of procedures by participants, involve families and young people (sections 10 and 11), and consider and follow the recommendations of the family group conference unless there is no agreement or there are good reasons under law for modifying it (section 279). The Youth Court also responds to the principles of the Act that prefer diversionary options and least restrictive sanctions, and aims to minimise the time taken to process cases and complete tasks. (Chapter 4 deals with this in more detail.)

*Youth offending teams*
Youth offending teams have been set up throughout the country (Ministerial Taskforce, 2002). These teams comprise a manager and a practitioner from Child, Youth and Family, the New Zealand Police, and the Ministries of Health and Education. In some areas, Youth Court staff and representatives of community agencies are also part of the team. The team's role is to coordinate and improve service delivery by supporting best practice, making sure the right people are connected and working together, monitoring data on offending and outcomes for the young people who become involved in the youth justice system, and developing initiatives to educate the community about youth justice and ensure that the needed services and back-up are provided to children, young people and families.

## The Youth Justice System in New Zealand

*Community response options*

Community response options are the final key to implementing the system. Suitable services and strategies need to be available to ensure families receive the support they need in caring for their children and young people, and that children and young people's needs in the areas of health, education and leisure are provided for.[6] Suitable arrangements also need to be made when the court orders the young person to undertake tasks in the community as an alternative to custody.[7]

### Family group conferences' key elements of practice

*Youth justice coordinators*

Youth justice coordinators are responsible for making arrangements for all children and young people referred for family group conferences by the police or Youth Court (section 247).

Youth justice coordinators are employed by Child, Youth and Family. They are chosen to ensure a representation of Māori, Pacific peoples and other ethnic groups to reflect the composition of the community they serve. They are expected to have an appropriate background and training in working with families and young people. In practice, most have trained as social workers.

The role of youth justice coordinators includes informing the young person, family members and victims about the family group conference and seeking their input on who should attend, the time of the conference, where it should be held and any other arrangements (for example, preferred customary practices and who should facilitate the conference). Ideally, this is done through meetings with all parties. This part of the conference is seen as essential to achieving effective outcomes (Levine and Wyn, 1991). Other aspects of their role include facilitating conferences, monitoring the outcome of plans and arranging for plans to be reviewed when necessary (sections 262–266).

---

6   Ideally, one would add victim support services to this list, but, although these are increasingly available in New Zealand, the provision for and management of these has been the responsibility of other players in the justice sector.

7   The top tariffs in the Youth Court are orders for supervision, supervision with activity (where the young person remains in the community but carries out a plan that involves supervised activities and 24-hour-a-day, 7-day-a-week monitoring), supervision with residence (in a residential youth centre for up to 3 months followed by 6 months' supervision), and transfer to the District Court or High Court for sentence (usually followed by a prison sentence or other adult penalty) (section 283(o)).

Those attending the family group conference will normally include the young person and their family, the victim and their supporters, a representative of the police, the facilitator, others who may be able to provide useful information (section 251), and, when the matter is referred from the Youth Court, a youth advocate (sections 323–325).

The process at the family group conference usually includes introductions, an account of what happened, a discussion of the offending and a discussion of possible responses to the offending. The family and the young person then retire to discuss matters privately, and develop a proposal for a plan to respond to the offence. The full conference reconvenes to discuss the family's proposals, and, if possible, reach a consensus on the final plan, including details relating to supervision and monitoring. (For a fuller description, see Figure 3.1.)

## Research on outcomes

Early studies of the New Zealand youth justice system described and evaluated it (Maxwell and Morris 1993), looked at aspects of best practice (Maxwell and Morris, 1996) and examined factors associated with reoffending (Maxwell and Morris, 1999b; Morris et al., 1997). In 2004, Maxwell and her associates published a major study of factors related to effective outcomes (Maxwell et al., 2004a, 2004b). The analysis presented here relies mainly on this most recent retrospective file study of more than 1,000 young people who had family group conferences, interviews with more than 500 of these young people, and a smaller prospective study of just over 100 cases where victims and families as well as young people were interviewed and conferences were observed. Collectively, these studies, enable reasonably firm conclusions to be drawn about the extent to which objectives have been achieved, the factors predicting outcomes, and the nature of the critical aspects of best practice. These results are summarised below. Unless otherwise stated, data come from Maxwell et al. (2004a).

### *Meeting objectives*

#### *Accountability, repair and wellbeing*

The goal of achieving accountability for young people is being achieved almost universally through the plans agreed at the family group conference (97% of conference plans include measures intended to ensure accountability) and through the orders of the Youth Court. Data from Child, Youth and Family files indicate that in more than 80% of cases all the required tasks are satisfactorily completed and in another 9% were mainly completed.

**Figure 3.1:** What happens at a family group conference

At a family group conference, the facilitator greets people and brings them into the meeting place. Usually the seating is arranged in an open circle and people are invited to introduce themselves.

The facilitator of the meeting then briefly reminds everyone of the purpose of the meeting: to discuss what has happened, to find ways in which the young person can be held accountable for their actions, and to discuss ways to prevent such happenings in the future.

Usually, the police officer is invited first to read the police summary of the facts. The young person is asked if they agree that these are accurate. If the young person does not agree, the details are discussed and may be amended, but, provided the young person accepts responsibility for the harm that was caused, the conference can continue. If the young person denies matters, the conference concludes and the matter is referred back to the police for further investigation or to the Youth Court for a trial.

If the conference proceeds, the victim is then usually invited to present their view of what happened. Others become part of the discussion, which naturally moves from the views of each of the participants about what has happened and what can be done to repair the harm. The young person is often asked why they did what they did. Family members often talk about their relationship with the young person. Ways of preventing such behaviour in the future are canvassed.

After a general discussion (which may take half an hour or more), the victim and professionals leave the family and young person to discuss privately what they think should happen and draw up a plan.

The meeting reconvenes with all the participants present. The family presents its plan and everyone discusses it. The plan is amended as needed. When all participants are in agreement, the decisions on the plan are recorded and the meeting concludes. If there is no agreement, the matter is referred back to the police or the Youth Court, depending on which agency referred the case for a family group conference.

Unlike the formal process of the court, where all the information to be presented has already been collected, a family group conference can involve people disclosing what has not previously been shared, so can be very emotional. The victim may express anger or fear or sorrow. They may ask for things to be done to help them or others, and they may be concerned that the young person is helped so that they do not reoffend. Among the family, there is often a lot of soul-searching over what might have been done differently and what they can do now and in the future. Sometimes, they too express their anger at the young person. The young person frequently apologises to any victim that is present but also often finds it difficult to talk easily. Tears are not uncommon.

At best, there can be laughter and reconciliation. Even if no strong emotion has been expressed, young people, families and victims will often afterwards describe being very much affected by what occurred.

When data on the accountability elements of plans are further broken down, the results show that some form of response intended to repair harm is part of 84% of young people's plans. Elements of plans that were fundamentally restrictive were present in nearly 60% of plans, although it is doubtful that these will have always been necessary for public safety or consistent with the goals of the Act.

Measures to enhance wellbeing were included in about two-thirds of the plans: 39% had a reintegrative element and 31% had a rehabilitative element in their plan.

However, the elements of plans intended to promote wellbeing are not necessarily being implemented, especially the rehabilitative aspects of plans. Both reintegrative and rehabilitative options are too rarely available for young people, and those that are available are not necessarily effective.[8]

### Empowerment

The main process goals of the family group conference – ensuring that the appropriate people participate, that victims and families are involved and that there is consensus decision making – appear to be being largely achieved. Young people almost always attended the conference (99%) and so too did at least one parent or caregiver (85%). Other family members were present in nearly half the cases (44%). Where a potential victim had been identified, just under half (47%) chose to attend. More than 80% of parents reported feeling fully involved in the process of reaching a decision, but this was only true for just over half the young people and the victims.

Despite the records showing almost universally that the outcome of the conference was an agreed decision, interviews revealed that the process of decision making did not always reflect a true consensus. There were often indirect pressures on participants to agree, and, at times, there was evidence that professionals dominated decision making.

### Cultural responsiveness

The data on the experiences of Māori and Pacific family group conferences show that they can be successful in engaging families and arriving at successful outcomes. Success appears to be facilitated when the process treats the family

---

8   Some increase in the proportion referred to programmes or training courses was, however, noted for the sample collected in 2000/01 compared with the 1998 sample. Since these data were collected, additional resources have been made available to improve services.

members with respect and acknowledges them and their role in a manner that goes beyond token gestures. The participants need to feel validated and central to the process rather than merely being provided with an opportunity to participate. They need to be able to take charge of decisions rather than have professionals suggest or make decisions for them. They need to be spoken to in a language and a manner they understand by people who understand and can respond to them in ways that are affirming and respectful. They may need encouragement to provide their young people in turn with the support, affirmation and forgiveness that the young person needs if they are to become part of a solution that sets wrongs right and builds towards a constructive future. In addition, speakers of English as a second language must always be enabled to understand the process.

There is clearly room for improvement in the way family group conferences are managed in these respects. Best practice would be for the facilitator to ascertain the specific cultural expectations of the participants before the conference and to clearly explain any culturally specific processes to all participants at the beginning. In particular, it is important that the convenor ensures that all participants in the family group conference are introduced to each other. When interpreters are not able to be present, non-English speakers should be identified and encouraged to seek clarification (perhaps from a family translator) throughout the conference.

### Time-frames

Criticisms have often been made of the time it takes to resolve matters, with blame being placed on one or other parts of the system. Overall, appropriate time-frames in convening and completing family group conferences are, for the most part, being met within Child, Youth and Family (three-quarters are completed within 4 weeks of referral). But time-frames in all parts of the system often seem unnecessarily long when considered from a young person's perspective.[9] Improved practice in all parts of the system is possible, but this

---

9   For example, Maxwell and colleagues (2004a, pp. 101–105) describe the length of time spent by Youth Court cases in various stages of the process. In the police, 30% of cases took more than 4 weeks to reach Youth Aid. In Youth Aid, 15% of cases took more than 4 weeks before being sent to the Youth Court. In Child, Youth and Family, 16% of cases took more than 4 weeks for the conference to be completed. In the Youth Court, more than half the cases took more than 12 weeks before the final court date. The mean number of days from first to final appearance was 108 days, and 15% took more than 140 days.

## Protecting rights

Information on the extent to which young people's rights were being protected was not available.

Procedures for recording the actions of police in arresting and interviewing young people were in place during the early years of the Act (Maxwell and Morris, 1993), but these appear to have been discontinued. In addition, records have not been kept on whether the young person was asked if they agreed with the summary of facts and, if they did not, the processes followed to correct the allegations of police or to arrange a defended hearing.

All young people who were charged in the Youth Court had a youth advocate appointed to represent them. However, there are no formal arrangements for monitoring the performance of youth advocates.

## Diversion and decarceration

Achieving diversion and decarceration are key objectives of the Act. The results of the new provisions have been dramatic. A smaller proportion of young offenders now appear in court in New Zealand than in any other Western country. Figure 3.2 describes the decline in the rate of Youth Court appearances from before the Act to 2001. This change has occurred partly through the increased use of police warnings, but the major change has come about through the use of police youth diversionary plans and family group conferences as primary responses to youth offending.

The diversionary changes have occurred, not only by developing new processes for making young offenders accountable outside the Youth Court, but also by changing practices within the Youth Court. Most cases that come before the Youth Court are now able to be dealt with by discharge after plans arrived out in a family group conference have been completed, and relatively few are resolved through orders made in the Youth Court (the impact of the Act on Youth Court practice is described in greater detail in chapter 4).

A second dramatic change in outcomes for young offenders is the very low rate of custodial sentence resulting from court appearance. Figure 3.3 graphs changes in the number of custodial sentences from before the introduction of the Act to 2001. The number of custodial outcomes in 2001 is less than a quarter of what it was in 1987. This has resulted from a decline in the use of residential custody for young offenders and a decline in the number of young offenders being transferred to the adult courts for consideration of a prison sentence.

The Youth Justice System in New Zealand

**Figure 3.2:** Rate of youth offender (aged 10–16 years) appearances per 10,000 distinct cases in the Youth Court, 1987–2001

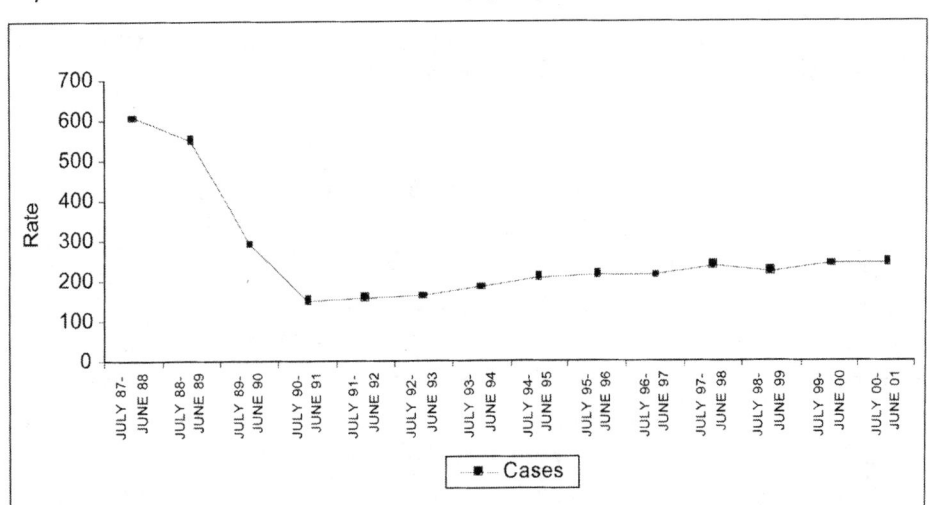

Source: Maxwell et al., 2004a.

**Figure 3.3:** Number of young people receiving custodial sentences as a result of a conviction and sentence in the District Court or High Court, 1987–2001

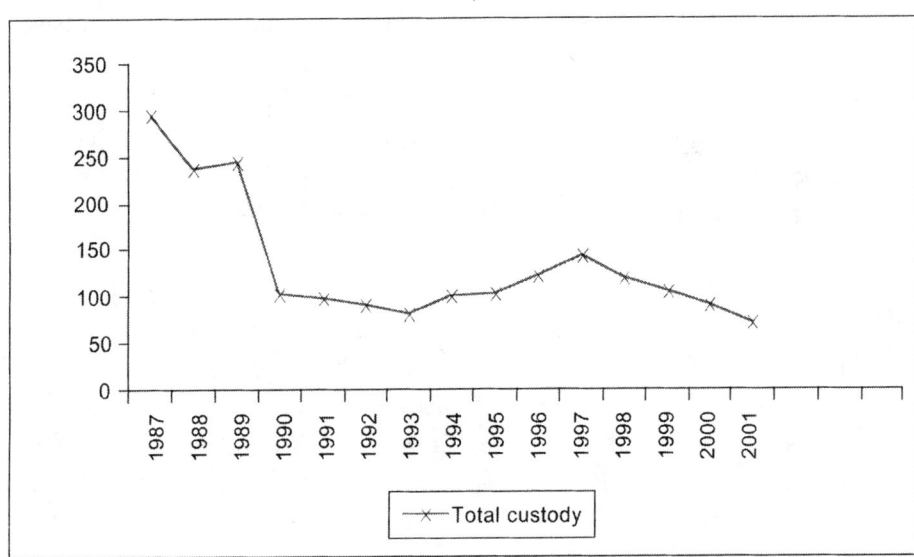

Source: Maxwell et al., 2004a.

At times, there has been a perception that these changes were 'soft' on young offenders and that the consequence would be an increase in reoffending (Robertson, 2003). On the contrary, evidence indicates that young offenders do not perceive the diversionary alternatives as a 'soft' option, and there has been no dramatic adverse effect on reoffending rates since the introduction of these diversionary changes (Morris and Maxwell, 2003).

On the other hand, it has been argued that it would be possible to resolve an even greater number of cases outside the Youth Court and for more young offenders to be accountable in the community rather than through the use of custodial sentences (Maxwell et al., 2004a). Such an increase in the use of diversionary decisions and non-custodial options would require a redistribution of resources away from courts, residences and prisons towards police Youth Aid, youth justice coordinators, social workers and community service providers. However, I would argue that there would be both direct financial savings from such a shift as well as an increase in the constructive outcomes for the young people involved.

## *Predicting outcomes*

### *Life outcomes*

Research results show that since participating in a family group conference, most of the young people were able to develop positive goals and achieve successes (Maxwell et al., 2004a). Seventy percent of those followed up had been constructively employed in the previous 6 months, and more than 80% reported having close personal relationships. About 60% did not want any further involvement in crime, felt life had gone well for them, and had positive views about the future.

However, negative life events and risk factors were also recorded for more than 60%. Furthermore, nearly two-thirds said that they were involved in further offending, and this figure agrees with court records. Data on convictions for offences committed as an adult showed that nearly half the offenders appeared before the courts in the first year after they turned 17, and after 3 years this figure had risen to 69%. Offences most often involved property, followed by traffic and violence offences. Within 3 years, 22% had received a prison sentence.

Reoffending is often the key criterion used for evaluating the success of a system. Undoubtedly, this is an important outcome, but there are problems with this as a criterion in research. First, there are no baseline data about reoffending before the Act. International data are of little value as they describe total groups of young offenders whereas only a limited subset of more serious offenders in New Zealand would normally be those at high risk of reoffending. Furthermore, these young people are in an age group and from backgrounds where the probability of reoffending would normally increase over the next few years. Perhaps what is more important about these data, is not the absolute level of reoffending but the finding that the probability of reoffending is less when the family group conference plans include restorative outcomes.

## *Strongest predictors*

Traditionally, research on young criminal offenders shows the importance in predicting both offending and reoffending of family background, schooling, early anti-social behaviour, and relationships with others. The research by Maxwell and colleagues (2004a, p. 204) also identified the statistical significance of these factors in predicting reoffending, particularly:

- family background, including whether:
  - family relationships were distant and children were in conflict with parents;
  - family members were involved in crime;
  - children were abused and/or severely punished; and
  - parental monitoring of children was absent or limited;
- school background, including:
  - negative experiences of school; and
  - a failure to gain school qualifications;
- anti-social behaviour, including:
  - bullying, substance abuse, stealing and fighting;
  - running away; and
  - involvement with child welfare and the police;
- relationships, including:
  - being bored and 'hanging around'; and
  - having a lack of positive relationships with others;
- being currently involved in offences.

What is new in the research by Maxwell and colleagues (2004a, p. 205) is that it also identifies the aspects of the young person's experience in the youth justice system that are predictors of future offending and life outcomes. Particular aspects of the process and its aftermath that showed significant correlations with not reoffending were:

- diversionary actions, including:
  - being dealt with at lower levels of system; and
  - receiving less severe penalties;

- the family group conference, including:
  - the father as well as the mother attending a family group conference;
  - a small number of professionals at the family group conference;
  - the young person feeling they participated in the family group conference;
  - the young person deciding to keep out of trouble in future; and
  - the young person not feeling stigmatised and excluded from the process;
- subsequent events, including the young person:
  - not having criminal associates;
  - not being involved with drugs and alcohol; and
  - experiencing positive life events, including close relationships or obtaining a qualification or a job.

These results indicate the potential importance of diversionary responses and participatory family group conferences for preventing reoffending. Other analyses suggest that a young person's feeling they were treated fairly and with respect at the conference; feeling remorseful and able to repair the harm they had done; and having reintegrative outcomes arranged (such as constructive programmes and educational plans) were significantly associated with constructive outcomes.

The results of the research on the impact of justice processes on reoffending and positive life outcomes as young adults are clear and consistent, both internally and with previous studies, to the extent that they have examined similar issues (Andrews, 1994; Andrews et al., 1999; Farrington, 1994; Fergusson et al., 1994; Zamble and Quinsey, 1997). The data provide strong support for the model described in the full report of this research that explains both reoffending and positive life outcomes from a variety of earlier life events (Maxwell et al., 2004a). Family background factors had an impact on the young people's lives, but so too did the responses of the youth justice system, including a restorative family group conference. Events after the conference also affected young people's future. Phrased like this, the conclusions seem to be common sense.

These data demonstrate that, if reoffending is to be reduced and the breach in the social harmony is to be repaired, diversion and decarceration are critical, and so too are constructive processes and responses. The findings here are a strong validation of restorative justice theory: repair, reintegration, fairness and respect, participation and empowerment, and forgiveness are key elements in effective outcomes, while punitive and restrictive sanctions and stigmatic shaming are ineffective or counterproductive. Key lessons from this research are that:

- early action is important and is likely to be effective in preventing reoffending and ensuring positive life outcomes;
- the focus of early intervention needs to be on building positive relationships in both the school and the family environment, rather than on simply responding with denunciation or punishment to early indicators of anti-social behaviour;
- using diversionary strategies, implementing the least restrictive sanctions and avoiding charges in the Youth Court whenever possible are likely to lead to more positive outcomes;
- a constructive family group conference can make an important contribution to preventing further offending, despite negative background factors and irrespective of the nature of the offending; and
- life events after the conference also matter: taking advantage of the opportunity to address psychological problems, alcohol and drug misuse, educational failure and lack of employment can reduce reoffending and increase positive life outcomes.

The data describe different aspects of the family group conference that are important in making reoffending less likely. There should be good preparation before the conference. At the conference, the young person should feel supported, understand what is happening, participate and not feel stigmatised or excluded. Those young people who were able to feel remorse for what they had done, to go some way to making amends and who came away from the family group conference feeling forgiven were less likely to reoffend than those who did not. In summary, processes that are diversionary, sanctions that are the least restrictive and outcomes that are constructive are associated with positive life outcomes. These findings provide a validation for the objects and the principles underlying the Act and of the features that those close to the youth justice system in New Zealand have identified as being important to good practice (Levine et al., 1998), and for the main tenets of restorative justice theory.

However, few of the young people in this study appear to have participated in positive and effective follow-up programmes for reintegration. Research strongly suggests that, if the restorative process were followed up with appropriate programmes of good quality, the outcomes would be even more positive (Andrews and Bonta, 1998; Andrews et al., 1999; Dowden and Andrews, 1999; Farrington, 1994; Sherman et al., 1997).

The findings identified clearly the most important precursors of good outcomes in respect of backgrounds and criminal justice events. They also identified critical factors in building on positive youth justice system experiences by:

- providing appropriate and effective mental health services;
- making employment a realistic possibility; and
- avoiding placing the young people in situations where they form close bonds with others involved in offending.

On the other hand, there is no support in these data for those who call for stronger justice system responses based on punishment and retribution as methods of protecting communities rather than on repair and reintegration.

## Moving forward

The research enables aspects of policy and practice to be identified if New Zealand is to become more effective in preventing and responding to offending by children and young people. In particular, there are implications for crime prevention strategies; improved policies are needed in key areas such as recording data, monitoring conferences, supporting professionals and setting standards of practice that are consistent with the key indicators of effective practice that are likely to achieve desired outcomes.

### *Crime prevention*

An analysis of the background factors most likely to be associated with conviction as an adult has implications for crime prevention strategies.

- As in other research, the factors in the backgrounds of young people that place them at risk include frequent changes of home and school, high levels of childhood abuse and punishment, and a lack of parental monitoring. Potentially, these could be addressed by early intervention programmes aimed at such children and young people and their families.
- Early involvement with Child Youth and Family, either for reasons of care and protection or because of earlier offending, is an important predictor of negative life outcomes. This finding suggests the importance of ensuring the quality and effectiveness of interventions when a child or young person first comes to the notice of Child, Youth and Family.
- A lack of school qualifications is another major factor in poor outcomes, indicating the critical impact of the effective management of problems that lead to school drop out and failure.

The level at which a young person is dealt with in the youth justice system emerges as an important factor in life outcomes. This finding underlines the importance of compliance with the diversionary principles of the Act by ensuring that children and young people are, whenever possible, dealt with at the least formal level possible in the youth justice system and without the use of punitive sanctions.

## *Effective practice*

Good outcomes depend on good practice (Levine et al., 1998; Maxwell et al., 2004a, 2004b). But rules for best practice are not easy to develop because good outcomes do not depend on following detailed procedures but rather on allowing the participants themselves to determine what happens. Nevertheless, some generalisations are possible.

Ideally, a conference will work best when the families, victims and young people have been well informed about what is likely to take place and their role in it, and are actively involved in deciding the arrangements and who will be present. The presence of all these people is important, but victims need to feel free to choose to stay away if they wish. If they do stay away, finding ways they can have their views presented to the group is important. Findings on best practice for youth justice coordinators emphasise enabling people to talk freely in the conference and minimising professional domination of the decisions that are arrived at.

Research indicates that particularly important features of practice in the family group conference from the perspective of the young person include (Maxwell et al., 2004a):

- having people present that support and care about them;
- being treated fairly and with respect;
- not feeling stigmatised and excluded;
- participating fully by presenting views and being involved in decisions;
- feeling remorse, including understanding the victim's views and feeling genuine regret for what happened;
- feeling able to repair the harm that was done;
- feeling that others forgive them and give them another chance; and
- deciding to keep out of trouble in future.

Research also identifies best practice from the point of view of the youth justice coordinators who arrange the family group conferences: the need for professional supervision and regular meetings with other coordinators and other local youth justice professionals (Levine et al., 1998; Maxwell and Morris, 1993; Maxwell et al., 1997; Morris and Maxwell, 1999).[10] Best practice also

---

10 Key professionals include police, those working in the Youth Court and Child, Youth and Family, and community agency personnel. Youth offending teams comprising

depends on quality programmes that are effective in rehabilitating and reintegrating young people.

## Conclusion

The youth justice system in New Zealand developed independently of restorative justice theory and in response to both pressure from Māori for participatory processes and the findings of international research on the negative impact of institutional responses to young people who offend. The system is now seen internationally as the first major example of restorative justice in practice. The outcomes from the research presented here indicate that a commitment to diversionary and restorative principles and values can enable the development of a total system of youth justice that is effective in reducing the numbers of young people appearing in court and being placed in institutions and result in improved life outcomes and reduced reoffending. Furthermore, a restorative system such as that described here is inevitably less costly financially as well as less criminogenic than are systems that rely heavily on courts to process youth offenders and institutions to incarcerate them.

Parallel to the development of the youth justice system in New Zealand has been the development of restorative justice theory and practice in the adult system here and throughout the world. In particular, a variety of different youth justice systems using some form of conferencing has been adopted throughout Australia. These have built on the New Zealand experience, developing a variety of different models of practice, and research carried out on effective outcomes in these jurisdictions supports the outcomes reported for New Zealand (Daly, 2001; Luke and Lind, 2002; Sherman et al., 2000).

The New Zealand youth justice system continues to attract great interest because it is the only national system in the world, and, because it has been in operation nationally for more than 12 years, judgements can be made about its ability to deliver what it promised in its early years. Furthermore, the research presented that has been carried out in New Zealand is the first examination of the impact of all aspects of the system as opposed to an analysis of specific aspects such as conferencing. What then is the verdict today?

In some respects, the youth justice system has continued to grow in strength and become more restorative in its philosophy and practice. The sanctions adopted by family group conferences remain at least as restorative in 2002 as

---

members of these groups are being set up under the Youth Offending Strategy (Ministerial Taskforce, 2002).

they were in 1990. The way in which police have developed their own diversionary practices reflects restorative philosophies rather than the punitive philosophies that underpin much police action in response to young people in other jurisdictions. The Youth Court appears to have become even more inclusive than it was in its earliest years if the views of young people and families are to be relied on. Now victims more often appear to feel positively about their experiences. Reintegrative and rehabilitative programmes are being offered more often, and current policies aim to strengthen this aspect of the youth justice system. Meanwhile, both community and government-sponsored models of providing restorative justice options in the adult justice system are flourishing.

On the other hand, restrictive sanctions are still being used in cases where these do not appear to be necessary for public safety. And the practice of laying charges in the Youth Court has increased in cases where relatively minor offending is involved and where relatively minimal sanctions are arrived at.

Furthermore, there remain considerable areas where improvement in practice is both needed and possible. Young people's needs are not being adequately met if their wellbeing is to be enhanced. Victims and young people are not always being effectively included in decision making at the family group conference. Youth justice coordinators and other professionals do not always manage the conference in a way that optimises involvement, encourages consensus decisions and provides an opportunity for remorse and healing. The role of the Youth Court in hearing relatively minor cases could be further reduced. And improvements in monitoring and the keeping of records on key processes and outcomes could allow the youth justice system to be assessed for its effectiveness in optimising key outcomes. Such changes could lead to greater satisfaction for participants, repair harm better and reintegrate more young people into the wider society.

# 4

# Restorative Justice in the Youth Court: A Square Peg in a Round Hole?

*Andrew J. Becroft and Rhonda Thompson*

## Introduction

The New Zealand youth justice system is widely recognised as a world leader in restorative responses to youth offending. The ground-breaking system is made up of very high rates of diversion, the acclaimed family group conference and the Youth Court process. Family group conferences have been described as the "jewel in the Crown" of the restorative response (Henwood, 1997). They have been extensively researched – and rightly so given that they are the essence or 'lynchpin' of the system. However, the operation of the Youth Court is seldom analysed in such depth, particularly on the question of whether its operation can be described as restorative. For this reason, this chapter is limited to an assessment of restorative practices in the Youth Court.

The Children, Young Persons, and Their Families Act 1989,[1] particularly the youth justice provisions of that Act, does not explicitly mention 'restorative justice'. However, both the principles of the Act and the practice that has developed around the use of family group conferences are largely consistent with the principles of restorative justice that emphasise participation, making amends and restoring those affected by offending to a constructive life in the community.

This chapter considers the extent to which the Youth Court is successful in achieving a truly restorative model within its *own* processes. It also discusses therapeutic jurisprudence and the role of the Youth Court in monitoring restorative justice concepts in the wider youth justice arena.

The family group conference process has fostered restorative practice outside the Youth Court but, arguably, the Youth Court has too often maintained a formal adversarial model of operation and failed to incorporate restorative processes. The formal system is important to at least maintain the rights of individuals and to determine guilt or innocence. This begs the question as to

---

[1] .Unless stated otherwise, all legislative references in this chapter are to the Children, Young Persons, and Their Families Act 1989 (reprint as at 16 November 2006).

whether restorative processes should be further incorporated into the operation of the Youth Court or whether they are inappropriate in that context – effectively, a square peg in a round hole. A second question is the extent to which the Youth Court should have a role in monitoring the extent to which the other aspects of process meet the principles and practices set out in the Act.

## New Zealand youth justice system

This chapter briefly reviews key aspects of the New Zealand youth justice system from the perspective of the Youth Court. As noted in the previous chapter, there are three key parts to the system: police warnings and 'alternative action' to divert young offenders away from being formally charged; the out-of-court family group conference process; and, formal in-court hearings. It is important to stress that, because at least 76% of youth offenders are dealt with by way of police diversion and 8% are directly referred to family group conferences, this chapter relates to only the 16%–20% of cases where charges are formally laid in court.

### *Role and responsibilities of the Youth Court*

When charges are to be laid, they are laid in the Youth Court by way of an 'information'.

The Youth Court assesses whether young people (of or over the age of 14 and under the age of 17) should be remanded at large, on bail or in custody (section 238(1)). These are important decisions as they may involve the young person being remanded to a secure youth justice residence or a police cell. The importance of these decisions is reflected in the fact that whenever the court opts to remand the young person in Child, Youth and Family or police cell custody, and the charge is denied, a family group conference must be held (section 247(c)).

Charges laid in the Youth Court are either 'denied' or 'not denied' by the young person. The young person opts to 'deny' or 'not deny' after they are given advice, usually by a court-appointed specialist youth advocate (section 323).

If the charge is denied then a hearing is held to determine whether the charge is proved beyond a reasonable doubt. This hearing is modelled on the traditional, adversarial common law model.

If the charge is proved after the hearing or the charge is 'not denied', then the court must order a family group conference. When the charge is 'not denied', a family group conference is held to determine whether the charge is admitted and a suitable outcome for the proceedings. If the charge is proved after a defended hearing, a family group conference is also held to determine a suitable outcome.

After the family group conference is held, the plan formulated at the family group conference is submitted to the court for monitoring and assessment. The court decides whether the plan should be adopted. In the vast majority of cases, the court accepts the recommendation of the family group conference. There is then an adjournment for the completion of the family group conference plan. If the plan is successfully completed, the young person may be discharged (section 282).

The family group conference plan may recommend the imposition of a formal Youth Court order under section 283. If there has been a disagreement at the family group conference about the most suitable course of events, the court must then decide which order should be imposed. These orders include an order for:

- discharge;
- the young person to come before the court within 12 months if called on;
- the payment of a fine and/or costs;
- the payment of reparation, the restoration of goods or the forfeiture of property;
- the placement of the young person under supervision for a period not exceeding 6 months;
- community work;
- supervision with activity that includes a plan for supervised activities for up to 6 months;
- supervision with residence, comprising 3 months in a secure youth justice residence with 1 month off for good behaviour, followed by a supervision order for up to 6 months; and
- conviction and transfer for sentencing under the Sentencing Act 2002 to the District Court or High Court if the young person is aged 15 years or over.

In the case of a purely indictable charge (a category of very serious charges), a depositions or preliminary hearing is held. Over recent years these cases have made up no more than 15% of all cases charged in the Youth Court. If sufficient evidence is found to put the young person on trial, the case is sent to the adult court for a jury trial and disposition. However, in certain cases, the Youth Court may give the young person the opportunity to forgo a jury trial, and the young person may elect to have the charges heard in the Youth Court. Among those given this option almost all (99.5%) elect to have their cases heard in the Youth Court.

The Youth Court may also review sentences when formal Youth Court orders have been breached. If certain, more serious, Youth Court orders are to be cancelled, a further family group conference must be held before a new order can be substituted (section 281(2)).

In summary, the role and responsibilities of the Youth Court in the youth justice process can easily be underestimated. In fact, the court is called on to make pivotal decisions about, for example, remand arrangements, the imposition of Youth Court orders in more difficult cases, and, in serious, purely indictable cases, whether Youth Court jurisdiction should be offered or whether the young person should be transferred to the adult courts. It is certainly a misconception to suggest that the Youth Court exists simply to monitor and support the decisions made at a family group conference, although this is a vitally important part of Youth Court work – perhaps 70% of its function. The Youth Court has a duty wherever possible to support options designed to respond to young people constructively as alternatives to more punitive sanctions likely to be put in place if matters are transferred to the District Court or High Court.

## *Types of family group conference*

A family group conference must be convened in six situations in the New Zealand youth justice system. The first three situations focus on whether or not charges are admitted and what actions should be taken to respond to the offending. The next two focus on what actions should be taken in cases where charges have already been admitted or proven. The sixth is where issues of custody pending trial need to be decided.

### *Court-directed family group conference: 'not denied'*

The most common type of family group conference in the youth justice system occurs when charges have been laid in the court for an offence that is not purely indictable and the young person does not deny[2] these charges. The court then refers the matter for a family group conference. These family group conferences have accounted for approximately two-thirds of all youth justice family group conferences over recent years.

---

2 'Not denied' is a somewhat odd, but very useful, mechanism. It triggers a family group conference without the need for an absolute admission of culpability. It may indicate the young person's acceptance that they are guilty of something, although not necessarily the charge as laid. In almost all such cases, the details can be resolved at the family group conference.

Those present at the family group conference must determine whether the young person admits the offence, and, if so, recommend to the court what actions should result (section 258).

*Intention to charge family group conference*
When the police have not arrested a young person (and therefore cannot lay charges directly in the Youth Court), but nevertheless wish to formally charge the young person, the police must first consult with a youth justice coordinator, and then a family group conference must be convened. This is the second most common type of family group conference, and accounts for approximately one-third of all family group conferences over recent years.

At an intention to charge family group conference, the group must determine whether the charge is admitted, and, if so, decide what should be done. This may include the completion of an agreed plan, which if successful will be the end of the matter, or a decision that a charge should be laid in court (sections 258(b) and 259(i)).

*Child offender care and protection family group conference*
Child offender care and protection family group conferences are held when a child of or over the age of 10 and under the age of 14 is involved in offending The police, after consultation with the youth justice coordinator, make an application to the Family Court for a family group conference to be held to address the child's offending (section 18(3)).

Those attending the family group conference, must determine whether the offence is admitted, and, if so, what steps should be taken, including whether a declaration that the child is in need of care or protection should be filed in the Family Court (sections 258(a) and 259(i)).

*Family group conference as to orders to be made by Youth Court*
When a charge is admitted or proved in the Youth Court and there has been no previous opportunity to consider the appropriate way to deal with the young offender, a family group conference must be held (section 281).

At a penalty family group conference, the group must decide what action and/or penalties should result from a finding that a charge is proved (section 258(e)).

*Family group conference at Youth Court discretion*
A Youth Court may direct that a family group conference be convened at any stage in the proceedings if it appears necessary or desirable to do so (section 281B). The most common example of this type of family group

conference is when a young person indicates a desire to plead guilty to a purely indictable charge and there is a possibility that Youth Court jurisdiction will be offered. In such a case, the family group conference will be asked to consider whether Youth Court jurisdiction should be offered, and what should be done.

### 'Custody conference' family group conference

When a young person denies a charge, but, pending its resolution, the Youth Court orders the young person to be placed in Child, Youth and Family or police custody, a family group conference must be convened (section 247(d)).

The task of this family group conference is to decide whether detention in a Child, Youth and Family secure residence should continue or recommend an alternative placement (section 258(c)).

## Restorative justice

The term 'restorative justice' lends itself to several definitions; the first chapter in this book deals with many of these issues. In this chapter, the following definition offered by Luna (2000) has been adopted as indicative of what a focus on restorative justice might imply in relation to the Youth Court:

> crime is not just an act against the state but against particular victims and the community in general. Offending, then, is primarily a breach of human relationships and only secondarily a violation of the law. As such the community, family members, and supporters, rather than the state and its justice machinery, are considered the locus of crime control. Toward these ends, the restorative model seeks the active participation of victims, families, and community representatives to address the causes and consequences of offending.

This active participation allows parties with a stake in a specific offence to collectively resolve how to deal with the aftermath of the offence and its implications for the future (Tony F. Marshall, 1999, quoted in Schmid, 2003, p. 93). Such a shift in focus requires new processes – rather than an adversarial court hearing there is usually a face-to-face meeting with the victim and other stakeholders. It also requires new responses – a focus on identifying needs and obligations so things can be 'made right' with the victim and the community, rather than the administration of 'doses of pain' (Zehr, 1995, p. 9). It requires new criteria of success – outcomes are judged by the extent to which responsibilities are assumed, needs are met, and healing (of individuals and relationships) is encouraged (Zehr, 1995).

In contrast, the adversarial court system has traditionally followed a 'retributive' approach to justice built on the view that (Zehr, 1990, p. 211):

(1) crime violates the state and its laws; (2) justice focuses on establishing guilt; (3) so that doses of pain can be measured out; (4) justice is sought through a conflict between adversaries; (5) in which offender is pitted against state; (6) rules and intentions outweigh outcomes. One side wins and the other loses.

Thus, the restorative approach of the family group conference often has different goals, processes and outcomes to those of the traditionally retributive approach of the adult courts. The Youth Court, being founded on the 1989 Act, aims to fulfil principles consistent with restorative justice and differs from the adult courts in many respects in its operation. In determining the extent to which various Youth Court processes are restorative, it is instructive to bear Luna's sub-principles in mind. These note that restorative processes involve (Luna, 2000):

- inclusion – all those with a stake in the criminal offence should participate in the process that responds to the offence;
- all parties should be included in decision making and included without improper coercion;
- voluntariness;
- participants, mostly victims and offenders, being entitled to support during the sanctioning process;
- the parties being able to control, to some extent, the process by which decisions are reached; and
- freedom of discourse among all participants.

Restorative justice allows offenders to be accountable for their offences and allows victims to participate and feel empowered as a result of their participation. It can lead to outcomes that address both victims' and offenders' needs and interests and increase the possibility of reintegration (Walgrave, 1998, quoted in Maxwell and Morris, 2002a). However, restorative justice has been criticised as, among other things, being insufficient in the face of serious crime, leading to inconsistent results and being inadequate in safeguarding the rights of young people (Walgrave, 1998). Given these criticisms, it is apposite to ask whether restorative justice is actually a statutorily mandated goal for the youth justice system at all.

## Restorative justice and the law

### *Restorative justice and the Children, Young Persons, and Their Families Act 1989*

The Act does not specifically mention 'restorative justice' in the Youth Court. His Honour Judge Fred McElrea (1994b, p. 45) noted:

> it is essentially the practice of youth justice, as experienced by practitioners, that is restorative, rather than the legislation underlying that practice. (Sections 4–6 and s208 spell out certain objectives of the Act and principles to be applied in youth justice. These are partly restorative, but mostly reflect a narrower emphasis namely the strengthening of the relationships between a young person and his family, whanau, hapu, iwi, and family group, and enabling such group whenever possible to resolve youth offending – see the short and long titles of the Act and ss408 and 208(c)).

McElrea went on, however, to say that the partly restorative aspects of the Act should not be downplayed. These 'partly restorative' aspects are noted by McElrea (1994a, p. 4):

(i) Section 4(f) propounds the principle that young people committing offences should be "held accountable, and encouraged to accept responsibility, for their behaviour" and should be "dealt with in a way that acknowledges their needs and that will give them the opportunity to develop in responsible, beneficial and socially acceptable ways". These provisions emphasise accountability and membership of a wider community.

(ii) By making criminal proceedings a last resort (s208(a)), the Act encourages the solution to come from within the community.

(iii) A "welfare" approach is discouraged by stipulating (s208(b) and (f)) that criminal proceedings should not be instituted solely for welfare reasons, and that any sanctions should take the "least restrictive form" that might be appropriate.

(iv) With almost breathtaking understatement, s208(g) requires that "due regard" should be had to the interests of victims of offending and s251 establishes the right of any victim or his/her representative to attend every family group conference.

(v) Young offenders are intended to be kept in the community, so far as that is consonant with public safety (s208(d)).

(vi) And finally, the whole machinery of the Act that propels the family group conference process is one that makes possible a restorative approach to justice.

Thus, an assessment of sections 4, 5 and 208 reveals several principles that are consistent with restorative justice processes. The Long Title to the Act and the general and youth justice principles sections all stress the importance of rehabilitation through family involvement (sections 5(a), (b) and (e)(i) and 208(c) and (f)(i)). Importantly, section 5 states that:

any Court which, or person who, exercises any power conferred by or under this Act shall be guided by the following principles:

(a) The principle that, wherever possible, a child's or young person's family, whanau, hapu, iwi, and family group should *participate in the making of decisions affecting that child or young person*, and accordingly that, wherever possible, regard should be had to the views of that family, whanau, hapu, iwi, and family group. [Emphasis added.]

The principles state that immediate and wider family groups should take part in decision making, where possible they should lend their support to exercises of the Act's powers, and measures should be taken to strengthen family groups. The wishes of the young person should be determined "so far as those wishes can reasonably be ascertained" (section 5(d)) and endeavours should be made to obtain the support of the young person to the exercise of powers under the Act (section 5(e)(ii)). Considering the sub-principles espoused by Luna (2000) these sections of the Act assist with inclusion in decision making, control of the process and, as participation is voluntary, voluntariness.

Nevertheless, the radical transfer of decision making to the family group conference is only partial, and the Youth Court retains the ultimate decision-making power and can, if it so chooses, modify or even override the decisions of the family group conference. Haines (1998, p. 105) describes attempts to provide an alternative restorative justice system in New Zealand as "haunted" by the formal court-based, punitive criminal justice system that waits "to catch the failures of the 'more progressive system'".

Restorative justice goals of inclusion and support for participants are further reinforced in the Youth Court through the Act's focus on cultural sensitivity and being more accommodating to Māori. This is achieved through the emphasis of wider "family, whanau, hapu and iwi" involvement in decision making and through a general understanding that facilities within the community should be "[a]ppropriate having regard to the needs, values, and beliefs of particular cultural and ethnic groups" (section 4(a)(i)). There is also provision for the appointment of lay advocates to assist the court in understanding cultural matters and to represent the interests of family groups (sections 326–328A).

However, it is important to recognise that restorative processes in youth justice are not (as is sometimes unrealistically touted) the wholesale adoption of an indigenous method of dispute resolution and a rejection of the Western legal system. It is, rather, a modern mechanism of justice that is culturally appropriate, and, certainly, a product of the dissatisfaction by Māori with the previous paternalistic, welfare-based system. It contains some elements of the traditional Māori system of whānau decision making, but also elements that are foreign to it (such as the presence of representatives of the state). It also modifies elements of the traditional system, such as the roles played by the family and victims, to give them a more restorative flavour. This is an important feature of the system because Māori children and young people comprise about half of all youth apprehended by police, having a youth justice family group conference or being prosecuted in court.[3]

## Should restorative justice principles be practised in the Youth Court?

The Act's principles are consistent with, even though they do not explicitly mandate, restorative justice processes in the youth justice system. However, the extent to which such processes should be in evidence in the court setting, in light of the Act's principles, is sometimes difficult to determine. Given that the out-of-court processes are practised in such a profoundly restorative way, there are strong arguments, if only for reasons of consistency, to adopt restorative practices wherever possible for the in-court processes.

The Youth Court is based on the traditional adversarial system. The retention of this formal system is arguably vital to safeguard individual rights and properly carry out the determination of guilt or innocence. Decisions on matters such as bail, top-end sentences and Youth Court jurisdiction are properly decisions for the court. These decisions may see a young person receive a criminal record or a custodial sentence, and an experienced and impartial judge is vital to ensure the rights of these individuals are upheld.

However, a sharp distinction is made in the Youth Court between (a) adjudication upon liability, that is, deciding whether a disputed charge is proved, and (b) disposition of admitted or proved offences (McElrea, 1994b).

---

3   Statistics suggest that in some regions (for example, Rotorua, Gisborne and Kaikohe) the rate of Māori youth offending is significantly higher, comprising 80%–90% of total youth offending (Ministerial Taskforce, 2002, p. 11).

All the safeguards are in place for the former (McElrea, 1994b). It is vital that the adversarial process is retained for the determination of liability. The Youth Court has an important role in dealing with offenders who are unwilling to participate in family group conferences, where a family group conference cannot agree or where the young person denies responsibility. Also, where an offence is very grave the need to deter and/or incapacitate remains (Goodyer, 2003). In these circumstances, arguably, the traditional court process is preferable in maintaining the rights of individuals through impartial legal processes.

The Youth Court is important in guarding against potential short-comings in the restorative justice process. For example, critics argue that restorative justice is too 'soft', but in the New Zealand youth justice system the Youth Court oversees parts of the process to ensure family group conference plans impose a level of sanction that is appropriate in light of the crime. And the Youth Court itself can impose heavy penalties, including a custodial sentence and a conviction and transfer to the District Court for sentencing. The Youth Court also assists in ensuring that disparity of outcomes is reduced – a criticism often levelled at restorative justice (Schmid, 2003). Proportionality is vital in upholding positive public perceptions of the justice system and the Youth Court is mindful of legal precedent to ensure like penalties are met with generally like responses.

Thus, the adversarial face of the Youth Court is probably important to safeguard a just legal process – yet the very nature of the adversarial process is antithetical to restorative practices. The family group conference focuses on restoring relationships, but the courtroom is concerned with the truth or falsity of allegations and assesses cases in a dispassionate and logical manner foreign to the restorative process. The court's adversarial approach has been criticised for failing to engage offenders and for failing "to stimulate any sense of respect for themselves or each other" (Carruthers, 2001, quoted in Schmid, 2003). The adversarial process, in seeking to divine the truth or falsity of allegations, necessitates a win or lose result.

It must be asked whether restorative justice techniques can ever truly 'fit' in the more traditional Youth Court setting. Perhaps a distinction must be made between the *process* and the *type of decision*. While some decisions, such as bail or jurisdiction, are for the court to make, the actual process used to arrive at many decisions could take more of a restorative tone. This would involve improving aspects such as inclusion, support and control for various stakeholders. This has the potential to improve outcomes for young people, their families and victims. However, it is accepted that restorative justice in its purest form cannot be achieved simply by the adoption and use of various restorative techniques (Haines, 1998).

An opportunity for reconciliation occurs in the family group conference process and this is essentially the 'power-house' of restorative justice in the youth justice system. Commentators have argued that the Act envisages that all the important restorative work is done outside the court and that the court's role is to fact find in contested cases, to safeguard the quality of family group conferences and to add official backing to the decisions of the family (Carruthers, no date, p. 34). However, the Youth Court is not only a 'referee' to family group conferences, but, as noted at the start of this chapter, has several important roles and responsibilities. The family group conference plan is only a recommendation and the judge may opt for any outcome that is appropriate. In considering the plan, the judge may be assisted by talking to the offender, their family and other participants to clarify matters such as the progress made on the case or changes in the offender's situation. However, such 'restorative' dialogue is carried out only at the discretion of the judge. Further, family and supporters of the offender, the offender and, if attending, the victim often feel overawed by the solemnity of the court and unsure when they may speak. For this reason, making regular opportunities for the parties to engage in dialogue would be a useful part of Youth Court practice and would bolster restorative practice in the Youth Court.

### *Restorative justice and international law*

The rehabilitative aims of the Act are also mandated by the United Nations Convention on the Rights of the Child 1989. The convention sets out key principles on the maintenance of the rights of children and young people. It is the most universally accepted human rights document in history, having been ratified by 192 countries, including New Zealand in 1993. Article 40 of the convention states:

1. States Parties recognise the right of every child alleged as, accused of, or recognised as having infringed the penal law to be treated in a manner consistent with the promotion of the child's sense of dignity and worth ... and the *desirability of promoting the child's reintegration* and the child's assuming a constructive role in society. [Emphasis added.]

Young people dealt with through restorative justice processes are less likely to reoffend (Beven et al., 2005), and are thus more likely to be reintegrated into society.

## Restorative practice in the Youth Court

### *To what extent are the goals of restorative justice achieved in the Youth Court?*

The question, then, is to what extent are Luna's (2000) principles such as inclusion, accountability, voluntariness, group involvement in decision making, support and freedom of discourse already in evidence in the Youth Court. A typical court hearing involves youth advocates, police, social workers, the offender and their family and supporters and, of course, a judge. Many judges encourage discussion and participation from these individuals, and a key goal of Youth Court outcomes is accountability. At first glance, then, a Youth Court appears to display features of restorative justice but levels of discussion and inclusion vary from court to court. What follows is an assessment of particular features of the Youth Court, and whether the law and actual practice assist or hinder restorative justice in the court.

### *'Not denied'*

The British adversarial concept of putting the prosecution 'to the proof' can be seen as a discouragement to people to plead guilty and accept responsibility for their actions (McElrea, 2001). As noted, the Youth Court avoids taking a guilty or not guilty plea and, instead, asks the young person whether the charge is 'not denied'. When a charge is 'not denied' it is transferred to family group conference where the young person may nevertheless opt to deny the charge but in the majority of cases the charge is proven by admission. The 'not denied' mechanism allows the parties to meet and discuss the charge (or charges) before the offender commits themselves to a plea. Once matters are admitted (including finalisation of the proper charge (or charges) and the summary of facts) the parties can then move along the reconciliation path (McElrea, 2001). Thus, the formal court process assists restorative justice processes, because if the Youth Court insisted on the making of a guilty or not guilty plea, this would inhibit prompt access to the family group conference process (McElrea, 2001).

### *Courtroom layout*

Few Youth Courts are purpose built, so the majority of hearings are held in adult courtrooms set up to operate in the traditional adversarial manner. Such courtrooms are arranged with rows of tables for prosecution and defence counsel, a public gallery at the rear, the Bench and something approximating a 'dock'. New Zealand courtrooms vary in shape, but the worst examples are long and thin, making communication between the judge at one end and the offender at the other very difficult. If a victim is permitted to be present, no direction is given as to where they should be seated. Despite the trepidation that some victims must feel facing their offender, they are likely to be seated in the public gallery among the offender's family and supporters.

In practice, it has proved almost impossible to alter adult courtrooms for Youth Court hearings due to in-built furniture and, for example, the placement of electrical fittings for microphones. This inhibits inclusion and freedom of discourse and may make it difficult for supporters to sit near the offender because they must be seated in the public gallery. The ideal Youth Court arrangement has the desks arranged in a U shape or horseshoe around which the social workers, youth advocates and police sit. Family and supporters of the offender are seated against one wall and other interested parties are seated along the facing wall. The offender stands behind the U shape of desks, facing the judge. This layout has been successfully adopted in courts such as the Wellington, Christchurch and Tauranga Youth Courts, to name but a few.

Paradoxically, the two newest courthouses that contain Youth Courts in Manukau and Albany are by far the least accommodating of restorative justice practices as they are 'junior' adult courtrooms. While Youth Court judges have attempted to adopt a more inclusive layout within the confines of their existing courthouses – in order to encourage participation by all parties – other decision makers within the justice system need a greater awareness of restorative practices and how those practices can be significantly impaired by courtroom layout.

### Involvement of victims in the Youth Court

The involvement of victims is an integral part of the restorative justice response. Their presence forces offenders to face the often crushing impact of their offence and give a genuine apology – an important first step away from a life of crime. Restorative justice approaches encourage dialogue and mutual agreement between the parties to restore the relationship between victim and offender. This can be an important part of healing for the victim. Youth Court judge Carolyn Henwood has described the victim's presence as a "powerful event" (Henwood, 1997, p. 17).

However, victims are *not* even entitled to attend a Youth Court hearing! (section 329(1)). The Act lists a range of people who may attend the court, including family, legal representatives and social workers, but victims are excluded. The judge may permit "any other person" to be present (section 329(1)(m)), and this description will obviously include victims, but this is at the discretion of the judge. Further, if the judge allows a victim to be present, they are not entitled to address the court as of right.

The victim's input into the discussion is vital in the restorative setting where the goal is the restoration of relationships and property. In the Youth Court, the goal is to restore the young person as a law-abiding citizen, but also to denounce, deter and punish. The victim's input is less relevant in this context and the principle that "due regard" should be had to the interests of any victims of offending (section 208(g)) may, in fact, conflict with the goal of rehabilitating the young person. For example, in cases of sexual offending, the victim may argue that a harsh penalty is warranted, but the court may instead opt for a therapeutic residential programme in an attempt to ensure the young person is rehabilitated and does not reoffend.[4]

It could be argued that victim's interests are considered at the family group conference stage and the court is aware of the impact on the victim in making its final decision.[5] Youth Court judges have a duty to take into account in sentencing "the effect of the offence on any victim of the offence, and the need for reparation to be made to that victim" (section 284(1)(f)). However, at a family group conference a victim who disagrees with the proposed plan for the young person effectively forces the case back to the Youth Court for it to make the decision, with the resulting ongoing stress and delay to the parties. For this reason, victims may agree to plans they feel are inadequate. This could be part of the reason why in one study only 49% of victims were satisfied with family group conference outcomes and 25% said they felt worse after the process (Maxwell and Morris, 1996, p. 100, quoted in Wright, 1998, p. 81).

Consequently, there are situations where the victim's input would be useful and yet they are excluded from the Youth Court even when the defendant admits the charge. Thus, the Youth Court does not follow the restorative model in terms of its treatment of victims. To allow their participation at this stage would give victims a new voice in the criminal justice process and give new emphasis to "the healing and restoration of victims" (Schmid, 2003). In

---

[4] See, for example, *R v Carmichael* CA521/94, 23 March 1995, summary retrieved 2 October 2005 from the New Zealand Youth Court website, http://www.justice.govt.nz/youth/decisions/years/1995/r-v-carmichael-23-03-1995-ca-52-94.html.

[5] Section 251 establishes the right of any victim or the victim's representative to attend every family group conference.

recognition of this, a law change is proposed to allow victims to attend Youth Court hearings as of right.[6] The proposed clause allows attendance by:[7]

(ca) a victim of the offence or alleged offence, or a representative of that victim:

(cb) if a victim is a child or young person, a parent or guardian of that child or young person, unless that parent or guardian is charged with the commission of, or convicted or found guilty of, or pleads guilty to, the offence concerned.

The commentary to the proposed legislation also states that measures for dealing with offending by children and young people should not merely (as currently) have regard to, but should instead recognise properly, the interests of any victims of that offending. This would include, for example, consideration of whether reparation should be made to those victims.[8] However, even the proposed legislation does not give victims an express right to address the Youth Court.

Victims' rights have received recognition in New Zealand law with the passing of the Victims' Rights Act 2002. This aims, among other things, to improve provisions for the treatment and rights of victims of offences, provide information for victims about services available to them or about the progress of the case through the courts, and place restrictions on giving information in evidence to the court that would identify or lead to the identification of a victim's address (section 16 of the Victims' Rights Act). However, most of this Act does not apply to the Youth Court. For example, the sections providing for the provision of victim impact statements to the court do not apply (sections 17–27 of the Victims' Rights Act). Youth Court judges often have limited information about the effect of an offence on a victim, so it would be useful for them to have victim impact statements available. Also, sections 29 and 30 of the Victims' Rights Act, obligating the police to inform the court of the victim's views as to bail being granted to an accused person facing charges of serious violence, including sexual violation, have not been seen by the police as applying to the Youth Court. Arguably, therefore, although victims are able to take part in a family group conference, they have fewer rights in the Youth

---

6 See Children, Young Persons, and Their Families Amendment Bill (No 4) 2004 (2004B159-1).

7 See Children, Young Persons, and Their Families Amendment Bill (No 4) 2004 (2004B159-1), clause 31.

8 See Children, Young Persons, and Their Families Amendment Bill (No 4) 2004 (2004B159-1), clause 6.

Court than in the adult jurisdiction. This seems anomalous, as it is of little consequence to a victim whether the law considers the offender is a 'young person' of 16 or an 'adult' of 18.

The Youth Court could improve its treatment of victims and thus improve restorative processes by finding ways to encourage victims to attend its hearings and to participate in the proceedings. Some judges encourage participation, but there is no standard procedure to ensure the victim's voice is heard in court proceedings. However, as Schmid (2003) argues, although statutes can be added that mandate victims having the right to address the court at different stages of the criminal process and restitution may be made mandatory, these are, in reality, just add-ons – healing the victim is often not considered a central and fundamental part of criminal justice outcomes.

### *Young people's participation and comprehension in the Youth Court*

The Youth Court has a duty to explain proceedings to a young person in a manner and language they can understand (section 10). And if the court makes an order against the young person it must explain that order to the young person and to any parent, guardian or person who takes care of that young person (section 10(1)(c)). Further, the court is under a duty to encourage and assist the child or young person to participate in proceedings (section 11). These are vital provisions for achieving the goals of restorative justice but they are too easily reduced to bare minimum requirements. The reasons for this include:

- Youth Court judges, although chosen for their special attributes and understanding, are not full-time specialists and Youth Court work is a small part of their caseload (usually less than 15% of their work and typically, Youth Court cases make up only 5%–6% of all cases coming before the District Court annually);[9]
- time and resource constraints; and
- some Youth Court professionals are less adept than others at communicating with young people.

The duties to explain and to encourage participation are statutory requirements; and the Youth Court should make time to explain proceedings at every stage of the process and encourage participation "where necessary and appropriate" (section 11). What is "necessary and appropriate" may differ from case to case, but, certainly, the input of the child or young person should be

---

9  Youth Courts exercise jurisdiction as a specialist division of the District Court under section 433.

sought before a decision is made. The extent to which these goals are achieved ultimately depends on the approach taken by the presiding judge.

### Importance of lay advocates

The Act contains provision for the appointment of lay advocates (sections 326–328A). Lay advocates must ensure the court is aware of all cultural matters that are relevant to proceedings and represent the interests of the young person's whānau, hapū and iwi (or equivalent) to the extent that those interests are not otherwise represented in the proceedings (section 327). Lay advocates may provide a voice for families and foster dialogue between families and young offenders, thus assisting in the restoration of those relationships. This is vital given that section 208(c) states that:

> any measures for dealing with offending by children or young persons should be designed—
>
> (i) To strengthen the family, whanau, hapu, iwi, and family group of the child or young person concerned; and
>
> (ii) To foster the ability of families, whanau, hapu, iwi, and family groups to develop their own means of dealing with offending by their children and young persons.

As noted, section 5 states that "wherever possible" the family group should participate in the making of decisions affecting that child or young person, and "regard should be had to [their] views" (section 5(a)). Wherever possible, the relationship between a child or young person and their family group should be maintained and strengthened (section 5(b)).

Lay advocates are potentially a powerful tool in achieving these goals but, in fact, lay advocates are rarely appointed. Attempts to introduce lay advocates into three New Zealand courts in 2004 at the initiative of the Principal Youth Court Judge, received a lukewarm response from the various professionals involved.

There are several possible reasons for this reluctance to adopt lay advocates in the Youth Court. First, legal professionals are competent at arguing their point of view and fail to see why young people who are represented by a youth advocate need a lay advocate to put forward the point of view of the offender's family and culture. In a busy and sometimes under-resourced court system that already has to accommodate the input of youth advocates, police, social workers, the young person and their family, yet another voice is considered unnecessary. Secondly, the majority of people in the court system are white and the system operates according to Pākehā culture. It may be difficult for key players within this system to understand the significance of cultural factors to other racial groups and therefore to make time to accommodate them.

Restorative justice is flexible enough to allow the incorporation of cultural or religious practices within the conferencing process. Researchers who have studied the Act and family group conferences acknowledge that there is considerable potential for cultural and ethnic accommodation.[10] Yet research has demonstrated that the New Zealand youth justice system remains "largely unresponsive to cultural differences" (Maxwell and Morris, 1996, quoted in Haines, 1998, p. 104).

The failure to appoint lay advocates is particularly galling considering that an express object of the Act is to establish and promote services that are "appropriate having regard to the needs, values, and beliefs of particular cultural and ethnic groups" (section 4(a)(i)). The Youth Court has struggled with the concept of giving weight to cultural values in its decision making.[11] An appropriate lay advocate would assist the court in understanding cultural matters and incorporating them into any orders made. This would bolster the values of inclusiveness, support, and control and enhance restorative justice values within the Youth Court system.

*Community involvement*

A truly restorative court process would ensure that all stakeholders were full participants at hearings. One stakeholder that is difficult to adequately represent is the community, which becomes weakened or embattled through rising crime levels. A large number of meanings can be ascribed to 'the community', depending on whether the context is a large city, a small town, a particular community of interest, or an indigenous community. It could be argued that the police, judges and social workers represent the community in some sense, and certainly victims and offenders are community members. Lay advocates potentially represent a sector of the community and this inclusion of a non-professional as a community representative has been encouraged by some commentators (Trépanier, 1998).

Whether the involvement of particular individuals as 'community' is sufficient, can be answered by questioning whether "the community [is]

---

10 See, for example, Olsen et al., 1995, quoted in Schmid, 2003.
11 See, for example, *Police v S and M* (1993) 11 FRNZ 322, summary retrieved 2 October 2005 from the New Zealand Youth Court website, http://www.justice.govt.nz/youth/decisions/years/1993/police-v-s-m-1993-11-frnz-322-yc.html.

stronger after the criminal justice intervention than it was before the crime was committed" (Pranis, a restorative justice planner in the Minnesota Department of Corrections, quoted in Wright, 1998, p. 85). Community representatives should ensure the offender understands the harm done to the community and put forward the needs of the community in particular situations. Several parties, particularly judges, are likely to express the harm done to the community, but whether the needs of the community are adequately expressed is a more difficult question. If these needs are expressed, responses such as appropriate community work may be imposed (section 283(1)). Further, sufficient community representation is useful in educating people about the need for preventative social policies to which community members can contribute (Wright, 1998). Representation may ensure that needs are recognised and that parties are galvanised into instituting social reforms.

*Power imbalance*

Consensus decision making is important to achieve the goals of inclusion and voluntariness in restorative justice. However, particularly where young people are concerned, there is a danger that power imbalances may lead young people to feel unable to contribute. This is particularly pronounced in the formal setting of the courtroom where a collection of lawyers, social workers, police, a court taker and a judge all watch the young person respond to questions. Haines (1998) notes that, from a young person's perspective, both the traditional courtroom and the family group conference involve facing "a room full of adults". It is not surprising, then, that young people tend to agree with charges or plans that are presented to them. This thwarts the goals of restorative justice because, rather than emerging from the hearing with a commitment to change, young people may leave such proceedings with a sense of injustice or dissatisfaction. To re-establish their sense of identity, young people can use a variety of adaptive mechanisms that distance themselves from the experience (Blagg, 1985, quoted in Haines, 1998, p. 101). At a family group conference, the primary stakeholders are empowered but under 'conventional' adversarial processes they are largely in the control of professionals (McElrea, 2001).

The young person's family may also feel daunted by the courtroom and its room full of professionals, particularly if family members are uneducated or have few English language skills. They are likely to be unsure whether they may speak or how to interject, for example, if incorrect information is given. To achieve meaningful participation by the parties it is vital that judges make families and supporters feel welcome and regularly give them opportunities to contribute. Similarly, offenders must be encouraged to participate. If the parties are mute throughout proceedings they will not take ownership of the outcomes and the process cannot be described as restorative.

*Restorative outcomes*

Outcomes of restorative justice processes are focused on the victims and perpetrators of crime. A change in reoffending is not one of the primary goals of restorative justice (Morris, 2002, quoted in Beven et al., 2005, p. 195), but certainly changes in reoffending behaviour are an expected outcome of the restorative process (Beven et al., 2005). This is often achieved in both restorative and conventional criminal justice responses by the referral of offenders to appropriate treatment programmes. The difference with restorative justice is that offenders are active participants in deciding what the reparative and rehabilitative outcomes should be (Beven et al., 2005). Research shows that individuals who participate in the process are more likely to comply with outcomes (Roche, 2003, quoted in Beven et al., 2005, p. 195). However, the young person is unlikely to be an active participant in determining the outcome in the Youth Court. It is vital, then, that the young person is heard at the family group conference level and in the Youth Court in order to ensure the process is truly 'restorative'.

For victims, restorative justice outcomes have three objectives: the restoration of a victim's sense of security, self-respect and dignity, and sense of control (Beven et al., 2005). As described above, victim's needs are insufficiently accounted for in the Youth Court and this part of the process cannot be described as restorative.

In circumstances where the Youth Court deems it necessary to impose a punishment on a young person, it has several orders open to it.[12] Responses such as reparation, restitution, community work and forfeiture of property appear more conducive to the restorative process. However, contrary to some definitions of restorative justice (Walgrave, 1998), punishment in the more traditional sense is open to the Youth Court. This may involve a custodial sentence or conviction and transfer to the District Court for sentencing. While best practice dictates that young people are offered therapeutic treatment during supervision with residence, in practice they may receive no more than 'childminding' in the relevant institution. Difficulties with custodial arrangements for young people spring from a shortage of residential youth justice beds in New Zealand. This shortage has the result that, before the final determination of their case, young people may be remanded in custody in police

---

12  Youth Court orders are listed on p. 71 of this chapter.

cells for a significant period. There is certainly nothing restorative about this incarceration, which is in a cell with no regular visitation, inadequate hygiene and poor food.

### Maintaining the dignity of participants

The Youth Court aims to uphold the dignity of participants and thereby maintain an atmosphere conducive to restorative justice through several statutorily based measures. First, the courtroom must be arranged so participants are not brought into contact with people attending any other court (section 331(a)). This ensures youth offenders are kept away from adult offenders and assists in maintaining their privacy. Further, the extent to which children and young people are able to associate within the court premises and the extent to which parents must congregate in common areas while awaiting their hearing should be "reduced to a minimum" (section 331(b)). This is achieved by Youth Court proceedings being arranged in a manner that keeps waiting times to a minimum (section 332(1)) and the time stated in a summons being a time that "accords with the reasonable expectation of the Registrar of the Court of the time when the proceedings in respect of which the summons is issued will be heard" (section 332(2)).

The dignity of participants is further maintained by the prohibition on the publication of any information about the young person, including their name, their school or any other details likely to lead to the identification of the young person or their school (section 438(3)). Along with upholding the dignity of young people and their families, these measures maintain the faith of participants in the system. They also ensure that young people are not overtly criminalised by the process.

### Therapeutic jurisprudence

A move to therapeutic jurisprudence has been particularly successful in courts around the world. This sees court processes and authority used to regularly monitor a defendant's progress and assist in bringing about change. The new problem-solving approach adopted by the courts involves treating offenders as human beings with issues that have causal effects on their criminality (Carruthers, 2004). The courts draw on community resources to assist in treating the underlying issues at the heart of criminal behaviour. The judicial mandate is used to enforce any therapeutic action taken. Judge David Carruthers, former Chief District Court Judge, argues that the machinery of the Act propelling the family group conference process "makes possible a restorative and so therapeutic approach to justice" (Carruthers, 2004, p. 4).

An example of the therapeutic approach is the pilot Christchurch Youth Drug Court where defendants are brought back for multiple visits to court to monitor their drug rehabilitation. The Youth Drug Court targets recidivist youth offenders with moderate to severe alcohol or other drug dependency that contributes to their offending. It aims to facilitate the treatment of the young person while under court supervision, with a view to reducing future offending and improving general functioning. The drug court model is based on an interagency approach involving practitioners from welfare, health, education and youth justice (Carruthers, 2004).

There are certainly aspects of restorative justice in therapeutic jurisprudence in that it restores or heals an individual so they can put things right with others. However, restorative justice should be seen in its wider context of assisting in healing relationships between the individual, the victim and family members. For this reason, the therapeutic aspects of the Youth Court can be seen as only partially indicative of restorative justice processes within the court system.

## Monitoring role of the Youth Court

### Role of the Youth Court in diverting young people away from criminal proceedings

The New Zealand youth justice system is focused on diversion. After an offence is detected, police must make every effort to divert young people away from court. Section 208(a) provides:

> unless the public interest requires otherwise, criminal proceedings should not be instituted against a child or young person if there is an alternative means of dealing with the matter.

The specialist Youth Aid section of the New Zealand Police bought into the ethos of the Act in a spectacular way. Diversion, or alternative action, rates have remained consistently high, around 76% of all cases since shortly after the Act was passed into law in 1989. A further 8% of cases are referred to a family group conference if there has not been an arrest and police intend to lay charges. However, in this situation, if outcomes are agreed and the young person carries out the family group conference plan, the matter can usually be resolved without referral to a court, although in rare circumstances a charge is still laid. In the other 16% of cases, if the young person is arrested and a charge is laid in the

Youth Court there must be a referral to a family group conference if the matter is 'not denied'[13] or proved after a defended hearing.[14]

The Youth Court has an important role to play in monitoring this diversionary process. When a judge sees that alternatives to criminal proceedings exist, they may order that charges be withdrawn and the matter be dealt with in the community. How this should be dealt with in the community must be considered by a family group conference at which 'alternative means' of dealing with the matter are formulated. This ensures the process is as restorative as possible.

## Role of the Youth Court in monitoring family group conferences

The Youth Court acts as a type of 'referee' to the family group conference process, in certain circumstances directing that family group conferences be held or deciding whether the plan formulated by the family group conference is sufficient.[15] If the family group conference plan is too lenient or too onerous, the Youth Court may alter elements of the plan. For example, it may reduce the number of community work hours required where the family group conference has recommended a large number of hours in response to a less serious crime. In this role, the Youth Court safeguards the restorative family group conference process and ensures that individual rights are upheld and that outcomes are proportionate to the crime.

## Youth Court's role in the wider youth justice arena

Youth Court judges often take a leadership role in convening interagency meetings to discuss court processes and issues around court operation for their area. In attendance at these meetings are representatives from the court, Youth Aid, and Child, Youth and Family and also youth advocates. The focus of these meetings, which should be held at least quarterly, is to ensure responses to youth offending are as restorative as possible. Along with discussing issues that arise, such as managing the congregation of youths in court foyers, court lists and how to keep the Act's vision alive, they give other interested community groups an opportunity to be involved in the process and discuss areas of concern

---

13  When a (non-purely indictable) charge is 'not denied' in the Youth Court, the court must direct that a family group conference be held (section 246). For an explanation of 'not denied', see footnote 2 in this chapter.
14  Less than 1% of all cases are dealt with at a defended hearing.
15  Although the Youth Court has no input into diversionary conferences.

(Henwood, 2004). Particularly through encouraging community involvement, the court takes leadership to ensure restorative justice principles are applied in the Youth Court.

## Conclusion

In this chapter we have argued that New Zealand's youth justice system is made up of three distinct components. The more significant and influential components take place outside the Youth Court: police diversion (or alternative action), which disposes of nearly 80% of cases, and 'intention to charge' and Youth Court–ordered family group conferences. As we have observed, the family group conference process has always been practised in an entirely restorative way, with an ethos reflecting a restorative justice approach, despite this approach not being statutorily mandated. (In fact, the family group conference process could have been introduced and carried out without any commitment to restorative justice at all and still have remained faithful to the legislation!) Now, however, the family group conference process is hailed as a world-leading example of restorative justice in practice.

The third component of New Zealand's system, the Youth Court, although secondary to the diversionary processes and the family group conference process, is nevertheless more significant than many commentators, particularly those from overseas, understand. However, the Youth Court procedures and processes are not based on a restorative model but on the traditional, common law adversarial system inherited from the common law of England. There is, then, a dissonance between the Youth Court (which has always remained faithful, sometimes uneasily, to its adversarial, traditional roots) and the 'out-of-court' processes, especially the family group conference, which is a full-blown and stunning advertisement for restorative justice.

In this chapter, we have concluded that there is a real challenge for the Youth Court to consider to what extent its processes can be modified or altered to reflect the restorative justice approach of the family group conference. Our view is that restorative justice, while not a statutorily mandated goal, is nevertheless a process that may, and should, usefully be embraced by the Youth Court wherever possible. The involvement of offenders, victims and other stakeholders has several positive effects, including a sense of 'ownership' of the process and, hopefully, even reducing recidivism. However, the formal adversarial system has an important role in maintaining the rights of individuals, determining guilt or innocence, and safeguarding the public interest where serious crime has occurred. In these circumstances, a judge must make decisions and a purely restorative model is inappropriate.

If a distinction is made between the process and the type of decision, the process used to arrive at many decisions could take more of a restorative tone. This is already in evidence to an extent in Youth Courts where judges actively involve the parties in discussion or allow victims to attend and participate, or, on rare occasions, when lay advocates are appointed. As discussed, there is room for considerable improvement in making processes more restorative, particularly in encouraging participation, improving the courtroom layout and improving the opportunities for meaningful victim participation in the Youth Court.

Restorative justice has a key role to play in an effective youth justice system, and restorative practices should be incorporated, where possible, into Youth Court systems. Restorative justice is also a good 'fit' with young people, and it should be made to 'fit' in the Youth Court, at least in part. This is not accommodating 'a square peg in a round hole'; appropriate use of restorative processes, even where decisions must be the prerogative and responsibility of the court, are perfectly compatible with Youth Court decision making and need not detract from the authority, dignity and mana of the court. Rather, their adoption will allow a flexible, meaningful, holistic and inclusive response to deal with the needs of young people who have broken the law, their victims and, indirectly, community interests as a whole.

# 5

# Restorative Justice for Adult Offenders: Practice in New Zealand Today

*F. W. M. McElrea*

## Introduction

For historical reasons, New Zealand interest in restorative justice has been driven primarily by practitioners, not by policy makers or academics. Three or four years before the term 'restorative justice' had become known in New Zealand, the Children, Young Persons, and Their Families Act 1989 introduced the family group conference for young offenders. The Act applied to Youth Court proceedings dealing with offenders of or over the age of 14 and under the age of 17. One of the primary objectives of the Act was to strengthen the ability of families to hold their young people accountable and encourage them to develop in law-abiding and socially productive ways.

Those like myself working with the Act soon saw the family group conference concept, talked about it and wrote about it as a new model of justice. When in 1993 I returned to Cambridge on sabbatical leave and read Howard Zehr's *Changing Lenses* (1990) it seemed he was describing a very similar approach. In early 1994 I wrote two papers, the first assessing our youth justice model as a restorative model and the second arguing for the application of its central principles to adults through community group conferences. From late 1994, these adult conferences were held on an informal, non-statutory basis encouraged by several like-minded judges with the blessing of successive Chief District Court Judges. There are currently some 30 restorative justice schemes in different parts of the country receiving some government funding, mostly set up by the Crime Prevention Unit[1] but also including the court-based scheme operating in four courts, including my own, the Auckland District Court.

The principal model of restorative justice used in New Zealand is the restorative justice conference – either a family group conference (for young people) or a community conference (for adults). A typical restorative conference involves the prior admission of responsibility by the offender, the voluntary

---

1  The Crime Prevention Unit was previously part of the Prime Minister's Office, but is now within the Ministry of Justice.

attendance of all participants,[2] the assistance of a neutral person as facilitator, the opportunity for explanations to be given, questions answered, and apologies given, the drawing up of a plan to address the wrong done, and an agreement as to how that plan will be implemented and monitored. The court is usually, but not necessarily, involved.

In the youth justice sphere, about one-third of conferences are not directed by the court but are diversionary conferences, initiated – and attended – by the police. If agreement can be reached as to an outcome that does not involve the laying of charges, then no charges are laid – so long as the outcome is implemented. I see the concept of a community resolution centre as able to operate in a similar way for adults, as explained below.

In this chapter, I discuss how restorative conferences operate in the adult criminal justice system. In particular, I discuss the Sentencing Act 2002 and the Victims' Rights Act 2002, which provide the legal mandate for restorative justice for adults. I then discuss some of the schemes that have developed for providing restorative justice programmes to respond to offending by adults, and how restorative justice has impacted on the sentencing process in New Zealand. Finally, I outline a proposal for the development of a more community-based model of restorative justice through the concept of community resolution centres.

## Sentencing Act 2002

In 2002, a new Sentencing Act was introduced that explicitly recognised restorative justice for adults. The scheme of the Act is permissive rather than mandatory, but where restorative justice processes have been followed the courts must take them into account in sentencing.[3]

The Act contains provisions that explicitly endorse restorative justice or the principles on which it is founded. They are in many ways remarkable and (as far as I know) unprecedented.

Section 7 lists eight purposes of sentencing. While they are not listed in any order of priority, the first four support the restorative approach, while the first two come directly from the language of restorative justice. This is the complete list of purposes:

---

2 Participants include victim, offender, their supporters, community representatives and (ideally) a police officer.
3 A fuller account of the provisions of the 2002 Act is in Eaton and McElrea (2003).

(a) to hold the offender accountable for harm done to the victim and the community by the offending; or

(b) to promote in the offender a sense of responsibility for, and an acknowledgement of, that harm; or

(c) to provide for the interests of the victim of the offence; or

(d) to provide reparation for harm done by the offending; or

(e) to denounce the conduct in which the offender was involved; or

(f) to deter the offender or other persons from committing the same or a similar offence; or

(g) to protect the community from the offender; or

(h) to assist in the offender's rehabilitation and reintegration; or

(i) a combination of 2 or more of the purposes in paragraphs (a) to (h).

Likewise, the section dealing with principles of sentencing (section 8(j)) requires the court to "take into account any outcomes of restorative justice processes that have occurred". More explicitly, section 10 requires the court to take into account any offer of amends made to the victim, any agreement between them as to how the wrong or loss may be remedied or to ensure it will not recur, any measures taken by the offender or their family to compensate the victim, make an apology, or "otherwise make good the harm that has occurred", and the extent to which such matters have been accepted as "expiating or mitigating the wrong". (This last aspect was also present in the previous legislation.)

Other principles of the Act are also relevant but are not new, for example, the desirability of keeping offenders in the community as far as that is practicable and consonant with the safety of the community (section 16(1)).

Very important also is section 27, which allows a defendant to call one or more people to address a sentencing court on:

(a) the personal, family, whanau, community, and cultural background of the offender:

(b) the way in which that background may have related to the commission of the offence:

(c) any processes that have been tried to resolve, or that are available to resolve, issues relating to the offence, involving the offender and his or her family, whanau, or community and the victim or victims of the offence:

(d) how support from the family, whanau, or community may be available to help prevent further offending by the offender:

(e) how the offender's background, or family, whanau, or community support may be relevant in respect of possible sentences.

Section 27 is a greatly expanded version of its predecessor (section 16 of the Criminal Justice Act 1985), with the contents of paragraphs (c) and (e) being entirely new.[4]

Section 25 allows the court adjourn sentencing until any such measure has been implemented. Alternatively, under section 110 a defendant may be ordered to come up for sentence if called on at any time within 12 months, and if the court specifies conditions that it expects to be fulfilled in that time then the non-performance of such conditions can result in the defendant being summonsed back to court to be sentenced.

Alternatively – and sometimes in addition – restorative conference outcomes can become elements in court sentences of supervision (as special conditions of supervision), community work (especially where the conference has recommended a particular type of work or a particular community sponsor), or even imprisonment (as special conditions of release in a sentence of 2 years or less). In the case of longer sentences of imprisonment, the Parole Board may require restorative justice elements to be fulfilled as conditions of parole. The Corrections Act 2004 is also relevant in this regard.

## Victims' Rights Act 2002

At the same time, section 9 of the Victims' Rights Act 2002 reinforced parliament's intentions as expressed in the Sentencing Act 2002, by requiring all judicial officers, defence and prosecution lawyers, court staff and probation officers to encourage the holding of a meeting between victim and offender "to resolve issues relating to the offence", provided the victim and offender agree, the resources are available for holding such a meeting and a meeting of that kind is practicable and appropriate. While section 10 provides that such a responsibility (to encourage the holding of victim–offender meetings) is not legally enforceable, it is nevertheless among the principles that should guide the treatment of victims.

---

4   Section 16 of the Criminal Justice Act 1985 referred merely to "the ethnic or cultural background of the offender, the way in which that background may relate to the commission of the offence, and the positive effects that background may have in helping to avoid further offending".

## Community restorative justice trusts

Since 1995, restorative justice trusts have been formed throughout the country, often with the support of the Crime Prevention Unit. These programmes differ somewhat in their practice model, the types of cases they receive and how they are funded, but all espouse at least some restorative justice principles and all accept referrals from their local District Courts.

First in time was the Te Oritenga Restorative Justice Trust formed by the Reverend Douglas Mansill, following his facilitation of the first adult restorative conference in Auckland in 1994.[5] This group operated without government funding or support, and was the model for other groups of trained volunteers providing facilitation services, mainly in Auckland. All of these groups brought together victims, offenders and others in a community setting, and remain within the core model of restorative justice.

The first government funding came from the Crime Prevention Unit and supported three pilot schemes for community diversion of adult offenders. These were Project Turnaround in Timaru, Te Whānau Awhina in Waitakere, and the Community Accountability Programme in Rotorua. The first two began operating in 1996, and the last some time later (as the Second Chance Restorative Justice Programme). They were not initially referred to as 'restorative justice', possibly because the then Department of Justice was not actively supporting restorative justice, but they applied some restorative justice principles.

The first two such programmes are still in operation today, although they have always operated somewhat differently from each other.[6] In Project Turnaround, on the offender's first appearance at court the judge may divert them to Project Turnaround and, if the subsequent community panel meeting is attended by the offender and if the plan agreed to there is completed, the offender makes no further court appearance and the police withdraw the charges. The panel members in Project Turnaround are volunteers who are selected to represent the community and they are the principal decision makers. A police officer is normally present at the meeting and the victim can also be present. At the panel meeting, the offender is confronted with their offending and its consequences. The plans from these meetings usually involve making amends to the victim and the community and making arrangements of both a reintegrative and rehabilitative nature.

---

5   See further Hayden (2001, section 2.6).
6   For more detail, see Smith and Cram (1998) and Maxwell et al. (1999).

As in Project Turnaround, offenders at Te Whanau Awhina are referred to the scheme by the judge at a court hearing. However, offenders who appear before a panel at Te Whanau Awhina are not necessarily diverted from further court appearances and court-imposed sanctions. Another important difference is that at Te Whanau Awhina, the panel typically consists of three or four members of the marae (Māori community centre), including one who takes the role of kaumatua (elder) and chairs the proceedings. The elders are the decision makers. The police do not usually attend the meetings at Te Whanau Awhina, nor usually do the direct victims, although those facilitating the meetings identify both the offender's family and the Māori community as victims. The whānau and friends of the offender, on the other hand, are likely to attend.

The focus of the panel meeting is first and foremost one of 'challenge': confronting offenders with the consequences of their offending for them, for their victims, for their family and whānau, and for the Māori community. The second main focus of the meeting and of the subsequent outcome is that of 'embrace': reintegrating the offender back into their family and whānau and into the Māori community and finding employment. The focus is reparation to victims and to the community and reintegration with family and whānau, and with the Māori and the wider communities. Thus, outcomes typically include plans relating to obtaining employment or job training and participation in marae-based programmes and activities as well as responses to victims.

Te Whanau Awhina has a strong ethnic base (specifically Māori), draws widely on Māori tikanga (culture), and is offered predominantly to Māori offenders. In contrast, Project Turnaround has no ethnic element (possibly reflecting the much lower Māori population in Timaru than in Waitakere), but draws on a panel of volunteers of varied backgrounds and skills, selected for the particular case. While having other admirable attributes, neither scheme (in my view) scored highly in the central restorative justice objective of involving victims, but since the 'restorative justice' label has been attached to the Crime Prevention Unit–funded groups, their attention to victim involvement appears to have increased.

It is also questionable how far a scheme in which the decision makers are panel members can be truly restorative. The ideal is for all participants, including victims and offenders, to be partners in the formulation of an agreed outcome. The notion of empowerment of the victim, in particular, does not sit comfortably with decisions being made by panel members.

The results of evaluation show that both schemes are effective in leading to the expression of remorse by those who offend, leading to them undertaking actions to repair the harm that they did, meeting victims' needs (when victims were involved), and reducing both the probability of reoffending and the costs to the justice system. (See, for example, Bowie, 2003; Maxwell et al., 1999; Smith and Cram, 1998.)

Subsequent community diversion programmes assisted by the Crime Prevention Unit have developed in several different ways. As at January 2006, the Crime Prevention Unit funded 19 community-based programmes of which eight offered the community panel model, seven offered victim–offender conferencing, and four offered both models.

## Court-referred restorative justice pilot

### Broad outline

The court-referred restorative justice pilot was initiated in 2001 and has now been professionally evaluated (Crime and Justice Research Centre and Triggs, 2005). Even though it is no longer a pilot, the scheme continues to be funded by the Ministry of Justice. Broadly speaking, the scheme, which operates in the Auckland, Waitakere, Hamilton and Dunedin District Courts, covers moderately serious offending where a guilty plea has been entered and both the defendant and the victim wish to take part in a restorative conference. Several 'provider groups' are approved by the Ministry of Justice (previously the Department for Courts), and these groups in turn have several conference facilitators trained by the ministry who arrange and manage restorative conferences. For this, the provider group is paid a fee by the ministry. Within each of the four District Courts involved, a restorative justice coordinator is the link between the court and the community.

### Suitability of the defendant

Counsel for a defendant need to discuss with the court coordinator whether the defendant is regarded as suitable for restorative processes. Most are regarded as suitable, but the coordinators will not accept defendants who have pleaded guilty but do not accept responsibility for the offence (that is, are still 'in denial'), or who would pose a risk to the victim, for example, through mental instability.

### Attitude of victim

If the defendant is regarded as suitable and (as nearly always then occurs) the court grants an adjournment and refers the matter for a restorative justice conference, the coordinator appoints a provider group to handle the case, which group may be selected for its particular suitability for the case. A facilitator from that group will approach the victim(s) to see if they wish to take part. If some victims do wish to participate and some do not, the conference can go ahead with those who do want to be involved.

### *Reports and monitoring*

A report is sent to the court as to the outcome, if any, of the conference. If the court then adjourns for a conference outcome to be implemented, the facilitator sends a supplementary report as to the completion of the matters covered by the conference agreement. (However, the actual monitoring of the outcome is done by people other than the facilitators and they should be named in the conference report.)

As noted, the court must take the report of the conference into account, in accordance with section 10 of the Sentencing Act 2002.

### *Results of the evaluation*

The latest evaluation of restorative justice for adults (Triggs, 2005) is described as a 2-year follow-up of reoffending. It showed a 17% reduction in the use of imprisonment coupled with a 9% reduction in reoffending measured after 2 years, and a 50% reduction in the seriousness of offences where participants did reoffend.[7] The 2-year follow-up did not measure victim satisfaction at that point, but in the earlier (main) evaluation very high rates of victim satisfaction were recorded, as has been shown in youth justice studies as well.

## Impact of restorative justice on criminal law practice

I would like to tell you that the provisions of the 2002 Act have brought about a vast difference in the way the courts approach sentencing, but the truth is that progress is slow. We have very far-sighted legislation, but lawyers (including judges), prosecutors, government advisers and others are slow to give up their old court-based, adversarial mindsets. Much of the impetus for change is to be found, as it was 20 years ago, in the impatience of the community with the formal system, and my view is that we need to develop a parallel but interlocked

---

[7] The figures just given are not stated in the evaluation but were calculated by me from the raw data provided. I respectfully disagree with the author's view that the results were not statistically significant, and have said so publicly.

system of community resolution centres that will become the first or 'default' system. I return to this below.

Despite the slowness of the general body of criminal justice practitioners to change, the impact of restorative justice on sentencing has been significant. One of the best accounts of this is a paper written by a visiting scholar from the United States, Yael Shy (2006). She discusses several cases from all levels of the New Zealand courts and suggests that restorative justice is in fact changing the jurisprudence of sentencing law in New Zealand.

Although initially the Court of Appeal[8] appeared to treat a restorative justice outcome as merely a mitigating factor in sentencing, to be set against traditional factors such as deterrence, Shy (2006) notes that several judges since then have applied the concept in a more comprehensive manner. She remarks (p. 17):

> Judges are also beginning to see restorative justice as a way to synthesise seemingly opposing sentencing values within these different areas. Accountability, responsibility, healing, denunciation and the opportunity for restitution are all being recognised to co-exist within one successful restorative justice conference, lessening the very difficult task of judges to ensure these goals and requirements are met through sentencing.

Let us therefore consider five specific goals or requirements of sentencing to see how this works in practice.

### *Remorse*

It is often difficult for a court to assess things like the degree of remorse experienced by a defendant or the sincerity of an apology, or to understand a victim's feelings about the case. The report of a restorative conference can make such aspects real to the court in a way that other means, for example, victim impact statements, simply cannot. As one illustration, take this extract from the decision on appeal in *Feng v Police*.[9] Here the defendant had been sentenced to imprisonment and denied leave to apply for home detention. He appealed to the High Court.

> [17] In the present case a factor telling against the appellant is his driving record. However, that is, in my view, not sufficient on its own to justify a refusal of leave [to apply for home detention]. There is no doubt that the appellant has displayed extreme remorse for his actions.

---

8   *R v Clotworthy* (1998) 15 CRNZ 651.
9   *Feng v Police* HC Auckland A127/02, 4 September 2002, Justice Salmon.

He attended a restorative justice conference. The facilitator of that conference records in his report the appellant's expressions of remorse. The report records that the appellant missed his friend and that every night he cried in bed and that he felt it was unfair that he was still alive when his friend was gone. He said that he was very, very sorry and was willing to receive whatever punishment was coming.

[18] In response to that, the mother of the dead young man said:

We are not here to punish you or judge you. That is for the law to decide.

She said she hoped that the appellant would have a good future.

[19] The facilitator records, under the head of Conference Outcomes, that the family of the deceased acknowledged the appellant's remorse and accepted his apology. The family said they were open to future visits by the appellant to their home, especially to see the album that they had compiled on their son's life. The appellant made arrangements to contribute to a trust which the parents have set up in memory of their son.

No judge, I suggest, could be given a clearer and more personal account of the remorse actually felt by an offender, and its impact on his victims. (The defendant was granted leave to apply for home detention, so he could serve his prison sentence in that form.)

## *Accountability*

Accountability has often been equated with punishment in Western criminal justice practice, but it is a much wider concept. What restorative justice allows is a very personal, face-to-face form of accountability that requires personal interaction, a willingness to explain one's actions, and the opportunity to make an apology and an offer of amends. Punishment may still play a part, but not the dominant part it has in Western criminal justice systems. (See further McElrea (2006) on the issue of accountability and punishment.)

The objective of accountability is illustrated by a prosecution brought under the Resource Management Act 1991, *Auckland Regional Council v Times Media Ltd*.[10] The case involved offensive fumes from a printing works at Warkworth, a country town north of Auckland. The restorative conference outcome included these elements:

---

10 *Auckland Regional Council v Times Media Ltd* DC Auckland CRN2084004885, 16 June 2003, District Court Judge McElrea.

- an apology to be published in the local newspaper;
- a donation to the local college for a native tree planting project;
- payment for regional council testing of health factors;
- a planted barrier around part of the site;
- a new odour entrapment device installed within 2 months; and
- payment of regional council costs.

Before imposing fines (at a reduced level) the court acknowledged (paragraph 20) that the defendant had been prepared to meet its victims face to face, to make an apology, and to be accountable for its actions; it had acknowledged the victims' concerns and agreed to a range of measures to try to meet those concerns. The court added that while it is there to see that justice is done, some crucial elements of justice had already been fulfilled.

## *Promoting a sense of responsibility*

The *Times Media Ltd*[11] case showed how restorative conferencing can promote a sense of responsibility in offenders in a very personal way. However, it is another advantage of restorative justice that a wider focus of responsibility can be considered. Although there were no previous convictions against the defendant there was a long history of infringements against the Resource Management Act 1991, and some of the residents' concerns were directed at the perceived failure of the regional council to properly enforce the requirements of the law. Indeed, the judgment comments (paragraph 44) that the defendant's lack of previous convictions:

> may be more a reflection on the slowness of the [Auckland Regional Council] to prosecute and its willingness to continue dealing with a persistent offender by way of infringement notices and abatement notices.

It is not uncommon at restorative justice conferences for the spotlight to go on 'officials' whom the victims feel have let them down – which I suggest is a healthy and democratic feature, making for a more accountable enforcement regime.

## *Interests of victims*

One of the major short-comings of the Western, court-based adversary model of criminal justice is that victims are largely excluded from the process. By

---

11 *Auckland Regional Council v Times Media Ltd* DC Auckland CRN2084004885, 16 June 2003, District Court Judge McElrea.

contrast, in the *Times Media Ltd*[12] case a large number of local residents turned up for the conference – more than could be accommodated in the room booked for the occasion. It was significant that some of the residents also attended both parts of the sentencing hearing – there having been an indication of likely sentence, and then an adjournment to allow the plan to be carried out before sentencing occurred. It was some of those present in court who explained to the presiding judge that an apology was agreed to be published in the local newspaper printed by the defendant because the newspaper had refused to publish letters to the editor complaining about the offending behaviour. (This illustrates another strength of restorative justice – the much greater variety and flexibility of outcomes than the court process provides.)

## Deterrence

The courts have in the past regarded deterrence primarily as a matter of the severity of punishment. Restorative justice is changing that. Examples of restorative outcomes that have a public deterrent effect include apologies and articles written in local or ethnic community newspapers (for example, *Auckland City Council v Raniga*[13]) and community work of an educative type, such as where a young drink-driver spoke to more than 8,000 secondary school students about what it was like to kill his two best friends by driving drunk. As one of the appeal judges asked in that (Canadian) case, "How is the principle of general deterrence better served [in such a case]?".[14] The appellate court upheld the sentence of community work, partly for that reason.

## Working with the community

A key feature of community policing found in several cultures, including those of the Pacific and in South Africa, is the notion of police and community working together pro-actively to find solutions to community problems, particularly crime. This finds its expression in local police stations that serve a neighbourhood with which the police are expected to be familiar. New Zealand has some of that community-policing element, but it is still underdeveloped compared with the practice in other societies. However, restorative justice can provide the means by which such partnerships are forged. I refer here

---

12 *Auckland Regional Council v Times Media Ltd* DC Auckland CRN2084004885, 16 June 2003, District Court Judge McElrea.
13 *Auckland City Council v Raniga* DC Auckland CRI2006-004-023-004-023560, 2 April 2007, District Court Judge McElrea.
14 *R v Hollingsky* (1995) 103 CCC (3d) 472.

particularly to the practice where, in some areas, youth justice coordinators work closely with the specialist Youth Aid police officers to involve the community.

This was done brilliantly by a youth justice coordinator (Allan MacRae[15]) and a senior Youth Aid officer in the Wellington areas in the late 1990s. They set out to increase community involvement in youth justice conferences. As well as family members and police, selected representatives of relevant agencies and/or voluntary organisations, perhaps two or three for a given conference, depending on the particular dynamics of the offending and the community, would be invited to attend and be part of the solution. Over this period, youth offending in the area dramatically reduced, because conferences were better informed as to the needs of both victim and offender, and better placed to find the local and state resources to deal with the issues.

## Proposal for community resolution centres in New Zealand

The following is the outline of a proposal I have made for the development of community resolution centres in New Zealand, and is currently under discussion. The topic is one I first advanced in Florida in 1998. (Until now, I have called these community justice centres, but that term has a different meaning in South Africa and the United States.) If established these would help us to get away from our heavy reliance on the courts, and would make victim-initiated restorative justice a reality.

The object of the proposal is to provide a community-based and consensual alternative to the courts for dealing with a substantial number of civil and criminal matters, using mediation for civil matters and restorative justice for criminal matters. This work, and disputes that might not have gone to court (such as neighbour disputes and alleged harassment or bullying), would be handled through community resolution centres that would operate as a partnership between local and central government, the police, the voluntary sector and various existing agencies. A pilot working in at least two different types of area would be ideal.

As far as civil disputes are concerned, the mediation function of the Disputes Tribunals would still be available for claims up to $7,500, but a community resolution centre would have no monetary limit. Agreements resulting from mediation would be enforceable through the courts if they were

---

15  Co-author of *The Little Book of Family Group Conferences* (MacRae and Zehr, 2004).

not honoured. For example, the claimant would be able to get judgement based on a signed settlement agreement, without having to prove the original claim.

For the category of 'disputes that might not have gone to court (such as neighbour disputes and alleged harassment or bullying)', the community resolution centre would serve more of a preventative or peace-keeping and peace-building function, thereby building safer communities and reducing the need for dispute resolution or the courts.

For criminal matters, the essential concept is that of diversion, but operating at a much more significant level than existing police diversion for first offenders. This is the major gap in criminal justice services for adults at the moment. It would not be limited to first offenders or to minor charges. It would use the proven New Zealand model of restorative justice, with offenders having to admit their responsibility and the matter proceeding only if there is the consent of victim and offender, and a trained facilitator able to supervise the process. The restorative conference would involve supporters of the parties and some relevant community representatives, selected for their ability to assist in the particular case. Lawyers would be entitled to attend, but as advisers rather than as advocates.

The police would be key people in this process. It is hoped that a community resolution centre would be located near a community constable's office. A police officer (for example, the community constable or the officer in charge of the case) would be entitled and encouraged to attend every conference, and for agreement to be reached as to outcome, all parties present, including the police, would have to be in agreement. It should be explained that there is no corruption in our police force, so I have no hesitation in requiring the support of a police office in each case. In most cases an agreed outcome would not involve charges being laid in court (provided the outcome is completed). However, in a particular case it might be agreed that charges should be laid in court – for example, to obtain an order disqualifying the offender from driving, or where a sentence of imprisonment cannot be avoided – but the outcome would be available for the court to take into account on sentencing.

As in the case of youth justice diversionary conferences, charges may have to be laid in a few cases to preserve time limits, but without requiring the defendant's attendance at court if the charges are ultimately withdrawn on completion of the conference plan.

The community resolution centre would oversee the monitoring of any outcome, civil or criminal, so that if agreements are not honoured the matter can be taken to court in the usual way. The courts would therefore act as a backstop for consent cases and a first stop for cases where there is no consent to the mediation or diversion process.

It would be ideal if the community resolution centre was located within or close to a complex that provided other community-based services, such as a community constable, social services, a Citizens Advice Bureau or community law centre.

Referrals to the community resolution centre could come from any source. In the case of criminal offending, this would fill a long-standing need for victim-initiated restorative justice cases, or indeed offender- (or even community-) initiated conferences. However, it is likely that the bulk of the referrals would come from the police, at least in early years. In that respect the process would be similar to diversionary family group conferences for young offenders, which are initiated (and attended) by police Youth Aid officers.

There would, therefore, be no 'gatekeepers'. No judge, police officer or other 'official' would say who could or could not enter the process. Whether a case continued on the restorative route would be decided by those taking part in the particular conference, on a case-by-case basis. Apart from homicide, treason and other cases that can be dealt with only by the High Court, all types of cases could be referred to the community resolution centre, although cases that require specialist skills (for example, domestic violence or sexual abuse cases) that are not available at the time, could not be accepted.

The essence of the proposal being community based, the initiative has to come from the community. This might be expressed through a local body (for example, a city or district council) or some other community organisation such as (for Māori) an iwi authority. The local body would have to take responsibility for providing accommodation for the centre and servicing a community committee to run the centre. This committee would have representation from all relevant sectors; for example, Victim Support, the local body (perhaps through its Safer Community Council or local ward committee), local mediation and restorative justice provider groups, central government (for example, the Crime Prevention Unit), a neighbourhood law office or Citizens Advice Bureau, the police, and representatives from churches and other community groups. Existing interagency initiatives could also have a focus at the community resolution centre, especially those dealing with conflict and the problems that produce conflict.

It would be necessary for the community resolution centre to employ some permanent staff (perhaps two people) and to contract the services of mediators and restorative justice facilitators on a case-by-case basis from suitably skilled and trained service providers. Because the community resolution centre will be reducing the need for the courts (and, indirectly, for corrections facilities), I feel it is appropriate that central government provides funding for such costs, and for some offender or victim programmes not available locally. A variety of other services may be provided by other agencies at no cost or by volunteers. In this category could be the monitoring of agreements, mentoring and the provision of community service projects or counselling services.

The primary tasks of the staff will be to provide information to the public, manage the flow of cases, ensure monitoring arrangements are in place, keep records of all matters dealt with, and generally act at the direction of the management committee.

## Conclusion

Already in New Zealand, restorative justice conferences have proved their value both in the youth and adult criminal justice systems. However, in the adult system, referrals still occur through the courts as pre-sentencing options. I would suggest that the adult criminal justice system could benefit by an increased use of restorative conferences as diversionary options before a court appearance.

If restorative conferences were regularly used when offending is admitted and the victim and offender agree to meet, then the community representatives who are present along with the prosecutor could build case by case on the information gained about offending in the local area, and shape the outcomes of conferences towards crime prevention rather than punishment for its own sake. The outcomes are likely to be a further reduction in the use of the courts, reduced reoffending, lower imprisonment rates, and a society in which victims will increasingly become real partners in making safer communities.

# 6

# Diversionary Policing of Young People in New Zealand: A Restorative Approach

*Gabrielle Maxwell*

## Introduction

Since 1989, the varieties of diversionary options for young people who offend have multiplied in New Zealand and there has been a move away from formal and restrictive sanctions to informal and restorative responses. Police have increasingly become the gatekeepers for diversion and, in recent years, they have also become actively involved in the management of the diversion processes.

Police warnings are the most basic form of police diversionary action and they have long formed part of the practice in countries based on a Westminster system. More recently, as restorative justice conferences have been introduced in many jurisdictions, the police have had a central role in determining a variety of other sanctions. Sometimes, as in Thames Valley, United Kingdom, and the Australian Capital Territory, conferences are operated by the police. More commonly, as in New Zealand, Northern Ireland and the various Australian jurisdictions, police are responsible for making the referral for a conference to another agency and also play a role as a key participant in the process (Maxwell and Hayes, 2007). Sometimes the restorative conference is used for mainly minor offences. At other times, as in New Zealand, it is reserved for more serious offences.

In addition to these options, the Youth Aid section of the New Zealand Police operates a diversionary option that allows a plan to be developed and completed within the community as an alternative to either prosecution or referral to a restorative justice conference. The extent and nature of police practice in diverting young offenders through the use of warnings and diversionary plans (variously referred to as alternative actions, informal sanctions or police youth diversion) is unparalleled in other criminal jurisdictions throughout the world. By far the largest proportion of child and youth offending is handled directly by the police themselves in several ways, either by front-line police or by police Youth Aid officers; 75% of all cases in 1999.

Given the centrality of police as gatekeepers who make the all-important decisions about how young people will be dealt with and the extent to which they have also become actively involved in decisions on the response and monitoring plans, questions need to be asked about the integrity of the process.

On the other hand, it has been suggested that the effectiveness of the youth justice system in responding appropriately to offending by young people stems as much from the use of warnings and diversionary plans as it does from the use of family group conferences and courts. In this chapter evidence is presented on the involvement of the police as gatekeepers, decision makers and monitors of outcomes in New Zealand. Key questions on the integrity of the system and its ability to protect children's rights are discussed. The material presented here draws principally on two research reports (Maxwell and Paulin, 2004; Maxwell et al., 2002). These studies aim to describe the total pattern of police responses to offending by children and young people[1] and to detail the responses that involve Youth Aid in arranging some form of diversionary plan or alternative action.[2]

## Police practice in response to offending by children and young people

Front-line police actions vary depending on the nature of the incident, the responses of the young person, and the officer's previous experience of the young person or their family. The officer at the scene responds to minor incidents with an immediate 'street' warning to the child or young person involved. Only the most serious cases involving young people (those aged 14–16 years) are dealt with by charges in the courts, usually after an arrest[3] and, in some cases, a remand in custody.

---

1  For convenience, I have usually referred to all this group as 'young people', although it should be noted that the Children, Young Persons, and Their Families Act 1989 defines 'young person' as a person of or over the age of 14 and under the age of 17. However, on occasion, I have used the word 'children' to refer to those under the age of 14.

2  I note that the term 'diversion' has a specific meaning in relation to adult first offenders. It is also widely used in New Zealand to refer to the diversionary actions arranged by police Youth Aid officers in relation to offending by young people. Some prefer the term 'alternative actions', which is used in overseas jurisdictions (for example, Canada). However, in the interests of simplicity and in accord with common practice, I have used the terms 'diversionary plan' and 'police youth diversion' in this chapter.

3  Cases of murder and manslaughter are referred to the District Court or High Court as appropriate, but all other matters are referred to the Youth Court in the first instance.

Others may be taken home after having their details recorded. Alternatively, they will be taken to the police station where they are interviewed in the presence of a parent or a nominated adult before being allowed to return home, or, if necessary, held until they can be bailed. These cases, including those involving child offenders (under the age of 14 years) are usually referred to Youth Aid for further investigation and action.

After examining file information, the Youth Aid officer may collect additional information from the young person, their family, their school and/or the victim. Youth Aid has five options for responding. It may decide to take no further action (especially if the offender is very young or there is insufficient evidence of offending) or simply to issue a written warning to the young person and their family. The third option is for Youth Aid to arrange a diversionary plan with the young person and the family that can involve actions that repair the harm (for example, apologies, monetary payments or work in the community) and/or referral to a programme to provide support to the young person or their parents. The last two options are to refer the case to Child, Youth and Family for a family group conference or, more rarely, to prefer charges in the Youth Court.

In making its decision, Youth Aid is largely influenced by the nature of the incident. The seriousness of the current offence is seen as the most important factor in deciding whether to warn, divert, refer for family group conference or charge in court. The young person's previous history of offending and responses to previous interventions are also highly relevant. The next most important group of factors relates to family circumstances, particularly parental responses to offending. The views of the victim, the young person's attitude and other current problems (such as truancy or alcohol use) can also be influential.

Police statistics record cases involving young people as being handled in one of four ways: warnings, referrals to Youth Aid, referrals to family group conferences and cases being charged in court. These data are presented in the left-hand side of Table 6.1. They indicate that there have been major changes in the pattern of disposals from 1990 to 1999. In particular there appears to have been a dramatic decline in the use of warnings, a large increase in Youth Aid referrals, a decline in referrals for family group conferences and an increase in the use of court; data that could be taken to indicate net widening.[4] However, there have always been problems both in understanding what these categories

---

4 'Net widening' is a term used to indicate a change in the disposal of cases in ways that increase the probability that young people are dealt with by restrictive sanctions and formal processes.

actually mean and with the reliability of these records. Verbal warnings are sometimes administered by front-line police and at other times by Youth Aid officers. Youth Aid has responsibility for deciding and administering written warnings, arranging diversionary plans and making referrals for a family group conference. Charges are normally laid by the front-line police officer in charge of the case, but they may also be laid by Youth Aid at a later stage in the process or even arise as an outcome of a family group conference. Furthermore, different districts have sometimes used these categories differently, and, because data may be entered into the system at various stages of the process, they do not necessarily reflect the eventual outcome in some cases.

**Table 6.1:** Police responses to youth offending: comparison of police national data and research data, 1990 and 1999

|  | National data | | | Research data | |
| --- | --- | --- | --- | --- | --- |
| Recorded response | 1990 (%) | 1999 (%) | Actual response | 1990 (%) | 1999 (%) |
| Warn | 63 | 23 | Warn | 51 | 43 |
| Youth Aid | 12 | 60 | Divert | 11 | 32 |
| Family group conference | 20 | 6 | Family group conference | 28 | 8 |
| Court | 5 | 12 | Court | 10 | 17 |
| Total | 100 | 100 | Total | 100 | 100 |

Note: Totals may not sum to 100% due to rounding.
Source: Maxwell et al., 2004a, p. 269; Maxwell et al., 2002.

More reliable conclusions can be reached from the research data that are presented in the right-hand side of Table 6.1. These data report the eventual disposal of the cases using samples that are largely representative of national patterns in terms of the type of offences and characteristics of offenders (Maxwell and Morris, 1993; Maxwell et al., 2002). They confirm that the period 1990 to 1999 saw an increased proportion of referrals to court and a decreased proportion of referrals for family group conferences. Further analysis indicates that the change in the balance of family group conference and Youth Court responses is not explained by changes in the seriousness of offending, but probably largely reflects changes in police practice. Over the 10-year period, shortages of resources in Child, Youth and Family have been accompanied by decreased confidence among many police officers in obtaining quick and appropriate outcomes unless the Youth Court is involved.[5]

However, the biggest change is the trebling in the use by Youth Aid of diversionary plans (see Table 6.1); from only about a tenth initially to about a third of all cases in 1999;[6] a finding that does not suggest net widening, but rather a greater tendency for police to arrange a diversionary plan as an alternative to referring for a family group conference. This change reflects both the growing recognition by Youth Aid that it can satisfactorily handle many minor cases, as well as the difficulties experienced over these years by Child, Youth and Family in managing an increased number of family group conference referrals when resources did not match demand.

Data on changes in reoffending over this period are not available, but data are available from the research on cases dealt with in 1998 and followed up 18 months later (Maxwell and Paulin, 2004). Table 6.2 presents these data.

In total, one in five of the young people reported to the police for offending in the 1998 sample were recorded as having reoffended in the following 18 months.[7] However, the results were very different depending on how the young people were dealt with. Only one in ten of those warned had reoffended and this figure was about one in six for the diversion cases. On the other hand, over a third of those referred directly to a family group conference had reoffended and the figure was about half for those charged in the Youth Court.

The differences between the outcomes reflect to a large degree the extent to which cases of a more serious nature and with a poorer prognosis are being dealt with at different levels of the system. However, even when the seriousness of offending and the background of offenders were taken into account, statistical analysis (using multiple regression techniques) showed that when young people were dealt with at the higher levels in the system, there was a statistically significantly greater probability that they would reoffend. This finding

---

5 Data from our research do not confirm the belief that more rapid and effective action is likely when the referral for a family group conference comes from the Youth Court rather than directly from the police. On the contrary, the research suggests that charge escalation is associated with poorer long-term outcomes (Maxwell et al., 2004a).

6 An important point to note in interpreting data based on police statistics is that a referral to Youth Aid will not necessarily involve a diversionary plan. Only about half of the cases recorded as referred to Youth Aid by front-line staff will result in a diversionary plan. The remainder are most likely to receive a written warning or be referred to the Youth Court.

7 This figure is probably an underestimate as there were difficulties in ensuring that the young people had not come to notice again in another police district.

demonstrates the importance of dealing with cases at the lowest possible level if reoffending is to be minimised. It also strongly validates the effectiveness of police diversionary plans as an alternative to more formal processes. On the other hand, there are caveats here, which become apparent in the next section of this chapter.

**Table 6.2:** Reoffending for a sample of cases dealt with by the police in 1998 and followed up after 18 months

| Police response | Reoffending (N) | Total (%) | Total (N) |
|---|---|---|---|
| Warning or no action | 60 | 9 | 649 |
| Diversionary plan | 74 | 16 | 464 |
| Refer directly for family group conference | 35 | 37 | 94 |
| Youth Court and family group conference | 118 | 51 | 231 |
| Total | 287 | 20 | 1,438 |

Note: Police data were based on an average 18-month follow-up period.
Source: Maxwell and Paulin, 2004.

## Nature of diversionary plans

The diversionary plans most commonly (for 75% of cases) involved only one, two or three elements and focused principally on responses designed to repair the harm that had been caused. About two in three involved an apology to a victim, about one in three involved some type of work in the community, and about one in four involved a financial contribution by way of reparation or donation to a charity (see Table 6.3). It seems likely that almost all those cases where actions to repair the harm were appropriate had such elements in the plan.

Responses of a more reintegrative or rehabilitative nature were less common: about one in five attended some type of programme. Such arrangements were much more likely when the Youth Aid officer had visited the home and explored the wider needs of the young person and their family. On the other hand, we found that some of the young people whose homes had not been visited had similar needs. Routine home visiting of all young people for whom a diversionary plan is being arranged is likely to increase the proportion of plans that include an appropriate response to needs and result in even less reoffending.

**Table 6.3:** Nature of police diversionary plans

| Element of the plan | Percentage (%) (N = 560) |
|---|---|
| Apology | 65 |
|    In person | 22 |
|    Written | 40 |
|    Both | 3 |
| Work in the community | 33 |
|    General | 15 |
|    Offence related | 18 |
|    Both | 7 |
| Monetary | 25 |
|    Reparation | 21 |
|    Donations | 4 |
| Attend a programme | 19 |
|    Cultural | 3 |
|    School or training | 6 |
|    Unspecified | 15 |
| Curfew or other restrictions | 11 |
| Other | 15 |

Note: Data may add to more than the total percentages as responses sometimes fitted more than one subcategory.
Source: Maxwell et al., 2002.

At times, various restrictions were placed on behaviour; for example, on driving, on other leisure activities, on associating with specific people, or curfews. Some of these could be seen as preventive in intent or designed to assist parents in re-establishing rules around teenage behaviour; for example, restrictions around times, places or companions associated with previous offending. Others seemed to be more in the nature of punishments – at least in the eyes of the young people themselves; for example, restrictions on leisure activities that were not related to the offending. A variety of other options included, for example, writing an essay about the consequences of their behaviour or undertaking some other type of activity that could seen as educational.

The impact of the diversionary plan on reoffending was examined using logistic regression, which held constant other factors such as the seriousness of the offending and the characteristics of the offender. The main finding to come from this analysis was that the more elements in the diversionary plan, the greater the chance of reoffending. This indicated that, other things being equal, simple plans are likely to be better than complex ones. The fact that other aspects of the plan did not prove significant in affecting reoffending in this study reflects the relatively small number of cases available for this analysis and the limited variability in the types of diversionary options arranged. It could be expected from other work examining the impact of the type of response on reoffending for those who were involved in family group conferences that longer time periods and heavier penalties in terms of money and hours of work could also increase the probability of reoffending (Maxwell et al., 2004a). Changes to record keeping within the police could enable the impact of the type of response on the reoffending of those dealt with by police to be examined in the future with larger samples.

Overall, then, the content of diversionary plans is very much in line with the generally restorative intent of the objects of the Children, Young Persons, and Their Families Act 1989, which emphasise the repair of harm and prevention of further offending. Furthermore, the use of these plans certainly serves to divert many young people from more formal justice procedures, avoid records that may affect their life choices when they are older, are able to be completed in relatively short time-frames, and, especially when they are relatively simple, are associated with relatively low reoffending rates compared to those associated with more formal options. These findings are consistent with other research on the potentially negative impact of more severe responses to youth offending. Additional information on New Zealand research can be found in Maxwell et al. (2004a) and some is summarised in chapter 2 of this book.

## View of Youth Aid officers

In 2003, interviews were conducted with Youth Aid officers that provided additional information on practice at that time in making decisions. They reported that, when it came to determining the nature of a diversionary plan, the views of the family and the victim were very important but the limited availability of programmes in the local area was often a major limiting factor in determining what could be done.

The principal goals described by the Youth Aid officers were primarily restorative: they aim to repair the harm to the victim, rehabilitate and reintegrate the offender, and achieve accountability and restoration. Punishment appeared for most to be subsidiary to these other goals, and many officers spontaneously expressed views consistent with the principles of the Children, Young Persons, and Their Families Act 1989; for example, emphasising dealing with matters at the lowest possible level and in ways that involve the least intervention in the lives of the young people.

## View of the young people

In 2003, interviews were also conducted with a sample of the young people who were dealt with by way of diversion. The interviews provided information on the family background of these relatively minor offenders. On average, they reported at least three of the adverse background factors identified in previous research as predictive of later offending and reoffending (Fergusson et al., 1994; Lipsey and Derzon, 1998; Maxwell et al., 2004a). While most of the young people reported positive relationships with others while growing up, many reported key factors that were significant predictors of later offending by them: in particular, early involvement in anti-social behaviour, problems at school and previous contacts with Child Youth and Family. These results indicate the potential for preventing further offending by responding effectively to school failure, early anti-social behaviour and referrals to the care and protection system.

The young people were also asked their views of what had happened. The results confirmed the file data and Youth Aid reports that the offending for which diversion is used is relatively minor. The descriptions by the young people underline this and indicate how unpremeditated most of the offences were. They also emphasise the important influence of peers and the roles played by alcohol and boredom in many of the offences.

When asked about the diversionary plan, most of the young people said the tasks were fair and appropriate to the offence and their capabilities. On occasion this was not so, and these findings underline the importance of reasonable and appropriate responses, particularly to younger children. Doubts have to be raised about requiring a young person to cut a lawn with scissors or asking a 13-year-old to do community work that involves handling rubbish in a recycling plant. Some of the young people felt they could have been helped more at the time of the diversion; for example, by having increased support or being able to apologise to their victim directly rather than in writing. Issues about the number of hours of community work and the length of time it took to complete diversionary plans emerged from the interviews, especially in relation to the younger offenders. However, these concerns affected only a small minority of those interviewed.

For most, the experience of a diversion plan was positive. Most felt supported and empowered by being involved in the decisions. Three-quarters felt they had been treated with respect, were remorseful, were forgiven and had not been shamed or stigmatised – all aspects associated with successful outcomes in research on the effectiveness of family group conferences. Nevertheless, between a fifth and a quarter did not report these experiences. Furthermore, about 40% had not been involved in the decision making or were unable to repair the harm they had done – both important features of the principles set down in the Children, Young Persons, and Their Families Act 1989 and endorsed by most Youth Aid officers. These findings point to areas where practice can be improved and where change may result in better outcomes in the future.

The responses of the police at the time of the offence had an important impact on the young people's views of the police. Many said they were treated fairly and responded to this with respect for the police. On the other hand, those who said that they had been treated roughly or abused still carried the hurtfulness of this with them and it has marked their view of police.

Since the diversion, most young people reported having had good experiences and having positive attitudes to their future, but a significant minority did not. For many the balance of negative events was still outweighing the positive in their lives. Of particular concern were those who reported unemployment and psychological problems, because these were aspects of life that could potentially be changed by constructive contact with the system. For others, the difficulties cannot easily be remedied: problems with their relationships with others, criminal associates, and alcohol and other drug abuse. It is this group of young people that needs to be given the opportunity and support that will enable them to choose more pro-social and rewarding pathways.

## Issues of police powers

Inevitably, when police are given powers that effectively enable them to not only apprehend but also to determine outcomes of offenders, there have to be serious concerns about the potential misuse of police powers and a system of checks is usually created to guard against this. On the other hand, the process in New Zealand has developed informally, and there has been a reluctance to set guidelines for a process that was evolving and appeared to be successful in achieving the goals of the youth justice legislation. Had more formal limits been placed on police in earlier years, the development of what appears to be a largely benign and constructive response to young people may never have occurred. However, after 10 years of evolution, it is timely to review the practice and ask questions about whether some limits should be placed on police powers to determine responses to offending by young people.

Maxwell and Paulin's (2004) report suggested that guidelines be set in relation to the upper limits for the contents of diversionary plans; particularly, with respect to the length of time necessary to complete the plan, the amount of money to be paid and the number of hours of community work required. An additional safeguard against increasing penalties inappropriately would be to require the approval of a more senior officer in the district when recommended limits were exceeded or using the option of a referral for a family group conference.

In the light of the data reported here, some obvious limits to the nature of the diversionary plan can be suggested by examining the cases that fell outside the amounts and time periods most commonly used. For example, one in five of the young people interviewed was required to pay reparation of an amount that was greater than $200, and about one in five was required to undertake community work of more than 30 hours. Perhaps a referral onward would be appropriate for amounts of reparation greater than $200 or 30 hours.

With respect to the time taken to complete a plan, legislation suggests that this should be appropriate to the age and maturity of the child or young person. Three months would certainly seem to be a desirable time-frame in which to meet such an objective. However, the data showed that the time taken to complete the plans was between 3 and 6 months for 20% and between 6 months and 1 year for 13%. In some cases, the longer time-frames enabled courses to be completed or were occasioned by a need to review an initial plan. However, a system for the review of time-frames exceeding 3 months would seem appropriate, providing the review process did not itself lead to further delays.

## Other issues relating to police practice

Three other issues arose from this research.

### *Better records are needed*

Better police records are needed to enable an accurate analysis of data on police practice in relation to young people. Since 2000, the police computer system (NIA – National Intelligence Application) has become the primary tool for recording information. However, at the time of the research there were still difficulties with the completeness and accuracy of the data available from the system; for example, discrepancies in young people's reports of their diversion experience and the police record sometimes reflected a failure to update changes to the original plan. Attempts to track instances of reoffending through the system also threw up many discrepancies.

### Meeting needs for services
The analysis of the diversionary plans showed that often there was no provision included for the support of young people and families with needs (for example, support for young people out of education or to deal with alcohol, other drug or anger issues, or for families needing assistance with parenting skills). Sometimes this reflected the fact that there had not been a home visit that established needs. Although a greater used of home visits would increase the demands on Youth Aid officers, the potential savings in preventing reoffending is likely to outweigh the costs of providing extra funding for staff at this stage of a young person's life. In other cases, a referral for a family group conference might have been a more appropriate option for making arrangements to meet the needs that were identified although in some areas, pressure on Child, Youth and Family may have mitigated against such a referral. The development of clearer guidelines indicating how needs can best be identified and responded to would seem desirable.

### Youth Aid officers need assistance
Youth Aid officers suggested that their time could be used more effectively if they received more help from non-commissioned staff with arranging and monitoring diversionary plans and entering data.

## Conclusions
Results of research on diversionary practice by the police indicate that actions are largely consistent with the restorative justice principles set out in the Children, Young Persons, and Their Families Act 1989. Satisfaction with outcomes is high both among police and young people and reoffending rates are low (9% and 16% respectively for the warning and diversion plan samples). Most matters are dealt with constructively through apologies together with other actions that repair harm or are likely to prevent reoffending by providing support to the young people and their families. There is relatively little use of

punitive sanctions. However, in many instances young people were not being fully involved in the decisions that were taken.

Conclusions from the research confirm other studies that support the value of restorative and diversionary responses to offending by young people. Best practice factors and potential policy changes that are likely to improve the quality of outcomes are identified.

Given the centrality of police as gatekeepers who make the all-important decisions about how young people will be dealt with and the extent to which they have also become actively involved in decisions on the response and the monitoring of plans, questions need to be asked about the integrity of the process.

On the other hand, it has been suggested that the effectiveness of the youth justice system in responding appropriately to offending by young people stems as much from the use of warnings and diversionary plans as it does from the use of family group conferences and courts.

This chapter presents evidence on the involvement of the police as gatekeepers, decision makers and monitors of outcomes. It examines key questions on the integrity of the system and its ability to protect children's rights. It demonstrates that the outcomes of police diversionary options are also undoubtedly positive in the view of most participants, consistent with the principles of the legislation and effective in avoiding reoffending. Finally, it concludes that police practice in New Zealand at the turn of the 21st century has been extraordinarily effective in achieving diversionary and restorative responses to about three-quarters of the young people who offend without resorting to the use of the more formal processes of the family group conference or the Youth Court.

# 7

# Restorative Policing

*Howard Broad*

## Introduction

In this chapter, I explore the connection between the current policing model in New Zealand and the concept of 'restorative policing'. Although there is plenty of literature to suggest how police might contribute to forms of restorative justice, I did not find a satisfying definition of restorative policing. And I am reluctant to boldly state a definition.

Therefore, in this chapter I have chosen to explore the extent to which there are restorative elements to the current style of policing in New Zealand. And I find that there is room to make some changes. However, that is not to say that the policing here is without a significant restorative connection – and I am particularly keen in this paper to advertise the excellent work of our youth services staff in the use of restorative techniques. Finally, I suggest that maybe we should aim a little higher than we currently do, and I have some ideas about how we might do that.

## Background

When a police officer graduates from The Royal New Zealand Police College and is posted to an operational station, typically their first role is one of incident response. They are assigned to a group of police staff under the supervision of a sergeant. Their work assignments will rotate around the clock over the full period of the week. Their duties will be a mix of emergency and non-emergency responses to reported crimes and incidents as well as a range of 'proactive' assignments. These include directions to patrol at particular risk locations and times, to make follow-up inquiries into crimes and incidents, and to monitor the activities of people on bail or suspected of current offending. They may also be tasked to perform a range of road policing functions such as crash attendance, and deterrent patrol targeting speed, drink driving and failure to wear seatbelts – all practices that impact on the number of deaths and injuries on the road.

I want to focus on the officer's response to a call to attend an incident. Although the individual tasks associated with this deployment are usually not extraordinarily difficult, the context in which the officer is expected to perform their duties varies significantly and adds complexity to the decisions required of them. The age and characteristics of the people involved, the type of crime or incident, the location, the time of day or night, the availability of support to control, coordinate or deal with the incident, and the extent to which the facts of the situation are immediately apparent all have a bearing on what option the officer may take.

The actions of the officer will also be determined by other factors. For example, it may be a busy night in the officer's patrol area, with calls backed up for the next available patrol officer. There is natural urgency too to have as many calls attended as possible, and this urgency transfers to the officer who feels pressured to make quick decisions and move on.

The main decision required is how to resolve the incident. If the matter is a crime report with no offender present, the details of the complainant and the circumstances may be noted down and later submitted as a formal crime report – the path to resolution is delayed. If the incident involving disputing parties can be resolved on the spot, as it often will be – the officers will note this situation as 'attendance sufficient' and move on. However, because of the rapid assessments often made this merely provides temporary resolution to an enduring problem. If, in relation to a reported crime, there is an offender available for apprehension immediately, then action will be taken to confront that individual. An explanation will be sought and noted, other evidence collected and then – decision time. What to do now? In many cases, the officer will arrest.

The officer potentially has other options. Where no offender is immediately apparent, the officer could prioritise time to make inquiries. If it is a dispute between two parties, they could prioritise time to mediate a practical, even if temporary, solution to the issue. If an offender is present, they could contemplate issuing a warning or deferring an arrest to broker an immediate rapprochement between victim and offender without resort to a formal process. At the very least, consideration of a summons to court as opposed to the blunt process of immediate arrest and incarceration could be considered.

From the officer's perspective, the decision to arrest is justifiable for several reasons.

If the offender is taken into custody, they will be identified through the taking of fingerprints and a photograph and any subsequent issue about identity resolved. Certain identification may lead to the connection of the offender to other crimes.

The arrest process is, among many processes available for officers to use, mightily efficient. The officer completes scene action and then lodges the prisoner into custody where other officers take responsibility for their welfare, and issues to do with bail and charging. The officer has to submit a file. It has a minimum level of information about the case and in some cases its preparation may be deferred.

The officers experience the frustration of the 'revolving door' of the current system. Those for whom a court appearance has not worked are frequently back in the same neighbourhood, causing the same problems. To the officer, this is 'someone else's fault' – and they are strongly supported by media commentary in this regard, that bail is given too easily, too many offenders get off on technicalities and prison sentences are too short.

Alternative actions to arrest are not as well supported by police. To be useful, the officer must have a clear process in which to divert an offender. But, to enter the alternative action process is to court uncertainty. What do I do? How long will it take? Who do I seek for support and assistance? Will I get in trouble for taking the 'soft' option? It would take a determined effort to overcome these issues in the current model.

Whatever decision is made, it is true that each officer is acting as the gatekeeper to the criminal justice system. While there are other actors in this gatekeeping role the police initiate the substantial volume of cases that proceed through the criminal justice system. The police play an immensely important role in finding and interpreting the facts of any case, deciding on the selection of charges, reviewing evidential sufficiency and proceeding the case to prosecution. In serious cases, the crown solicitor discharges a number of these roles in addition to the police.

To completely understand how extensive the influencing role of the police is we must also reflect that the police organisation's deployment and tactical options decisions also play a part in the type and quality of decision that a 'gatekeeping' officer actually makes.

For example, the police can, from time to time, assume a very 'control-oriented' posture. Increasingly the language of some police field strategies borrowed from overseas are couched in control language – 'zero tolerance', acquiring a 'grip' on crime, and attacking 'resolution targets'. There are also 'strategic campaigns' – operations designed to lift citizens' compliance with the rules through fear of penalty such as arrest or infringement notice. Each of these strategies typically emphasises apprehension and prosecution. Now, these strategies have their place, there is no doubt that in some areas there is a need for the authorities to exert control as a precondition for more effective and longer term crime reduction strategies. However, a police agency that overemphasises such measures will over time risk losing 'legitimacy' – the willing cooperation of the public.

Police have always, and understandably, struggled to adequately resource those staff deployed for reactive duty. Within the police a number of tensions are at play. The issues are similar to those found in other critical public services such as health.

The demand for immediate attention to calls for service has the potential to consume all resources – the public's expectations keep rising and their intolerance of 'poor' service keeps diminishing. Police have reserved resources to target the causes of problems that result in this demand, but when successful simply find that the public demands more. Therefore, the goal of being so sufficiently creative so as to not only stabilise demand, but also reduce it, has proved elusive.

There is also a demand to extract staff from response duties to 'specialist' units in order to lift quality or to add features to the previously basic service provided by front-line staff. Essentially, the role of the constable on front-line duty has become so wide that it is extraordinarily difficult to prepare new staff to competently effect all duties and, as pressure from both inside and outside the police develops around an issue, to effectively respond. Therefore, police management responds with the establishment of a specialist group. To do so effectively requires an extraction of staff from front-line units, which are therefore less able to meet demand, and, under further pressure, the risk to quality service increases.

The point is that decisions relating to the procedures and support made available to front-line staff as well as decisions as to where staff are deployed have a significant influence on the decisions they make, which then so greatly influence the criminal justice system. These decisions are in their own right eminently justifiable, variously on the grounds of efficiency or perceived effectiveness, but there is an increasing volume of opinion suggesting that the efficient response mode to policing constrains rather than promotes the outcomes sought from the system and that the effectiveness claimed is not enduring. There are two main grounds for the scepticism.

The evidence in support of the current system for *rehabilitating* offenders is quite weak. Many offenders leave the court or the place to where they were sentenced and begin to reoffend immediately. It has not changed their behaviour. The process is quite impersonal. It substantially avoids the involvement of the aggrieved party in the crime (the victim). It is a contested process in which the parties manoeuvre to position their own interests rather than to achieve the best result for all concerned. It selects from a small range of sentencing options that are able to be efficiently provided rather than seeking to identify the option that will address the causes of offending and ensure it stops.

This approach is an expensive option. Costs in the criminal justice sector continue to increase. In some respects this reflects an increase in the number of offenders being processed through the system. But there is an increased processing cost as additional procedural requirements are introduced – possibly also reflecting an increase in the standard or quality of justice being provided, and the costs of increasing the time spent in the system by participants as the impact of reduced opportunities for bail and tougher sentencing options, among other drivers, also take effect. The relative cost of adding to infrastructure (staff, prisons and so on) as the capacity in the economy shrinks and prices rise (building costs, pressure on wages and so on) is a further burden on government at this time.

There are, therefore, strong incentives to find alternatives to arrest and prosecution in the hope that a virtuous circle might be developed. Better options taken by the gatekeepers to the system will reduce the costs of the system and allow for the transfer of resources into more effective early interventions, so reducing the flow of potential cases into the formal criminal justice system.

However, New Zealand is not without a significant set of diversionary options. I want to describe several of these approaches already operational in New Zealand.

## Restorative and diversionary practices in youth offending

Towards the end of the 1980s, and as I recall that was a decade in which police practices in relation to suspected offenders were seriously questioned by the courts, the government revised its policy in relation to youth offending and moved to a restorative model. The Children, Young Persons, and Their Families Act 1989 required police to consider options other than arrest. Indeed, the threshold to arrest was raised considerably. With 15 years of experience of the Act, police practice has now settled down to a reasonably effective model.

As it happens, most young people who offend do so for minor offences. Over 80% of youth crime reported to the police is now dealt with in a diversionary manner; that is, the young person is diverted from formal reporting to the youth justice system. Police Youth Aid officers visit the home of the offender, make a risk assessment, and most frequently issue a warning or develop a plan that usually involves some form of apology to the victim, a form of reparation, and a sanction such as a withdrawal of privileges or the need to

perform some additional tasks, usually in the nature of community service. The rate of reoffending from this approach is very low. There are five reasons for this in my view.
- It is a form of early intervention, before offending becomes too serious.
- It holds the young person to account.
- It generally involves a responsible adult from the young person's family, so that the offending is acknowledged and the probability of the plan being implemented increases.
- The process avoids over-reaction and the negative effects of shaming, which are known to be unhelpful to behavioural change.
- Provided the interaction is performed well, it introduces a police officer to the young person as an authority figure, providing a constructive influence on their behaviour.

Where the offending is of a more serious nature, or is part of a pattern of repeated offending, police may report the young person to a youth justice coordinator, an official from Child, Youth and Family, with the intention that a family group conference be convened. If the young person has been charged with a crime, so has to make an appearance before the Youth Court, the court may also refer the young person to a family group conference.

A family group conference is a formal process designed to hold the young person to account and involve the family and youth justice professionals in an examination of the causes of the offending and the preparation of a plan that will be *formally monitored* with the intention that the offending stop.

Overall, the results from these conferences have been very positive. The approach we use, also a form of restorative justice, has attracted worldwide attention. We must acknowledge that the rate of reoffending is higher than the rate with earlier intervention diversionary methods, but you would expect this given that family group conferences are dealing with a population of young offenders prepared to commit more serious or serial offences. Certainly, conference-based planning to stop reoffending is more successful than the usual options raised from time to time that involve shaming, detention, boot camp or other 'aggressively tough' approaches. Young people who have embarked on serious or serial criminal activity need determined action, but of a particular kind that confronts who and what they are to be as adults.

Recent reviews of the operation of the youth justice process indicate there are some areas where improvements could be made.

First, the amount of time that is able to be spent on each case by youth justice professionals is important, as is the speed at which cases can be brought through to a conference – delays in bringing the young person to account reduce the impact of any plan. For that reason the government increased the number of youth aid officers in its 2005 budget and Child, Youth and Family has for several years been on a capability development process involving more youth justice workers and better processes.

Secondly, another critical factor is the availability of services to which a young person may be directed as part of the plan. For example, literacy programmes, life skills or outdoor activity courses, and alcohol and other drug counselling. Not all of these programmes are available everywhere in New Zealand, and in the bigger population centres the services are under pressure. Connecting young offenders to good services is a key part of the response.

In the event that a young person has committed the most serious offences, or where they are an enduring risk to the community, they can be arrested (up to this point police are under direction to find alternatives to arrest) and placed before the Youth Court. Dealing with these young ones is a real problem, and I will speak of our involvement in respect of more serious offenders shortly. One area of concern for us, however, is that there are difficulties scheduling young people in custodial remand and accordingly too often we have young ones in our cells. Our lock up is not a place for youth offenders. The government's steps to increase the number of youth justice facilities will be welcomed in the police.

Then there are our youth development initiatives. We have nearly 20 of these nationally. The basis of these programmes is that they aim to provide a wraparound service to known and potential young offenders and their families. The programmes are built around those factors that are known to correlate with offending and victimisation, so the elements of the programme touch on their family life, their attendance and performance at school or work, their associations with their peers, and the choices and commitments to leisure activities they make within their neighbourhoods. Police support the programme with a dedicated police officer and the salaries for two social workers as well as an operational grant. Usually there is community support, which provides for additional operating funding and sometimes additional staff. A significant part of the approach is the development of relationships with the family. This often brings into focus the needs of siblings of the at-risk youngster, and of the family as a whole. Links with and between social services (health, housing, welfare, education and other services) are developed. Overcoming bureaucracy and the silos into which bureaucratic organisations can fall, becomes an essential skill for the programme team. The same problem also features as a 'must fix' at the policy level.

The link to community, through committed citizens groups such as Rotary, or the myriad of linkages that the programmes build up over time, are absolutely critical to these projects. First, the community link offers legitimacy, because programmes that operate in support of the offender population are often viewed very negatively. Secondly, that the programme operates by grant and favour of the local community increases the manner and extent to which the programme is supported – the voluntary donation of time, effort and material that goes so far to glue these programmes together.

The programmes have been evaluated, some several times, and have been shown to have a significant level of success in diverting young people from offending or reoffending. They are difficult programmes to run, requiring real professional expertise but they offer real promise. We have been blessed by the number of committed people who we have employed in the programmes and the professional skills they have shown.

The message from our experience with a restorative approach to youth offending is that there is potential to develop effective interventions from minor offending through to more serious offending, maybe then this gives some hope that an arrangement may be made for adult offenders, other than the arrest and prosecution model.

## Adult diversion

At this stage, for people aged 17 and over, the only intervention option is the police adult diversion scheme. The objectives of the scheme are to:
- prevent reoffending;
- avoid a conviction for first offenders;
- provide another chance for the offender;
- help the offender's rehabilitation by tailoring the diversion to the individual and imposing conditions and requirements that assist rehabilitation and discourage further offending;
- use community resources to assist rehabilitation; for example, to provide marriage guidance or counselling for anger management, drugs, alcohol, grief or sexual dysfunction; and
- ensure that appropriate reparation is made to the victim of the offence.

Police in each prosecutions office appoint a diversions officer, usually an experienced prosecutor, who ensures that the criteria for diversion are met and then manages each case through the process.

The criteria for diversion are that the:
- offence must be a first offence, unless special conditions apply;
- offence must not be serious or the circumstances must be such that a conviction would be out of all proportion to the gravity of the offence;
- offender must admit guilt, show remorse and be prepared to pay full reparation;
- offender must agree to diversion;
- victim in the case must have been consulted; and
- officers involved in the case must have been consulted.

Diversion usually involves an apology, the payment of reparation if appropriate, and the completion of some element of community service or personal development (counselling and so on).

Adult diversion schemes do reduce some of the impact of the courts, shifting some of the case-handling responsibility to the police. The offender does report back to the court following the completion of the agreed plan, and if unsuccessful the court can retake responsibility for sentencing. As in the case of family group conferences, the pressure of case volumes can reduce the intervention to an 'efficient' model in which the range of options to select from in preparing the plan are few and similar – and the lack of customisation and personal oversight of the plan can be assumed to reduce its effectiveness.

## Restoring communities

In order to be more relevant to any form of restorative, or even 'community' approach to policing, an in-depth and sensitive knowledge of the community is required. There is a great deal of literature available on the subject of community policing that I will leave to you to consider. Suffice it to say that New Zealand, like many overseas agencies, is endeavouring to improve the level of connection to communities, and to improve the amount of knowledge of those communities, in order to improve the accuracy and completeness of the policing approach in those communities.

The challenge has been particularly great in respect of the indigenous Māori community, and in respect of immigrant communities from the Pacific and elsewhere. The development of the relationship with Māori and their cultural concepts related to the connection of people to each other, to the land and communal problem solving have been very useful. These concepts fit naturally with the ideas of problem-solving policing, and of the restorative approach to the administration of justice. The involvement of the extended family in family group conferences has shown to be effective in overcoming the shortcomings of the nuclear family in which the causes of the offender's problems are probably to have been based.

My touching on the restoration of communities would not be complete without a brief reference to the concept of 'reassurance' in policing, and in particular 'signal crimes theory'. This addresses a phenomenon evident in most Western countries at this time. 'Crime is coming down – but no one believes us', is the forlorn message from senior police. Reported and recorded crime is reducing in New Zealand and throughout the United States, the United Kingdom, Canada and Australia – our most comparative jurisdictions. Various reasons for this are suggested, from improvements in physical security, to the social changes of the 1960s onwards including the availability of the contraceptive pill and more readily available abortion, to the improving participation of vulnerable people and communities in the economy. And police agencies would also say that there has been markedly improved policing practice. So, why is credit for this not reflected in public opinion?

The first main reason is that there is a demonstrable shift in the reporting of crime. The amount of 'column inches' reporting on crime is known to have expanded in the last several decades, and the type of reporting has shifted to the controversial and combative. Television, in particular, is bringing the faces of victims and perpetrators into the living rooms of our homes. Consequently, it is easy to deduce from the information that is available that crime 'must be getting worse'.

If the message does not make the point, then the citizen's own frame of reference certainly does. At the same time as government officials are lauding crime reduction, citizens look out the front door and see plenty of evidence of criminal behaviour and incivility. Typically, this evidence is of lower order crime such as graffiti, noisy and abusive young people, bad driving and abandoned cars. Why would you believe the government when you can see the breakdown of society for your own eyes? And then, particularly, when a major criminal event happens in or near your own neighbourhood, you are quite justified in becoming afraid.

The research into the phenomenon has developed reasonably clear responses. First, there is value in governments taking action on run-down neighbourhoods to restore them, and eliminate the visual pollution and other evidence that crime is at hand. You will have heard of the 'broken windows' approach to crime espoused initially by George Kelling and James Q. Wilson, and there are many examples of neighbourhood renewal programmes. Secondly, the signal crimes research advocates rapid and emphatic action on local criminal behaviour that is having a disproportionate impact (an impact that 'signals' a step change) on the peace of mind of local residents. Determining what is a clear 'signal' requires good relationships with key observers in that community and a sound analytical approach. Further, when a major event happens locally, swift response action to bring the people in the community together to talk about the issue and develop an effective 'signal response' is necessary. This approach is one the New Zealand Police is in the process of developing in line with international trends.

Is how I have described this ubiquitous? That's difficult to say. One of the features of police work is that officers conduct most of their work away from the direct oversight of a supervisor, and do not report each and every activity that they perform. However, I am reasonably confident in asserting the following.

In most major centres where the level of specialisation is higher than in smaller centres, general duties response staff work under considerable pressure and the opportunities to be more creative, while they do exist, are few. This extends to the logical place in which a restorative approach might otherwise (than in the field) be actioned, that is the point at which prisoners are received at a police station. In the major centres at least, the demands on custody suite staff have increased over the years and their ability to tackle an additional duty such as the development of a restorative option for an arrestee is unlikely.

The work approach of detectives, staff who are in most places also working under considerable pressure of time, could be assumed to offer more opportunities for an alternative approach given the amount of time they spend with the offender and the commitment of time to court processes already an expected part of a detective's handling of cases. However, the type of case dealt with by detectives is more serious and does not usually fit current access criteria for diversion, and the suggestion that time spent preparing cases for court could be substituted for time spent on an alternative approach does not allow for the fact that the time of detectives is mostly spent proving guilt. The admission of guilt is a primary starting point for any form of restorative, diversionary or alternative approach.

In provincial and rural areas, there is more likelihood that alternative actions take place. With greater knowledge of the people involved, and possibly with a greater number of more experienced officers, opportunities to warn, divert and apply a form of restorative approach could be more readily taken.

## Towards a restorative police

In my view, and I hope it is clear from the opinions I have about the current system, some critical factors have to be present if the police are to be positioned to be more 'restorative' in our approach, and to contribute to more effective outcomes from the criminal justice process.

A new, or revised, vision of the approach to policing criminal cases is required. The elements of the approach lie in what is already known in respect of restorative justice already:

- allowing time to be taken on cases, so a restorative approach can be implemented as soon as possible in the lifecycle of the case;
- assembling sufficient information about the causes of crime;
- avoiding factors that demotivate the participants in the process to commit;
- selecting options that will address the problem;
- providing sufficient resources to enable the plan to be implemented; and
- recognising and celebrating the success of the plan or allowing for the ready availability of a fall-back option.

A critical factor is one of attitude. While I have spoken of the gatekeeping role of the police, this role is presently undertaken without sufficient linkage to the overall objectives of the criminal justice system. It is insufficient to state the goal of the police is to 'detect and apprehend offenders' without also acknowledging an equal and compelling goal of 'preventing or reducing crime'. It is insufficient for corporate directions of police to state these goals, the attitude that serves those goals must be owned throughout the police, and the various acts that contribute to overall crime reduction must be performed by all staff. In this respect, the front-line staff must see benefits in the approach, and be attracted to use this as a voluntary application of their discretion.

The second factor is 'connectedness', for a shift to restorative policing needs to be embraced by a group of agencies, including the judiciary. All parties 'singing off the same songsheet' is an essential precondition for such a change.

The case for change needs to be developed; that is, a baseline measurement of the performance of the current approach. A primary reason to have this information is to be able to track progress.

The systems of setting and measuring priorities within the police need to be in alignment with this direction. This includes developing procedural models that can be easily and practically acquired by front-line staff. The 'ease of use' factor is critical.

Sufficient resources need to be added to those parts of the system where countervailing pressures would otherwise subvert the opportunity for police to engage in more restorative activity. Further, resourcing needs must be met to ensure the 'ease of use' principle is achieved. If front-line police continue to see arrest and prosecute as the easiest option, it will be the one selected.

A wider range of staff need to be developed in terms of restorative policing practice – beyond the Youth Aid and diversion officers currently practising forms of the approach.

The approach needs to be communicated effectively. To the extent that this is seen as a 'soft' option by those participating and by those who will be called to comment (the media and so on) is a risk. Unless there are clear and compelling grounds, those in influential positions market the approach, and sufficient early progress is made to support those publicly promoting the approach, the fear of the community would be easily activated by those who will be promoting the 'tough, hard-line, throw away the key' model.

The approach has to be implemented gradually, working from simple and clear-cut cases through to those more difficult and contentious. One of the lessons from the youth justice model is that the stark transfer from one system to another created a risk. In the youth justice case it was in respect of serious, persistent youth offenders, for whom the new model seemed not to cater. Criminal justice is no place for other than a well thought through and cautious approach to change.

This is not an impossible task. There are grounds to reflect on the positive changes that have occurred in youth justice and that have been positive over a sufficient period. It is an approach that in my view, is well worth considerably more thought.

# 8

# Resolving Conflict and Restoring Relationships: Experiments in Community Justice within a New Zealand Faith-Based Prison

*Kim Workman*

## Introduction

In October 2003, a faith-based prison unit, He Korowai Whakapono (a cloak of faith), was opened at Rimutaka Prison, a prison for male offenders, near Wellington, New Zealand. It was a joint Department of Corrections and Prison Fellowship of New Zealand programme to promote peace and reconciliation. The model of biblical peacemaking and processes for conflict resolution and the restoration of community peace, presented both staff and prisoners with conflict in terms of established disciplinary procedures and the impact of 'prisonisation' on prisoners.

This chapter explores the role of restorative justice in prisons, and the applicability of 'best practise' restorative justice principles and practices within an institutional setting. It also examines the implications of this model for prisoner family/whānau restoration, and victim–offender reconciliation. The paper concludes with a discussion on the implications of this model for the wider correctional system.

## Exploring the context: history of faith-based prisons

In 1972, Brazilian lawyer Mario Ottoboni, inspired by his understanding of God's unconditional love for him, developed a programme to actively demonstrate that same unconditional love in the darkness of a prison. Dr Silvio Marques Neto, then a local magistrate, Dr Hugo Veronese, a prominent educational psychologist, and a group of committed lay people joined him.

Over the next 10 years, this team developed a methodology that was applied first at Humaita Prison in San Jose dos Campos, in the state of Sao Paolo. By the end of 1973, the programme was caring for prisoners in half the cells at Humaita. In 1979, the prison was closed, but political pressure led to an offer by the government to reopen it as a private facility. It reopened in 1984, as the first fully functional faith-based prison.

In October 1994, Prison Fellowship Ecuador established a faith-based unit called Hogar San Pablo in Garcia Moreno Prison in Quito, and another at the adult male prison in Guayaquil. Prison Fellowship volunteers in Peru opened the Saint Augustine Community at Socabaya Prison outside Arequipa in February 1997. Similarly, Prison Fellowship Argentina has established faith-based prisons in Cordoba and Concordia. Prison Fellowship Ministries (United States) opened the InnerChange Freedom Initiative in Houston, Texas, in April 1997 and in Newton, Iowa, in October 1999, and the Winfield Correctional Centre in Kansas in January 2000.

Prison Fellowship of New Zealand began actively negotiating with the Department of Corrections in 1995, and, following 7 years of negotiation, opened the first faith-based unit, He Korowai Whakapono, in the British Commonwealth, at Rimutaka Prison, on 16 October 2003. The Department of Corrections provided the facility and custodial staff, and Prison Fellowship developed and implemented the core programme through its programme staff and church volunteers.

## Characteristics of He Korowai Whakapono

He Korowai Whakapono, the faith-based unit, is a 60-bed prison unit with the overall objective of reducing the reoffending of prisoners, based on international evidence of the effectiveness of programmes based on a Christ-focused, community-centred, environment characterised by prayer and a process of Christian development and spiritual transformation.

The unit has three core operational characteristics. First, it is explicitly Christian based, with the faith ethos reflected in an 18-month programme delivered in the unit, a prayer-centred daily routine, and a combination of faith development programmes and regular worship involving a variety of external church groups and Christian volunteers.

Secondly, although the Department of Corrections' Integrated Offender Management System mandates interventions consistent with behavioural-cognitive theory, the department has explicitly accepted that there should be room to test other compatible interventions.

Thirdly, offenders are confronted with the harm they have done in committing crime, and work toward restoring relationships with their victims, with family members and with the wider community. They are challenged to restore key relationships and come to terms with the harm they have caused others. That in turn motivates them to address the behaviour and beliefs that drive offending, including violence, drug and alcohol abuse and other inappropriate behaviours.

Through Operation Jericho, a Prison Fellowship prisoner after-care programme, trained Christian mentors work on a one to-one basis with the prisoners up to 8 months before they leave the prison, and for up to 2 years after they are released. The mentors are supported by their church, which undertakes to provide the offender and their family with moral and spiritual support after release. Built on a firm foundation of Christ-centred leadership, the faith-based approach empowers offenders and volunteers alike to take responsibility for solving their personal and communal problems. Careful programming ensures that the incremental change process is successful in restoring the offender to their peers, family and the community. Lower recidivism rates, lower levels of prison incidents and savings to taxpayers are clear benchmarks of effectiveness.

## The core programme

The programme goes through four phases over an 18-month period, namely:
- phase 1: induction and orientation;
- phase 2: spiritual transformation;
- phase 3: restoration; and
- phase 4: reintegration.

### *Phase 1: induction and orientation*
Once a prisoner is transferred to the faith-based unit after an initial assessment, he enters phase 1, induction and orientation, which lasts 3–4 weeks. It is the start toward rebuilding and transforming a prisoner's values, beliefs and character.

### *Phase 2: spiritual transformation*
In phase 2, there is a strong emphasis on Christian development, combined with work programmes and internal support that facilitate the internal transformation process. The overall goal of this phase is for each member to begin life transformation through the Gospel. Each module has specific goals that, if achieved, enable participants to rebuild their value system and establish a solid foundation for spiritual growth.

### Phase 3: restoration

During phase 3, transformation and restoration are deepening, and a prisoner's newly developing value system is tested in many ways. In this phase, there is an emphasis on the restoration of the offender with family, the community and, where appropriate, the victim, in accordance with recognised restorative justice principles and practice. Prisoners will ideally have completed the Sycamore Tree Programme and will, where appropriate, have made reparation and be actively seeking reconciliation with family, the victim(s) and the wider community.

### Phase 4: reintegration

Phase 4 is the aftercare phase of the programme and begins the day the member enters prison. The transformation of the prisoner continues through this phase and is never really over. Faith-based unit core values are now transferred to a new community. In this phase, mentors are the primary point of contact with prisoners. They serve as a bridge for prisoners. The goal of this phase is to successfully reintegrate the member back into the community and have productive relationships in the family, the church, and the workplace.

## Outcomes

At the outset, Prison Fellowship posited that each offender who underwent the faith-based programme would:

- develop an understanding of, and commitment to, the Christian faith, and, through the support of a faith community, understand the implications of that in the development of a Christian worldview and lifestyle;
- achieve a positive attitudinal and behavioural change of orientation, values and beliefs through a process of spiritual transformation;
- demonstrate improved institutional behaviour, and treat other offenders with increased respect, demonstrating empathy for the circumstances of other prisoners, and for their victims;
- be motivated to change their behaviour, so offenders who had previously resisted taking part in rehabilitative programmes, or had resisted changing their behaviour, would exhibit improved behaviour, and be more likely to set positive goals for the future;
- take personal responsibility for the harm they had done to others in committing crime, and work toward restoring relationships with their victims, family members and the wider community through a process based on forgiveness, love and reconciliation;

- reintegrate successfully with their families and whānau and the community, through a programme of mentorship and church support; and
- demonstrate reduced offending behaviour.

## Concept of spiritual transformation

Within the context of the faith-based unit, 'spiritual transformation' refers to a subjective and private change of orientation and values through religious or spiritual allegiance (Gillespie, 1979). The idea of spiritual transformation reflects the theological understanding that we are spiritual and eternal beings, who share humanity's God-consciousness. It may sometimes be suppressed, but it keeps coming to the surface.

## Spiritual transformation: a developmental process

The faith-based unit uses a biblically based programme with an overt emphasis on spiritual growth and moral development. The expectation is that this will increase the likelihood that prisoners will achieve the secular and correctional goal of rehabilitation. As prisoners proceed through the programme, we are able to observe changes in attitude and behaviour among programme participants and those who interact with them.

In recent research, Byron Johnson and David Larson (2003) identified five themes of spiritual transformation that not only correspond with, but provide the impetus for, various characteristics and attributes associated with the process of rehabilitation.

### *Theme 1: I'm not who I used to be*

Theme 1 is the recognition on the part of the offender that their previous behaviour was justifiably unacceptable to society. In fact, the person they have become actually condemns their previous behaviour because the new person now appreciates and promotes pro-social rather than anti-social behaviour.

According to Shadd Maruna's (2001) research on British offenders, this process of "wilful, cognitive distortion" helps offenders desist from crime and to "make good" with their lives. For those who have been in prison before, maybe multiple times, this time they feel they are on a mission as they prepare to leave prison.

### Theme 2: spiritual growth

Theme 2 is the recognition on the part of the offender that they are very much a work in progress. While many report they have made a great deal of progress in putting their life back together, most acknowledge they still have a long way to go. Importantly, they are quite surprised and encouraged about their own spiritual growth, and this progress is confirmed and validated by staff, volunteers and mentors – further strengthening their resolve to continue this path of spiritual development.

In order to transform their deviant histories into the present good, desisters employ 'redemption scripts' (Laub and Sampson, 2001). This process establishes the goodness of the individual and marks the emergence of the desisting self. Particular events like being 'born again' or the recognition that God and others actually love and care for them appear to be critically important turning points in their spiritual development.

### Theme 3: God versus the prison code

Many correctional staff concede that the penitentiary mentality or prison code is so pervasive and strong as to be beyond the possibility of reclaiming. The prison code runs counter to the various components of offender rehabilitation programmes. To be able to successfully oppose or even reverse the influence of the prison code is a significant achievement.

### Theme 4: positive outlook on life

Theme 4 reflects a paradigm shift for many offenders that is typified by hope and purpose. Instead of viewing their life in a fatalistic way, where offenders might relapse or decide to commit crime due to a minor setback with a friend, a family member, or an employer, those with a positive outlook are much more likely to be resilient in the face of adversity during their societal re-entry. Believing that their life now has meaning and knowing that they are loved and accepted by God and others, they are much more likely to view their life and circumstances in an upbeat rather than negative or hopeless way.

### Theme 5: the need to give back to society

The need to give back to society is something many prisoners seemed to be overwhelmed by. They reported feeling compelled to give back, to make a contribution to society in a way that improves the situation of others, especially others who come from similar backgrounds and experiences as their own. Respondents viewed their circumstances positively. Noted criminologists John Laub and Robert Sampson (2001), who work on factors that contribute to the desistance of crime, discuss 'transformative action' and 'subjective reconstruction of the self,' concepts they found to be quite common among people who develop new commitments and find purpose and meaning in life and consequently stay out of trouble.

### *Summary of the five themes*
In sum, all five spiritual transformation themes reflect behaviour and attitudes consistent with those one would hope for in achieving offender rehabilitation. It bears some resemblance to the emerging Good Lives Model of rehabilitation (Ward and Brown, 2004).[1]

### *Evaluation*
The faith-based unit is to be evaluated by the Department of Corrections through 2005–08. Once that is completed, Prison Fellowship will be more certain as to whether these themes are reflected within the community living in He Korowai Whakapono. The subjective and anecdotal evidence, through discussion and interviews with participants, staff and volunteers, is that they are.

## Potential for conflict
At the outset, we anticipated that there would be potential for personal and interpersonal conflict, as both participants and staff worked together to move beyond the prevailing prison culture, and create a community based on Christian principles and values. In fact, the faith-based unit's change environment is designed to create conflict. It was, therefore, important to set mechanisms in place to manage and resolve conflict, and to avoid the escalation of conflict. The potential for conflict was identified in six areas, namely;
- the impact of prisonisation;
- building trust;
- pro-social compared with anti-social values;
- discipline compared with conflict resolution;
- community building; and
- a biblical peacemaking model.

---

1  Ward and Brown (2004) argue that there is too much emphasis on the negative aspects of the offending process (that is, reducing risk factors), which fails to address the necessary preconditions for effective interventions. They advocate a 'strength-based approach' that focuses on the transition of offenders to a meaningful and richer life characterised by high levels of wellbeing.

### Impact of 'prisonisation'

The existence and adoption of a distinctive prison culture, referred to as 'prisonisation' or 'the prison code' is widely acknowledged by those who live and work in prisons (Clemmer, 1963). The existence of gangs, race-based groups, violence, widespread drug use, sexual aggression and other anti-social behaviour represent just some of the widely known aspects of the prison culture. There are others. Displays of machismo are often considered acceptable – showing love, affection or compassion can be viewed as a sign of weakness and is not acceptable. The prison culture provides fertile ground for the breeding of a mentality that supports the notion of rehabilitation or reform as something very much needed by the prison – not the prisoner. The issue of trust, or more precisely the lack of trust, is a central feature of the prison code. For example, a new prisoner learns very quickly that outside a select group of prisoners, prisoners should not trust other people. This is especially true when referring to prison staff or others who work in or represent some aspect of the criminal justice system. Further, the prospect of 'opening up' or becoming transparent about one's needs or shortcomings – a major feature of the faith-based programme – can be problematic, because it not only shows weakness, but it may require one to trust in something or someone else – a prospect that may well run counter to the prison code.

One of the biggest obstacles to more regularly achieving successful outcomes in various treatment programmes is the inability to counteract the deleterious effects of the prison culture. At the core of the faith-based context, is the premise that a faith-based programme will eventually erode the negative or harmful tendencies of the 'prison code' or 'penitentiary mentality'. In essence, this approach is based on the assumption that the prisoner's spiritual transformation and spiritual growth will help to provide an antidote to the present prison subculture. Thus, a spiritually transformed prisoner will be more likely to choose a pro-social response over an anti-social response when faced with a moral dilemma. The programme is based on the belief that spiritually transformed prisoners will, in fact, accept good over evil, or 'God over the prison code'.

### Building trust

One of the key principles arising from the 'prison code' has to do with 'trust'. Prisoners are supposed to mind their own business. For prisoners who had been in prison multiple times (and many had) this was a deeply embedded rule. However, the philosophy of the faith-based unit is just the opposite of that promoted by the prison code. Namely, members are taught they have the responsibility to hold each other accountable for various kinds of faith community infractions. The issue of trust, therefore, is something that did not come easy for many prisoners, since 'the code' taught otherwise, especially where custodial staff were concerned. Particularly among the new participants, there was still the firmly held belief that 'informing' on another prisoner, regardless of the situation, violated the prison code.

### *Pro-social compared with anti-social values*

The faith-based unit is a values-based programme. In the context of this chapter, 'values' mean specific, overall purposes and guiding principles in the programme. A value is a standard or quality that is good, needed and wanted. In the faith-based unit, values are Christ centred and Bible based.

As transformation took place, offenders debated, accepted and experienced the seven core values of the programme, namely:

- affirmation;
- integrity;
- accountability;
- spiritual transformation;
- restoration;
- community building; and
- productivity.

Each value was constantly reinforced through biblical teaching, through daily interaction with staff, and during evening community meetings. These values were referred to during any conflict resolution process. A values framework in the staff manual, described each value, identified the guiding principles for their implementation, and described when the value was being implemented (that is, by way of a performance indicator). As participants struggled to adopt these values, staff, through processes of discussion, case study and dialectic, worked through actual situations with prisoners.

### *Discipline compared with conflict resolution*

The custodial staff are responsible for prisoner discipline, and are required to enforce the Department of Correction's Code of Discipline. The introduction of a biblical peacemaking model required some dextrous thinking, and an ability to work collegially with prison staff, so that their custodial function was not compromised. Custodial staff were unable to exercise discretion where a serious breach of evidence was revealed (for example, physical assault, drug use or behaviour that threatened public safety).

## Community building

The community model that we envisaged provided a greater opportunity for prisoner participation and involvement in community-based decisions than is usually the case. We wanted to introduce a tiered system, in which prisoners would have the opportunity to resolve lower-level conflict themselves. To do that, we needed to build a community infrastructure that provided for those opportunities and reinforced community values and living principles.

## A biblical peacemaking model

We needed to introduce a biblical peacemaking model that could be understood and implemented by both staff and prisoners on a daily basis. We did not want to escalate the conflict resolution process into a formal and time-consuming exercise, but rather teach participants how to address conflict themselves, through a process that could be replicated when they re-entered society.

# Issues and challenges in conflict resolution: new beginnings

He Korowai Whakapono opened on 16 October 2003, after Department of Corrections staff had been selected and completed a 5-day training programme, jointly implemented by corrections staff and personnel from Prison Fellowship. The original intention was to phase the 60 participants into the unit over about 3 months, with an initial group of 15 men 'hand-picked for their Christian maturity and leadership qualities – the 'first 15'. Because of a national muster blow-out, the staff selected 60 participants from 89 prisoner applicants at Rimutaka and Wellington Prisons.

The first 6 months were difficult, as staff struggled to create a critical mass of participants who understood Christian values and principles, and actively engaged in and contributed to the development of a Christian community. The general staff view was that 30 of the participants were fully supportive of the programme and wanted to change, 15 were positive but struggling, 10 were neutral and had adopted a 'wait and see' approach. The remaining group of 5 was disruptive, manipulative and had an adverse influence on the other prisoners. The balance righted itself after 9 months, through a more rigorous prisoner selection process, and the exiting of participants who refused to comply with the community rules or committed serious breaches of discipline.

## Biblical teaching

The spiritual transformation component of the 18-month programme is of 8 months' duration. The eight modules taught a basic understanding of the scriptures, with a strong emphasis on challenging participants to change, and to adopt pro-social biblical values and lifestyle changes.

Participants were divided into four 15-person groups, known as Living Unit Groups (see p. 152), who studied under a facilitator and met each evening to discuss progress, affirm each other and resolve community issues. Participants shared their issues, prayed for each other, discussed the teaching programme and learned to live and work as a faith community.

After 4 months, staff realised that the biblical teaching programme was too intense, with some participants unable to process the information and apply the teaching to their daily lives. The teaching programme was reduced from four 2-hour sessions a week to three, and the spiritual transformation programme was divided into two segments of four modules, introducing the 'Forty Days of Purpose' Christian living programme in between. This provided the opportunity for a period of reflection and consolidation, which relieved the programme intensity.

## A biblical peacemaking model

The biblical teaching made it clear 'what' was expected of participants in seeking to reconcile differences. What was unclear for most was 'how'. Many of the prisoners had been raised in families where the fist ruled, and had been victims of physical and sexual abuse. That environment, and the prevailing prison code, meant that participants had to be taught a process by which interpersonal and disciplinary issues could be resolved. We chose the methodology developed by Peacemaker Ministries, a non-profit organisation founded in 1982 to equip and assist Christians to respond to conflict biblically. The methodology suited the unit community, as it was grounded in biblical principles that were already being reinforced through daily teaching and the core values.

Briefly, the process was underpinned by the following principles.
- As Christians we believe that conflict provides opportunities to glorify God, to serve other people and to grow to be like Christ.
- Glorify God: Instead of focusing on our own desires, we seek to please and honour God by maintaining a loving, merciful and forgiving attitude.

- Get the log out of our own eye: Instead of attacking others or dwelling on their wrongs, we will take responsibility for our own contribution to conflict.
- Go and show your brother his fault: We will choose to overlook minor offenders, and will talk directly and graciously with those whose offences are too serious to overlook. When a conflict can be resolved in private, we will ask others to help us settle the matter in a biblical manner.
- Go and be reconciled: Instead of accepting premature compromise or allowing relationships to wither, we will actively pursue genuine peace and reconciliation, forgiving others, and seeking just and mutually beneficial solutions to differences.
- By God's grace, we apply these principles, as a matter of stewardship, realising that conflict is an assignment, not an accident. Success is a matter, not of result, but of faithful, dependent obedience.

The process was difficult for both the staff and the prisoners to implement. Some staff feared that the process might undermine the official disciplinary process. Staff from other units, not fully aware of the process, took the view that all prisoners had to do was to apologise to avoid disciplinary action. Initially, prisoners were reluctant to invoke the reconciliation process, fearing that it might result in standover tactics, or worse.

The concept was introduced during the initial orientation and induction module. Gradually, the more mature prisoners started to experiment with the process. A major advance was made after 3 months, when two participants, leaders from competing gangs, were placed in a room to resolve a major difference. They emerged after 20 minutes and walked around the yard, signifying reconciliation and affirming the process.

## Staff involvement in conflict resolution

One of the first challenges was to encourage staff to implement a graduated process of conflict resolution, based on the biblical principles of peacemaking. As each incident occurred, the issue was discussed with and between staff, in terms of the most effective way of maintaining community peace and upholding the community's values.

Prison Fellowship staff had anticipated that this approach to conflict resolution would be difficult to implement. That was not to be the case. The corrections staff selected for the unit were chosen on the basis of their support of the unit's values. About two-thirds were Christians, and all staff grasped the opportunity to exercise discretion in order to resolve interpersonal conflict and breaches of discipline. Initially, some struggled with issues of repentance, forgiveness (and seeking forgiveness) and reconciliation. But as they became more familiar with the concepts, it became easier to refer issues to the community meetings and the eldership for resolution.

Over time, a graduated process for resolving conflict emerged. Briefly, the following principles were developed.

- Most offences committed by one prisoner against another could be addressed between those two prisoners with the eldership being the mediator in many cases. First, the men were separated and calmed. Then the victim was required to call attention to the offence in a calm, direct way. Participants would help each other by exercising accountability and responsibility to the group.
- If the offence was committed by one prisoner against another, the victim could bring the matter to the attention of the prisoner's Living Unit Group or the eldership.
- If an incident was against the community in general, or could not be resolved through a one-on-one meeting, then the prisoner could take the matter up with the eldership or the Living Unit Group.
- If the matter could not be resolved by the eldership, the matter was referred to the programme officer (pastoral support) for mediation.

## The eldership

Over the first 6 months, the unit began to take on the identity of a 'church community' within the confines of the prison. By design, leadership and staff sought to create an environment that drew upon the best features of a church setting.

After the first 6 months, a clear leadership emerged within the participants. Through consultation with staff and participants, a group of eight prisoners, together with the programme manager, pastoral adviser and principal corrections officer were selected as the community's eldership. They assumed a role similar to that of deacons or elders referred to in scripture.

The eldership served the community by upholding the values base of He Korowai Whakapono. They encouraged and actively helped those in the community by example and encouragement, and by meeting with those who were struggling. They encouraged and placed strategies in place that assisted and built value back into the individual. They also worked with the faith-based unit's faith community (management, staff, volunteers and fellow prisoners) to encourage full attendance and participation from community members in all aspects of the programme and community values.

The eldership also served to reconcile differences at the community level, and were consulted in order to identify participants who were ready to take leadership responsibilities. They were also consulted when a participant was proving difficult to manage within the community and not prepared to comply with the community's rules. In some cases, the recalcitrant participant's attitude showed marked improvement after discussion with the eldership and/or the Living Unit Group.

## Living Unit Group

Every prisoner was part of a Living Unit Group, the basic family unit of He Korowai Whakapono. Each group of about 15 prisoners stay together for almost all activities. The group served as a surrogate family where prisoners could experience Christian love, concern, trust and commitment. It was accepted that, as in any normal family, there would be conflicts, disagreements and hurt. Participants were helped to accept responsibility for their choices and actions and worked to solve problems collectively.

The Living Unit Group met five times a week, and prisoners regularly evaluated each other's contribution to the community through group discussions. Each group had elders within the group, but they did not necessarily run the group. It became the place for people in the unit community to share and feel safe. From the outset, staff emphasised the need to respect each other, knowing that each person's hurts, joys, achievements and victories were about that person's journey. Information was shared so people in the group could build each other up and encourage each other in their journey.

## Volunteers: breaking down the walls

One unique feature of the unit is the high level of volunteer participation and involvement in the unit. All the biblical teaching and many of the daily programmes are facilitated and taught by volunteers from churches throughout the Wellington region, from a wide range of denominations. The also contribute to constructive activity within the unit: choir leadership, an art class, music tuition and pastoral visiting.

One unique feature of this programme is the matching of a prisoner with a trained mentor about 8 months before the prisoner is due for release. The mentor meets regularly with the prisoner to help plan the details of his release, and assist with employment, accommodation, financial planning, relationship issues and other concerns. The mentor and their church commit to supporting the prisoner and their family for up to 2 years following release.

In speaking on the issue of penal reform, Vivien Stern (2004) emphasised the importance of normalising the prison environment:

> I now think there are two basic things for which one should aim. One, get as many people as possible out of prison, and two, get as many people as possible from the outside, non-prison world, into prisons.

## Disciplinary processes

Over the first 6 months, staff developed a process for dealing with disciplinary issues. The overriding principle was that rules broken or inappropriate behaviour offer opportunities for teachable moments – a time to reflect on actions and learn how they reflect or deny Christ-centred, biblically based values.

Where a participant continually breached the rules or values of the unit, it usually became an issue for the Living Unit Group and/or the eldership. Unit staff usually formally counselled or cautioned the participant, and where there was a serious breach of discipline, a continued lack of contrition or a continued refusal to comply with the community rules, participants were exited from the unit. All exited participants were given an opportunity to apply for re-admission to the programme. Of the 11 exited for disciplinary breaches in the first year, two have since been readmitted, and have demonstrated markedly improved conduct.

## Providing pastoral and counselling support

After the first 4 months, some participants were struggling personally with the mechanics and challenge of change, and needed to dialogue with significant others. Because they were still wary of corrections staff, the prisoners inundated the Prison Fellowship programme manager and volunteers with requests to discuss personal issues, resolve interpersonal disputes and provide spiritual guidance. These staff were unable to meet the demands of the participants, and it became clear, that the unit needed to build additional mechanisms to provide opportunities for dialogue and conflict resolution.

The Department of Corrections responded to the need by resourcing the appointment of additional part-time staff; that is, a pastoral support person and counsellor. Prison Fellowship engaged an experienced Samoan church elder to provide pastoral support for the participants. He provided spiritual guidance, discipleship and mediated on matters of interpersonal conflict. A part-time counsellor dealt with referrals relating to relationship and personal issues. The staff and the counsellor referred more deep-seated issues (for example, a history of sexual abuse) to a clinical psychologist or other specialist agencies.

## A turning point: murder in the unit

At 10.30 am on Thursday 4 April, 6 months after the unit opened, an event in He Korowai Whakapono became a turning point in the unit's history. A prisoner was found dead, with a garden fork thrust through his throat.

The incident that triggered this event could only be described as the sort of encounter that prisoners have many times each day. A request was made and declined. No one could have predicted the savagery and violence of this attack, either from the nature of the incident itself or the assailant's previous history.

On the day after the murder, the prisoners were unlocked for a 2-hour service organised by Prison Fellowship and the chaplaincy. The prison unit staff, devastated though they were, moved among the prisoners, hugging them, crying with them and praying with them. Christians and non-Christians alike, including prison staff from other units, joined to support each other. There was a sense of unity and anointing, as prisoners and others struggled to establish God's purpose in all this. The prisoners as a group resolved that this was a call on their lives to godliness, to stop grizzling and complaining, to desist from pettiness and power plays, and to follow Christ with more determination than ever before. The shock and disbelief of the tragedy was eventually overtaken by recognition that this event served to bond staff and prisoners alike into a group with all determined to treat each other differently. It proved to be a turning point in the life of the unit.

The regional manager for the Department of Corrections visited the unit later that morning, and was amazed at how settled and 'together' the prisoners and staff were. It can often take weeks for prisoners to settle after such an incident; he acknowledged that there was a supernatural power at work.

Visitors, the police and staff were deeply touched by the prisoner's response. A kaumatua (Māori elder) who took part in a blessing of the unit following the incident wrote:

> I was so touched by the support and endorsement displayed by the men. As we blessed each house they acknowledged by taking off hats, bowing their heads in prayer, and at the end gave a little wave of appreciation. It added essence and value to what we were doing. And to then hear them singing hymns was like the icing on the cake.

Over the next week, the prison chaplaincy and Prison Fellowship shared in taking evening services in the home of the victim's family, taking the opportunity to share their faith with them, and to share in the grieving and healing process.

And so the staff moved forward, their resolve strengthened, and demons put to rest. As one prisoner noted, if there was one scripture that gives us direction and inspiration, it surely must have been Paul's words in Romans. The Living Bible puts it simply (Romans 8:28):

And we know that God causes everything to work together for the good of those who love God and are called according to his purpose for them.

## Embedding the peacemaking model

Our review of progress over the first 12 months suggests we may have been more successful in embedding the peacemaking model within the community, if we had adopted the following measures.

- Implemented formal and regular training on the framework and application of the peacemaking model with all corrections staff and during the initial orientation programme for new participants.
- Implemented a case study review of issues as they arose, to consider whether the peacemaking model was being applied effectively.
- Emphasised to corrections staff that the peacemaking approach was entirely consistent with the department's 'active management' philosophy. 'Active management' is the interaction between staff and prisoners where every contact is viewed as an opportunity for positive influence. It encourages the use of discretion in a rules-based environment.

As a result of our experience, a project team developed a set of guiding principles for the management of offenders in the unit. It includes guidelines for the resolution of conflict.

## Two years on: achievements

The results produced so far support the overseas experience; namely, that if we can encourage prisoners to explore and develop a sound belief system based on Christian principles and values and surround them with mature Christian support on release, then the chances of them reoffending after 2 years drops from around 60%–70% to something like 30%.

### Key indicators
Four key indicators suggest that the programme is working.

### Low drug use
Drugs are rife in prison. If someone is determined to use drugs, they can usually find a way to access them. In the last 12 months, none of the faith-based unit prisoners randomly tested for drugs showed positive results. Of all those tested outside the random-testing regime, less than 2% tested positive. That compares favourably with a national prison average of about 14%.

We find that prisoners are prepared to challenge those who may be suspected of using or supplying drugs, and make it clear that such behaviour is unacceptable in the unit. That is a reversal of the way prisons usually function – God is winning over the 'prison code'.

### Low reported incidents
The unit had four reported incidents (one murder and three assaults) in the first 6 months of operation, but none since. This is an extremely low level of incidents, and an indicator that something special is happening in the unit.

The high level of volunteer–prisoner contact contributes to the 'normalisation' of the prison environment. Visitors always comment on the peaceful nature of the unit and the efforts of the staff to assist prisoners through a process of biblical peacemaking when conflict arises.

### Values compared with rules
Much of the success of this unit must be attributed to the corrections staff, who have worked with Prison Fellowship to develop an environment where prisoners and staff treat each other with mutual respect. The standard is high – 11 prisoners who were not prepared to comply with the standards were exited in the first year. Two of those have been readmitted at their own request, and their attitudes have totally changed. There is a waiting list of about 50 prisoners who have requested entry to the unit, and an equally large group of prison officers keen to work in the unit.

### Reduction in reoffending
The ultimate Department of Corrections measure relates to a reduction in reoffending. Nationally, 25% of all men leaving prison are back in prison within 12 months. That number increases to 35% after 2 years. While it is too early to produce any statistically significant results, the current information indicates that the reoffending rate for men leaving the unit is lower than the national average.

### *Implications of positive indicators*

The implications are significant. If the department could achieve a reduction of 5% in the national reoffending rate, it would mean 350 fewer prisoners in the system – the equivalent of a new prison. One less prison saves the taxpayer $150 million in construction costs. Each prisoner costs around $60,000 a year to maintain. If there are 350 fewer prisoners in the system, that represents an annual saving of $21 million for prisoner upkeep.

It would be wrong to present the faith-based approach as a panacea to the challenge of rehabilitating offenders. The prisoners who come into the unit volunteer, and most of them volunteer because they want to change. Many of them have been in the system a long time, and have reached a point in their lives where they want something better. The existence of the faith-based unit offers them a haven, a sanctuary in which they can explore their spiritual lives, and go through a process of transformation without having to cope with the negative aspects of prison culture. We believe that the faith-based response is making a valid contribution to breaking the crime cycle. We further consider that its potential within the criminal justice system has yet to be fully explored.

## Beyond prison: the role of restorative justice in prisoner reintegration

Once released from the faith-based unit, ex-prisoners find themselves in a totally different environment. The high levels of accountability, solidarity and support are gone. Without a proactive plan in place before release, few ex-prisoners will solidly connect with a church after release. Without this source of spiritual and social support, there is little else to do except to return to old friends, old habits and eventual failure.

Recent research shows that where former prisoners are well integrated into a faith community, it contributes significantly to the reduction of reoffending. It might be of little consequence that a given prisoner 'finds' religion in prison unless this also involves or is followed by immersion in a like-minded group. Prison conversions will not have lasting influence unless people retain or replicate religious group support on their release. The Prison Fellowship aftercare programme, Operation Jericho, provides support and continuing pastoral care for prisoners released from He Korowai Whakapono and other released prisoners.

For those faith-based ex-prisoners familiar with the concepts and practice of restorative justice, Prison Fellowship staff have experimented with the development of restorative and community justice practice, where an ex-prisoner transgresses or reoffends. Experience so far, demonstrates that the foundations set within the prison, and the processes learnt by prisoners for resolving conflict, can be usefully transferred to the community setting, to resolve domestic and relationship issues, facilitate discussion on such issues as substance abuse and conflict with employers or probation staff, and resolve infractions of the law.

Aftercare practice has been stymied historically by an insular focus on the needs and risks of offenders. Having identified these needs and risks, intervention professionals then proceed to develop supervision plans that gear levels of surveillance to the documented levels of threat presented by the offender. In New Zealand, corrections staff also conduct offender needs assessments and attempt to match offenders with appropriate services and treatment or remedial programmes designed to address the deficit in question. Though various aftercare models talk about community-based agencies, and occasionally about the role of work and educational institutions, the aftercare enterprise is primarily a highly individualised one. The Department of Corrections in New Zealand is in the process of appointing Work and Income case managers and work brokers who will, by the end of 2005, be based in every prison to help prisoners find work in time for their release. The policy framework that is emerging places the coordination of the reintegrative activity at the core of the reintegration strategy, rather than as a component of a comprehensive reintegration framework which involves iwi, hapū and community organisations in the support and sanction of offenders within the community (that is, a 'continuum of care' approach).

The concept of *reintegration* implies a recognition that returning offenders to the community raises larger issues than those associated with offender surveillance and service. Indeed, reintegration has always been as much about the community as the offender. Historically, however, the traditional literature of aftercare remains devoid of broader policy visions and of theory that places the offender in the context of community and gives specific consideration to the role of church and faith-based organisations, whānau, hapū or iwi groups, and other socialising influences in the reintegration process. The risk management and service needs focus limits debate about re-entry practice to alternative means of applying varying amounts of government intervention to bring about offender change while typically failing to address community transformation. Moreover, current approaches seem disconnected from research-based or normative data that demonstrate successful negotiation of desistance pathways throughout the life course of offenders – independent of the influence of correctional intervention.

Policy makers need to give strategic consideration both to the community role in reintegrating offenders and to the impact of offender re-entry on communities. It also raises the possibility of a different framework for reintegration grounded in the principles of restorative justice (Zehr, 1990). Broadly conceptualised as a new way of thinking about crime that gives emphasis to the harm caused by offences, restorative justice will provide an opportunity to move beyond the individualising tendencies of offender-focused treatment and punishment paradigms (Bazemore et al., 2000). Such a broader focus may open doors to what Sampson and Wilson (1995) refer to as "a community-level perspective". Though somewhat marginal to mainstream criminal justice practice, restorative justice practice could be effectively linked to the issue of offender reintegration through the related concepts of informal social control (Hunter, 1985) and social support (Cullen, 1994).

Three 'big ideas' provide the basis for a normative theory of restorative justice. These core principles – repairing harm, stakeholder involvement, and the transformation of community and government roles in the response to crime (Van Ness and Strong, 1997) – most clearly distinguish restorative justice from other orientations, and define the core outcomes, processes, practices and structural relationships that characterise restorative models (Bazemore and Walgrave, 1999).

The last principle reminds us that offenders grow up and live most of their lives in communities – not corrections programmes – and it is families, extended families, teachers, neighbours, ministers and others who provide support and guidance in socialisation and maturation processes. These 'natural helpers' accomplish the primary work of reintegration informally by identifying mentoring adults and community groups that help offenders to develop new skills and understandings and to connect with other community organisations, or small businesses that may provide employment opportunities as well as creativity and access to vital resources (Sullivan, 1989).

## Restorative justice as criminological theory

The new Sentencing, Parole, and Victims' Rights Acts of 2002 each make extensive reference to restorative justice and/or principles of restorative justice, recognising that this concept is now a critical component of our criminal justice system. These provisions not only impact on offenders before and during the sentencing process, but after an offender has been sentenced to prison or remanded in custody.

Section 6(1)(d) of the Corrections Act 2004, which came into force on 1 May 2005, reflects the government's support for restorative justice, by providing that prisoners must, where appropriate and so far as is reasonable and practicable in the circumstances, be provided with access to any process designed to promote restorative justice between offenders and victims.

It is clear that the implementation or proposed implementation of restorative justice provisions and principles will impact on offenders while in prison. The law envisages facilitated meetings between the offender and their victim, and prisoner involvement in restorative justice programmes or processes while in prison. Under the Parole Act 2002 it is a guiding principle that the Parole Board considers any offender involvement in victim awareness programmes or victim–offender restorative justice programmes while in prison.

What *is* the place of a prison unit that focuses on peacemaking, conflict resolution and the restoration of relationships? The faith-based methodology grew out of experience and experimentation. It was not the result of deduction by intellectuals from a particular school of criminology. Consequently, there is a still a need to develop a theory of justice within which it can be understood and implemented. Restorative justice may be that theory.

Restorative justice creates processes through which parties are able to discover the truth about what happened and the harms that resulted, to identify the injustices involved and to agree on future actions to repair those harms. Secondly, restorative justice argues that the response to specific crimes should emphasise the recovery of the victim through redress, vindication and healing, recompense by the offender through reparation, fair treatment and rehabilitation, and the reintegration of both into the community.

Repentance and reconciliation are understood to be important parts of a prisoner's spiritual transformation and restoration. Affirmation is viewed as critical to effective reintegration, creating opportunities for prisoners to break free from old habits. Restorative processes can offer greater sensitivity to indigenous needs as they enable cultural diversity to be recognised, and may be a mechanism for affirming and strengthening the power of indigenous communities.

It is not yet clear the extent to which restorative justice theory will be accepted as the criminological context within which to place the faith-based methodology. If so, it may also help staff, volunteers and prisoners to identify new programmes that will strengthen its overall restorative effect as well as to clarify when it is appropriate as an intervention.

## Conclusion

The faith-based unit provides a place where prisoners can learn new ways of resolving conflict and restoring peace. That context leads naturally toward an environment that promotes restoration between offenders and victims.

It is a place where the secular and correctional goal of rehabilitation is achieved through a process of spiritual transformation. It is a sanctuary in which prisoners learn to resolve interpersonal conflict through a process of confession, redemption, forgiveness and reconciliation in order for relationships to be healed and restored.

If it is anything, it is a place where the community promotes behaviour and attitudes consistent with those one would hope for in offender rehabilitation.

Our experience suggests that it also a place where prisoners can learn the skills and values that will enable them, on release, to smoothly integrate and usefully participate in society, and equip them to resolve life issues both within and with the community, thus contributing to their reintegration as fully functioning members of the community.

# Part Three

# Restorative Practices in Civil Society

# Introduction to Part Three

The ideas underpinning restorative justice have had an impact throughout New Zealand. Increasingly they are being given expression in almost every area where conflicts are being resolved, particularly in those areas where the state is one of the parties. Notions of fairness are broadening, concepts that are consistent with restorative values are developing and the use of restorative practices is becoming more common.

Civil disputes, especially in the area of employment, are increasingly relying on a social consensus around good faith bargaining, conciliation and mediation. Restorative practices in the education system aim to increase inclusion and resolve disciplinary problems. In both these areas of conflict resolution practices vary in the extent to which decision making is participatory and consensual or adversarial and reliant on the decisions of authorities or arbitrators: David Hurley (chapter 9), Wendy Drewery (chapter 10) and Sean Buckley (chapter 11) suggest that more satisfying, lasting and reintegrating solutions tend to be associated with strategies that are inclusive and involve making amends and healing the hurts that have been incurred.

Maureen Hickey (chapter 12) and Nicola White (chapter 13) echo the same themes. The responses to the settlement of historic grievances of Māori through the Waitangi Tribunal and the Office of Treaty Settlements emphasise establishing the truth of the past, apologising to those who were wronged and putting in place some form of settlement to redress the damage that was done. The same features can be seen in the other approaches taken by the Crown to past injustices for which the state has been responsible. White examines the problems and pitfalls that stand in the way of achieving a resolution that will pave the way for genuine forgiveness by those who were wronged.

# 9

# Restorative Justice in the Civil Jurisdiction

*David Hurley**

> Always forgive your enemies; nothing annoys them as much.
>
> (Oscar Wilde)

## Introduction

Mediation and other forms of alternative dispute resolution that explore the needs and interests of the parties are becoming standard in legislation in areas of civil law that previously have been dealt with by way of rights and through courts or tribunals. Legislative provisions have more than doubled in the last few years, although with little consistency of either nomenclature or process. Alternative (or as some argue 'appropriate') dispute resolution processes have attracted considerable research and attention from a range of disciplines over the past 25 years. These changes have been paralleled by the increasing diversity of New Zealand society. This chapter discusses emerging themes in theory and practice in the field, the issues to be considered in suitable legislative design, and their relevance to concepts of restorative justice.

Providing systems of remedying wrongs – conflict resolution – for its citizens is a core function of government. In criminal matters, government provides decision making for all prosecutions (although private prosecutions can be filed), thus ensuring that any decision is based on justice, and not revenge. This is in contrast with civil litigation where there has always been a choice of public justice or private resolution through arbitration or other processes. Differences between the two systems include whether a binding precedent is established, public or private outcomes, the choice of decision maker and the costs of the process.

Historically, mediation was a private process. However, an early example of state-funded mediation in New Zealand was collective bargaining in the 1890s.[1]

---

\* I record my indebtedness to those who assisted in the preparation, formatting and proof-reading of this chapter. In particular, I acknowledge the respective contributions of Barbara Wilson of Hampshire, United Kingdom, and Fran Williams in New Zealand.

The present system of statutory processes and remedies for personal grievances in employment situations, such as claims for unfair dismissal, is much more recent (1970s) (Goddard, 1993). Before this present system, such matters were often dealt with by wildcat strikes with severe economic disruption far beyond the individuals involved. The 1970s also saw the introduction of counselling services (usually involving conciliation and/or mediation) as a way for couples to avoid litigation when separating.

More recently, mediation has become an accepted strategy for responding to any conflict. Over the past 20–30 years, there has been an explosion of legislation that provides for mediation services of various kinds driven, one suspects, as much as anything by the need to reduce the costs of litigation. Claire Baylis (1999) drew attention to the potential problems of such diversity and lack of consistent definition. She identified (with the assistance of two researchers, Kerensa Johnston and Caoline Hicks) some 30 statutes with varying provisions. Since then, in early 2005, the Parliamentary Counsel Office commissioned its then summer clerk (Nuala MeKeever) to prepare a list of statutory provisions for alternative dispute resolution.[2] This showed that the number of Acts containing such provisions had grown to 77.[3] Most of these statutes do not define mediation or the process, but instead have provisions variously called adjudication, arbitration, conciliation, facilitation, mediation or review. Some are mandatory, and only some have a form and manner of process prescribed.

An allied development is the introduction of the option of arranging a restorative conference to resolve personal and neighbourhood disputes.

The major exception to the types of issue currently being dealt with by some form of government-provided alternative dispute resolution is in the area of civil litigation.

## Focus of chapter

This chapter overviews the key features of mediation in New Zealand today. It asks questions about the advantages and limitations of mediation and other

---

1 Industrial Conciliation and Arbitration Act 1894, the specific section uses the terminology of "settlement of the issues".
2 Neither Baylis nor the Parliamentary Counsel Office–commissioned study included such provisions made under regulations (for example, the commodity Orders).
3 Under some analyses this may not be complete. For example, the list does not include the Health Act 1956 under which "officers" have the role of assisting mentally ill patients to be reintegrated into the community – undoubtedly a mediation function.

forms of alternative dispute resolution in resolving conflicts; discusses issues about the public funding of alternative dispute resolution options; and identifies key questions about core values, best practice standards and guidelines, arrangements for monitoring consistency in legislation, and funding in this important area of conflict resolution.

Throughout the chapter, the underlying principles of various forms of mediation are compared with those of restorative practices and are contrasted to the alternative processes of bargaining and financial redress for damages. Attention is also paid to key critical issues in practice such as differences in power, money and skills of participants, and the training and skills of those managing the process.

## Conflict

All conflict is but different perspectives illuminating the same truth.

(Adapted from Mahatma Ghandi[4])

Conflict and disputes are not bad in themselves. They can trigger desirable change, focus on injustice and, in any event, are inevitable. It is not my intention to focus on the various ways in which conflict can arise,[5] but rather on the quality of response to such challenges.[6] People have always responded to conflict in a variety of ways from 'freeze, flight or fight' in which conscious thought is overtaken by primitive survival instincts to using complex judicial systems in which highly skilled advocates argue on a party's behalf for weeks at a time.

While several conflict resolution strategies are available, some are dysfunctional such as 'freeze, flight or fight'. Paralysis in the face of an oncoming train is unwise. Emigrating to Australia may mean no more than that you take your problems with you, and mortal combat has its risks. Nevertheless there is merit in considering the dispute resolution processes of social group animals, especially the great apes, to gain insights into our own patterns of behaviour.

---

4   Ghandi's insight was directed to war, but it is suggested that this is an unnecessary limitation and the quotation is of general relevance.
5   See, for example, Moore (1996).
6   Though there are some interesting framings of how conflict does arise (see Cloke, 2001). Examples include, "Negative intimacy when positive intimacy is no longer possible" and "Conflict is the sound made by the cracks in the system, the manifestation of contradictory forces coexisting in a single place".

Lee Dugatkin offers just such an intriguing insight involving goats, hyenas, primates and dolphins, and the costs and advantages of reconciliation in their interactions.[7] Dugatkin suggests (2005, p. 37):

> The different reconciliation styles of chimpanzees and bonobos could also offer a pointer to human behaviour. Bonobo society is particularly harmonious, and one way they achieve this is through reconciliation. This is a notoriously sexy affair ... Chimps follow the usual pattern, with the loser trying to make amends. For bonobos, however, it is the winner, the individual wielding the power, who makes the first move. Now there is a lesson for us all.

The functional and legally allowable forms of conflict resolution are based on three areas: exploring interests and needs; pursuing legal rights; and exercising power. In the industrial field needs and interests are met when the parties (employer and employee) are able to work together for their mutual benefit; rights are where the institutions (the Employment Relations Authority and Employment Court) hand down decisions; and power is in the use of strikes and lockouts, or pressure of other kinds such as the mobilising of public opinion through the media. In this chapter, I do not examine the uses of power, although I note that there is legislative control over the way this may be exercised in some instances, such as proscriptions around strikes and lockouts in essential industries.

A continuum of appropriate forms of needs/interests and rights-based processes can be described as follows.

- *Discussion* – initial problem solving where the parties sort things out at the first stage. It can be as simple as 'Who does the dishes?' or 'Who takes the notes of the meeting?' to complex problem resolution.
- *Facilitation* – where the parties problem solve within the group and have the resources and ability to do so themselves, sometimes with the use of techniques such as brainstorming, using a whiteboard or using a skilled facilitator.
- *Third-party fact finding* – where the group requires outside input (for example, an architect's advice, a legal opinion or more information) to be able to finalise its plans and agreements.[8]

---

7   Behavioural ecologist at the University of Kentucky. His latest book is *Principles of Animal Behaviour* (Dugatkin, 2004).
8   Arguably the Waitangi Tribunal fulfils such a role, albeit with specific procedures and powers of recommendation. It establishes the historical record based on which the Crown and respective iwi then negotiate a settlement.

- *Negotiation* – where the parties traditionally sit around a table, but are in control of the process, topics, outcomes, agreement and concluding the process.
- *Third-party negotiation* – where, for example, lawyers or other advocates conduct the negotiation on behalf of their clients, often by telephone.
- *Conciliation* – a word that has been used generically for a large number of processes, but is used here in the more limited sense of when an outsider works independently with the parties to resolve issues (often emotional) that prevent them from meeting in negotiation, so that they can return to the table.
- *Mediation* – a description that covers a wide variety of styles and processes[9] from facilitation to virtual arbitration, but with the common theme that an outsider assists the parties with appropriate processes to resolve their differences.
- *Med/Arb* – a hybrid process (of mediation and arbitration) that ends with the mediator making a decision for the parties if they cannot agree.[10] (But see the discussion of risk in this process below.)
- *Arbitration and litigation* – for this purpose being similar in that the process and outcome are determined by a decision maker.[11]

## Med/Arb: its problems

Much has been written on the process of Med/Arb over recent years (for example, Goldberg et al., 1985). It does have the advantage that the problem is determined after the parties have had a chance to agree. It is a process that is available under the Employment Relations Act 2000 and has been used to resolve a particular conflict, but in less than 1% of the cases filed with the mediation service. In short, there is little demand.

My own view is that there are dangers in blurring the line between two good processes and thereby possibly damaging both. A mediator cannot properly

---

9   See, for example, Menkel-Meadows (1995).
10  There are other variants such as 'peek-a-boo' mediation where a mediator is chosen for expertise in the area of dispute, and offers an opinion on what has been presented during the session. The parties can then take this view into account in a manner that is not binding but may be persuasive.
11  There are a variety of differences in aspects such as the choice of decision maker, the time-frames for the hearing, how costs are borne and the formality of the process. It is partly because of its comparative informality that arbitration is commonly included in the concept of alternative dispute resolution.

caucus with one party, because a decision maker should not breach the rules of natural justice – to see one party in the absence of the other. It removes the ability to be quite challenging if the party then thinks you have lost impartiality and 'gone over to the other side'. An arbitrator is unable to properly test conflicting evidence in mediation – some witnesses may not be present. My experience is that if parties can agree for me to decide, in the knowledge that there are no appeal rights and that I may not have to give reasons for my decision, and they have to hand over their right to decide to a stranger, then they may as well decide on the main issues themselves. If they can agree on that much, then given a little more time in mediation they will normally achieve substantive agreement. Such decisions as I have made have been either a pure arbitration process, or I have given a public decision for the parties (after they have made it themselves) where, for whatever reason, it is better for the mediator to 'take the blame' for the decision, rather than the parties.

## The Court system and the development of alternative dispute resolution

While the law is renowned for conservatism (and valuable for that reason for keeping boundaries and principles intact), it would be a mistake to think that it has been immutable for centuries. From the early days in England, law was literally 'fight', as in trial by combat, or 'flight', as in self-exile. Later it became trial by champions; and duelling remained available for private dispute resolution long after courts were established. Two court systems evolved under the Crown (the King's Bench Division) and the Church (the Chancery). Initially, the equitable and good conscience outcomes of the latter served to ameliorate the quite rigid approach of the former, until, in time and in the interests of certainty, equitable rules also became rigid. When New Zealand established its systems, it combined those two court structures into one, and then, while retaining the concept of common law, began to codify branches of the law through legislation rather than requiring the distillation of numerous case precedents.

When I started in the law the magistrates of the day spoke of their court[12] as being 'the people's court' and placed emphasis on its accessibility. Over the years its jurisdiction increased to take over some of the lower end responsibilities of the then Supreme Court (later renamed the High Court),

---

12  In the 1960s and 1970s the Magistrate's Court was still the first point of entry into the judicial system in civil matters.

salaries increased as did the legal costs of taking cases. Among the factors generating change was that law firms that were well rewarded by the conveyancing scale for house transactions were thereby enabled to offer pro bono services in the Magistrate's Court as a public commitment.[13] (As a comprehensive service, this had its limitations.) In response to need the New Zealand Law Society took several initiatives such as the Duty Solicitor Scheme, the Visiting Solicitor Scheme in prisons, and the provision of free legal advice through Citizens Advice Bureaux. Community initiatives included Nga Tamatoa and community law centres. The government initiated or upgraded legal aid schemes in both criminal and civil jurisdictions. Significantly, the Ombudsman's Office was established. Government also created an avenue for small claims through the (now) Disputes Tribunal. An essential feature of the latter was the attempt by the parties to resolve cases themselves, but with the mediator making a decision for them if there was no agreement. Subsequent legislation in other jurisdictions separated the mediation function from the decision-making process (for example, the Tenancy Act 1986) or specified that a mediator could not sit on the same case if the case required a decision (for example, the Employment Contracts Act 1991).

Some processes have evolved from situational imperatives. For example, the Privacy Commissioner's mediation service operates primarily by phone (due to the geographical separation of the parties); the Human Rights Commission's mediators interview the parties separately (their cases often involve harassment and this avoids the risk of further traumatising the victim/survivor); while the Employment Service's mediators normally meet the parties for the first time when they are brought together on the day of the mediation (due to the pressure of work and traditional practice).

## Limitations of courts and tribunals

May you be involved in litigation in which you know you are right.

(Old Arabian curse)

Over recent years the courts have come under increasing criticism for the high cost of litigation and their imperviousness to human feelings. Access to the High Court and above is beyond the means of all except the rich and the legally aided. This lack of accessibility has lead to the creation of low-level specialist courts and tribunals from which, in some cases, lawyers are excluded (for example, the Disputes Tribunal), and a greater emphasis on mediation for

---

13  As many lawyers still do.

parties to resolve their own disputes (for example, the Watertight Homes Mediation Service).[14] In some cases, the adversarial process has been amended to allow for an investigative one, a notable example of which is the process of the Employment Relations Authority.

I note here some five factors that distinguish litigation processes from alternative dispute resolution and restorative justice principles.

First, the law is concerned with the past; not the present or future. It may have a salutary consequential effect on future behaviour, but only as a threat against repeat behaviours.

Secondly, the law applies restitution primarily in the form of money. For people with emotional problems money does not meet the hurt, nor is it adequate to meet their assessment of personal pain (see Case studies 9.1 and 9.2). *Money becomes a metaphor for pain* and because pain is a personal experience people tend to think in terms of massive sums unrelated to any reasonable expectation from litigation. Even if such remedies were to be ordered, once the money is gone the pain is still there. Money may also have to take the place of revenge or punishment.

Thirdly, the law cannot provide unique outcomes, whereas agreement can (see Case study 9.1).

**Case study 9.1:** Agreement can provide unique outcomes

An employee was made redundant from a pig farm, but claimed the process was unfair. One of her senses of loss was being unable to work with the animals.

The dispute went to mediation. The agreement reached included a provision for the pig farm to give the ex-employee "one healthy weaner piglet".

Fourthly, the law is concerned less with the truth than with provable facts. It is adversarial, not investigative, which means the decision maker is limited to assessing the selected issues put before them.[15] Credibility issues can be very difficult to sort out when competing parties have genuine, but selective, memories over past events, and both appear with complete integrity. It can be

---

14 For descriptions of such systems, see, for example, Spiller (1999) and Boulle et al. (1998).
15 Judges and lawyers are well aware of the 'tricks of the trade'. In a recent farewell to a retiring and very successful United States advocate, a judge described, in admiring terms, how the lawyer's cases represented "the greatest number of miscarriages of justice the Court had seen in the last 30 years".

described as an exercise to find out 'where the truth lies' (pun intended).[16] The 'game' is not so much about the truth, but about what can be proved to be true. David Lange (former lawyer and Labour Party Prime Minister of New Zealand), in his 2005 autobiography, described his experience on his last day in the District Court when he successfully argued somewhat spurious points on behalf of two accused. He felt disgusted how easy it was for him to do "bad things".

Finally, the law is concerned only with rights. Interests and needs go far beyond these limitations, and therefore both substantive and monetary outcomes from litigation are likely to be less satisfying or satisfactory to (usually) both litigants (see Case study 9.2).

**Case study 9.2:** Outcomes from mediation may be more satisfying than those from litigation

Two women were made redundant in similar circumstances. Both women went to mediation.

One woman settled for $6,000 and an apology. Shortly thereafter, she applied for and was appointed to another job.

The other woman took the matter to the Employment Relations Authority, and, after many months' delay, received an award of about $22,000, including a contribution to costs. After deducting actual costs (for mediation, trial preparation, the hearing and so on) her net return was about $10,000. But the case had consumed her time, she had not been in a good space to apply for a new job, and she remained angry with the employer and about the outcome.

Moreover, some have argued that litigation brings out the 'dark side' – the worst – of people (Stahura, 2001):

> The traditional adversarial system separates you from all other people, and so it really disempowers you. Once you feel that you're right and everyone else is wrong, you have an us–them attitude, a survivalist attitude. It allows you to say someone is bad. It really plays into your ignorance. It takes you to those places where you're mean and angry and jealous.

The International Alliance of Holistic Lawyers has as its logo the Goddess of Justice, Thema, but holding only one instead of two scales. She is weighing the soul of the individual party. The meaning is akin to the thesis (espoused by Kubler-Ross (1997), among others) that we are all here on Earth to face

---

16 In discussing possible outcomes with parties in mediation I expand on the old example of "What is truth? If you see an egg end on – then it is round. From an angle, it is obviously oval". To which one can add, "For a chicken, it is at least the start, if not the meaning of, life; and for the judge it is what they ate for breakfast – scrambled!".

challenges from which we must learn and grow. If we do not learn, then we will face the same challenge over again. The questions to be asked are not legal so much as: Why is this challenge facing me? What in my background has led me to this point? How should I respond in a way that will enable human growth to occur for both me and the other? If I lose and learn a hard lesson now, will this enrich me in future dealings? Can I lose with dignity?

The International Alliance argues that the legal process does not search sufficiently deeply. The issues placed before the courts are those brought by the parties. They can be symptoms of underlying needs and interests that, if exposed, could lead to mutual gain. If two parties are arguing over an orange, if the dispute is properly and safely explored it might be found that one wants the pith and the other the flesh of the orange. (This example is a standard in mediation training to illustrate this point.[17] It does not answer the problem of when both parties want the whole orange!)

The courts of course still have their essential place. No one is suggesting they be abandoned. Mediation in many situations is conducted 'in the shadow of the law'. The courts provide a sanction against inertia (why come to a voluntary process if content with the status quo?), and provide indicators of likely outcomes within the judicial process. They provide the ultimate resolution process when there cannot be agreement; they establish through precedent principles by which the community can operate; and they provide fundamental protection for human rights. They also provide the back-up enforcement systems to mutually agreed solutions resolved through other dispute resolution processes. Fundamentally, they provide systems of integrity, procedural fairness (the rules of natural justice) and objectively sound outcomes that alternative dispute resolution services cannot necessarily ensure. Their future role, indeed survival, in a world potentially dominated by alternative dispute resolution systems is, however, becoming a matter of debate (Redfern, 2005).

## Can justice be defined as 'a satisfactory outcome'?

Some have argued that the application of the law has little to do with social justice and may indeed perpetuate the unjust systems that gave rise to the initial conflict (Fox, 1999):

> What counts in legal decision making are discrete provable facts relevant to the logically derived abstract principles – not humane, individualized decisions. Indeed the insistence on procedurally correct,

---

17  See also Rothfield (2004).

context-free decisions by neutral, autonomous legal institutions, devoid of subjectivity and emotion is commonly portrayed as one of law's strong points, distinguishing it from more 'primitive' systems where individuals allegedly suffer at the whim of despotic or arbitrary rulers.

In a relatively homogeneous society where people have similar backgrounds and expectations, justice may be commonly understood in terms of expectations of likely outcomes. If society is made up of disparate groups who think in fundamentally different, even frighteningly different, ways then there will be no consistency of what fairness might mean.

Virginia Phillips in her 1995 paper 'Mediation: the influence of style and gender on disputants' perceptions of justice' discusses what 'justice' means from the disputant's point of view. Reviewing the literature to that date, she finds that justice means both satisfaction and fairness. Each element is composed of three related components: a procedural component relating to the process; a distributive component relating to the outcome; and an evaluation of the neutrality of the mediator (or judge) by the parties.[18] Each of these elements is readily identifiable in the court system. The process is well established, and subject to review by higher courts if unfair (breaches of natural justice); likewise there are appeal rights if substantive mistakes are made; and care is taken in the selection and maintenance of the independence of the judiciary.

Thibaut and Walker (1975, cited in Hedeen, 2004, p. 120) developed a measure known as "satisfaction with the process", which is now the mainstay of evaluation of mediation and other forms of dispute resolution. This is critical to representing the participants' sense of procedural justice, and correlates well with their compliance with the outcome.

My own experience in discussing with disputants what they mean by 'wanting justice' is that they express the desire for an outcome that is satisfactory to them. In some cases, this is no more than the chance to have their say and know they have been heard, even if not agreed with (see Case study 9.3).

## Levels of satisfaction in conflict resolution

Maslow places justice and order in the level of B-needs (just below physiological needs) as one of several driving needs for 'self-actualisers' to be happy. He writes that without the presence of truth, goodness, beauty, meaningfulness and other meta-needs, then people can develop meta-

---

18 See also Van Gramberg (2003).

pathologies such as depression, despair, disgust, alienation and a degree of cynicism.[19]

**Case study 9.3:** Disputant's desired outcome is often not money

> A young man came to mediation the day before attending the District Court on a charge of theft as a servant to which he planned to plead guilty.
>
> His union represented him, and wanted the employer to recognise that it had not followed its own handbook for internal investigations over the incident. It was also concerned, in part, about the employer getting it right in the future for the benefit of its other members of staff. The union felt money would sink the message home; and the young man had debts.
>
> The employer was ready to recognise its mistake, wanted to avoid costly litigation that it thought it would win, but was not going to reward bad behaviour. When asked his needs, the young man asked for the opportunity to apologise to his work mates who had supported him, and whom he felt he had betrayed.

So how is satisfaction achieved in any dispute resolution? In terms of disputant satisfaction with outcomes, an externally handed down decision normally gives the lowest level of satisfaction as one party or the other will have 'lost'. Certainly some may prefer not to take responsibility for a decision so that no one can blame them – but by and large there will have been cost despite this advantage. Winning can get the disputant the reputation for being litigious; losing can be ruinous. This is not to say that mediation and other forms of dispute resolution do not have their critics, both from feminist and judicial perspectives. See particularly Laura Nader,[20] Deborah Hensler,[21] and Lisa Bingham.[22]

A continuum for satisfaction with outcomes may be described as follows.

- *Settlement* – where the parties agree to disagree, but 'cut a deal' for the sake of moving on and not dealing with each other again. This is the equivalent of a decision.
- *Agreement* – which is more positive than settlement, but may be limited to a single presenting issue (this may be merely a symptom of some deeper underlying malaise), and has the risk of behaviours that gave rise to the problem in the first place being repeated.

---

19 See, for example, Maslow (1968/1999). For a biographical note on Maslow, see Boeree (2006).
20 See, for example, Nader (1969).
21 See, for example, Hensler (2002).
22 For biographical notes, see Indiana University (2005).

- *Resolution* – where all issues have been explored and resolved and the relationships have been restored. I understand such resolution to be the ultimate aim and outcome of a restorative justice system.

## Emotional impact of conflict

Those from counselling professions have long recognised the great benefits of their processes in helping people cope with traumatic events in their lives. Conflict can have a traumatic effect on human wellbeing. In recent years physiological studies have shown that changes in the amygdala (that part of the brain that deals with strong emotion) are observable following counselling to resolve trauma (Van der Kolk, 1994).

A second element in the biological field is the view that some scientists hold that humankind is equipped with a gene for altruism as well as for violence. Would we have advanced as a species to the extent we have without such an inbuilt capacity for working together? This theme is echoed in the social scientist debates over cooperative and competitive approaches to conflict resolution. Morton Deutsch (2002) discusses the view that most conflict is conducted with a mixture of these two approaches, with success or not depending on the extent that the cooperative approach is to the fore.

Both restorative justice systems and mediation provide for parties to talk through their feelings, and this is often called 'venting'. The advantage is that if people are bottling up anger or other distress then they will not be able to think rationally until that emotion is released. Moreover, there are often better ways to address those feelings than offers of money (see Case study 9.4). For example, a genuine apology that is seen and accepted as such can have remarkable effects (Hurley, 2002; Schneider, 2000; Young, 2000).

Gordon Hewitt and Rhonda Pritchard in their unpublished paper 'Healing grievances model' (1992) offer a four-step process in acknowledging the grievance and a further four-step process for making reparation. These steps are echoed in the work of Reverend Marie Fortune who works mainly with sexual abuse cases within churches.

- *Regret* implies that the abuser is sorry only that the victim is feeling hurt; but there is no accountability for causing pain.
- *Remorse* is no better than regret – it is saying you are sorry you were caught.
- *Repentance* is acceptance and recognition that you were responsible; that there were other options; and other people might have made different choices in the same situation, so there are no excuses.

- *Reparation* is restoring the victim to where they were before the incident. This can be to reinstate them to the position they held in society before the offence occurred, so reparation may not be confined to money. The concept of doing a little more than is required (supererogation) should be included, and there should be a genuine statement of intent to act differently in the future.

If these steps are taken, then it is up to the victim to consider accepting the perpetrator's apology as the perpetrator is now worthy of forgiveness. This may lead to reconciliation, and perhaps redemption. But if the victim rejects the approach and wants revenge or retribution, then the roles of victim and perpetrator can be reversed.

**Case study 9.4:** Addressing the emotional impact of conflict

A man had been injured in a work-related accident. At the time, he had been working night shifts, which attracted a penalty rate of pay. On his recovery, he had returned to work, but on day shifts. The employer got him back on nights quite quickly, but at the time of mediation there was a claim for back pay of about $400 for wages he might have earned had he gone back on night shifts immediately. The worker wanted the cash.

The employer could not compromise on the principle that it was the employer's right to allocate workers to different shifts, because this would have major precedent impact. Paying the money would jeopardise that principle.

In discussion at mediation, the worker talked of the pain he had suffered and how difficult it had been to be at home unable to do much more than sit on the couch for some weeks while his wife was in the last stages of pregnancy.

How many children? They had three under the age of 5 – all at home.

What was all this like for the two of them? He went very quiet for a while and acknowledged life had been tough.

Would a counselling programme for the two of them help? In the end, the employer was glad to pay for up to eight sessions for the couple (about $1,000) and the worker could go home to his wife having achieved a real benefit; and the employer received the gratitude of the worker over a matter that might otherwise have festered.

## What do disputants want from any dispute resolution process?

This is not a question that can readily be asked in a court setting (save perhaps the Family Court), because the pleadings will have covered applications for specific outcomes within the court's jurisdiction. In mediation, however, the question 'What do you want?' is likely to receive a reply about what the disputants have been told they can expect from a court. 'What do you want to achieve from this process?' will provoke more holistic responses around restoring the party's good name; making sure their experience will not happen to anyone else; and getting matters resolved (see Case study 9.5).

**Case study 9.5:** 'What do you want to achieve from this process?'

> Two men had come to mediation over the allegation that one had been unfairly fired. The response was that the employee had hit the boss.
>
> The matter had gone to the criminal courts on a charge of assault, but had been dismissed for lack of corroboration. All this had lasted over a year. The two men's sons played in the same football team, and the parents had had to stand on opposite sides of the playing field for the whole season.
>
> After the lawyers had talked for the parties for some time, it was clear that there was an impasse, but also that the parties' body language was of pain and reaching out to each other. It was agreed that they would speak to the mediator alone.
>
> As soon as they sat down the employee leaned across the table and said, "I know my lawyer is claiming $7,000, but you know, I would accept $1,000. The other stood and spoke for several minutes in a manner that was inarticulate but from the heart. The message was that "I'm hurting here too, and $1,000 is too much". He then sat down.
>
> What to do? The mediator said, "What about treating the end of the employment as one where you both agreed to end it without allocation of fault?".
>
> The employee looked up and said, "You know, I would have accepted 2 weeks' notice – what about that?". (He was a part-time employee, so this was about $400.) The employer got up, walked around the table and held out his hand. Then, as one, the two men put their arms around each other and wept on each other's shoulders. As they left, they were heard promising to share a meal together.

In more than 2,000 cases I can remember just four in which the first and only thing desired was money, and they settled quickly for smallish amounts. Ian Macduff of the New Zealand Institute for Dispute Resolution and I adapted an acronym from one developed by Mitchell Hammer, a professor at American University,[23] to encompass the range of answers to the 'achieve' question. The acronym is ASPIRE, where:

A stands for altruism – those who come with a generosity of spirit and seek results beyond pure self-interest.

S stands for spiritual issues – in many intra- or cross-cultural cases we may start with karakia or prayer, or the issue for one party may be their

---

23 Mitchell's acronym was FIRE where F stood for Face. Ian and I thought the acronym unfortunate for a dispute resolution process and did not cover all the issues we had experienced.

relationship with God in how they treat this other human being rather than justice between the parties. For others, apologies, acceptance and forgiveness have a spiritual component.

P stands for personal factors – such as face, mana or human dignity. It allows for cultural backgrounds. It can also represent the need to be heard; personal involvement in developing the outcome; and issues such as one party's need to feel justified about the pain they are feeling (where the other party or their lawyer is blaming them for the conflict).

I stands for instrumentality – the costs and risks of litigation.

R stands for relationships – even if these are irreconcilable these may be important for a person to be able to walk down the street without having to cross the road if the other party is coming the other way.

E stands for emotions – the real issue in all conflict. The mediation process provides an opportunity for the 'venting' of feelings in a safe environment only after which a disputant can begin to think rationally about outcomes.

This taxonomy also indicates the extent of matters traversed in restorative justice processes.

As a forerunner to the next section I note that lawyers and advocates are formally trained in only one of the six ASPIRE elements set out above. Equally of note, is that most mediators in New Zealand come from a legal, management, construction industry or counselling background. To the extent that experience and training can influence a mediator's approach, it is arguable that outcomes for the same set of facts (whilst possibly all satisfactory to the parties) could vary, depending on whether the mediator explores legal results, human growth, or practical and administrative issues.

It is not the purpose of this chapter to explore matters of accreditation, certification or training beyond noting that the first duty of a mediator is to make the process safe. That means the mediator must be a safe person, and that means having self-insight. (While I believe this view, or ability, is fundamental to mediation practice, it may not be thought so universally.) To telescope an important issue to a sentence, I suggest that while one cannot avoid one's genes and life experiences and therefore be neutral, one can at least be self-aware and therefore practice impartiality.

## Lawyers and advocates

As long ago as the 1980s, Riskin and Westbrook (1988) were writing about the "map references" that lawyers have for dispute resolution as being to identify a relevant rule of law, to find provable facts that apply, and winning and losing measured in money. These they pointed out had little in common with mediation where the law is relevant only to the extent the parties agree (subject to lawfulness and ethical considerations), winning or losing is damaging to each side achieving dignity in the process, and the intent is to find solutions that mesh mutual needs and interests.

Today most lawyers graduate without having studied jurisprudence – the theory of law in society. For some, the practice of law is accordingly more about business than the old concept of professionalism where the family lawyer was turned to for wise advice. There are many lawyers (and lay advocates) who display great skill and common sense in helping their clients through conflict, but also some who do not understand or pay attention to their client's psychological needs. Some do not distinguish their own needs (to feel they have got the best deal possible for their client) from the client's needs (to get a reasonable deal with dignity for both sides and to move on quickly).

While this chapter concentrates on those aspects of alternative dispute resolution that most closely adhere to restorative justice principles, this is not to overlook the fact that much negotiation is conducted in a manner calculated to be anything but openhearted. That dynamic is also receiving attention (for example, Gordon, 2000; Wade, 2005).

I suggest that in the future, advocates of all disciplines will need wider, more holistic training than that which is imparted at the moment. This leads me to emerging developments in other disciplines that are of direct relevance.

## Philosophy: phenomenology and the law

> Men are not conditioned to live by reason alone, but by instinct. So they are no more bound to live by the dictates of an enlightened mind than a cat is bound to live by the laws of nature of a lion.
>
> (Spinoza)

Phenomenology teaches us that people are the product of their genes and life experiences and have unique needs and interests. As the late Paul Ricoeur said, the critical questions to ask oneself are "Who am I?" and "What should I do with my life?".[24] (Arguably, people can spend too much time on the first question, when getting on with the second might help answer the first.) These questions predicate unique answers. Those individual answers can require unique solutions in the event of conflict.

---

24 For a description of his writings and thought, see Dauenhauer (2002).

## Neuro-biology

Edward Ergenzinger Jr, in his 2002 paper 'Conversations with Phineas Gage: a neuroscientific approach to negotiation', has this to say:

> In recent years a relatively neglected aspect of decision making and judgment has secured greater interest among scholars and researchers; the automatic, experiential, affect-based side of our mental life. Neurological research has highlighted the fact that the region of the human brain primarily responsible for rational judgment and decision-making cannot function properly without input from the region responsible for emotion. Much of the time this input and its influence may not even be noticed on a conscious level, but it nevertheless shapes our decisions and judgment in drastic ways. Although emotional influences have been analysed by legal scholars in areas such as jury deliberations, appellate advocacy, judicial decision-making and consumer products liability, there has been little or no direct discussion of the applicability of these findings to the field of dispute resolution.

The linkages with phenomenology are obvious. It gives some insight into why personal involvement in decision making is generally preferred over that of an outsider. Why risk another's perception of justice when you can work things out with the other party?

This theme has also been taken up by legal scholars (though without reference to Ergenzinger's paper). Jones and Hughes (2003, pp. 487–490) advance and discuss four ideas. First, that the mind is inherently embodied. Secondly, that thought is mostly unconscious; and thirdly, that communication about abstract ideas is largely metaphorical. Finally, they discuss that human beings are feeling beings with thoughts, not thinking beings with feelings. They point to the importance of the scientific method (that can lead to the unravelling of the human genome), but that complex adaptive systems (such as understanding immunology) are resistant to analysis, description and prediction using traditional analytical tools.

> Complex adaptive systems – among them the human mind, an ecosystem, or a community of individuals – represent a wholly different set of systems from those that are merely complicated and cannot be understood with traditional analysis.[25]

The authors offer no answers to the implications of how to replace the traditional approach of objective, lineal, reductionist analysis with something

---

25  See also Ruhl (1997).

more appropriate. Instead, they argue that "true wisdom is in the question not the answer" (Jones and Hughes, 2003, p. 191). But they point out that for mediators (as for decision makers) the task is to understand the reality of conflict when:

> it is being dynamically co-formed by the disputants both internally and interactively. How does the formula change when a mediator is introduced and the parties and the mediator are jointly co-forming the conflict reality.

They go further and suggest that the training of mediators with metaphors such as 'the tools of trade' is outdated and ask with what should we replace them.

Jones and Hughes (2003) further argue that a revolution in thinking has begun and it may be as far-reaching in its effects as the Age of Enlightenment. So we can be explorers of this new world, or defenders of conventional wisdom (flat-earthers?).

In treating the brain as a 'complex adaptive system', however, there are further consequences and insights to take into account. Robert Benjamin (2002) posits that people take their cues in approaching conflict from national and international stages. Even what they saw on television the night before mediation might affect the way in which they approach the process. If on the world stage, negotiation is failing to make a difference in say the Israel–Palestinian conflict, then why would it work for them? Perhaps they think it is time to draw a line in the sand. Mediators should be aware of this factor in daily work. "Some care needs to be taken to assure that neither they nor the people with whom they work are sucked into the nihilistic vortex of no-negotiation" (Benjamin, 2002).

## Restorative justice

Gabrielle Maxwell (personal communication, 2005) identified four key elements of a restorative justice process as being:

- the involvement of those affected by the offence;
- the empowerment of those involved in the decision making;
- acknowledgement and repair of harm; and
- the reintegration of those affected into their society in ways that restore the harmony of the group.

She stated:

> It is about changing hearts and minds. It is about putting matters right, it is about healing and forgiveness, it is about a new start. And it provides

an alternative set of values that can underpin social relationships between people in all areas of community life.

While the language used is directed to the criminal area, the principles are readily applicable to the civil scene.

Conflict arising in interpersonal relationships (family, employment and neighbourhood) can generate feelings of betrayal, hatred, violence (verbal and physical), harassment and bullying to name a few of the 'offensive' behaviours that can occur. Likewise, civil case conflict will normally also involve emotion. Even if a party is a company or other institution, some individual's actions will be under review.

Normal mediation practices can address all the four key restorative elements identified above.

The linkages between restorative justice, conflict transformation and trauma healing have been discussed by Howard Zehr (2004) and he suggests some 10 lessons from exploring these issues holistically rather than independently:

1. An experience of victimisation and even trauma is involved in most situations of conflict and wrongdoing.
2. Most, if not all, situations of conflict and harm involve questions of justice and injustice, and situations of injustice frequently involve trauma.
3. Processes to resolve harm of conflict often must find ways to explicitly address both needs and responsibilities. Too often, resolution processes focus on the former and not the latter.
4. Personal and communal narratives [referred to as story and 'restorying'] play critical roles in conflict resolution, trauma recovery and restorative justice.
5. Successful resolution and transformation often turns on the creation of empathy of one another by the participants.
6. Humiliation or shame plays a role in most conflicts, traumas, and harms ... [P]rocesses ... often require proactive steps to remove or transform shame.
7. Both restorative justice and conflict transformation reflect a common set of values ... which include respect, humility, empowerment, and engagement [and] can be seen as reflecting an underlying worldview based on a sense of interconnectedness.
8. Structural injustices and problems play a role in many crimes, conflicts and traumas. Both fields are in danger of overlooking or

# Restorative Justice in the Civil Jurisdiction

even perpetuating such injustices by individualising conflicts and harms.

9. Both fields are susceptible to unconscious biases – of gender and culture for example.[26]

10. ... Both fields are susceptible to forces of co-optation and diversion that can sidetrack them from their intent. [This requires] conscious vigilance on the part of practitioners and advocates.

Such processes, however, do need advocates to have a range of skills and knowledge that lies outside those of traditional rights-based systems. There are recent developments in these areas as well.

## Therapeutic jurisprudence and related initiatives

David Wexler, who has training in both psychology and law, has introduced the concept of 'therapeutic jurisprudence', a concept that might be thought an oxymoron.[27] Briefly, he observes that the experience of law of a litigant or an accused person will be affected by the treatment received from their interaction with all the people involved in the process. This impact can be either therapeutic or the reverse. If such results are observable, then they are worthy of study, and adoption of those behavioural changes that enhance positive outcomes, and reduce negatives (such as recidivism). His website has links to many articles that have been published in furtherance of this insight.

Likewise, lawyers are exploring many alternative styles of practice of which the Renaissance Lawyer Society has a comprehensive list and description on its website.[28]

Collaborative law is a new idea based on traditional processes of joint meetings between parties and their counsel (Scott, 2004). Apart from prescriptions about the process it has one major difference; namely, that the lawyer who handles the direct negotiations should not be the one who handles the litigation if that is required. This is not the place to discuss the advantages and disadvantages of such a scheme, but among the subtleties of such a

---

26 'Bias" may be an overstatement here. Conflict can be gendered in terms of how the different sexes typically report differently on how they have dealt with it. This is different slant on conflict, and there have been a few feminist critiques of the dominant male model. See Holt and DeVore (2005).

27 Wexler is the director of the International Network on Therapeutic Jurisprudence, see http://www.therapeuticjurisprudence.org.

28 See http://www.renaissancelawyer.com.

situation, there will be a desire by the lawyers involved to achieve resolution, which otherwise might not be evident to the same extent.

## Communication and linguistics

While the theory and practice of communication are not new, its importance in both being the source of much conflict and the logical means of resolving same are becoming more recognised. The basic concepts of 'encode' (formulating words that you think will be understood by the recipient), 'transmit' (the means of communication) and 'decode' (what the recipient makes of the message) are clear enough; together with 'attribution error' (where a person assumes a meaning based on their own life experience that varies from that intended by the speaker (resulting in miscommunication)) (see Case study 9.6).

**Case study 9.6:** (Mis)communication

> A senior manager had fallen out with the board of directors and chief executive. Mediation occurred at a crisis point when the parties saw no outcome other than the termination of employment and litigation. The employee did not want to leave for a variety of reasons, including the impact on his superannuation rights for himself and his wife. The employer did not want to lose a good performer or have to face replacement and litigation risks and costs.
>
> By working through the complaints each had of the other, a clear pattern emerged. Each, over a series of about seven events, had acted in a way they had thought either innocuous or helpful. But the other had interpreted their motives as being underhanded and malicious.
>
> One of the most powerful tools of a mediator is to observe and then name what is going on in the process. Such dynamics are called 'attribution error'. Naming the issue was the 'ah ha!' jaw-drop moment for both sides.
>
> What could we do about our respective assumptions in the future? "Well we could check it out with each other I suppose." Six months later, feedback was received that the relationship was fully restored.

Recognition of the importance of metaphor is another issue in the light of the neuro-scientific approach discussed above. Metaphor is a useful strategy to ensure communication through shared experiences, but it is easy to make mistakes. For example, men often use metaphors of war, physical sports and sex, all of which may be of little relevance, or may even be offensive, to women. The conscious use of universal metaphors such as journeying, geographical features, mazes and prisms of light have a greater chance of success.[29] Words have their own power. For example, the English word 'enemy' comes from the two Latin words Latin *in* (not) and *amicus* (friend). *Inamicus* evolved to the English 'inimical', and that in turn led to enemy. In Māori the word for enemy 'hoariri' is also made up of two words – hoa (friend) and riri (angry); that is, angry friend. The Latin denies a relationship, while the Māori acknowledges both relationship and emotion.

## Emotional intelligence and Neuro-Linguistic Programming

Emotional intelligence is based around three personal competencies: developing self-awareness; developing an ability to regulate one's own thoughts and behaviour; and developing an ability to motivate oneself following setbacks. These dimensions lead to social competencies of improved empathetic responses to others and the ability to develop healthy relationships (Schreier, 2002; Shearhouse, 2003). These are all-important skills for a mediator and can help in recognising deficits in the parties in conflict, and suggesting future outcomes. The ideal mediation is one in which underlying issues are identified, and the parties are thereby equipped to avoid future conflict arising from the same sources.

Neuro-Linguistic Programming provides principles of communication, how we take in and process information, how our minds work and how we make meaning of what we hear. It places a major emphasis on reading body language, and addresses issues such as the mediator's and parties' states of mind in mediation.

Natasha Serventy (2002) tells the autobiographical tale of a lawyer who believed strongly in litigation and third-party negotiation, then became entranced with mediation, and subsequently convinced of the importance of Neuro-Linguistic Programming in the practice of mediation.

Healing and human growth through conflict resolution is another research area. Marie Hoskins and Jo-Anne Stoltz (2003) describe a research programme in which the parties had experienced long-term conflict in the workplace. Three to six months later, they were asked to explain how the process affected their beliefs, values, expectations and behaviours, and to reflect on how they had changed since mediation. Findings included that change (in terms of personal change) does not happen in the mediation but may well appear in the months

---

29 For a valuable analysis of how mediators can use language usefully or not, see Bagshaw (2003).

following. There are some useful insights for mediators in such ongoing relationships around support systems for the individuals, and a similar emphasis on the importance of the use of metaphors, which has been described above.

External analysis can give a rather different impression of disputants' motivations. Tyler Harrison (2003) describes the experience within an Ombuds Office in a large American university (35,000 students). Harrison highlights the need for differing strategies to be used by mediators in dealing with different individuals and to recognise that some may potentially move from one identified category to another. For example, he states (p. 326):

> the discourse of destroyers suggests they take the grievance very personally and are more likely to strike out in retaliation if the opportunity arises. This would suggest a strategy that avoids face-to-face confrontation (or the use of the legal system).

> Future research should also focus on what leads to the different characterisations of the dispute by the disputants. For example, victims, targets, and destroyers all seem more likely to attribute the other's actions to malicious intent, than are information seekers, exception seekers, protectors and enforcers. The discourse of victims, targets, and destroyers often portrays the other as malevolent, and the motivations attributed to the other disputant are more egregious.

## Spirituality, mindfulness and presencing

The great religions have always been involved in dispute resolution and over the past 40 years or so particularly, the Mennonite and Quaker communities in the United States have developed very advanced and sophisticated treatises and training manuals in mediation, but the theme of spirituality has also moved away from a purely religious basis. Linda Lazarus chairs the Spirituality Chapter of the Academy for Conflict Resolution and writes of a conversation with Professor Leonard Riskin on the topic of *mindfulness* – or staying in the moment – and its value to mediators (Lazarus, 2005). This concept has many links with Eastern religions and values.

*Presencing* is a capacity-developing process for enabling new ways of learning to inform future action. Some seven capacities have been described (Senge et al., 2004, p. 225). *Suspending* is arguably akin to mindfulness in that it is 'seeing our seeing'; namely, appreciating the limitations in perceiving what is, and allowing for new possibilities. *Redirecting* is seeing matters from a holistic whole, which leads to *letting go* of the old vision. *Letting come* is being open to new options, which leads to *crystallising* those opportunities.

*Prototyping* is experimenting with the new, and *institutionalising* is the adoption of the new way. The book has many spiritual references and allusions that illustrate the messages, and is valuable in that the process as described follows a course that can be experienced in many mediation sessions. Ultimately it describes an impasse-breaking code.

Carrie Menkel-Meadows (2001) discusses a similar creative process in a book review that covered (among other creative dispute resolution issues) the design of a new supermarket shopping trolley, and drew parallels with harnessing the same energy in finding new and unique solutions in conflict resolution.[30] That is not to say that spirituality does not have an important place in helping people think deeply about conflict and its resolution. For example, the Bushmen of the Kalahari Desert have had very sophisticated conflict resolution processes in place for thousands of years due to the risk of a small community losing two members as a result of violence. When both are equipped with poisoned arrows each has the potential to inflict an inevitable but lingering death – which gives the victim time to reciprocate. Some 50% of all conflict within the group is resolved at the first stage of creating a spiritual environment and then exploring interests, then rights and then power. But if unsuccessful through to that stage the process is recycled through interests, rights and power until agreement is reached (Ury, 1995).

## Other indigenous processes and values

It would make an interesting thesis topic as to why the early British social system of feudalism evolved a rights-based dispute resolution process rather than one based on interests. Some might say that it reflects the need for the privileged powerful group in charge of the legal system to protect property rights. Most indigenous systems are needs and interests based and involve all persons affected (the need for at least equilibrium if not harmony in the community rather than justice between individuals) and that can be the whole community. Examples include Hawaii (Barnes, 1994), North American Indians (LeResche, 1993), the Bushmen of the Kalahari Desert (Ury, 1995), Australian

---

30 Her paper reviews three books, two directly in the mediation field (Mnookin et al., 2000; Kolb and Williams, 2000) and the third in industrial design (Kelley and Littman, 2001). The review has valuable comments and insights, among other things, into the thinking processes of advocates and participants, and how both they and the context of the dispute affect outcomes.

Aborigines (Pringle, 1996) and New Zealand's tangata whenua (people of the land), Māori.[31]

The reason for spending time on indigenous systems is to recognise that any dispute affects not only the individuals concerned, but all those around them. No one is left unaffected by a personal grievance, whether they be the manager, the employee, their respective families, or other work colleagues or other stakeholders in the business. It is of particular interest in New Zealand where demographics are changing rapidly so that the mainstream culture (Pākehā) by the middle of this century may remain the major group, but be less than half the population. Māori dispute resolution has much in common with restorative justice principles, and this may be seen as another example of the Pacific reclaiming its own following colonisation.

Many of indigenous values are also of universal human relevance. Joe Epstein (2005) describes 12 values of North American wisdom that would have equivalence in other countries. They are illustrated with proverbs or short stories as follows.

- Listening:

    Blue Jay noticed that Bear had not said a thing. Finally, Blue Jay asked Bear why was she so silent and Bear replied "I'm listening and learning. I don't need to talk; I already know what I know."

- Respect:

    Respect for all forms of life, unfortunately, is not common value in many cultures today. It is easier to respect someone stronger, faster, or richer. Likewise it is easier to respect someone who is like us in every way possible. Respecting someone with different beliefs, different dress or different customs, or something entirely different from us is not easy.

- Generosity:

    Generosity is a good thing to have as we are all travellers on this earth.

- Humour:

    Humor is one of the most powerful tools that the Creator has given human kind.

---

[31] It is recognised internationally that the case conferencing method was originated in New Zealand and based on Māori customary processes.

- Compassion:

    Human beings cannot understand another's life until they have carried the weight of that person's burdens, listened to that person's words, felt that person's pain, observed that person's actions, and walked along that person's path, sharing the other's greatest longings and aspirations. Understanding those things, we must then be able to sleep at that person's fire, sharing every part of the other human being's dreams and nightmares.

- Silence:

    Silence was meaningful with the Lakota, and his granting a space of silence before talking was done in the practice of true politeness and regard for the rule that 'thought comes before speech'.

- Non-verbal communication:

    The wise individual looks and hears the unspoken signals that scream for the need to be recognized. The gentle and sensitive listener is adept at the art of creating safety and space for sharing that allows others to express their needs.

- Atonement:

    The sincere desire to deal fairly with others. To admit our shortcomings and to make amends where needed is the mark of a person worthy of trust.

- Trust:

    The art of speaking harmoniously is a bit more difficult because people who are honest and direct tend to forget that brutal honesty is not always appreciated. If sensitivity is paired with intelligence, we are using our power of perception to notice where we can bring harmony in a potentially upsetting situation. Respecting the vulnerability of those who trust us to be honest and gentle is the key to the art of speaking the Truth in Harmony.

- Healing:

    Part of healing was the way she listened ... she always reacted with sympathy and compassion. So it isn't just the treatment that heals it's the hands on understanding and cooling that sometimes make the mediation do its work. In truth, the caring and attention are part of the medicine.

- Wisdom:

    Being wise, having wisdom, is knowing what to do with what you know, when to do it, and how to do it. Or sometimes a person must know enough to do nothing.

- Peacemaker:

    A person who can take the ordinary and illuminate it, invoking deep feelings in others often is called a creative genius. The Ancestors call those who carry that talent The Gifted Ones.

Epstein (2005), quoting Kenneth Cloke (2001),[32] argues that:

mediators who will not take the risk of bringing "a deep and dangerous level of honesty and empathy" to the dispute resolution process leave a void in the circle of justice.

I am indebted to my colleague and fellow mediator Tauiliili Paul Stowers for noting that these themes are repeated in Pacific cultures such as the Samoan ritual of ifoga. This has the following elements (Stowers, 2005).

- It is spiritual.
- It expresses genuine feelings and acts of remorse.
- It involves family.
- It is an accepted ritual.
- It empowers the victim's family.
- It seeks forgiveness.
- It brings reconciliation.
- It re-establishes harmony.
- It provides closure.

I have seen many of these values incorporated into mediations with Māori, both intra-culturally and cross-culturally. I am also aware of many whakataukī (proverbs) that would illustrate similar values. I would love to see the identification of such principles and how they should be illustrated from within Māoridom.

## Designing processes: the elements

It has often been observed that good theory goes hand in hand with good practice and vice versa. There needs to be more interchange between researchers

---

32 Whereas mediators are taught that the first duty of a mediator is to provide a safe environment, Cloke (2001) quotes Johann Wolfgang von Goethe, "The dangers of life are infinite, and among them is safety".

and practitioners. David Lipsky and Ariel Avgar (2004) argue this point and explore what such research might entail in the future. They posit that the first generation of dispute resolution research was at a societal level – legal questions and the implications for our legal system and social justice. The second (in the mid-1980s) was at the macro-organisational level – internal mechanisms of dispute resolution in non-union settings. The third generation they argue is at the micro-organisational level – the operation of procedures and processes and their relative effectiveness. This has included, for example, a comparison of facilitative, evaluative and transformative types of mediation.[33]

The challenge for the next generation of researchers, Lipsky and Avgar believe, will be to synthesise the disparate theories and empirical findings of the first three generations. Questions arise such as "has the transformation of employment dispute resolution in the United States strengthened or weakened employee rights and [the] system of social justice?" (Lipsky and Avgar, 2004). They note that in the United States there has been a dramatic shift to private dispute resolution away from public forums. Some commentators have expressed concern about this phenomenon, especially regarding the decrease in precedents and diminishing skills of trial judges and lawyers (Higginbotham, 2004). There has been no rigorous analytical research on the implications of this trend. Lipsky and Avgar also believe that there should be examination of micro-variations in dispute procedures on macro-level outcomes such as recruitment, retention, employee performance, productivity, employee satisfaction and even profits and other bottom-line measures.

As a minor comment on 'facilitative' mediation as opposed to 'evaluative'[34] I offer the suggestion that there can be a half-way house; that is, 'analytical' mediation (although purists would see this as evaluative in any event). I see no point in a mediator offering advice. It exposes one to charges of negligent advice or blame for the outcome. But sometimes a party does not have enough

---

33 'Facilitative' can be described as a 'pure' form where the mediator helps the parties by staying only with the process – even so far as facilitating the common rules under which the parties will negotiate. 'Evaluative' is where the mediator offers more than information on what might happen in court and effectively becomes an advice giver. 'Transformative' is based on the work of Folger and Bush (1994) in which they explore the ways in which helping the parties recognise the other's position, and then enabling them (which includes power balancing) to negotiate effectively leads to transformation of the conflict and even of the parties themselves. The United States Postal Service has adopted the transformative style for all internal mediations. These styles require very different approaches from the mediator.

34 See footnote 33.

knowledge to make a wise decision. Here I think there is an argument for a mediator to indicate areas of concern that a party will have to overcome at litigation, but without making a recommendation. An example might be a claim for constructive dismissal (where the employee has resigned for allegedly good cause) where the onus of proof is on the employee to show why they had to resign; as opposed to a dismissal where the onus is on the employer to justify the sacking.

## Practical implications

As indicated at the start of this chapter, initial problem solving is by far the cheapest and most effective way to resolve conflict. Programmes that equip potential disputants with communication skills, and skills in understanding emotion and its management are the most cost effective, but may be the least apparent when successful.

However, requiring the parties to talk to each other is a normative step. Where this is not possible, having an intervener (or perhaps a conciliator) to facilitate a safe environment becomes basic.

Peter Adler and Christopher Honeyman (2005) have recently identified the common values and political beliefs of most conflict management strategies as follows (in an American context):

i. Inclusion of the fullest possible diversity of voices and viewpoints
ii. Participation in both the formulation of the process and the content of discussion
iii. High quality information and data, including grappling with scientific and technical uncertainty and the limits of current knowledge
iv. Questioning and critical inquiry to reveal, understand, and test key underlying assumptions
v. Mutual listening and understanding as [a] bedrock for productive dialogue, the invention or practical reconciliation of competing ideas, and the hunt for practical outcomes
vi. Fair decision rules that do not tilt the playing field or the marketplace of ideas
vii. Transparency so that the tradeoffs are understandable to those affected by but not present for decisions
viii. Accountability so that those who are making decisions participate in their implementation

ix. Amendability so that decisions can be adaptable to new information or changed conditions
x. Assent/Consent/Acceptability so that new ideas can move forward with the highest levels of political traction
xi. Implementability so that solutions are pragmatic and do-able.

These form a useful basis for an assessment of processes, but I note the alternative dispute resolution committee of the Wellington District Law Society has under action a project for developing guidelines for policy makers and others involved in such new legislative provisions. Pele Walker (executive director of LEADR NZ) is preparing the guidelines and I note from a draft the following principles (Walker, 2005).

Strive to keep decisions in the hands of those closest to the problem.

Seek not only the rational but also the reasonable.

Seek to 'supplement' not replace the legal system.

Anticipate and try to prevent escalation of the dispute.

Explicitly assess the alternatives to using alternative dispute resolution and negotiation forums.

Provide options that will enable/empower parties to negotiate and solve problems by satisfying interests, rather than capitulating to positions.

These principles should result in processes that place primary responsibility back on the parties to work out their conflict themselves; and if that is not possible through fear or lack of trust, then to provide third-party participation to ensure safety while they do so. In limited circumstances, decision making through informal processes such as arbitration may be appropriate, but the court system is likely to be the last resort.

## Conclusion

The breadth of study of conflict resolution that is now occurring has much more in common with restorative justice and other alternative dispute resolution processes than with traditional litigation. It is to be hoped that such study does not remain 'siloed' in discrete disciplines as cross-fertilisation of ideas could yield new insights. Such a holistic view is entirely consistent with the principles of restorative justice.

The congruence of restorative justice, mediation and other alternative dispute resolution processes can be seen in the following.

We now know that humankind comprises 'feeling beings who think' (or perhaps creatures who think and feel), and that the part of our brain that thinks cannot operate without input from the part that feels emotions. This insight challenges the basis of decision-making processes such as the courts, which are designed to apply objective logical judgement in the absence of emotion. This is not to say that the courts are not an essential part of the dispute resolution process, but can be seen as a last resort.

We know that people perceive 'justice' as occurring where the process is procedurally fair, the outcome substantively sound and the third party (whether facilitator or decision maker) is seen as unbiased. A diverse community will perceive different outcomes as being 'fair', so systems for the future should allow for the fact that each case may require unique outcomes to meet the parties' ideas of substantive fairness. This is more likely to be achieved when the parties are involved in the outcomes.

There needs to be ongoing evolution of processes; for example, the issue of the third party being impartial is not always a given. According to Dame Joan Metge (2001) takawaenga (mediators in the Māori community who operated as a link between the tribal group and an outcast) were chosen for their standing, skills and knowledge. John Lederach (2005) writes of the efficacy of "insider partial" mediators, who may be more appropriate facilitators/negotiators in some cultures or conflicts.

The current omission of a free mediation service from private civil litigation may be explainable for economic reasons (why should the taxpayer subsidise such processes) but this appears inconsistent when it is provided for in so many specialist areas in the private civil dispute field (for example, in relation to tenancy, employment, family, human rights, privacy, and disability issues). One question that may arise in the future is whether a plethora of mediation services attached to many government departments, each with individual agendas and responsibilities is as desirable as a single, independent mediation service available for use in all disputes and for all courts and tribunals.

One of the key issues to be resolved will be the interface between the courts and the other dispute resolution services that evolve.

We especially need to be conscious of the closeness of Māori (and other cultural communities) universal values to restorative justice principles and the contribution they can make – especially in contributing to the design of inclusive processes (Metge, 2001).

To te kanohi tona kite

To te hinengaro tona kite

To te mauri tona kite

(The mind, the eye and the soul/Each has its own perspective)

# 10

# Restorative Practices in Schools: Far-Reaching Implications

*Wendy Drewery*

In 1999, the New Zealand Ministry of Education contracted a team from the University of Waikato to develop a process for conferencing in schools. The brief was to utilise restorative justice principles to develop a conferencing process for use in schools. The purpose was to test whether such an approach to wrongdoing could reduce the exponential increase of suspensions, particularly of Māori boys, who were, and still are, disproportionately represented in reported numbers of suspensions, stand-downs and exclusions.

We introduced the process into five schools initially, and a further 24 schools subsequently sent staff for training. In the participating schools, numbers of suspensions went down, as they have declined in most schools where similar initiatives have continued. Reasons for this reduction in suspensions may well include the well-known Hawthorne effect – the effect of being in the spotlight.

Our projects were strictly professional development for staff, rather than research per se. In developing our process, we drew upon the practices of family group conferencing developed by the Department of Social Welfare in the early1990s in New Zealand, principles of restorative justice then being brought forward by Howard Zehr (1990, 1994), and the theoretical and practice resources of narrative therapy (Monk et al., 1997; White and Epston, 1992).

The values and principles of restorative justice were described in the first chapter of this book. However, the primary purpose of schools, namely the learning and development of children and young people, is very different from the correctional focus that is central to the legal system. Exploration of these differences would be a valuable project, regrettably one that is beyond the scope of this chapter. Here, I shall simply raise some conceptual issues that arise in approaching the use of restorative principles in schools.

Details of a process for conducting a restorative conference in a school setting are provided in chapter 11. Different approaches to conferencing use subtly different processes, and they may also emphasise different outcomes. Similarly, different people expect different outcomes from the introduction of these practices into schools. Policy makers and school principals, parents and academics will, not surprisingly, emphasise different aspects. For some, the primary outcome sought is the development of a specific plan for managing and monitoring behaviour in the future. Others may want to see achievement in learning as a test of success.

The University of Waikato approach to the conferencing process – more recently applied to 'small' or 'deans'' conversations – does not deny the importance of these objectives, but it does place primary importance on two things that are prior conditions for cooperative behaviour and collaboration in learning: one is preserving and/or restoring the dignity of those involved in the conference, the other is peaceful coexistence through respectful relationships (Restorative Practices Development Team, 2004).

My professional interest is in theorising the notion of restoration in a way that explains both the individual and the social psychology of restorative practices, including the process of conferencing, without resorting to a deficit account of the young person (Drewery, 2004). The way language is used in conferencing is a primary focus of my theoretical interest, because it is primarily through language that new meanings, new relationships and new personal identities are produced (Drewery, 2005). In a restorative conversation, therefore, what is said, how it is said, and when and in what order it is said are theoretically and practically important because the process is what produces new identities and new relationships.

The introduction of restorative conferencing into schools in the late 1990s was initially part of what the Ministry of Education called the Suspension Reduction Initiative. More recently, the ministry has been focused on the Student Engagement Initiative.

The intention of the Suspension Reduction Initiative was to reduce the numbers of students who were being suspended, expelled or excluded. In 1999, around the time our new conferencing process was being trialled, the Ministry of Education published *Guidance for Principals and Boards of Trustees on Stand-Downs, Suspensions, Exclusions and Expulsions*. These guidelines introduced new definitions and a new category, stand-down. Stand-down means the removal of a student from school for a specified period of no more than 5 days, and no more than 10 days in total in one year.[1]

---

[1] Suspension means the formal removal of a student from school until the board of trustees decides the outcome at a suspension meeting. The principal is the only one who can make the decision to stand down or suspend a student from a school. The board may decide to lift the suspension, with or without reasonable conditions, or to exclude

These initiatives have been only partially successful. Over the last few years, suspensions and expulsions have decreased slightly, but the number of stand-downs has continued to increase. Early leaving exemptions for students who wish to leave school before they reach the legal leaving age are also on the increase.

According to the Ministry of Education (2007a), 22,467 stand-downs were reported in 2006. This compared with 21,862 in 2005. The most common reasons for stand-downs in 2006 were continual disobedience (26%), physical assault on other students (24%) and verbal abuse of staff (15%). These behaviours accounted for 65% of stand-downs each year from 2000 to 2006. There were 5,008 suspension cases in 2006 compared with 5,145 in 2005. Continual disobedience (27%), misuse of drugs (20%) and physical assault on other students (18%) accounted for 65% of these in 2006.

Students who are male, Māori or 14 years old continue to be over-represented in stand-down and suspension statistics compared with their proportions in the general school population.

Pasifika students, both male and female, have comparatively high rates of stand-down.

Secondary schools are more likely to use stand-downs and suspensions than are primary schools. Between 2002 and 2006, about 25% of all schools (primary and secondary) used suspension. In 2006, this figure included 65% of secondary schools. In 2006, 25% of secondary schools suspended students at an average rate of twice the national average (Ministry of Education, 2007a). In 2004, 83% of primary schools had no suspensions. Of all schools that suspended students (25%), about 10% were responsible for 43% of all suspensions (Ministry of Education, 2005). I calculate this to mean that 2.5% of all schools were responsible for 43% of suspensions. It would have been interesting to analyse this figure in relation to the claim that students from decile[2] 1 and 2 schools

---

or expel the student. Exclusion means the formal removal of a student aged under 16 years from the school, with the requirement that the student enrol elsewhere. In this case the principal of the excluding school "must try to arrange for the student to attend another school" within 10 days, and to inform the Ministry of Education if they are not successful (section 15(5) of the Education Act 1989). Expulsion means the formal removal of a student aged 16 or over from school, and the student may enrol elsewhere (Ministry of Education, 1999). There is another category, exemption, which permits students under the school leaving age to leave school without a requirement to re-enrol.

2   A school's decile indicates the extent to which the school draws its students from low socioeconomic communities. Decile 1 schools are the 10% of schools with the highest proportion of students from low socioeconomic communities, whereas decile 10

were 4.9 times more likely to be suspended than were students in the highest quintile (deciles 9 and 10) (Ministry of Education, 2007b), but there were insufficient data available to do so. *A Report on New Zealand Student Engagement 2006* states that decile 2–5 schools make up the bulk of schools standing down students (Ministry of Education, 2007a). Equivalent data were not reported for suspensions. Although the age-standardised rate of suspensions per 1,000 students went down from 2000 to 2006 (8.0 students per 1,000 in 2000 compared with 7.0 students per 1,000 in 2006), the rate of stand-downs has not (26.1 students per 1,000 in 2000 to 31.4 students per 1,000 in 2006) (Ministry of Education, 2007b).

Thus, in spite of the overall reduction in suspensions, there are still rather large numbers of students who are temporarily excluded from schools under the heading 'stand-downs'. How should we interpret these numbers, each instance of which reflects significant disruption to the lives of the students concerned and their families, as well as significant misery in the working lives of teachers and school managers? Why would 14-year-old, male, Māori and Pasifika students be excluded (however briefly) in greater numbers than others? Is it true that students from low decile schools are more likely to be excluded? And finally, how shocking is it, in fact, that a little over one in 30 students is given the equivalent of timeout each year?

The matter of discipline in schools has previously been treated as a child development issue, and as such left to teachers, parents and other education professionals such as counsellors and resource teachers for learning and behaviour. Adolescence is a formative time. One developmental theorist, Anna Freud, even went so far as to suggest that not experiencing storm and stress during adolescence is itself abnormal. Moral development also features during this period: young people are inevitably faced with many conflicting questions about what is right and in whom they should place their trust.

The world has changed significantly in the last half century, and this must have an impact on growing up in a post-modern world. One interpretation of the whakataukī (proverb), "Ka pū te ruha, ka hao te rangatahi" (When the old net is worn out and cast aside, the new net is put into use), encapsulates the expectation that at some time, the older generation might have to step aside and let the young take over (Keelan, 2004). Of course, every generation faces the problem of transmitting its values and assisting young people to learn how to manage situations where they come in conflict with social norms. At the same

---

schools are the 10% of schools with the lowest proportion of these students. Census information is used to calculate the decile (Ministry of Education, 2006b).

time, history shows that each generation also has its own 'truth', its own 'take' on the social conditions it meets, and almost by definition, it will of necessity not only learn from, but also surpass, the experience of previous generations.

Teachers' skills in behaviour management are also in focus in relation to this problem. Both the teaching profession and policy makers (and possibly the general population) tend to view the problem of managing behaviour in the classroom as a professional skill to be learned by teachers, and link this directly to the figures on stand-downs and suspensions. The most recent statement of intent from the Ministry of Education links personalised learning, presence, engagement and achievement (Ministry of Education, 2007c). Transgression of classroom and school norms of behaviour by students may also be thought of as resulting from problematic peer group influence or poor parenting.

My colleagues Russell Bishop, Mere Berryman, Sarah-Jane Tiakiwai and Cath Richardson (2004) asked students and teachers what was the most important thing affecting students' achievement. Students said they work hard for teachers with whom they have a good relationship, and teachers overwhelmingly blamed lack of student achievement on parents who do not value schooling and education. This finding has prompted the Ministry of Education to fund a large professional development programme, Te Kotahitanga, which is aimed at addressing this apparent mismatch, particularly in relation to Māori students (Ministry of Education, 2006c). By implication, that project also lays some of the blame for poor student achievement at the feet of teachers. One cannot dispute that student attendance is one of the most significant variables influencing student achievement in senior secondary school (Hughes et al., 1999). But whilst Bishop and colleagues have suggested that there could be a systematic discrepancy in teachers' expectations of Māori students, poor student engagement overall is almost certainly not down to any single cause, and could well relate to a variety of factors, many of which are beyond the control of either parents or teachers.

In a post-modern world – where the pace of social change and the multiplicity of influential factors have outstripped anyone's capacity to keep up with them – it is possible that the disaffection of young people from schools may also incorporate a message for those of us who are trying to maintain stability within the status quo. The figures for stand-downs, suspensions and exclusions are unprecedented, to a point where discipline in schools has become a broad social issue. Thus, it would be worth inquiring how much of this problem is a reflection of young people's resistance to schooling practices, including both behavioural expectations and curriculum. The fact that young people are maturing earlier than before, yet are expected to stay at school for longer, may be placing unexamined strains on our schools, families and students themselves. If developmental theory is right, that this is a time when identity formation, including moral development, is thought to be a primary psychosocial task, then it is normal to see it as a time of protest, questioning rules and challenging set boundaries. Continual disobedience, verbal abuse and physical assault are unacceptable, yet sometimes they are also hallmarks of protest. The way schools respond to these incidents is an important modelling opportunity for young people to learn how to respond appropriately and effectively to conflict. Schools are an important instrument of socialisation – a fact that is very present for those working in them, but which often seems to be forgotten in current debates about learning and achievement related to outcomes in the National Certificate in Educational Achievement.

From a school's perspective, the problem of reducing suspensions, rather than being about increasing student engagement, often translates into a question about how to get its students and their families to conform to the expectations of the school – to follow the rules. If stand-downs and suspensions are indicators of 'a form of behaviour management', and restorative conferencing is brought in to address this problem of escalating exclusions of one sort or another, then restorative conferencing and other practices such as restorative conversations are being understood as disciplinary measures designed to maintain a particular regime of morality. This sounds more draconian than most of us who espouse restorative principles would like – indeed, it appears to run contrary to the principles.

This is because, intuitively, restoration is not centrally about discipline. Our team found as our projects have gone on that when a school takes on the idea of restorative conferencing, it is by implication embracing in some cases a very different approach to relationships between staff and students, and sometimes among staff, from that which may have prevailed until that time. I think that this is because the notion of restoration draws attention to the ways in which both staff and students show respect for one another – or not. A focus on restoration contrasts starkly with processes of conflict resolution based on opposition and competition, or on conferencing that is focused on criminal wrongdoing and commensurate punishment.

One of the principles of restorative justice is respect: at the University of Waikato we believe one of the outcomes of a restorative process should be to restore the mana of the young person who has offended, of those who have been offended against, and of anyone else whose care for the young person has also been offended against. Indeed, our first project was named Te Hui Whakatika by our colleague Angus Macfarlane, who introduced us to the peacemaking process of his Te Arawa ancestor Hikairo (see Macfarlane, 2000). Mana is a word that signals not only respect and personal dignity, it also refers to the agency of the young person. I believe that sometimes the Pākehā-dominated education system treads unwarily on the mana of our young people. A Māori approach to education has always sought to build on or scaffold what is good about mokopuna (Tangaere, 1997) – rather than to punish them. There is an openness about the way young people are cared for in many families: this includes an expectation that the mana of all involved should always remain intact. Many people, including many Māori, are very sensitive to transgression of this value, whether it be against one of their own, or by them. This may be especially so when a family is frequently and systematically placed in this position.

Nevertheless, it is a family's job to be on the side of their young: to empathise with them and to see that they grow up well. Schools too are charged with this responsibility. Arguably, a primary outcome of any form of education for young people is about becoming a sovereign person, an individual with opinions and ideas, who can contribute to society in personally unique ways. This outcome includes but transcends the notion of achievement or learning encapsulated in the National Certificate in Educational Achievement. At the same time, the process that occurs within the exchange, whether it be a restorative conference or a similar kind of conversation – or, more likely, many such conversations – is a process that will contribute to the formation of both personal and community identity. Thus, a restorative process is transformative of relationships, builds identity and community, and is therefore profoundly educational.

The process that we devised begins well before the actual meeting, where the designated person finds out who should be party to the meeting. Once the meeting is convened, there is a set sequence of questions that are addressed: the problem is named, with as many descriptions as possible. Eventually the group agrees on what the problem ought to be called. A name is chosen that does not make the problem an inevitable characteristic of the offender, but offers some space between the young person and the problem.

Then the effects of the problem are also named. The young person is often so ashamed at what is being said at this point that they cannot hold their head up, and the grandparents (or other supporters) might start to get very concerned that this is turning into a bashing. This is the turn of those who have been affected, to let out and name their worst experiences.

Then alternatives to the current story are sought: are there times when this young person acted differently, or is this negative story all that can be said about this young person? Once some differently focused stories are told, the facilitator asks what these alternatives suggest about the young person. The supporters start to relax as they give their loving and empathic view of their young one. Gradually, the young person's body language changes. They might say what the effects of the problem are on them: and they may even volunteer what they think can be done about it. They may apologise. The formal part of the meeting should end with a clear and do-able plan that has the support of all, with clear responsibilities for reporting and follow up. Often this is the role of the school counsellor. Informally, afterwards, over a cup of tea, it is not unusual to hear the two families make connections, apologise and make plans to follow up themselves.

What I have described here is an orchestrated, emotional journey, taken by a group of people who do not normally come together. It is designed to ensure that all present get to say what they need others to hear; it is also designed to keep hope alive. The separating of the problem from the person of the offender maintains the dignity of the latter as a sovereign person who can do differently. The young person has undergone a psychological process that is capable of transforming their identity as a wrongdoer to someone who has the opportunity to retrieve a status that carries respect. The space given to the voices of those affected, the new, alternative perceptions of the young person that are offered, and their witnessing of the contrition of the young person and their family, inevitably change their demeanour towards the offender. When the parties learn about the weaknesses and humanness of those who have previously been seen only as offenders, opponents or competitors, there is often a kind of catharsis. People can forgive a lot when they understand how something came to happen. But this is not magic. Their generosity is often conditional, and the young person must often be helped to take advantage of the opportunity that has been created for them to make amends. Making a satisfactory plan and seeing it through is also central to the process for all. Sometimes the plan includes agreed punishment: this may even be suggested by the offender or their supporters.

Interest in the use of principles of restorative justice in schools using 'restorative conferencing' began with a question about whether the formal use of conferencing in disciplinary matters could lead to fewer suspensions. The association with the success of family group conferencing with young people by the then Department of Social Welfare is clear. Initial evidence showed that there was a lot of satisfaction with the process among participants in our initial project, but that conferencing used up a lot of time on the part of all involved (Adair and Dixon, 2000). The Ministry of Education has so far declined to introduce the process into schools in a systematic fashion. Many schools have taken the initiative, meanwhile, investing their own funds to engage private providers to train their staff to use a conferencing process. More recently, the term 'restorative practices' has become fashionable, indicating a move in emphasis, away from the correctional connotations of the family group conference and the criminal associations of the legal system, towards a more educational focus on ways of interacting that have at their centre the learning and development of the young people involved. The range of practices now referred to under this heading may or may not also have some explicit form of correctional or disciplinary intent. Restorative practices in schools include less confrontational discipline, and a focus on relational practices earlier in the chain of command, for example in the classroom, between students and teachers, between students in the playground, and in the dean's or principal's office. In short, the introduction of restorative practices involves the entire culture or ethos of a school. This move accords well with our experience: after doing numerous conferences, we ended up feeling that conferencing should be the last in a long chain of formal and informal interactions that are characterised by a desire to engage in respectful relationships at every level. This focus on a 'restorative' school culture is quite a different concept from that which sees conferencing as simply a disciplinary measure.

However, this interpretation of the concept is itself not clearly agreed on. Battles for the ethos of the school frequently ensued during our introduction of restorative practices: the primary objection by those opposed to it was that it was 'nothing more than a slap on the wrist with a wet bus ticket'. Anecdotal evidence and the report by Buckley and Maxwell (2007) support this perception. This kind of objection is borne of a (mis)understanding of the practices as simply a (weak) form of punishment. It also overlooks the (once again anecdotal) accounts of students who have gone through a conferencing process, and who attest to how hard it was for them to do so. In spite of the difficulties, however, some amazing things can come out of a conference. These include better teacher–student relationships, better relationships between school and home, better understanding between students, and increased participation by the community in the school.

Perhaps because conferences often happen after school or in the evening, or perhaps because they did not appreciate these other objectives, classroom teachers sometimes resisted participation – even when it may have been their own interactions that had brought the student to this point. Yet when they did come to a conference, teachers almost always found out something about the 'problem' student that they did not know before, which changed their view completely. Several teachers were so overcome by what they heard that they cried. At one such conference, one young man sat between his mother and sister, with his father and his father's girlfriend on the other side of the table. His teacher, who had been driven to distraction, said that she hated the days when she had his class, and lay awake the night before dreading it. The young man told of how pissed off he was that his father is no longer around, because he loved fixing cars with him, and wanted to become a mechanic. The pleasure of mucking about with cars had now gone. He told of his hatred of the father's new girlfriend, and how his life now felt as though it had no purpose. The conference ended with the student apologising to the teacher, saying he had no idea she would care that much. The girlfriend committed herself to the young man's growth and development, and the father made plans to spend time helping his son fix a car he had left behind. The plan included a programme for helping the student to catch up, and help from the school counsellor (also present) for him to write letters of apology to other teachers not present, outlining how he was proposing to catch up, and asking for their support. The presence of the dean, and his mother and sister were central to the success of this conference, because of the communal relationships that were involved. In such instances, we saw relationships not only between teacher and student transformed before our eyes, but also in the entire family, such is the power of the process. These teachers then helped to promote the use of conferencing in their schools.

Conferencing can also transform the relationships between school, home and community. We saw a school learn, for example, that a young man, brought to conference because of frequent lateness and fighting in the playground, was actually taking responsibility for his younger siblings, and all were being cared for by their grandfather, who was working to keep the family going, against great odds. A useful response to such a situation is surely not to blame such a man, but rather, to find ways to support him. Through a conferencing process, which by its nature brings together the community of care around a young person, the school can learn about the effects of its rules on students' families, and also on relationships between students. By including peers in the conference, it is possible to get a very different perspective on both the problem, and what to do about it. For instance, regular fighting in the playground might be shown up as the effect of bullying on someone who was in a weakened position in their peer group because of non–school-related responsibilities, when all this had previously been hidden and called something else. A further spin-off from this kind of conference has been that the kaumatua (elder) who supported the family was invited to talk with the deputy principal, and eventually they worked together for better links between the school and the local rūnanga.

The way the school communicates with its constituency may also be transformed by what happens in a conference: one of the first bits of feedback we received on our training was from a secondary school counsellor of a large urban school, who reported bringing together the parents of two boys who were at loggerheads. After the formal conversation one of the parents said, "Well, that is the best conversation we've ever had with this school!". However, such transformations of relationship depend on the capacity of the school to learn and change. To use restorative conferencing solely as a one-way, top-down process is to mistake a major point, which is, that the transformation and restoration of a relationship is a multi-directional process. These practices are not for schools that are not interested in learning about, and potentially improving on, the effects of their own regulatory and other professional practices on students and their communities.

One of the things we developed in our projects was a description of a restorative school, which emphasised:

- working for respectful relationships among all members of the school community;
- focusing on encouragement and possibility rather than failure and deficit;
- having teachers see themselves as in relation with students and their parents, not as authorities over them;
- having a focus on restoring order by restoring relationships rather than restoring authority when disciplinary offences occur;
- including parents and visitors, who are welcomed as part of the school community; and
- ensuring the environment is one where children and staff can enjoy their school life and have fun (Restorative Practices Development Team, 2004).

This is a list that almost all school personnel recognise as reflecting their values. And yet our experiences in introducing restorative practices to schools show some very disparate interpretations of, and ways of approaching, these goals. It is also clear that some schools and perhaps many teachers do not see their mission as necessarily related to the expectations of the parents of their students. This is born out by the findings of a study by one of my master's thesis students, Fran Cahill, who interviewed Samoan parents about their expectations of the schools and the teachers who had charge of their children. She found that Samoan parents entrust their children to the care of teachers to deliver education on their behalf. They expect teachers to be there for their children in the same way that they themselves are there for the children at home. And they believe teachers are failing in this responsibility (Cahill, 2006).

The research by my colleague Russell Bishop and others referred to above showed a major discrepancy between the perceptions of the teachers and those of the students about who holds what kinds of relational values. Of course, it is not possible for all teachers to care for the children in their classes the way the children's parents would do, but these results show that there is a problem here nevertheless. These are issues that are internal to the education system, relating to the way its constituent professionals conceive their work, and cannot be simply remedied by the formal or mandated introduction of restorative practices.

The notion of restorative justice originated in the justice system, and applying it to education must involve the recognition of the very different context of the school. Justice is about determining whether a crime has been committed and who is responsible. Education is about trying to produce young people who will become good citizens. Educationalists are not trained to judge whether young people have committed crimes. In some ways, the idea of restoration in schools is already very familiar to education professionals. The examples given have a quality of care about them that is not about judging whether a crime has been committed, but about how the young person(s) involved can best be brought back into the 'fold'. The parties to a conference in a school are most likely to be school administrators, family members, neighbours and classmates; these people will potentially see one another for substantial proportions of each day, into the future. Students are required by law to go to school from age 6 until they reach the age of 16 years. Parents are required to send their children to school, unless they go through a significant process to be excused. Families are therefore also often integral to resolving problems being experienced by pupils. More importantly, the purposes of education are very different from the purposes of justice, notwithstanding the latter's interest in rehabilitation. The context of justice is crime and punishment, where the context of education is development and learning. The starting point of the education system is that all children are there to be cared for and supported to grow and develop. I doubt that this is the primary stance of the legal system.

Schools are required by law to stand 'in loco parentis', and most teachers and administrators take this duty very seriously. A re-examination of this fundamental concept is long overdue. Such relinquishment of parental power may have been acceptable once, but it is doubtful whether all parents might reasonably be expected to share the values of the disciplinarians of the school in just the way that the concept appears to require. And this is the rub. Restorative practices lie across the boundaries between discipline and care. They call for a more 'authoritative' or democratic form of parenting on the part of the school, whereas most disciplinary systems are based on a more authoritarian, top-down form of power (Marshall and Marshall, 1997). With increasing diversity in our communities, we cannot presume homogeneity of either parenting styles or values, just as we do not all have the same way of showing that we care. What is clear is that the form of the duty of care must change as the child grows. How it should change is at issue.

Policy at the national level has acknowledged and attempted to address the problem of growing diversity, not just in our schools but in our society. In schools, at the same time as there are calls for clear boundaries and better discipline, there has been an almost opposite tendency: schools and classrooms are also required to be 'inclusive'. Teacher education programmes are required to invest student teachers with the skills to manage inclusive classrooms. 'Diversity', like equity, has almost become a buzz word. Disparity of outcomes must be addressed. This means, among other things, that classroom teachers and school administrators must not discriminate on grounds of culture, race or ability. Teacher education students are also taught that they should meet the needs of each student, and approach each student's learning needs starting from where the student is, rather than where they 'should' be by any particular measure. Nowadays classrooms can have up to 30 nationalities (and 30 languages) represented, and a teacher may be at the same time required to teach inclusively mainstreamed students with a disability. As school communities become more diverse, teachers and administrators have an extremely complex, possibly impossible, job to satisfy the great array of expectations laid on them.

Surprisingly, there are some schools that seem to be managing to achieve these aims. I have not researched this, but I would hypothesise that these are (probably smaller) schools that (in a benign sense) take ownership over their students and behave as though they all belong to the same family. Many primary school classrooms have this quality: I believe that fewer secondary schools do (with the possible exception of some area schools).

Our experience in Northland suggested that many of the smaller, often poorer schools, that see themselves as integral to their communities, also saw it as their responsibility not to suspend if possible, and to take back students who had been suspended. These schools protested at being listed in the Suspension Reduction Initiative as 'high-suspending' schools. The absolute numbers of suspensions said little about the fact that their students were always expected back, and they were often managed by the school during their period of suspension. This seemed to be particularly the case where there was a strong link between the school and the community. Often these were predominantly Māori communities. These same schools, and many others like them around the country, work to keep their children and young people in school, and to bring them back in, even after exclusion. They use suspensions much like an ordinary family might use 'time out'. These schools often treat all students, including miscreants, as 'their own', thus taking very seriously their duty of care. In fact, across the country, only a few schools exclude or expel without taking some responsibility for what then happens to these students. For students under the legal leaving age this follow up is required by law, but I am referring to the many generous and ongoing demonstrations of concern for the future of these students. This kind of care is not accounted for in the statistics.

As indicated above, there is currently a huge amount of interest in the introduction of restorative practices in schools. However, there is not a lot of reliable research yet available to demonstrate the long-term effectiveness of these practices, or the favoured conditions of their introduction – or even what, exactly, they are. Indeed, we would be hard pressed to decide what, out of a complex number of interweaving and often immeasurable and uncontrollable factors, to study, besides suspension figures.

In one of the schools where we delivered a workshop, for example, one dean kept a file of the 'small conversations' he held in one term. Of the nine files, only one student came to his notice a second time. He thought this was significant, and praised our 'circle' process (Restorative Practices Development Team, 2004). Whether it is down to the conversation process or not I have no idea, though I would like to think it is. Intuitively one might expect that more engaged students will show a higher rate of achievement, and there are some suggestions that this is borne out in practice (Bishop et al., 2007; Buckley and Maxwell, 2007). But whether restorative conferencing and restorative conversations have a bearing on student engagement, I do not know.

Rutter (1979) suggests that student performance often depends more on the culture of the school and whether or not it develops a climate of care. This is the model that most educators have been raised on, and what they currently already work for. I do believe that the achievement of academic goals is more likely to be enhanced by creating a constructive school climate where conflict is resolved in ways that build and enhance relationships. However, I would raise a note of caution, because the factors involved are extremely difficult to study, and for any positive response to a questionnaire there is often a contrary opinion and contrary evidence. For all we know, there may be other quite different factors influencing the growth in our society of resistance to schooling by what seems to be a growing number of students. Nevertheless, there are sufficient exciting stories to suggest that the introduction of restorative practices into schools is worth further investigation.

In many ways, schools are already communities of care, but there is a need for a re-examination of the notion of care that predominates. A community of care is not necessarily one where we have a 'natural' or even a learned empathy for others: a true community of care comes into its own when respect is maintained and there is disagreement and strangeness (Young, 1990). This is a very different version of the caring community from that promoted by Rutter all those years ago. Such a (post-modern) community understands (or might have to learn) that meanings are negotiated, and that this can take both time and patience. It understands too the importance of having in place processes for the working through of such disagreements. Where schools care for their students as if they are part of the communal family – including the miscreants, the misfits, and the resisters (of which every family has some) – they are already well on the way. People who strive for and maintain such schools already deserve our respect.

Education is one of the Pākehā imports that Māori and Pasifika families value: and it is compulsory for children and young people aged 6–16 in New Zealand. Thus, schools have a unique and powerful place in our civic life. Most of today's schools are complex communities, reflecting the make up of our society, and they are in a powerful position to influence the way forward, towards whatever is meant by a restorative society. The role of education in such a vision ought not to be confined to ensuring that more students achieve set goals within a fixed curriculum. Education can be a major vehicle for the ongoing development of New Zealand as both a peaceful and a respectful society. Such a lofty objective will not be achieved by 'behaviour management', suspensions and exclusions (though no doubt these must also go on). I am arguing for a concept of restorative society that is about peaceful relating among diversity, and not simply about how we 'do' our disciplinary functions. In such a society, a primary objective of schooling could be to develop an understanding of how to achieve legitimate goals within relationships of mediation in complex communities. Unravelling what that means in practice will take a while. My vision for schools is also my vision of a restorative society, and schools could have a central role in reaching for this objective. This would imply a review of the role of schools in our society, which in turn would entail a much broader conversation.

# 11

# Restorative Practices in Education: The Experiences of a Group of New Zealand Schools

*Sean Buckley*

## Introduction

In 2005, my colleague Gabrielle Maxwell and I examined the experiences of 15 New Zealand schools using restorative practices (Buckley and Maxwell, 2007). These schools differed in socioeconomic backgrounds, and all identified themselves as using restorative practices. While representing only a small group of the many schools in New Zealand, they provided us with the opportunity to study the experiences of a sample of restorative schools and add to the findings reported in chapter 10.

This short account of the project outlines how these schools described the values that underpinned their practice, the contexts in which restorative practices were used, the elements that were key to their operation, and the outcomes that were reported.

## Practice

We found that the motivation for designing and implementing a programme of restorative practices differed, depending on the needs of the school, its community and the concerns of its management. For most schools though, the primary motivation to adopt a restorative approach was a concern for students at risk of failure and exclusion, and the belief that existing methods of responding to these issues were not effective. These beliefs, therefore, provided the fundamental catalyst for change.

All schools involved shared similar concepts about what philosophical principles were key to running a restorative programme. These included trust, pride in one's school, tolerance, striving for achievement, responsibility and, most importantly, respect for oneself and others (Figure 11.1).

**Figure 11.1:** Shared case study values and beliefs

| |
|---|
| Participation of all school community members – family/whānau, members of the wider community, students and staff – is key. |
| Cultural diversity must be recognised and affirmed. |
| Student needs and the development of core skills must be a focus. |
| Clear expectations for all who are part of the school community are needed. |
| The approach towards learning and achievement must be inclusive and holistic. |
| Respect, rights, responsibility and honesty are core aspects of the school's philosophies. |

Source: Buckley and Maxwell, 2007.

Schools reported a wide variety of strategies that enabled the principles in Figure 11.1 to be transferred into restorative practice. All schools used variations of one or more of the following five restorative practice methods.

- The *restorative chat* is a one-on-one private conversation between staff and student where an issue is discussed using a series of questions based on a restorative approach that aims to explore the events, their consequences and how any harm could be repaired (that is, 'what happened?', 'what were you thinking at the time?', 'who do you think has been affected?', 'how could you have acted differently?' and 'what do you need to do to make things right?' (see Moxon, no date).[1]

- The *restorative classroom* is an open dialogue held within the classroom to discuss specific conflicts as they arise and how members of the class should approach potential conflict situations before they happen. Often a class will write down its agreed set of guiding principles and display these within the classroom. At any stage, the class can revisit these principles and make changes.

- The *restorative thinking room* is a room specifically set aside for students who have become involved in a conflict situation and who may need time away from peers in order to regain their composure. Time is spent in the restorative thinking room working through several restorative questions with a staff member and discussing the conflict and how to repair any harm caused.

---

[1] Some of these questions, for example those about the motivation of the offender, are not necessarily seen as essential by many restorative practitioners because of the extent to which they increase the sense of shame rather than encourage an emphasis on repair and reintegration.

- The *restorative mini conference* is held for more serious conflict situations. It includes the victim, the offender, a staff member and perhaps one other individual. The number of those in attendance is limited in order to make it easier for the conference to be quickly arranged and held.
- The full *restorative conference* is loosely based on the youth justice family group conference (see chapter 3). It may take several days or weeks to organise, because participants are likely to include, though are not limited to, victims, offenders, staff, family/whānau, officials and other support personnel. Conferences are used for the most serious of conflict issues and can take several hours. (See chapter 10 for a more detailed outline of typical conference outcomes.)

Each school agreed that the overall goals for each of these methods was to:

- facilitate a safe environment for communication between those involved in a conflict;
- achieve consensus on how any wrongs committed might be made right in order to repair damaged relationships; and
- reintegrate all those involved back into the school community without stigmatising labels such as 'victim' or 'offender' being attached to the parties.

Other strategies were also used to achieve these goals; for example, educational support services such as counsellors, resource teachers for learning and behaviour, social workers and psychologists, peer support groups, and other community and state sector services as appropriate. It should also be noted that all schools sought to achieve non-exclusionary behaviour management strategies (Figure 11.2) (Buckley and Maxwell, 2007).

**Figure 11.2:** Shared case study elements

| |
|---|
| All action pinned to a belief in trust, respect and reciprocity. |
| The use of restorative communication and language, normally manifest in a conference process. |
| A critical mass of staff who use and are committed to restorative practices. |
| Networked and specialised support systems. |
| A commitment to non-exclusionary behaviour management strategies and to finding re-integrative solutions. |
| The involvement of community and particularly families/whānau at all levels. |

Source: Buckley and Maxwell, 2007.

The time spent examining these schools revealed that they were all achieving similar outcomes. These included better student engagement as indicated by less truancy and absenteeism; greater achievement in all areas of school life (sporting, cultural and academic); safer, more inclusive and tolerant school climates; greater community, family and caregiver participation in school activities; and fewer suspensions, expulsions and exclusions (Figure 11.3).

**Figure 11.3:** Shared case study benchmarks

| |
|---|
| Fewer expulsions, exclusions and suspensions. |
| Less absenteeism and increased retention and reintegration. |
| Higher educational achievement levels. |
| Improved whole school–community relationships. |
| Increasingly positive Education Review Office reports. |

Source: Buckley and Maxwell, 2007.

## Policy issues

The schools we studied found that a complete 'paradigm' shift needed to occur so restorative practices could be seen as a *whole school management system* (Buckley and Maxwell, 2007). However, Drewery, in chapter 10, highlights a key barrier to achieving this outcome, which was also apparent in our study. This is the inability to implement restorative practices as a stand-alone process for *whole school* change and to sustain that paradigm shift.

Currently, the schools that want to implement full restorative programmes are often incapable of doing so because of limitations related to funding and access to numbers of staff trained in restorative practices. In the Buckley and Maxwell (2007) study, most of the participating schools had only one or two individuals properly trained in restorative practices, only partial 'buy-in' from staff or community, no space for facilities such as 'restorative thinking rooms', no or limited finances to maintain or expand training, and not enough staff to cover for others who do attend training.

This has meant 'restorative' schools have been forced to operate between management paradigms, either reverting to one based on exclusionary processes or mixing this with a restorative process when only limited support exists for restorative options. Thus, schools have often been unable to fully implement a restorative approach as a total philosophy for the whole school. Despite their preference not to, at the time of writing, each of the 15 restorative schools that participated in the Buckley and Maxwell (2007) study continued to use stand-downs and other exclusionary measures, although predominantly on far fewer occasions than in the past.

Therefore, two essential changes are needed to effectively cement the restorative practices paradigm as a viable and effective option for schools in New Zealand schools. The first and most important change is in the way educationalists in schools view the use of exclusionary measures. While most schools never need to resort to exclusionary measures, for some it has become common practice for responding to difficult situations (as noted in chapter 10). Even legislative change will not likely be able to change this, as Fleming (1999) notes those who "currently find it more convenient to suspend for long periods or expel are likely to continue to do so".

There will inevitably be situations that warrant the exclusion of a student from a school environment. Some students may even be better off outside of school and in, for example, an apprenticeship scheme. However, it is important to recognise the dangers associated with exclusion, particularly for those students already failing. Not only is exclusion in direct conflict with the objectives of the United Nations Convention on the Rights of the Child 1989, the Education Act 1989, the Children, Young Persons, and Their Families Act 1989, and the Ministry of Education's statement of intent for 2006–2011 (Ministry of Education, 2006a), but research (Skiba and Peterson, 1999; Skiba et al., 2003) indicates that exclusion does not necessarily make a school safer or more educationally productive, rather an excluded student is more likely to experience poor future life outcomes (see also NAACP, no date).

The second change that is necessary to enable the growth of restorative practice is increased support for the programmes and strategies that provide an alternative to exclusionary measures. In part, this means greater funding for restorative programmes. Direct funding is needed for the training of staff and the employment of additional staff who can respond quickly to problems, arrange conferences, mentor students, support parents and follow up on absentees. In addition, schools need better access to effective community non-government organisations and state services that can meet other student and family needs. Such funding and service support would also enable schools to provide a range of restorative tools (such as those earlier discussed) and the training of more staff in restorative practices, as well as enabling them to better engage extra services that would respond to the wider needs of students and families.

Chapter 10 highlights one other issue that is critical to our thinking about the relationship between restorative justice and restorative practices. This is the perception that because restorative justice has been embedded within our criminal justice system, it is somehow fundamentally linked to judgment and punishment, so cannot be transferred to the educational sector. This suggests conferences are different in the two sectors because the emphasis is on crime in the justice sector and on caring in the educational sector.

I have a different perception of the relationship between the two sectors. In both education and justice there are often wrongs to be righted. However, in both sectors it is also necessary to respond constructively in ways that allow the reintegration of young people and the restoration of the social group. Inevitably, the differences in the two contexts result in different ways of working. But, ultimately, in both sectors the answers lie in moving away from judgement and punishment when there are breaches of the social order. As in education, the goal of the justice system is to build a safe and caring society. Therefore, in both sectors the answers fundamentally lie in finding out "how the young person(s) involved can best be brought back into the 'fold'" (chapter 10, p 210). In both sectors the success of the restorative conference lies in responding to needs through constructive and non-punitive repair and the reintegration of all those involved.

## Conclusion

The past decade has seen restorative justice approaches spread into a wide variety of sectors. Underpinning this has been legislation such as the Children, Young Persons, and Their Families Act 1989, which has influenced practice in those sectors directly affected such as child welfare, courts and police. Perhaps even more importantly, is that with the spread of restorative justice within New Zealand has come an effective alternative tool for resolving some of our more challenging social troubles.

Educationalists in particular have shown a growing interest in restorative concepts. Above all else it is this interest that will bring New Zealand closer to a society built on restorative values, because it is the young people of today who will shape the society of tomorrow. Social harmony is core to restorative practices, and if harmony is what we want for the society of future generations then restorative practices offer schools a powerful tool for achieving this. As others such as Varnham (2005, p. 2) have noted, this is because, "It is arguable that the model presented by a school provides a crucial template for the value system which students will live by for the rest of their lives". If such an argument stands, then the outcomes achieved by New Zealand's restorative schools should be a comforting but clear sign to those directing educational policy today.

# 12

# Negotiating History: Crown Apologies in Historical Treaty of Waitangi Settlements

*Maureen Hickey\**

## Introduction

> The settlement of the grievances of an indigenous people arising from colonisation is not an easy task. Yet to ignore valid grievances is not only unjust but leaves unreconciled the relationship between the descendants of the settlers and the tangata whenua. Race relations in such a climate will always be fragile.[1]

At an international historical conference in Sydney in 2005 several historians who had been involved in, or studied, reparation cases for historical injustices took part in a roundtable discussion entitled 'Injustice, memory and politics: cases of restitutions'. Their experience spanned reparation movements for the Holocaust, Japanese and German military sexual slavery, African American slavery, communism and more recent wars in several countries.

One common theme of the cases discussed was that where reparation had been paid or apologies delivered there was usually little direct discussion between the parties. As a government official involved in the New Zealand historical Treaty of Waitangi settlement process, I was interested in whether the panel considered notions of reconciliation between the aggrieved and offending parties could be a factor in, or an aim of, the provision of redress or reparation for historical grievances.

I broadly described the New Zealand process, whereby claimant groups and representatives of the government directly negotiate with each other, including attempting to write a joint account of the historical injustices. The panel's reaction was mixed. The concept of direct negotiations between the offending and aggrieved parties and of attempting to achieve some level of reconciliation between those parties was seen by many to be inappropriate and possibly even

---

\* An earlier version of this chapter was published entitled 'Negotiating history: Crown apologies in New Zealand's historical Treaty of Waitangi settlements' (Hickey, 2006).
1 Rt Hon Sir Douglas Graham, Minister in Charge of Treaty of Waitangi Negotiations (in Office of Treaty Settlements, 1999, p. 3).

## Restorative Justice and Practices in New Zealand

asking too much of a reparation process. Some could not countenance the idea of Māori and the Crown, the victim and the offender, sitting down together to negotiate redress for historical injustices.

This reaction illustrated that there are many models for redressing historical injustices. One model is the 'settlement' of claims, where fiscal redress is provided by the offender without a direct admission of responsibility or liability. Another model is what is often called 'reparation'; generally involving an apology from the offender as well as some level of physical redress. A 'restitution' approach carries a different implication. It suggests that the position of the claimant has been restored to what it was before the historical injustice occurred or that what was physically taken from them has been fully restored. Each of these may be an appropriate response to the historical injustices and the needs or demands of those who experienced them (Brooks, 1999a, pp. 8 and 9).

This chapter argues (by looking at both the broad negotiation framework and the apology redress component of settlement negotiations) that although the resolution of historical Treaty grievances in New Zealand is commonly termed 'settlement', the established settlement framework and negotiation process have strong elements of a restorative justice approach. The result is a 'reparation' model that aims to achieve some level of reconciliation between the Crown and Māori, and the descendants of settlers and tangata whenua. Reconciliation, and the building of a strong, ongoing relationship between the Crown and Māori, has been a key driver for New Zealand governments in setting up and continuing the historical Treaty settlement processes.

## Development of Treaty of Waitangi settlement framework

The framework for negotiating and settling the historical grievances of Māori in New Zealand was developed after a combination of protest, litigation and negotiation in the 1970s–1990s saw successive governments accept the need to resolve historical Māori grievances and improve statutory protection of Māori land.[2] Following the Waitangi Tribunal's jurisdiction being changed in 1985 to

---

2   The Waitangi Tribunal was later given the power, under particular circumstances, to order the Crown to 'resume' certain lands for use in a Treaty settlement. The two classes of land the tribunal can order the Crown to use in Treaty settlements are Crown forest land that is subject to a Crown-forestry licence and 'memorialised lands'. The latter are lands that are owned or formerly owned by a state-owned enterprise or a tertiary institution or were former New Zealand Railways lands, which have a statutory memorial or formal notation on their title that the tribunal has the power to order the

allow it to inquire into and report on historical Treaty grievances, the National government was elected in 1990 on a manifesto that included a pledge to settle the major historical Treaty claims (Graham, 1997, p. 50; Office of Treaty Settlements, 2002, p. 19). The rationale was both pragmatic and idealistic: the desire of most New Zealanders to enjoy positive race relations was unlikely to happen if the grievances of the past still blighted the relationship between the Crown and Māori (Office of Treaty Settlements, 1994, p. 5). Sir Douglas Graham, the Minister in Charge of Treaty of Waitangi Negotiations, later argued that "[t]he simple fact is that we have to deal with these grievances. Can any country allow 16% of its population to continue to feel deeply aggrieved about serious injustices?" (Graham, 1997, p. 89).

The government formally started negotiations with the Ngāi Tahu and Waikato–Tainui tribes in the early 1990s while still considering its approach to the resolution of Māori grievances (Graham, 1997, p. 51). It was aware that previous governments' ad hoc attempts to settle Māori claims from the 1940s onwards had been unsuccessful "because there was little understanding of the totality of the issues". The government, therefore, resolved to try to approach Treaty claims in a "rational, cohesive and constructive way" (Office of Treaty Settlements, 1994, p. 7). This culminated in the release for public consultation in 1994 of detailed Crown proposals for the settlement of Treaty claims, which outlined key principles to guide future settlements, including that they would have to be fair, sustainable and remove the sense of grievance felt by Māori (Office of Treaty Settlements, 1994, p. 7).

Māori were intensely critical of these proposals and universally rejected them at regional consultation hui (meetings).[3] Despite this, many tribal leaders also acknowledged and welcomed the Crown's resolve to attempt to settle the claims and sought to continue discussions with the government. The Crown proposals were modified as a result of the consultation process with Māori and others, and have subsequently provided the broad framework and process for 20 settlements, which have generally included a Crown apology and both

---

Crown to take back the property for use in a Treaty settlement, under certain circumstances, even if that land has since been transferred to a third party (Office of Treaty Settlements, 2002, pp. 19–21 and 154–156).

3  More than 100 pre-consultation hui were also held throughout the country in order to inform Māori communities of the detail of the Crown's proposals. Thirteen regional hui were planned to give Māori an opportunity to respond to the formal presentation of the proposals by ministers of the Crown, but two were cancelled at the behest of local Māori (Office of Treaty Settlements, 1995, p. 2).

commercial and cultural redress.[4] Since 2000, the Crown has also been guided by six negotiating principles: good faith, restoration of the relationship, just redress, fairness between claims, transparency, and that Treaty settlements should be government-negotiated) (Office of Treaty Settlements, 2002, p. 30.). While a broad framework is necessary to ensure that the Crown is able to maintain fairness across its dealings with multiple claimant groups, the Crown also has to retain the capacity to be innovative and react to the different grievances and interests of each claimant group as they work through the settlement process at different times.

## Restorative justice elements of Treaty settlement process

The settlement process and framework has several elements that draw on restorative justice principles or approaches. The first is that the Crown has a strong preference for grievances to be settled through negotiation rather than through arbitration by the court (although the latter is an option in some situations that Māori can pursue). This means that the Crown is committed to getting to a mutually agreed outcome with the claimant group. The process of working through and resolving well-founded claims can be difficult and uncomfortable for both the Crown and the claimant group but they are the only two parties who can, by agreement, achieve the settlement of historical claims.

The Crown also generally prefers to take an interest-based approach to the negotiation of settlement packages, particularly the commercial and cultural redress. Commercial and cultural redress is intended to address the specific effects of, or issues that have arisen out of, historical grievances. The Crown recognises, through commercial redress for instance, that generations of Māori have suffered financial and other losses as a result of Crown breaches of the Treaty. Financial and commercial redress takes into account the fiscal and economic constraints of the country while aiming to be sufficient to redress the claimant group's sense of grievance. The nature and amount of redress the Crown offers in each settlement package largely depends on the severity of the

---

4   The Crown has concluded settlements with Ngāti Whakaue, Ngāti Rangiteaorere, Waikato–Tainui (in relation to their raupatu land claims), Ngāi Tahu, Ngāti Tūrangitukua, Pouakani, Te Uri o Hau, Ngāti Ruanui, Ngāti Tama, Ngāti Awa and ancillary claimants, Ngāti Tūwharetoa (Bay of Plenty), Ngaa Rauru Kiitahi, Te Arawa (over their lakes claims), Ngāti Mutunga (Taranaki), Te Roroa, and a grouping of Te Arawa iwi and hapū (over their non-lake claims). It has also negotiated settlements over Waimakuku, Rotomā, Waitomo, Hauai and Te Maunga lands.

Crown's breaches of the Treaty, the amount of land lost and the size of the current group that holds the grievance.[5] Cultural redress is provided to recognise the claimant group's spiritual, cultural, historical or traditional associations with the natural environment. It aims to address historical grievances about the loss of ownership or guardianship of sites of spiritual and cultural significance, loss of access to traditional foods or resources, and the exclusion of the claimant group from decision making regarding important sites or resources. Negotiations on cultural redress have dealt with wāhi tapu (sacred places) and other sites of significance, including mountains; rivers and lakes; wetlands, lagoons, indigenous forests and tussock lands; customary freshwater and marine fisheries; geothermal and mineral resources; plant and animal species; moveable taonga (artefacts) and traditional place names.

Taking an interest-based approach to cultural redress means that the negotiations explore the desires, concerns and values that are important to each party. This enables the parties to mutually design redress that meets the interests and aspirations of the claimant group and addresses any constraints on the Crown. Such an approach involves a high level of participation and discussion and ensures that the aggrieved party receives redress that is meaningful to it (Office of Treaty Settlements, 2002, p. 97). Claimant groups have negotiated cultural redress packages that include the return of land, greater participation in the management of culturally important areas or resources, and statutory acknowledgements of their historical, spiritual and traditional associations with an area (aimed at enhancing the group's ability to participate in certain consent processes) (Office of Treaty Settlements, 2002, p. 84).[6]

One of the key restorative justice elements of the Treaty settlement process is that Māori have the opportunity to publicly tell their story and air their grievances through the Waitangi Tribunal process, before they begin negotiating the resolution of those grievances with the Crown. If that is not the approach a claimant group wants to take, it also has the option of proceeding to direct

---

5   Settlements have included financial redress totalling $720 million, which is usually taken in a mix of cash and Crown assets such as property. Commercial properties included in settlements have included Crown exotic forest land, police stations, schools and properties within the Office of Treaty Settlements landbank (which holds properties, at the request of claimant groups, that have been declared surplus to requirements by government departments). Claimant groups also sometimes negotiate a right of first refusal over surplus Crown property for a certain period. See Office of Treaty Settlements (2002, pp. 87–95).

6   For a full outline of cultural redress, see Office of Treaty Settlements (2002, pp. 96–144).

negotiations over its historical grievances with the Crown. Throughout the negotiation process it also has the opportunity to discuss its grievances with the representatives of the Crown, including ministers. The Crown has also made a commitment to take responsibility for its breaches of the Treaty by providing commercial and cultural redress, and by explicitly acknowledging its breaches of the Treaty.

## Apology redress

### *Development and purpose of the apology*

Almost all settlements have included some form of Crown apology. While it was clear from the start that the Crown would have to acknowledge the legitimacy of Māori grievances, the idea of the Crown formally proffering an apology came after it accepted that redress was due for historical grievances. According to Sir Douglas Graham, the negotiations between Waikato–Tainui and the Crown taught the government that reconciliation required something more intangible than monetary or physical redress. It was suggested that the Crown should "formally acknowledge the wrong done and tender a full apology" as only then would it be possible to put the events of the past in "their proper place – not forgotten but accepted" (Graham 1997, p. 74).[7] As a result, the Crown proposed to explicitly acknowledge historical injustices in future settlements.

The apology is an essential part of the settlement process for the Crown because it is only through taking explicit responsibility for its past actions, which have breached the Treaty of Waitangi that the Crown can begin to restore its honour. An insincere apology would lack good faith and would not contribute to a lasting reconciliation so the Crown has to carefully consider whether it agrees with claimant arguments that particular Crown actions, or its failure to act, were wrong or unjust in Treaty terms. As part of that process, the Crown will consider the implications of any apology it makes. The apology can be considered to set standards for the future behaviour of the Crown. Sir Douglas Graham noted of the Crown's decision to apologise to Waikato–Tainui that "there needed to be an understanding that in the future the relationship between Waikato and the Crown would be as envisaged by the Treaty – one of cooperation and good faith" (Graham, 1997, p. 74). The apology also serves a secondary, but important, function of explaining to the public why the

---

[7] The Waikato–Tainui Deed of Settlement was signed in May 1995.

settlement is due. This is necessary both for maintaining public confidence that the settlement process is addressing legitimate historical grievances and for increasing public understanding of the particular historical actions of the Crown that have impacted on the claimant group.

The Crown apology can be powerful and highly symbolic redress for claimant groups. The Ngāi Tahu negotiators placed importance on the Crown's apology confirming the validity of the Ngāi Tahu claims, which had been borne by seven generations. They considered it part of a healing process, which would (Te Rūnanga o Ngāi Tahu, no date):

> go a long way with our elders to atone for the past. It does not mean we forget the past, but it gives the Crown the opportunity to make amends, and for Ngāi Tahu and the Crown to move on with the healing process. It is also something that could only have been obtained through a negotiated settlement. No legal process could bring about such opportunity for reconciliation. To some Ngāi Tahu this is the most important part of the settlement.

These sentiments have been echoed by Robert Joseph, who has written that the importance of the Crown's apology to Waikato–Tainui could not be overstated because it overcame the political and legal denial that had existed about their grievances. It was seen as an opportunity for both parties to move on with the healing process in a new relationship (Joseph, 2001). Pat Heremaia, chief negotiator for the Ngāti Ruanui claims, has also remarked that, "without the apology, the settlement would have been incomplete" (Wethey, 2002, p. 62).

## Negotiating the apology

The process used to develop the apology redress can contribute to the resonance it has with the claimant group. The form of the apology redress has developed over time, but generally includes some form of historical account in which the Crown and the claimant group aim to agree text that outlines the history of their interaction, focusing on historical events that have caused grievance. This broadly provides the context for, and is followed by, a statement of the Crown's acknowledgments of its Treaty breaches and an apology from the Crown to the claimant group. The Crown's acknowledgments and apology are, in the final stages of the settlement process, recorded in the settlement legislation passed by parliament. The historical account (or an abridged form of it) may be included as a preamble to the settlement legislation. Given that the apology becomes a permanent record in legislation, the content and language can be extensively negotiated. Layne Harvey, a member of the Ngāti Awa negotiation team, has commented that "claimants do not want the Crown's view of every claim detail to prevail in the deed and legislation and negotiations over even the smallest word can become terse and hard fought" (Harvey, 2005, p. 109).

Apology theorist Aaron Lazare has argued that some of the most successful apologies are the result of complex negotiations over several variables between the aggrieved and the offender (Lazare, 2004, p. 43). It is only through such discussions the offender can fully understand both the meaning of the grievance but also what is needed from the apology process. In Treaty settlements the apology negotiations give the claimant group and the Crown the opportunity to talk together about both the grievances and claimant group's expectations of the apology (this may include the form of the apology, what it will address, and how and when the claimant group wants it to be delivered). The two Treaty partners talking directly to each other and discussing their perceptions and interpretations of the history that has caused grievance lays the groundwork for reconciliation and a more positive future relationship. It also enables the Crown to apologise to the claimant group in a way that is meaningful to the group.

The process of discussing the grievances with Crown representatives is usually welcomed by claimant negotiators, but it can also be challenging for both parties. The offering of an apology is a clear statement that the Crown, in providing redress for past grievances, is seeking not just a legal settlement of the claims but also the more morally charged notion of some form of reconciliation between the parties. Claimant groups enter the settlement process because they want to settle the grievances of the past but may have some ambivalence about the notion of reconciliation. They may question the sincerity of the Crown's intentions and whether the settlement negotiations and their outcome will be sufficient to address the sense of grievance and enable the beginning of a new relationship. This can be particularly evident at the start of negotiations when the past relationship between the parties may mean that trust levels are not high or where the Crown has not agreed with all of the Treaty breach allegations made by the claimant group. In such cases, the negotiations present an opportunity for the parties to discuss those issues, listen to each other's perspectives and try to find some resolution.

Every apology negotiation is unique. They tend to be shaped by the grievances of the claimant group, the research base for their claims, the extent to which there is agreement between the Crown and the claimant group's views of the ways in which the Crown breached the Treaty, and the importance the claimant group places on the apology redress. In most cases, the parties establish an apology working group. The Crown is usually represented by officials with historical, policy and legal skills. Claimant group negotiation teams vary, but are usually led by the mandated claimant negotiators. They may also draw on the expertise of kaumātua (elders), legal advisers, people within their claimant community who have particular knowledge of the grievances, and people who were involved in the research for the claim, including professional historians. The negotiators may also have drafts reviewed by appropriate people from within the claimant group from time to time. Negotiations are usually face to face, either in the claimant group's rohe (area) or in Wellington, and can take many months of intensive meetings.

### *Historical account*

Apology negotiations often begin with the parties discussing the drafting of the historical account, because the process of discussing the history and agreeing the text of the historical account will inform the eventual discussion of Treaty breaches and the Crown's apology. On the Crown's side, the expectation is that the historical account will reflect available historical evidence, so that it can withstand external scrutiny. There is also, however, an expectation that different parties (even different claimant groups who experienced similar Crown actions) may have different interpretations of that evidence depending on their own experiences. There is, therefore, also an understanding that both parties will present alternative evidence or interpretations on particular aspects of the claim during negotiations. The overall aim is to gain agreement on an historical account to be placed in the Deed of Settlement. The Crown also generally advocates for the language used in the historical account to be reasonably neutral and non-emotive and for any judgement of the events outlined in the account to be reserved for the section detailing the Crown's acknowledgements of Treaty breach, as this allows the reader to formulate their own assessment of the historical events and may facilitate public trust in the document.

Claimant expectations differ, but are generally that the historical account will reflect the claimant's grievances. The detailed negotiations will usually start with both parties agreeing on the issues that will be considered for inclusion in the historical account, whether the account will be broad and high level or more detailed, and some assessment of whether there is sufficient research to inform the discussions. If the Waitangi Tribunal has issued a report on the claimant group's historical claims it will form the basis of the negotiations, as will research reports produced by the claimant group and the Crown for tribunal or settlement negotiation purposes and a range of secondary literature and primary sources. The parties also agree on which of the parties will produce a first draft and what it should cover. Both parties have to agree to the final text, so once a draft has been started the parties will meet regularly to consider the draft and negotiate agreed text.

The historical accounts developed by the Crown and claimant groups in Treaty settlement negotiations are shaped by their purpose. The accounts agreed have been short summary documents (usually about 3–20 pages) shaped on a narrative of what happened. The content, the way it is expressed and what matters are given emphasis reflect the purpose of informing an apology. Apology theorists have discussed how attempts by those who caused offence to explain the reasons for their actions can be seen by the aggrieved as trying to mitigate the impact of their actions (Lazare, 2004, pp. 120–127). While both the Crown and claimant groups usually agree that it is important to include relevant context and outline the complexities of Crown and Māori actions, there can be a perception that such context or explanation for events may mitigate the overall grievance. Conversely, the omission of context can draw criticism that the historical account does not fully reflect the complexities of the situation.[8]

The process of negotiating text that is considered by both parties to fairly recount the history and accurately address the grievances has some particular complexities. For a start, the parties are writing an historical account in a distinctive emotional, cultural, political and legal context. It will usually be the first time that the claimant group has had representatives of the Crown listen to it talk about the group's grievances and the impact on its people of past Crown actions in a face-to-face situation where the aim of both parties is to work out a mutually agreeable way of settling the grievances (Wethey, 2002, p. 56 and chapter 10). Claimant negotiators also carry the responsibility of ensuring the grievances of their ancestors and their people are appropriately represented. They will also usually have personal experience of the grievances (because 'historical' claims are defined as claims that arise out of Crown acts or omissions before 21 September 1992) or the impact of the grievances they are bringing to the table. There is more personal attachment to the history and to the results of the discussion than is the case in academic or public history writing. There are also, inevitably, methodological issues to be navigated. The desire to reflect the historical intentions of all the parties and the context for their actions (as far as can be deduced from the available evidence) can sometimes come into

---

8  For example, historian Bill Oliver has criticised the historical preamble to the Waikato Raupatu Claims Settlement Act 1995 for not providing enough context on the actions of Waikato–Tainui before the war that led to the raupatu (Oliver, 1993, p. 15). In a minority opinion to the Waitangi Tribunal's report on the Kaipara claims, tribunal member Michael Bassett argued that the Crown acknowledgements in the Te Uri o Hau settlement were sweeping and appeared to exclude Māori from any responsibility for their ultimate landlessness (Waitangi Tribunal, 2006, pp. 359–362).

tension with the often 'presentist' lens through which both parties are assessing and judging that past, with the aim of resolving past grievances.[9]

The number of people contributing to and reviewing the drafts means it is history writing by committee and, moreover, by negotiation towards an agreed outcome. Those negotiations inevitably mean that both parties learn more about the other's perspectives. Both parties to the negotiations will also have particular issues to manage that may affect the events included in the historical account or the wording chosen. Claimant negotiators, for example, may have to consider whether all the people they represent will be able to see their experience in the historical account or in the settlement more broadly, and they may have to manage sensitivities about the naming of particular hapū or chiefs or individuals. They also have to ensure that the historical account reflects the issues that really resonate with their people. The Crown may have to consider issues such as the naming of individual Crown officials and whether the Crown is taking a broadly consistent approach to similar issues across settlements.

The negotiations are also informed by the cultural perspectives each party brings to the table, including sometimes differing interpretations of the meaning of the same events. Both parties will also have to grapple with the usual issues of the uses, limitations and meanings of historical evidence. There are often questions about the extent to which the documentary evidence, whether written by Crown officials, settlers or Māori, fully reflects the motives and understandings of the claimant group's ancestors. It can also be difficult to reconcile oral tradition and written sources, even sources written by Māori. The parties may have to assess and try to agree what weight should be placed on different types of evidence and what statements can be made when the grievances are significant but the available evidence is scanty, ambiguous or heavily debated. In some cases, information may only be within the realm of the claimant group's knowledge and the drafting will reflect that by attributing the statements to them.

While the aim of the negotiations is to get to an agreed historical account to be included in the Deed of Settlement, it is common for specific Crown or iwi (tribe) perspectives on the history to be reflected in the text. Claimant groups have also sought to record their feelings about the impact of the Crown's actions on them in their historical account. Ngāti Ruanui and Ngāti Mutunga, for example, have negotiated the inclusion of waiata (songs) in their historical

---

9 These tensions, often generated by the mix of legal, political and historical imperatives in the settlement process, have been well canvassed in relation to the role of historians in the Waitangi Tribunal process. See, for example, Ward (2001) and O'Regan (2001).

account that record the feelings of their people about various events in their history. Ngāti Tuwharetoa (Bay of Plenty) have included statements in their historical account noting the impact of Crown actions on their connection to the land.

### *Crown acknowledgements of Treaty breach*

The Crown's breach acknowledgements are where it makes an explicit judgement on the past. The assessment of Treaty breach involves a mix of legal, historical and political judgement. While the Crown may have made breach acknowledgements to a claimant group during Waitangi Tribunal hearings or at the start of the negotiations, the wording of the breach acknowledgements included in a claimant group's Deed of Settlement is usually developed after substantive discussion on the historical account has occurred. Because they are the Crown's acknowledgements the Crown leads the drafting process, but the draft acknowledgements are generally discussed extensively with the claimant group in negotiations. The Crown breaches acknowledged include breaches relating to war, the confiscation of land, human rights breaches, including the execution of prisoners without trial in times of war, the impact of the native land laws, and the inadequate protection of land Māori wished to retain. In some cases, the Crown has acknowledged the sense of grievance that claimant groups have about Crown actions that the Crown does not consider breached the Treaty.

Claimant negotiators usually want the Crown to formally recognise, and record in the acknowledgements, the ongoing impacts of its actions for their people. The Crown has, for example, explicitly acknowledged to Ngāti Tūwharetoa (Bay of Plenty) that its confiscation of their land:

> had a damaging effect on the welfare, economy, and development of Ngati Tuwharetoa (Bay of Plenty), deprived the iwi of access to its traditional natural resources and wahi tapu, and contributed significantly to the subsequent dislocation and fragmentation of the iwi.[10]

There is often also a desire for the Crown to recognise that wider New Zealand society has benefited from some of its actions that have caused grievance to Māori. The Crown acknowledged in the Ngāti Awa settlement that the land iwi had lost through Crown confiscation and other means had:

---

10  Ngati Tuwharetoa (Bay of Plenty) Claims Settlement Act 2005, section 8(2)(b).

made a significant contribution to the wealth and development of the nation, whilst Ngati Awa has been alienated from and deprived of the benefits of those land and resources.[11]

## *Crown apology*

The text of the actual apology is drafted by the Crown and presented to the claimant group for comment. The Crown tries to apologise to the claimant group in a way that will be meaningful for the group. In some cases, this has meant the Crown has recognised the past and the ongoing impact of its breaches of the Treaty by apologising to the claimant community today, to their ancestors and to their descendants. The apology may use language that has particular meaning for the claimant group and reflects the Crown understanding of the group's grievance. For example, in the Ngāi Tahu settlement, the Crown stated that its failure to act reasonably and in the utmost good faith towards the iwi was "referred to in the Ngai Tahu saying 'Te Hapa o Niu Tireni!' ('The unfulfilled promise of New Zealand')".[12]

Claimant groups also commonly make representations about the most appropriate way for the Crown to deliver the apology. Some consider its inclusion in the Deed of Settlement and legislation is sufficient. Other claimant groups, like Te Uri o Hau, have requested that once legislation has been passed and implementation of the settlement is under way, representatives of the Crown deliver the apology directly to the claimant community.

To accept that its past actions have been wrong necessarily places the Crown in a morally humble position. As the offending party the Crown can only extend the apology and express that it is, with the settlement, seeking to atone for past wrongs and begin a process of healing. Reconciliation is a process that involves both parties and the response to the Crown's offer of an apology differs between groups according to their experiences. Willingness to settle the grievances will also depend on the extent to which the total settlement package, including commercial and cultural redress, meets the claimant group's interests.

There is, however, evidence that the Crown's acknowledgement of and apology for past actions that were unjust may assist in making Treaty settlements a reconciliatory process. In March 2003, representatives of the eastern Bay of Plenty tribe Ngāti Awa and the Crown met at Parliament Buildings in Wellington to sign their Deed of Settlement. It was the completion of a long journey. Ngāti Awa had actively sought redress for their grievances

---

11 Ngati Awa Claims Settlement Act 2005, section 8(8)(a).
12 Ngai Tahu Claims Settlement Act 1998, section 6.

against the Crown, including the confiscation of approximately 245,000 acres (about 99,000 hectares) of their land, since 1866. Professor Hirini Moko Mead, the chief negotiator for Ngāti Awa, spoke to the gathering, reminding them that the Deed of Settlement outlined a number of the acknowledgements that the Crown had made about its confiscation of Ngāti Awa land. He stated (Mead, 2003, p. 9):

> In a final statement the Deed adds: *"the Crown seeks to atone for these wrongs and begin the process of healing and looks forward to building a relationship of mutual trust and co-operation with Ngati Awa"*.
>
> In the spirit of these final statements of apology Ngati Awa acccpts the Crown's apology and on our part say that we forgive the Crown for what it did to us and we, too, want to begin the process of healing and we look forward to building a relationship of mutual trust, respect and co-operation. We will hold the Crown to that promise.

# 13

# Saying Sorry Effectively: Government Apologies for Historical Wrongs

*Nicola White**

## Introduction

Picture a common domestic scene. Two young children are arguing, descending into shouting and tears. A parent – swooping in to arbitrate – notes one child at fault and invites the other to say sorry. The offender mumbles, "Sorry", with a supercilious rolling of the eyes and toss of the head. The parent's next line is, of course, "Say it again, and say it like you mean it".

In the family example, the importance of 'meaning it' is obviously that the incident would otherwise remain un-repaired: neither recipient nor giver would believe that anything 'real' had taken place, but simply a *formality* to satisfy others. The underlying issue would probably re-emerge at the first opportunity and the behaviour would continue. At this simple level we all know the power – and connection – of someone meeting your gaze and saying sorry without artifice or qualification. That acknowledgement and sincerity is the key to being able to let go of the grievance, rather than brooding and (in the case of young siblings at least) planning retribution. In other words, apologies work to settle grievances when they are meant, and when they are received and accepted.

The core question tackled by this paper is how the impersonal apparatus of the state can apologise effectively – in short, how does the government of New Zealand say sorry 'like it means it' so that 'victims' will accept the apology? The perspective here is primarily practical, focusing on examples that took place between 2000 and 2005. For reasons of space, only limited attention is given to important and closely related questions, including in what circumstances

---

\* This chapter is based on a paper I initially gave when I was Senior Research Fellow at the Institute of Policy Studies, School of Government, Victoria University of Wellington (2004–06). As a public servant between 1993 and 2004, I was involved, to varying degrees, with the processes discussed in this chapter. The chapter, therefore, records what took place, including commentary from others on the merits of each process, but does not attempt a detailed analysis or critique of any of these initiatives. Naturally, the views are my own and do not reflect any formal position of any agency of government, including my current employer, the Office of the Auditor-General.

apologising is appropriate in the first place, and the relationship of the Labour-led government's apparent restorative agenda to deeper constitutional questions about the citizen–state relationship. The detail of these processes nevertheless suggests important lessons in terms of effectiveness and risks, and briefly situates those lessons in some of the literature on the topic of state-based reconciliation processes and restorative justice theory.

The most obvious reconciliation processes in New Zealand, in which apologies play a very significant role, concern the settlement of historical breaches of the Treaty of Waitangi. These processes began in the 1990s by a National government and have continued under the Labour-led governments since 1999. They are now accepted by all political parties in the New Zealand parliament, with the main debate now being about what can be done to speed the processes up, so that the 'apology and redress' period can end.[1] The Treaty processes have already been described in the previous chapter, their importance, however, is hard to exaggerate. The gradual acceptance of Treaty of Waitangi settlements over the past 20 years almost certainly paved the way for the reconciliation initiatives that followed.

The specific processes discussed here are the:
- apology to the descendants of early Chinese settlers in New Zealand for past discrimination;
- apology to Samoa for aspects of New Zealand's colonial administration;
- apology and settlement to former patients at Lake Alice Hospital; and
- Confidential Forum for Former In-Patients of Psychiatric Hospitals.

These four processes have all been undertaken since 2000 by the Labour-led government. There are others too, which are not discussed in detail here. They include a settlement with the victims of a failure in the cervical screening programme; a working group on concerns of Vietnam veterans, where it has been clear from the outset that the process would conclude with an apology by the Prime Minister (with the mode of delivery to be agreed during the process); and an investigation into allegations of abuse at an army cadet camp.

## *Range of restorative processes*

It is important to be clear on the context, and what is and is not being considered here. There are a wide range of situations in which apologies are given, or

---

1  At the 2005 general election, no political party had a policy to stop the process. Rather, most had policies to speed it up or refine it. See, for example, the summary of the policies of all major parties on the *Political Policy Online* website (see 'Treaty of Waitangi', 2002–05).

restorative processes are adopted by a state or some other significant institution. The two extremes of that spectrum are:

- transitional justice processes for societies emerging from conflict, such as truth and reconciliation commissions; and
- apologies given to individuals in the course of resolving a specific dispute, as part of either the formal settlements of legal claims or the relatively immediate and informal responses to grievances in the course of the day-to-day business of government, where someone has been the victim of administrative confusion or error.

This chapter is concerned with neither of these situations, but with a phenomenon that sits somewhere between them. New Zealand is a settled and stable democracy. Unlike the questions before many truth commissions, the issues at stake in each of these examples are not about the very survival of a new and fragile nation, attempting to forge a basic social contract. They are more subtle questions about the nature and quality of the ongoing society. The apology processes considered here are each directed to a group in society that suffered a wrong in the past. Some of them brush up against the legal system and court-based dispute resolution system, but most do not. Put differently, these were all issues that did not involve legal responsibility in the conventional sense, easily judiciable by a court of law.

### *Rationale for state apologies*

The sudden arrival of several significant apologies on the New Zealand stage since 2000 suggests that the Labour-led government has been looking for new ways of responding to historical wrongs. New Zealand is not, of course, alone in this process. Internationally, examples abound of states and other social institutions apologising for serious wrongdoing, particularly in the context of institutional abuse.[2] To take just one indication of the scale of the practice internationally, one database collecting examples of what it terms 'political apologies' indexes more than 600 documents.[3] And there are many similar website and collections. We appear to be in the 'age of apologies' (Brooks, 1999a).

---

2  See, for example, Alter (1999), who describes in some detail many Canadian examples of apologies by governments and churches.

3  See the *Political Apologies and Reparations* website created and maintained by Rhoda E. Howard-Hassmann, Canada Research Chair in International Human Rights at Wilfrid Laurier University in Waterloo, Ontario, Canada (http://political-apologies.wlu.ca).

In New Zealand, there has been remarkably little public discussion about this new-found engagement with 'saying sorry'. The only significant elaboration of the reasons behind the processes appears to be a speech delivered by New Zealand Prime Minister Helen Clark in an address at Cape Town University in 2002. She discussed the historical settlement processes of reconciliation with Māori, the Chinese process and the Samoa apology, acknowledged that each has been controversial, and commented (Clark, 2002a, p. 4):

> New Zealand will be better able to build a nation which values and respects all its citizens and communities if it acknowledges its past and takes steps to redress it ... As a government we endeavour to lead from the front in promoting respect and tolerance for people of all ethnicities, beliefs, and backgrounds.

Clearly, the Prime Minister's big picture goal here was 'nation building' in the context of an increasingly diverse society. A key part of that process appears to be about building respect, both between citizens and between the state and citizens. To that extent, therefore, these initiatives are a logical follow-on from recognising human rights, in particular, freedom from discrimination, and the promotion of tolerance and inclusiveness that accompanies a commitment to making those rights a reality.

How does one work towards such large goals? The approach that has been taken in New Zealand in recent years clearly draws on restorative justice concepts. In particular, the Cabinet papers behind the Chinese and Samoan apologies refer to work by Professor Roy Brooks (1999b), who has written extensively on attempts at reparation and settlement of human rights injustice. The papers (Clark, 2002d; Clark and Hawkins, 2001) assess both those claims against the framework used by Professor Brooks, which includes:

- political will and political pressure for the settlement process;
- strong internal support amongst the victims for pursuing redress; and
- genuine merit in the claim itself.

To meet this last test, the papers suggested that an 'injustice' must have been committed and be well documented, the victims must be identifiable as a distinct group, the current members of the group must continue to suffer harm, and that harm must be causally connected to the past injustice.

Suppose all these tests are met – what then? Brook's own views have been summarised neatly by a reviewer of this substantial work (Kim, 1999, pp. 558 and 559):

> Once the merits of redress claims are established, the remaining question is the proper form of redress. Brooks distinguishes between redress

responses that are remorseful, in which the government seeks atonement for the commission of an injustice, and those that are not. The remorseful responses are properly called reparations and others settlements. Both reparations and settlements can take the form of monetary and nonmonetary responses. The latter type that includes amnesty, affirmative action, and various municipal services, Brooks notes, can be more effective than cash payment in meeting the individual and collective current needs of the victim group. If reparations and settlements, monetary or otherwise, are directed toward individual victims, they are intended as compensatory measures "to return the victim to the status quo ante." If directed toward the group, they are designed to be rehabilitative of the community "to nurture the group's self-empowerment or the community's cultural transformation, or at least to improve the conditions under which the victims live".

The substantial literature in this field[4] explores myriad examples where historical wrongs are (and are not) addressed, including by governments. The commonality is simple: addressing historical wrongs in the appropriate manner is 'healing', and 'restorative'. This should enable the government, the society as a whole, and the victims and their descendants to 'move on'. The process is not to enable 'forgetting', but learning. The goal is to acknowledge harm, take responsibility for it and clearly articulate that the causes should never be repeated. Obviously, there are significant religious elements to these processes, seen in all major religious traditions – and most famously epitomised by Archbishop Desmond Tutu in South Africa.[5] The approaches of the New Zealand government, at least, have been studiously secular.

The key point here is that the New Zealand initiatives were clearly driven by the core restorative goals from the wider literature, although these were mostly not articulated in public. I turn now to examine the detail of what happened in four recent and significant examples.

## Facing up to the past: New Zealand case studies

### Early Chinese settlers and the poll tax

Chinese people were among the first migrants to New Zealand, coming initially to the goldfields in the 1860s. Their welcome here was not warm. They have the

---

4  See, for example, the extensive bibliographies set out in Peacemakers Trust (no date) and Barkan and Karn (2006).
5  See, for example, Enright and North (1998) and Helmich and Petersen (2001).

distinction of being the only ethnic group where discrimination against them was so explicit, and so directly sanctioned by parliament.

The Chinese Immigration Restriction Act 1881 attempted to limit the number of Chinese coming here by two devices: it imposed a poll tax of 10 pounds per person, so that every person had to pay what was in those days a very large sum to be allowed to come here, and it imposed a quota on carriers, restricting the numbers able to come here to one person per 10 tonnes of ship cargo. In 1896, the poll tax was increased to 100 pounds per person, and the restriction on numbers was increased to one person per 200 tonnes of cargo. The poll tax was last collected in 1934, but was not repealed from our statute books until 1944.

Other related government actions included the requirement imposed in 1908 that Chinese people, and only Chinese people, were required to leave a thumbprint on their 'certificate of residence' before leaving the country, and a removal of the right to naturalisation for Chinese people. The ability to become a naturalised New Zealander was not restored until 1951. Through the 1930s and 1940s the number of permits available to Chinese people for the reunification of family and partners was significantly restricted.

Similar measures were adopted in Canada and Australia, each time just against the Chinese. Nigel Murphy (2003) and others have collated many examples of newspaper reports, cartoons and even speeches in the House of Representatives where people articulated their fear of 'the Yellow Peril'.

These restrictions may have achieved their policy goals, but they also had a dramatic and negative effect on the development of the Chinese community in New Zealand. In particular, the practical consequence was that families tended to send one or two members here each generation, as that was all they could afford to pay for, and those members would work to send money back to the family in China. Family links were maintained, but families lived a divided life – the husband and father was in New Zealand, but the price of bringing others here was too high. The disruption to normal social and family structures was significant.

In 1995, the New Zealand Chinese Association published historical research that it had commissioned (Murphy, 2003). With the history and its impact documented, the association began to raise with politicians the possibility of a formal apology. Interest waxed and waned over the next 7 years, but in late 2001 the government decided to act on the request. On 12 February 2002, at a celebration of Chinese New Year, the Prime Minister gave a speech where she recounted the background and announced (Clark, 2002b):

I wish to announce today that the government has decided to make a formal apology to those Chinese people who paid the poll tax and suffered other discrimination imposed by statute and to their descendents.

With respect to the poll tax we recognise the considerable hardship it imposed and that the cost of it and the impact of other discriminatory immigration practices split families apart.

Today we also express our sorrow and regret that such practices were once considered appropriate. While the governments which passed these laws acted in a manner which was lawful at the time, their actions are seen by us today as unacceptable. We believe this act of reconciliation is required to ensure that full closure can be reached on this chapter in our nation's history.

The Government's apology today is the formal beginning to a process of reconciliation. The Minister of Ethnic Affairs and I have been authorised to pursue with representatives of the families of the early settlers a form of reconciliation which would be appropriate to and of benefit to the Chinese community. To that end we wish to meet with key representatives of the descendants to discuss the next step in this process of reconciliation.

The Office of Ethnic Affairs and Department of the Prime Minister and Cabinet worked together over the next 2 years on a lengthy process of community discussion. The first question was who to talk to. The second question was how.

The two agencies began by bringing together a group of community leaders to advise them. With their help, a consultation process was eventually developed that incorporated:
- a series of 10 community meetings held throughout the country; and
- public submissions, which were received in writing or through a website.

The process paused in mid-2002 while the general election took place, as there was a strong message from the community that they did not want the issue to become embroiled in national politics. Submissions finally closed on 5 January 2003.

A full analysis is available on the Office of Ethnic Affairs website (http://www.ethnicaffairs.govt.nz). The summary records that 1,008 people attended the community meetings and 420 submissions were received. More than 94% of those who responded were descendents of poll tax payers, and 79%

indicated that they would like the government to take some form of action (Office of Ethnic Affairs, 2003).

At each meeting the community was invited to nominate a representative to be part of an advisory group that would work with officials to sift the suggestions and come up with recommendations to government on an appropriate form of reconciliation. The advisory group that resulted had 31 members, from all over New Zealand. They met in Wellington several times, and there were numerous phone discussions between all or some of the members.

The process was not free from difficulty. Commentators from within the Chinese community have spoken and written of some of the concerns, which included the following.

- Cynicism about the government's motive, and speculation about the interplay with raw electoral politics.
- Suggestions that the process was back to front, and had been sprung on the community. Steven Young (2005) has described it as "an accidental apology", controlled by the government rather than by the group being addressed. Indeed, most community meetings included a discussion about whether to accept the apology, fortunately culminating in a polite resolution in each case that the group would graciously accept it, notwithstanding the perceived clumsiness in the manner of delivery.
- A perceived need to allow time for the community to discuss this history among its members and in particular with the young people, in order to enable some measure of consensus to build about the appropriate way forward.
- Worries about the effect of the process on the profile of the Chinese community in New Zealand, and concern about whether it would lead to the community becoming a renewed target for criticism, particularly given the state of public debate at the time about Asian immigration. In part as an attempt to manage this risk, each meeting strongly agreed that no financial compensation should go to individuals as a result of this process.

Nonetheless, there was clear agreement that it was preferable to be addressing the issues through direct political engagement of this kind, rather than through litigation in the courts, as the equivalent community in Canada has been attempting (Young, 2002). The advisory group, assisted by officials, eventually produced recommendations for Cabinet to consider.

The Minister of Ethnic Affairs formally announced the result on 11 February 2004 – Chinese New Year – 2 years after the apology was given. The government announced:

- a $5 million seeding grant for a new government-administered community trust;
- new school resources to tell the stories of Chinese settlers in New Zealand; and
- the preservation of a significant Chinese heritage site in Central Otago.

The community trust is to fund projects to boost the study of Chinese New Zealand history, encourage maintenance of the distinct early Chinese culture and the Cantonese language, promote greater awareness of ethnic diversity and support projects that strengthen the unique identity of Chinese New Zealanders. The Prime Minister commented that "the establishment of a trust signifies the determination of the government to secure the place of the Chinese community and its role in our nation's history" (in Carter, 2004).

It is still early to attempt evaluative comment on the effectiveness of the process; nor is it easy to evaluate progress towards such diffuse goals. That said, it is noticeable that there is greater awareness of this part of New Zealand's history, and that it is now more visible in school topics and general social and political commentary. Chinese New Zealanders have been regular participants in various recent seminars and panels discussing questions of diversity and social identity in New Zealand. It is also material that the redress that was finally decided on was an initiative that the community wanted, and that relates directly to the goals of the government and the community. And finally, the Chinese community itself recognises that the discussion process that accompanied the reconciliation initiative was significant in helping build a sense of community and a more broadly shared understanding across the community of this part of the Chinese New Zealand story. In short, the building blocks now appear to be in place for valuing the differences that Chinese New Zealanders bring to this country, and for strengthening the threads that bind Chinese New Zealanders into the social and political fabric of the country as a whole.

### *The New Zealand–Samoa relationship*

The 1899 Treaty of Berlin gave the German government control of Samoa. As part of the events of World War One, New Zealand troops entered Samoa in August 1914 and occupied the islands. After the war, New Zealand had the task of administering Samoa. The relationship was fairly acrimonious until 1935. Following a change in government in New Zealand at that time, and a developing relationship with the united Western Samoa chiefs, efforts were made to move to a more mutually agreeable system that mixed colonial-style administration and local governance. In 1946, the relationship formally became governed by the United Nations trusteeship system, which enabled the transition to full political independence for Samoa on 1 January 1962.

In 2002, the New Zealand government perception was that a deep sense of resentment remained about events from the period when New Zealand administered Samoa. The Cabinet paper on this issue succinctly states (Clark, 2002d, p. 2):

> The administration of Samoa by New Zealand was not trouble free, especially in the early years. The poor colonial administration was in part due to the racist and paternalistic attitudes of the administrators as well as to their ineptitude and lack of experience.

Three events in particular were cited as significant. First, the 1918 Spanish influenza epidemic arrived in Apia on a passenger ship that the administration cleared to dock. The epidemic resulted in the death of about 8,500 people, or 22% of Samoa's population. Medical assistance for Samoans was poorly organised, and was very obviously second to that provided for Palagi (white people), and cultural and religious ceremonies were overridden without explanation as the Samoan dead were piled and thrown into mass graves.

Second, between 1922 and 1928 matai were banished and stripped of their titles by administrators using discretionary powers under the Samoan Offenders Ordinance. The discretionary powers were designed to deal with Samoans deemed to be a source of danger to the peace, order and good government of Samoa. However, they were used extensively by the administration, particularly towards the end of this period, as a tool for the general control of the population and the containment of political activism and the emerging Mau movement in particular.

Third, lives were lost during a peaceful demonstration in 1929. Samoan resentment to the use of the banishment and title-stripping powers and to the suppression of the Mau movement came to a head on 28 December 1929, in a confrontation now known as Black Saturday. About 300 demonstrators were marching along the waterfront. Police had warned that they would arrest any wanted men they identified in the group. But when police tried to arrest men, the demonstrators resisted. Samoans threw stones, and police fired into the crowd before retreating to the station to get rifles, bayonets and a machine gun. The scuffle escalated. One police constable was killed in an alley. Police opened fire from the station and killed the Mau leader Tupua Tamasese and those who went to his aid. Nine Samoans died.

Prompted by the forthcoming Samoan celebrations of 40 years of independence, discussions took place in 2002 between New Zealand and

Samoan officials and politicians on the possibility of an apology. In May 2002, the Cabinet Policy Committee (p. 1):

3  agreed that as an act of reconciliation to the people of Samoa, the government [would] offer a formal apology that:

3.1 acknowledges the injustices arising from New Zealand's administration of Samoa in its earlier years;

3.2 expresses sorrow and regret for these injustices; and

3.3 is in a form that is unlikely to incur any legal risk;

4  agreed that the Prime Minister offer the formal apology during her visit to Samoa for the celebration of the fortieth anniversary of its independence, based on the recommendations above;

5  noted that the offer of an apology would be made within the context of the good bilateral relationship between New Zealand and Samoa.

The Prime Minister duly delivered a speech in Apia in June 2002, which included the following comments (Clark, 2002c):

before coming today I have ... been troubled by some unfinished business. There are events in our past which have been little known in New Zealand, although they are well known in Samoa. Those events relate to the inept and incompetent early administration of Samoa by New Zealand ... my government believes that reconciliation is important in building strong relationships. It is important to us to acknowledge tragic events which caused great pain and sorrow in Samoa ... On behalf of the New Zealand Government, I wish to offer today a formal apology to the people of Samoa for the injustices arising from New Zealand's administration of Samoa in its earlier years, and to express sorrow and regret for those injustices ... It is our hope that this apology, will enable us to build an even stronger relationship and friendship for the future on the basis of a firmer foundation.

The speech triggered tears in the audience in Apia, and in many of the crowds who watched the speech on live broadcasts in Auckland, Wellington and Christchurch.

Again, the process was not free from criticism, however. Coming hot on the heels of the apology to the Chinese settlers, and immediately before the announcement of a date for the general election, there was some cynicism about the motive. This was fuelled by the impression that the apology had been relatively swiftly put together: only weeks beforehand the Minister of Foreign Affairs had appeared to publicly rule out the possibility of an apology (Field, 2002; Ward, 2002).

Moreover, it was unclear what was to happen next. Given that the Chinese apology of 4 months earlier was being followed by a reconciliation process, some expected something equivalent for Samoa.

It also subsequently became clear that, for the Samoans living in New Zealand at least, the major issue on people's minds was immigration. There was still great distress over the treatment in the 1970s of Samoan immigrants to New Zealand, and the legal changes to the New Zealand citizenship laws as they affected Samoans in 1982. Domestic political attention rapidly turned to these events, and the apology caused some to expect that the government might act to respond to the perceived grievance. A petition was presented to parliament on 27 March 2003, accompanied by a large demonstration in parliament grounds, calling for the repeal of the 1982 legislation (Braddock, 2003).

The select committee that considered the petition reported in May 2004. Despite the Prime Minister's apology nearly 2 years earlier, the committee reported that (Government Administration Committee, 2004, pp. 35 and 36):

> It became apparent in the course of our consideration of the petition that underlying it was a sense of grievance amongst a significant number of New Zealand's Samoan community and Samoans in Samoa arising from incidents during New Zealand's administration of Samoa, and post this period, New Zealand's immigration policies. We believe this is an issue that must be taken seriously and should be addressed in good faith regardless of the legal rights and wrongs of the issues raised by the petition. This part of our report therefore looks at a way to progress forward New Zealand's special relationship with Samoa, in view of the matters raised by the petition.
>
> ... We acknowledge that New Zealand has benefited over the years, and continues to benefit, from the talents and skills of Samoans. We regret that New Zealand's administration of Western Samoa under the Mandate and then Trusteeship was, at times, traumatic. We note that throughout the period of foreign, including New Zealand, administration of Western Samoa, a significant number of Samoans had strongly advocated for full independence. We also note and regret that the immigration policies of past Governments were seen as targeting Samoans.
>
> We consider that the Samoan Prime Minister's desire to concentrate on the future, and on ways that New Zealand can assist with Samoa's nation-building, is we believe relevant in addressing the issues raised by the petition.

Although the stated aim of the apology was to acknowledge the past and build a strong future relationship, it was clear from these comments that among many people the sense of grievance remained some 2 years later. The air may have been cleared between the two governments, but that was manifestly not yet fully or effectively achieved with Samoans in general.

When set against the experience of the Treaty settlement and Chinese reconciliation initiatives, it is possible to speculate on the differences that may have contributed to a more mixed outcome. For example, it is clear there was much less dialogue in advance to build an agreed context for the apology, including an agreement on the parts of history that warranted a formal acknowledgement of this kind. The government-to-government aspect also clouded the focus and added a level of complexity that was not present with the other two examples. Although the apology was delivered as a matter of a state-to-state relationship, it appears that some of the core tension that needed to be addressed was internal to New Zealand, and was really a question of citizen–state relationships. Given the closeness of the links between the populations in New Zealand and Samoa, it was probably not possible to isolate the relationship and the initiative in this way. Related to both these points was the fact the core issue causing contemporary tension was probably the ill-feeling surrounding immigration, rather than the events of history that were the subject of the apology. Therefore, although the apology was welcomed, it was perhaps not an effective way of addressing the tensions in New Zealand about the treatment of Samoans.

## *Lake Alice Hospital*

The Child and Adolescent Unit at Lake Alice Hospital operated from 1972 until 1978. It treated children with a wide range of behavioural problems, from children with significant psychiatric problems to children who had been made wards of the state, been passed through foster homes, or started to exhibit 'challenging social behaviours'.

By the 1990s, stories were emerging about the way these children had been treated. In particular, there were allegations of cruel and abusive treatment, including the use of electric shock treatment as a punishment, administered without anaesthetic and in front of other children.

By 1998, legal claims had been filed (Anderson, 1998a). The Minister of Health at the time was initially reported as being "horrified" and of the view that the claims should be settled immediately (Anderson, 1998b). But by 1999 the government decided to let the claims run through the courts (Anderson, 1999). The cases were unquestionably weak in legal terms, because there were difficulties with the age of the claims under the Limitation Act 1950, significant boundary issues with the accident compensation regime (which bars legal claims for those within its cover), and major difficulties with amassing sufficient evidence to prove the allegations. Moreover, the precedent risks of settling with those who had received dubious treatment in or through state institutions, outside the bounds of clear legal liability, were significant. Many people have passed through state health, education and welfare institutions over the past 50 years or more, and standards of acceptable treatment have changed greatly over that time. Opening all of that up to potential scrutiny and compensation claims was regarded as potentially a very big step indeed.

That attitude changed in late 1999, with the change of government. The Labour Party in particular had already made a commitment to settle the claims. After extended negotiation with the lawyer representing most of the claimants, the government established a process for the direct settlement of the claims. An independent person (a retired High Court judge) was appointed to review the files and hear from each claimant, assess which claims were valid, and allocate a fixed compensation fund between the various claimants. The total fund was $6.5 million, which was allocated across 95 claimants, according to the nature of their experience in the unit. Each claimant had the opportunity to be heard by the judge, and each claimant received a personal written apology at the end of the process signed by the Prime Minister and Minister of Health (King, 2001; Clark, 2001).

When the settlement was announced in 2001, the Prime Minister and Minister of Health stated that (Clark, 2001):

Whatever the legal rights and wrongs of the matter, and whatever the state of medical practice at the time, our government considers that what occurred to these young people was unacceptable by any standard, in particular the inappropriate use of electric shocks and injections.

At the end of this process the judge who had heard the claims wrote an unsolicited report to the government, which later became public, in which he recorded his view that the claims were well founded. In particular, he commented that the children at Lake Alice "lived in a state of terror" (Sir Rodney Gallen in Collins, 2001).

The process was then repeated a second time, during 2002, to enable all those who had passed through the unit but who had not joined with the initial legal action to receive equivalent redress and an apology.

A key part of the negotiation process for this particular settlement process was managing the boundary with the legal system. In particular, it was considered essential that the claimants waived any ability to bring a legal claim before they could receive a settlement out of this parallel process. In addition, the wording of the government's apology was very carefully crafted to avoid any suggestion of acknowledging a legal as opposed to a moral responsibility.

Many claimants commented that the most important part for them was the acknowledgement of what had happened – the ability to tell their stories and have them believed. The direct apology was an important part of that acknowledgement. That acknowledgement by the government was also perceived as important in reducing the chances of something similar happening again – if the government accepts it has happened in the past, it can consciously guard against it. The financial redress was considered by most to be welcome, but less significant. The quantum in most cases was also not sufficient to make a dramatic difference to people's lives (Bridgeman, 2003).

## Confidential Forum for Former In-patients of Psychiatric Hospitals

The concern about the precedent effect of the Lake Alice claims proved well founded. Within a few years, more claims were surfacing alleging abuse in state institutions. A large group of claims was centred around the Porirua Psychiatric Hospital, but other institutions were also involved.

This time the government moved to establish something new: the Confidential Forum for Former In-patients of Psychiatric Hospitals. The forum was initially chaired by a former judge and ombudsman, Anand Satyanand. He was appointed Governor-General in early 2006, and was replaced by Judge Patrick Mahoney, a former Principal Family Court Judge. The other panel members were two people experienced in the mental health care sector and a lawyer with significant health sector experience. Hearings began in July 2005. According to the forum's press statements (Confidential Forum, 2005):

> The Forum is designed to give patients who were in psychiatric hospitals before November 1992 an opportunity to talk about their experiences in a non-critical and confidential environment with the intention of assisting them to come to terms with their experiences and to achieve closure.

The forum was not designed to establish truth or guilt, but to assist people in other ways. In practical terms, the forum aimed to help former patients make the most of existing support, complaint resolution and counselling services. It did not aim to replace the ability to bring claims through the court system and people could continue with any legal action they might have under way while participating in it.

The government considered, but decided against, an inquiry process similar to the Lake Alice Hospital inquiry that would distribute financial redress. An initial investigation had suggested that it would be appropriate to defend many of the claims, as the alleged abusers often denied the allegations, and there were complex legal questions about immunity and limitation periods. It concluded that each claim would require individual assessment before compensation could be awarded, and that the courts were the best place for that detailed evidence-based task.

The forum was, therefore, designed to meet other needs – primarily the need to talk about experiences in a supportive environment. The forum did not have any remit to seek or give apologies, but the possibility of apologies arising further down the track was left open.

When registrations closed in late 2006, 554 people had registered their interest in meeting with the forum. Over nearly two years, the forum held hearings throughout New Zealand, and met with 493 people. The final report of the forum records that there were three major groups of participants: former inpatients (82 percent), family members of former inpatients (17 percent), and former staff members (6 percent) (Confidential Forum, 2007). The forum report describes the major themes that emerged from the stories that it heard, many of which gave a very negative picture of institutional culture and treatment regimes. There was some positive recognition of care received from staff members and others.

The forum organised assistance for participants where possible, including referrals to counsellors and access to some free counselling sessions, individually tailored information about support services, links to other agencies able to provide assistance, information on patient rights, and support for a range of other matters associated with the medical system.

People gave a range of reasons for participating, including a desire to make sense of their own experiences, wanting government to know of their experiences and the effects on them, and hope that others might benefit as a result of the process.

The key innovation was that the forum process did not construct the issues as a dispute between two combatants, requiring resolution. It was a process focused on the individual and their experiences in the mental health care system. It focused on what could be done to assist that individual, as they continue to navigate that system or manage their health and other difficulties, or simply to come to terms with their experiences. There may be a dispute, and there may be other processes for resolving any dispute, but this process took a different approach.[6]

Indeed, on the day the forum was announced, Attorney-General Margaret Wilson commented that the aim of the forum was to try to get away from an adversarial notion and the "compensation culture where past wrongs can only be resolved by the writing of a cheque" and to concentrate instead on the real issues affecting the former patients (Wilson, 2004).[7]

Many of those who have spent time in psychiatric institutions are marginalised members of society, and the fact of being given the space and time to tell their stories, individually and privately, to representatives of the government, is seen as significant. Implicit in the process is that their experiences are important, and that they as individuals deserve to be treated with dignity and respect.[8] Given the nature of many of their previous interactions with state agencies, including abuse of authority, failure to seek consent, and physical and sexual assault, this message alone is important (Satyanand, 2006).

When the forum concluded, the panel offered its own views on what had been achieved (Confidential Forum, 2007, p. 3):

> The panel concluded that the formalised listening process of the Forum, as well as the personalised follow-up actions taken, provided a useful vehicle for participants in their journey of coming to terms with past experiences. Many of those who attended had never before had an opportunity to recount their experiences.
>
> Many participants also expressed appreciation of the follow-up actions tailored to the needs of individuals and said that the assistance had been helpful to them.

---

6  In this regard, there is some parallel with the birth of the accident compensation system, which transformed the court-based system of tortious liability for personal injury from a legal dispute, requiring fault and harm to be proved, into a state-funded system for remedying the injuries and restoring the individual to health and full social (and employment) participation.

7  The difficulty of charting this path and of managing the interface with those wishing to claim through the legal system was illustrated by the interview that followed with Sonja Cooper, a lawyer representing former patients. Cooper (2004) criticised the forum for its inability to determine facts and liability, award compensation, or even acknowledge and apologise.

8  These comments draw on discussions with Anand Satyanand and Katharine Greig, a forum staff member, in March 2006, as well as on media and other commentary, including comments after the release of the forum's periodic reports to government.

On the question of apologies, the report concludes with the following "Hopes for the future" (Confidential Forum, 2007, p. 42):

> As already noted, many participants hoped that the Forum process would bring further improvement to the mental health services in New Zealand.
>
> Another hope of many former patients who came to the Forum was that the Government would give a public acknowledgement or apology showing that the Government understood that many former in-patients of psychiatric hospitals had had experiences that were deeply humiliating and demeaning, often taking a lifelong toll. Many who spoke of this said that a public acknowledgement/apology would make them feel valued and accepted in a way that was very important for them, often saying that such recognition of the experiences of former patients would help bring closure.

It is too early to tell whether this experiment with a new process will mark the start of a new way of dealing with individual grievances against the state. At the time of writing, the final report was still relatively recent, and there had been no response by the government to the implicit invitation to follow up with an apology. Several legal claims by former patients are also still being pursued in the courts. Initial impressions, however, suggest that there has been value, and that there is cautious interest in the idea that there may be another, more constructive, way of responding to grievances of this kind.

## Reflections on the New Zealand experience

### *Relationship with the court-based dispute resolution*

Why follow a restorative path rather than a traditional court path? The answer for the historical claims, of course, is that the age and political nature of the grievances mean court action is not available: the actions in question are too old, and too rooted in the statute law of the time, to be open to legal challenge. Therefore, if action were to be taken to respond to the claims of grievance, a different model has to be used. Given the policy goals – of promoting respect and tolerance within New Zealand society and of bringing aggrieved groups into the general framework of the state for settling disputes – a restorative path was the logical direction.

For the more recent claims, court action was not only possible, but claims were already under way. The choice to adopt a restorative approach was accordingly more complex. In each example, however, the claims were shaky in legal terms and the court process was likely to be complex and drawn out. It was fairly clear that, whoever 'won' at the end of it all, the process itself was likely to cement bitterness and grievance. On the one hand, the government could legitimately claim that the court system existed in order to determine the bounds of legitimate claims, and that it was prudent and a rational management of taxpayer funds to refuse to settle outside the bounds of legal risk as defined by that process. On the other hand, the argument was that the legal process would be long, expensive and counterproductive in terms of broad goals, and that a more direct engagement might be able to produce a much better outcome for all. This latter argument obviously prevailed.

### *Benefits of a restorative approach*

The benefits of a restorative approach across all of these examples are reasonably apparent.

Direct engagement builds a direct relationship between the state and the group in question, thus bringing people within the democratic fold.[9]

The application of governmental time and energy to the relationship with the particular group, as well as the public acknowledgement and redress that result, increases the social visibility of the group and sends a clear message to society as a whole that this group belongs and is valued.

The public acknowledgement of a wrong and the acceptance of responsibility manifested through the apology demonstrate respect for the group and a willingness to listen to its point of view. These elements are basic for building a stronger forward-looking relationship.

The direct negotiation process, untrammelled by legal rules about forms of compensation, enables redress to be developed that is relevant and wanted by the group. This in itself is a benefit, but it is also a measure of the empowerment of the group that is achieved by the restorative process.

All of these benefits contribute directly to the overall goal of building a healthy and tolerant society.

### *Risks of a restorative approach*

But it is not all plain sailing. There have been many risks.

There are difficulties with managing the interface with the court system. The common law is not static, and if a government repeatedly and publicly takes

---

9 See Ladley (2005) for a discussion of the role of democracy in mediating claims between different groups in society, and the importance of all groups opting to work within that framework to pursue claims.

responsibility for particular types of harm, then that may, over time, provide a basis for the courts to start to recognise legal liability. There is a dynamic and evolutionary interaction between the two branches of government that the executive ignores at its peril.[10]

Moreover, when there is potential for a concurrent legal claim, there is a fundamental conflict that must be managed. For an apology to be effective in psychological terms, to achieve the restorative goal, there needs to be clear acceptance of responsibility for the action in question and for the harm suffered. Yet clear acceptance of that responsibility is precisely what any good defence lawyer will be trying to guard against, lest it become 'exhibit 1' for the plaintiff in the courtroom. Hence the regular requirement for those engaging in restorative processes to waive any rights to bring legal claims: without that step, the government is likely to be inhibited in its admission of responsibility, thus jeopardising the restorative goal.[11]

Apologies given too freely or too often, or without clear foundation, risk feeding cynicism and, ultimately, devaluing the currency of apologies and the restorative process as a whole.[12]

In terms of overall social conduct, it is possible that a demonstrated readiness to settle with aggrieved groups, notwithstanding a lack of clear evidence, will feed a 'claims mentality' or, in the New Zealand political parlance, a 'grievance industry'.

If the process does not have a clear purpose, aims and limits, it may backfire and fuel further grievances within the claimant group. Restorative processes are concerned with building a relationship that can move forward. Central to that is acknowledgement of the harm and of responsibility for the harm. In general, any redress is symbolic of that acknowledgement rather than aiming to compensate for the harm or the loss suffered. If those pursuing the grievance remain focused

---

10 This risk may explain why the most recent process for former psychiatric patients is very clearly running in parallel with the court system, rather than seeking to replace it with a more comprehensive settlement process.

11 And note the terms of the government's statement on the settlement of the Lake Alice claims quoted above, "Whatever the legal rights and wrongs of the matter" (Clark, 2001).

12 The importance of this factor was underscored in New Zealand by an apparent off the cuff remark during a media interview by the Prime Minister, which resulted in reports that she had also apologised to the gay community. Coming hot on the heels of the Chinese and Samoan apologies, it led to many cynical comments about the willingness of the government to apologise to all and sundry. See, for example, Bassett (2002).

on the past, on the harm, and on full compensation or reparation they may come away frustrated, with the grievance compounded rather than resolved.

If others in society cannot see the justification for the settlement, there is a risk of generating a grievance in those other groups. The action, therefore, does have to meet a basic test of according with a sense of fairness or justice. This test is also relevant to the nature of the redress: full reparation for historical wrongs might be inconsistent with a sense of what is just in the current circumstances, hence the delicacy of negotiating redress that is sufficient to give weight to the acknowledgement of the past wrong, but not sufficient to create fresh injustice for others.[13]

All of these risks show why it is important for governments to move carefully as they develop restorative processes, including apologies and redress. To avoid these risks, there are many aspects that need to be explicitly discussed and negotiated with the claimant group, and explained to the wider community.

### *How do governments apologise effectively?*

There is one further difficulty, signalled at the outset of this chapter, that needs to be tackled in every case. That is the question of how an impersonal and eternal bureaucracy – the state – can ever apologise in sufficiently direct and personal terms to achieve the psychological healing that is the goal of every restorative process.

The theory underpinning restorative practice highlights the importance of individualised tailoring of the process, so it is 'owned' by the participants. Effective apologies also require the person apologising to take responsibility for the actions in question and, ideally, some kind of personal connection to be achieved between the two parties. Research in the criminal justice context shows that restorative aims are best met when the victim and offender both participate in the conference. Apologies have much more credibility when conveyed face to face, so the victim can see that the offender's discomfort and shame are genuine. Apologies conveyed indirectly can have less credibility, and therefore less effect.

Achieving a similar psychological outcome is clearly difficult when the restorative process is between the government and a large social grouping. Both are necessarily working through representatives, and no individual is sitting behind the representatives, only a more or less well-organised group (on the part

---

13 See, in particular, Jeremy Waldron's (2002, 2003) careful analysis of redress for past wrongs in terms of theories of justice, and the development of a theory of supercession to explain how past injustices do not automatically render the status quo unjust also.

of the social group) and a somewhat amorphous concept and legal entity (on the part of the state). Moreover, particularly in the Treaty settlement process, the state is trying to work through a whole list of claimant groups and has inevitably systematised the process. It is simply not possible for the state to have organised the 21 agreed separate settlement processes, nor the 20 that remain to be settled, without some standardisation. To do otherwise would risk creating a whole set of fresh problems, including allegations of fresh injustice when groups received different treatment. At the outset in the Treaty process, therefore, some of the benefit of an individually tailored and owned process has had to be sacrificed.

What both these simple points tell us is that these state-to-group processes are never going to be perfect in terms of restorative theory and practice. There must be adaptation as these concepts are taken from the realm of criminal justice and the healing of relationships between individuals into the more abstract world of healing relationships between the state and social groups.

There are, however, key lessons that can be taken from the New Zealand experience so far, which can help us to manage some of the risks and limitations and increase the chances of a reasonably successful outcome.

First, it matters *who* says sorry on behalf of the state. Most of the recent apologies have been conveyed by the Prime Minister, as the political leader of the government. Sometimes, however, the relevant portfolio minister may give the apology, if that seems more suited to the particular group and its relationship with the government.[14] On at least one occasion – the settlement of the Tainui Treaty claim, there was a concerted push to have the apology tendered by the head of state – Her Majesty Queen Elizabeth II. The rationale from Tainui was that that would better reflect the status of Tainui, as the home of the Māori Queen, Te Arikinui Dame Te Atairangikaahu. In the end, a classic compromise was reached: the Prime Minister tendered the apology when he attended the ceremony to sign the final Deed of Settlement. The text of the apology was recorded in the implementing legislation, which was later given the royal assent by Queen Elizabeth II in the course of a royal visit to New Zealand in 1995. The short point is that specific consideration needs to be given to who is the best placed, from the range of actors within the government, to be an effective representative for the purposes of apologising to a particular group.

Second, the timing and mode of the delivery of an apology benefit from careful and explicit negotiation beforehand. The contrast between the Treaty and Chinese settlement processes makes this point sharply. The press statements

---

14 For example, most Treaty settlements, including the tendering of the apology, are signed by the Minister in Charge of Treaty of Waitangi Negotiations.

about the process under way with Vietnam veterans suggest the government has learned this lesson.

Third, the apology needs to be seen not as an end in itself, but as part of the overall restorative *process*. It matters when in the process it is given, and how. There also needs to be clear connection between the terms of the apology and the issues that are at the root of the contemporary grievance. Thus, the failure to deal with immigration issues at the time of the apology to Samoa left the key contemporary issue festering, arguably undermining the apology process. And the Chinese process was put at risk by the apology being given too suddenly and too early. As many restorative justice practitioners have learned, an apology given at the wrong time or in the wrong way can be wasted or even counterproductive.

Fourth, it is important not to give apologies too often or too easily. Credibility and sincerity are important. If they are to have significant value, state apologies must be given sparingly and for manifestly good reason.

## Conclusion

New Zealand is experimenting in interesting ways with some big ideas: nation building, respect, tolerance, social justice and reconciliation. None is a small concept and none has proved easy to implement in practice. The key lessons so far are twofold.

First, there is ample room to take quite effective symbolic action as part of a restorative process, including a full apology, if there is no question of contemporary legal liability for the actions in question. Where legal risk still exists, careful negotiation is needed in advance of the process in order to isolate that risk and create the space for frank acknowledgement of wrongdoing. If the confidential forum process proves to have been successful in its parallel track, operating alongside legal claims and presumably with the hope of defusing them, then that may open up an interesting new direction for further exploration.

Second, it is important how one goes about making such gestures. If the actions of apologising and providing redress are primarily symbolic, to convey acknowledgement, regret, respect and an affirmation of belonging, then every detail of what is done and how it is done can matter. Although it may feel artificial, it is preferable for every aspect of the process to be negotiated and choreographed in advance. If this is true for ordinary people engaged in restorative processes, it is doubly so for governments. The popular suspicion of politicians is well documented, as is the ability of bureaucracies to bungle. Governments, therefore, have to work twice as hard to ensure that they are taken as being sincere, and that they do not inadvertently undermine their efforts with errors of detail.

As noted, the Cabinet papers launching these apologies drew mostly on Brooks' (1999a, 1999b) framework, suggesting the three key ingredients for apologies appropriate for historical wrongs are:
- political will and political pressure for the settlement process;
- strong internal support among the victims for pursuing redress; and
- genuine merit in the claim itself.

Sober assessment of the four examples discussed suggests that most of these elements were present to some degree in all of them. The political pressure for the Chinese apology was tentative, and the internal community support for it was mixed. But there was enough to render the process successful. The most questionable against this framework was the Samoan apology, where there was no obvious history of political pressure for an apology, and subsequent events showed that the community was not necessarily convinced by what had been done. The Lake Alice process clearly had all these elements, and they were probably also present for the former psychiatric inpatients process.

Both the Samoan and Chinese reconciliation processes show that having the basis for action is not sufficient. The action must also be delivered in the right way. As has been discussed, the Chinese process stumbled at various points, although it ultimately appears to have achieved its goals. The success of the Samoan process is more questionable. In both cases, the speed of the process at the beginning, and the fact the apology came early and apparently at the instigation of politicians rather than the community, meant that some 'backfilling' was needed to reassure the recipients and achieve the restorative goals.

Stumbles aside, since 2000, New Zealand has absorbed these various processes with relative calm. As noted at the outset, the ground had been laid with the Treaty settlement process of the previous decade: as a society we had already become comfortable with the notion of facing our collective past, and with the idea that the Crown was a vehicle for 'putting right' historical wrongs, as best it could. Indeed, there is some national pride in the ability of the state here to say sorry, whereas the same does not appear to be possible for governments across the Tasman.

The comparative literature suggests that this ability is fundamentally healthy for the collective psyche, as well as for victims and their descendants. The smallness of New Zealand means that any disaffected group has a potentially significant impact on simple notions of trust between citizen and government. A disaffected group can create unhealthy fissures in that basic trust, which is the foundation of government by consent in a democracy. If left to grow, those fissures can put the integrity and effectiveness of the state and its institutions at risk. Thus building an inclusive society is not only a social goal; ultimately, it is a constitutional goal as well, cementing people into the democratic framework.

It is too soon to say whether these processes have fulfilled the larger 'nation-building' agenda, although it can be argued that they are a promising beginning. Besides, the country is still in the midst of the ongoing processes involving Māori and the Treaty of Waitangi. As that process moves on to the more difficult settlements (including those involving complex cross-claims), and as the early settlements mature and found new and perhaps different expectations of citizen–state relationships, we can expect to confront further challenges. In the end, the merits of the claims behind each of the case studies in this chapter were reasonably clear once the facts had been established. Where justice lies in some of the more complex Treaty claims is a much harder question. Finding resolution in those cases will truly test the restorative capacities of the national character.

# Part Four

# Reflections on Restorative Justice

# Introduction to Part Four

In this part, the authors draw from a diverse set of influences to reflect on how the practices and principles of restorative justice resonate with basic human needs (Tony Taylor, chapter 14), empirical social psychology (James Liu and Katja Hanke, chapter 15) and philosophy (Karen Baehler, chapter 16).

Taylor reviews contemporary concepts of justice in arguing for his view that justice is "an essential precondition for approximating the good life that ensures the reciprocal quality of relationships between people for their mutual wellbeing". He argues that despite the variety of definitions and approaches taken to justice, they all point towards the direction that justice has a deeper purpose, to satisfy the basic human need for security and belongingness to a community.

This rather simple, but profound, idea is developed more fully by Baehler. Baehler reviews the historical progression of ideas in Western societies to assert that some form of re-balancing is at the root of many of the philosophical underpinnings of justice. She moves from the ancient ideas of Aristotle and Hammurabi's Code, where proportionality of punishment (that is, let the punishment fit the crime) is used to re-balance the scales, to the Enlightenment era philosophies of Hegel and Kant, where the concept of restoring equal rights rather than imposing equal suffering becomes the basis of re-balancing. Hegel's idea that a crime harms society, not just an individual victim, because it infringes against the rights of citizens to feel secure within their communities is consistent with Taylor's thesis that justice satisfies a basic need for security.

Baehler cites Enlightenment era philosophers to assert that civil society depends on a mutual recognition of rights, and that punishment should not be arbitrary, but in proportion to the crime, and serves to reinforce the idea of the moral agency of the offender. The offender should be required to take moral responsibility for their misdeed; and justice is an attempt to re-balance the equal rights and standing of the victim and perpetrator.

Liu and Hanke draw from empirical research in social psychology to underline the validity of several of Baehler's philosophical conceptions. First, the idea of distributive justice focuses on the rules used to ascertain fair outcomes. The most popular justice rule is equity, which is another term for proportionality. Liu and Hanke, like Baehler, consider some form of equity or proportionality to be fundamental to justice, but warn us that the empirical literature shows that sometimes equity is not required, and rules based on equality or need may predominate instead. In the language of social psychology, Baehler's concept of justice being based on rights applies something like an equality rule rather than an equity rule: everyone should have the right to feel safe and secure and worthy of the company of others in society. In the language of restorative justice, the concept of circle sentencing or family group conferencing applies something like a need rule rather than an equity rule, by taking into consideration the circumstances surrounding a misdeed before applying any sentence.

Baehler's idea that agreement between victim and offender is a more appropriate standard for deciding proportionality of sentencing than is a blind application of a fixed standard, is completely consistent with the procedural justice findings from social psychology where having a say and feeling the legal procedures were fair are more important than outcomes in determining satisfaction with the law. There has been a recent explosion of interest in forgiveness, this quality of clemency that a restorative approach may be able to engender on the part of the victim. Clearly, taking the victim's views into account seriously is an important component of restorative justice, the consequences of which have only recently begun to be understood as an important component of a more inclusive system of justice.

# 14

# Restorative Justice Serving the Need for Justice

*A. J. W. Taylor*

## Introduction

Restorative justice is a remedial and a reparative process that engenders expressions of forgiveness and benevolence from victims and encourages the reintegration of offenders in the community. With some exceptions, the outcome gives participants on both sides the satisfaction of having experienced justice. In so doing, restorative justice meets a basic need that has only recently been conceptualised and brought into a theoretical structure of human development.

Consequently, this chapter goes beyond the perception of justice deriving from the procedure and process of restorative justice, to consider the more fundamental need for justice that restorative justice serves. In so doing, it touches on the origin of the concept of justice as a necessity for community cohesion, and for comparative purposes it raises definitions of justice, morality and human needs. It mentions the reluctance of academic psychologists to enter the fray, except for Abraham Maslow, who came close to incorporating justice in his motivational framework of human behaviour. As a result, it restructures Maslow's model slightly to incorporate justice more fully, and imposes a requirement for the 'self-actualised', at the supposed pinnacle of mature psychological development, to address the concerns of injustice under which some of the less fortunate members of society might labour.

The chapter also raises the question of extending restorative justice from the domain of criminal justice to those of civil and social justice, and it touches on the different kind of orientation that mediators will require to make the extension work.

## Restorative justice

As previous chapters have shown, restorative justice is a powerful initiative that that has been introduced into the New Zealand justice system as an alternative to more traditional ways of responding to crime. Instead of relying on state-sponsored retaliation with the threat of more to come should there be a repetition of criminal activity, it strives to create a meaningful dialogue between victims and offenders in an orderly setting. In the process, restorative justice has generated feelings of social responsibility in offenders by engaging them in taking responsibility for the impact of their behaviour through an interaction with their victims in the presence of families and community representatives.

In ways that have yet fully to be understood, the evocation induces a desire on the part of offenders to put matters right wherever possible, to reorder their lives and to bring their values into alignment with those of their largely law-abiding community. It also induces others to restore the security of victims and to help in whatever way they can to retain or reclaim offenders as members of the community, instead of rejecting them irrevocably as beyond redemption.

Overall, the judicial initiative has proved its worth at home, and caught the imagination of many other jurisdictions abroad. It also seems to have met the fundamental human need that people have for justice.

Although today the specific notion of justice is rarely addressed, the classical Greek philosophers regarded justice as one of the foremost virtues alongside courage, prudence and temperance. The early Christian Fathers also declared such virtues to be universally applicable (see 'Virtues', no date). The very existence of codes of conduct (for example, Hammurabi, Moses, Brehon and Ancient Rome, to say nothing of those that operated in the Far East and Pacific) suggests that good law is an essential prerequisite for the maintenance of virtue in any society. It helps to safeguard a variety of human needs essential for human development, constructive community life, happiness and well-earned contentment.[1]

It follows that justice has three main strands, civil, criminal and social, although to the person in the street, criminal justice often seems to be the most important concern until major examples of deprivation, discrimination and intolerance are exposed (see Human Rights Commission, 2004). Social justice – the youngest member of the judicial family (and in some ways still the runt of the litter) – is only now coming to the fore, with a range of studies such as those linking economic deprivation to the onset of lawbreaking, and poor health and life expectancy (Howden-Chapman and Tobias, 2000; Marmot, 2005; Weiss, 1998).

It follows that restorative justice, which began as an alternative model for dealing with criminality, could conceivably be extended with benefit to the

---

1 For a succinct appraisal of the functional prerequisites of society, see Aberle et al. (1949/50).

other spheres in which justice is sought. Consistent with that thought, cross-cultural psychiatrist Derek Summerfield (2000) asserted that the post-traumatic reactions of victims of war and atrocity were not simply "a private problem, with the onus on the individual to recover, but an indictment of the socio-political forces that produced them". He went on to say that social reform was the best medicine, "this means ... *Justice*" (emphasis added). The World Commission on the Social Dimension of Globalization (2004, p. 8) went so far as to declare that a "fairer and more prosperous world is the key to a more secure world. Terror often exploits poverty, *injustice* and desperation to gain public legitimacy. The existence of such conditions is an obstacle in the fight against terrorism" (emphasis added). Subsequently, the United Nations General Assembly (2005) endorsed the world commission's theme, and urged member countries to redress their priorities to avoid further catastrophe.

In New Zealand, as in many other countries, the 20th century social policy of committing psychiatric patients to callous and dehumanising care in mental hospitals is commanding public attention (see Confidential Forum, 2007). Rather than leave the mountain of complaints for testing in an adversarial manner through the conventional courts of civil law, in 2004 the government established a confidential forum in which former psychiatric hospital patients, their families and members of staff could present their accounts of the 'treatment' they had suffered. The outcome convinced the government of the enormity of the abuse, and led it to create a comparable forum to investigate the serious complaints of adults who had been committed to institutions as needy, orphaned and wayward children.

As indicated in chapter 13, it remains to be seen what forms any compensation might take, but at this stage it seems that the government has initiated a process of truth and reconciliation, consistent with the principles of restorative justice, and comparable to that undertaken in South Africa (Truth and Reconciliation Commission, 2003). In so doing, it might have opened the way for similar forums to address crucial social problems. Were that the case, future adjudicators would require mediational rather than adversarial training, with procedures established to enable complainants and their families to play a more direct role than before to satisfy their need for justice.

The case has to be opened, because justice is sometimes difficult to discern behind laws and their enforcement. As John Warr said in 1649, "At the foundation of governments justice was in men before it came to be laws ... Laws upon laws do bridle the people" (cited in Hill, 1972, pp. 272 and 273). Systems introduced for apparently worthy purposes can also become self-serving and encrusted with irrelevance, and they require revisions of a kind the

New Zealand Law Commission (2004), parliament and reformers sometimes proclaim.

## Approaching the concept of justice

Here a word should be said about justice per se, because justice is a nebulous but far from negligible concept. It underlies the operating system of individuals, families, tribes, communities and nations both separately and collectively. According to the moral philosopher John Rawls (1971, p. 302), justice rests on two principles. The first being that "everyone has as an equal right to the most extensive total system of equal basic liberties compatible with a similar system of liberty for all", and the second that "social and economic inequalities are to be arranged so that they are to the greatest benefit of the least advantaged and attached to offices and positions open to all under conditions of fair equality and opportunity". He argued that in determining justice, people should abandon their vested interests and adopt an "original position" for testing social contracts, in which the terms would be acceptable to everyone regardless of their personal financial position, race, religion or health. In effect, he was advancing the case for justice to be seen as a basic human need, but he stopped short of saying so.

Later, Rawls (1993) substituted the term 'fairness' for justice – a decade ahead of the world commission reported above. No doubt for some people the substitution revived nostalgic memories of middle childhood and sportsmanship when the notions of right and wrong were unsullied by selfishness, bitter life-experience, specious argument, financial concerns or vested interests. More recently along the same vein, the worthy desire to create 'a level playing field' has often been heard.

But professionalism and the desire to win at all costs are known to corrupt the most noble of such intentions. Competing teams are also rarely well matched, and for the weaker side the game seems interminable, with no half-time allowing them to benefit from changing ends. Finally, as Judge Fred McElrea (2002) said in an address to a legal conference in London, too often the process is itself portrayed as a game, "with the lawyers playing the system (the rules) while the court acts as umpire, and justice [is] the loser".

For such reasons it seemed better both to try to retain the earlier conception of justice than to substitute the sporting analogy, and to disentangle it somewhat from the definition of morality – the one being more pragmatic and applied, while the other is more abstract and ideal. To complete the package it was also thought advisable to include a definition of 'needs' in a batch of definitions of key terms.

## Definition of terms

The legal and philosophical definitions of justice, morality and needs have generated a wealth of scholarship (see Coate and Rosati, 1988; Fisk, 1993). Without being too pedantic, the offerings from *Oxford English Dictionary Online* reflect the convention that presently obtains.

- *Justice* is "the exercise of authority or power in maintenance of right; vindication of right by assignment of reward or punishment".
- *Morality* is the combination of "personal qualities judged to be good or bad".
- *Needs* provide the impetus to "be under a necessity to do something".

But to focus on justice as being more than the process designed to deal with breaches of common law and statutory law, the definitions can be rephrased as follows.

- *Justice* is as an essential precondition for approximating the good life that ensures the reciprocal quality of relationships between people for their mutual wellbeing.
- *Morality* is the quintessential code by which behaviour might be ordered, with the distinction between morality and law resembling the difference between idealism and pragmatism.
- *Basic human needs* are the mainsprings of action for personal and social development that are energised by depletion and satiated by repletion.

## Theories of human motivation incorporating justice

Not unreasonably, McElrea (2002) thought one "should be able to find, or create a theory about the innate sense of justice". In a valiant attempt to legitimate the academic study of human values, that conceivably could include justice, William O'Donohue (1989) appealed to clinical psychologists to incorporate values as a third component of the scientist–practitioner model. Although the incorporation would garnish rather than tarnish the reputation of psychologists, it has yet to gain favour. But it was interesting that after the 11 September 2001 attacks, the American Psychological Association (2001) advised its clinical members to respond to disasters by attending to self-care strategies that include their own *spiritual needs* (emphasis added).

Here in New Zealand, for quite different reasons, the Public Health Advisory Committee to the National Health Committee (2004, p. 8) nailed its colours to the mast by going beyond the World Health Organization definition of health as the complete state of physical, mental, and social wellbeing, to include "family/whanau, community and spiritual wellbeing".

Clearly, to account for human behaviour, human values in general and justice in particular, warrant recognition in a theoretical framework. Towards that end, parsimony dictates that it were still better to try to build on existing theory than to construe justice as being so important as to warrant a separate theory of its own (Taylor, 2006).

Turning first to theories of social and community development and then to those of personality development and motivation, the social psychologist Melvin Lerner's (1980) concept of a 'just world' looked promising. Yet Lerner restricted the term simply to a description of the initial tendency for individuals to maintain the status quo after any adverse incident by blaming the victim, unless the magnitude of the distress were substantially disproportional to the action that might have caused it.

To its credit, some 30 years ago the United Nations lent support for justice through the use of *social indicators* to monitor matters of concern about individual and community wellbeing.[2] The indicators had several characteristics, such as relevance to the topic of interest, having broad support, being grounded in research, allowing for disaggregation, having consistency over time, being statistically sound, and providing international comparisons. They were introduced in New Zealand by the Department of Statistics as part of national census taking (Shields, 1979), and used by the Royal Commission on Social Policy (1988a) to gather empirical evidence from the community about perceptions of justice, health and hospitals, education, housing, employment, and personal social services, to determine whether New Zealand society was 'fair and just'.[3] Since then, the indicators have become regular assessment devices of the Ministry of Social Development (2004, pp. 7–11). But they have yet to be fully explored with regard to attaining the fundamentals of justice.

---

2  In the words of Peter Davis, an adviser to the Royal Commission on Social Policy (1988a, vol. 3, pp. 345–362), "Social wellbeing – its achievement, promotion, enhancement – is the goal towards which social policy is to be directed and by which it should be judged ... it is social in that it goes beyond the private concerns of individuals to a dimension of public and collective significance; and it involves assessments not only of individuals but also of groups, institutions and other social forms and processes, including society itself".

3  In passing, it has to be noted that in its executive summary, the Royal Commission on Social Policy (1988b, p. 52) concluded that a "good justice system should provide a fair and efficient means of resolving disputes. It should ensure that individuals receive justice, and that society is protected. It should punish appropriately those who commit offences".

In the 1980s, community psychologists construed justice as a prominent motivating force in human behaviour, the attainment of which, according to them, depended primarily on negating adverse environmental factors. But they abandoned the concept two decades later, with Gregory (2001) reporting that "the lofty spirit, awakening of morals, and arousal of conscience [had] dimmed [and] wealth and power [had replaced] principles about what is right, or the pursuit of justice for all, or simply the greater good".

From the 1990s, Lyman Porter and colleagues (2003, chapter 2) took advantage of developments in social theory to refer to justice as it reflected the fair distribution of rewards and penalties in industry, the fairness of the processes through which the distributions were made, and the fairness of the interpersonal consequences. But they made no mention of the adverse psychological effects on general staff and stakeholders of the plundering of resources by management and corporate dictatorships for personal gain, that is, corporate malfeasance, or the unjust enrichment on a gigantic scale resulting from the abuse by business directors and executives of their financial responsibilities, the results of which can be regarded as tantamount to those of any other kind of disaster (Taylor, 2003). Similarly, theories that conceptualise public policy were limited to scrutinising the process of justice (see Kurtines and Gewirtz, 1991), instead of the fundamental need it served, as also were the most recent contributions in forensic psychology (Ross and Miller, 2002b).

Turning from social and community theories and practices concerning justice to those of individual personality development, the most accommodating of them merely alluded to the acquisition of moral behaviour (see Lundin, 1996) without regard to its motivational aspect. In fact, Maslow (1908–70) was the only one of all the major motivational researchers and social theorists to come close to nominating *justice* per se as a human need. He even mentioned specific attributes of justice, such as "the child's need for some kind of undisrupted routine or rhythm ... a predictable, orderly world", adding that "*injustice*, unfairness, or inconsistency in the parents seems to make a child feel anxious and unsafe" (emphasis added; Maslow, 1954, p. 86).[4] He also warned of the consequences of *injustice*, the evidence of which would be seen in the "neurotic or near-neurotic individuals" who had been endangered as well as "the economic and social underdogs" (p. 87). He went on specifically to describe conditions such as "freedom to do what one wishes, so long as no harm is done to others, freedom to express oneself ... to defend oneself, justice, fairness, and

---

4  Although all three editions of Maslow's text were consulted, for the sake of consistency the references are given to the first edition in which they appeared.

orderliness in the group [as] preconditions for basic need satisfactions" (p. 92). But he stopped short of giving justice full recognition, when saying "These conditions are not ends in themselves but they are *almost* [sic] so since they are so closely related to the basic needs, which are apparently the only ends in themselves".

Maslow also fell short of expecting the most psychologically mature people – whom he called the 'self-actualised' – to have moral obligations for helping the rest of humankind to address the injustice they might be suffering. Instead, he epitomised them in mystical terms as people capable of understanding everything but resolving nothing. Many of the self-actualised became his "personal growth" disciples, but very few his critical companions.

## Proposed revision of Maslow's theory

Despite the shortcomings of Maslow's theoretical constructs and their lack of empirical validation that the originator himself acknowledged, it seemed sensible to revise Maslow's conceptualisation of justice, by:

- including justice – all three civil, criminal and social components intertwined – in the group of safety needs that Maslow identified, while also accepting its relevance in the need for 'belonging' that he outlined;
- redesigning the familiar illustration of progressive layers of basic needs to show the physiological needs, safety needs, and belonging needs as the separate legs of a milking stool, the precarious structure of which makes clear the equal and fundamental importance of all three, with the functional development of the later stages of self-esteem and self-actualisation depending on all three legs being strong enough to carry the load; and
- placing an obligation on the more fortunate and psychologically secure individuals to help people who might be under a heavy strain.

## The assertion and implications

The assertion is that justice is more than a matter of affirming contractual rights, giving protection from criminality, neutralising the aversive effects of socio-political policies, making the courts and procedures less forbidding, and involving a cadre of responsible citizens in the processes of mediation and reconciliation. Necessary as they are in conflict resolution and restorative justice (Ladley, 2006; Maxwell and Morris, 2006), such procedures serve the deeper purpose of satisfying the part of the basic human need for security that overlaps with that of belonging to a community. Marlene Young (2001) demonstrated as much through her authoritative work on the provision of personal assistance to many different categories of victim that she underpinned with Maslow's theory.

Already a few scholars and researchers have braved the opposition to revive interest in morality and value systems (see Burns, 2006; Jose, 2006, Marshall, 2006; Tolman, 2006).[5]

Their work has become the more essential because of the urgent need to find common ground in the prevention of terrorism (see Ali, 2003; Zaoui, 2005). The theologian and human rights lawyer Melodee Smith (2005) broached the topic in relation to restorative justice in her paper to the April 2005 United Nations Congress on Crime Prevention and Criminal Justice that was held in Bangkok. Also in the present volume, the political scientist Karen Baehler (chapter 16) gives a refreshing appraisal of a few key philosophical theories to show their relevance in the attainment of 'justice', and social psychologists James Liu and Katya Hanke (chapter 15) explore the contemporary research that has a bearing on the subjective perceptions of justice.

The combination of such subjective and objective studies has epistemological consequences for the development and teaching of behavioural and social science that should redound to the benefit of both. It remains to be seen how soon the defensive battlements of behavioural science in the universities will be abandoned in favour of interactive endeavours that speak to the 'real' condition of people.

---

5 Apart from those already cited in the present text from the same volume, see Eccleston and Ward (2006), Fischer and Skitka (2006), Oruvwuje and Taylor (2006), Sluka (2006) and Wexler (2006).

# 15

# Reflections on a Social Psychology of Justice: Implications for Restorative Justice Practices

*James H. Liu and Katja Hanke*

## Introduction

Virtually all human societies are based on the premise that people should be governed by standards of conduct that appeal to principles of right and wrong rather than to simple might or self-interest. A social psychology of justice focuses on subjective perceptions of right and wrong. It examines what people think is just and unjust, fair and unfair, their reasons for holding such views, and the behavioural consequences of violating standards of justice. It focuses on subjective or psychological reactions to and justifications for these principles rather than an analysis of the institutions that administer them or their underlying philosophy. Perceptions of justice provide an important link between objective circumstances (for example, deprivation) and people's reactions to them (see Stouffer et al., 1949).

Although the practices of restorative justice did not develop in dialogue with theoretical concepts of justice identified by social psychology, they do appear to be mutually informative. Hence, this chapter reviews the literature in social psychology on justice and examines its interface with practices of restorative justice.

In every domain of human judgement, satisfaction with one's lot in life seems to depend on more subjective perceptions than on the absolute values of any given criterion (Tyler et al., 1997). People regularly compare themselves to others, and satisfaction appears to depend on a process of social comparison. Concern with justice, or fairness, appears to be part of this ubiquitous tendency to compare one's outcomes relative to others'. Because perceptions of justice are made in relation to something or someone, social psychologists have found no single universal principle of justice, but rather a set of rules that apply with different force across situations.

Justice pulls together the fabric of society by providing different rules to regulate different relationships and social functions, at the micro-level (for example, between family, friends or co-workers) and at the macro-level (for example, between genders, social classes, ethnic groups or countries; see Brickman et al., 1981). Hence, while justice may be defined as a set of abstract moral principles or rules for regulating the conduct of relationships in society, their content is so varied as to defy unitary description. The first and most important distinction is between distributive and procedural justice. Distributive justice is concerned with the allocation of resources or outcomes between individuals (or groups), whereas procedural justice is concerned with the processes used to reach the decision.

Much of the research conducted in social psychology on justice over the years has been concerned with understanding how different rules of distributive and procedural justice influence perceptions of satisfaction and fairness, at both the individual level and at the systems level. Other research focuses on why people sometimes do not seem to care about justice at all and why specific groups or people are outside one's *scope of justice*. Those people or groups not 'morally included' are vulnerable to unfair or even harmful treatment (see Coryn and Borshuk, 2006; Opotow, 1994). There is a much smaller literature that deals with retributive justice. The 'market metaphor' of justice, based around inputs and outputs and rewards and costs, has dominated the literature rather than the perhaps more primal language of crime and punishment. Hence, we focus our review on distributive and procedural justice, as well as the scope of justice, and only touch on the issue of retributive justice.

## Distributive justice

Classic social psychology of the 1950s to the 1970s focused around issues of distributive justice (for example, Adams, 1965). Research identified three types of distribution rules (equity, equality and need) that all could be applied to different situations, but varied in their force across different relationships and circumstance (Deutsch, 1975). This work was built on social exchange theory and interdependence theory, which have been and continue to be among the dominant theories in the social sciences (for summaries, see Foa and Foa, 1974; Kelley and Thibaut, 1978).

Equity rules follow a market pricing metaphor (Fiske, 1992). According to equity rules, the ratio of inputs to outputs (or rewards and costs) between two people should be equal for perceptions of maximum satisfaction and fairness within the relationship. This apparently simple rule of justice (you get what you pay for, you get what you put in) has received considerable support (Adams, 1965; Walster et al., 1978), and provides the counterintuitive prediction that people who are over-benefited will be less satisfied than those who are receiving an appropriate level of benefits relative to their costs. Although this prediction has received support (Walster et al., 1978), it is qualified by the self-serving bias, or a tendency for people to overestimate their own contributions and costs, and underestimate the contributions and costs of others (Taylor and Brown, 1988). In general, people are less unhappy about being over-benefited than being under-benefited, although they are always sensitive to maintaining a 'fair' level of reward for their work or investment into a relationship. There does seem to be some sort of internal calculus of rewards and costs even for close relationships, but how this is determined is highly subjective and difficult to pin down.

It is difficult to apply equity rules in real life because it is hard to determine an exchange value for many actions, especially actions that have caused harm to others. As noted by Karen Baehler (in chapter 16), compensation of even purely monetary damage done is complicated by the fact that emotional damage could have been done as well, and that the victim feels less safe and less trusting after having been defrauded or robbed. Heather Strang (2002) observes that often victims do not demand complete restitution of financial harm done to them if they understand the circumstances that led the offender to commit their offence and if the offender offers a heartfelt apology. Payment in kind is even less appropriate if the harm done involves physical damage. The form of equity expressed in parts of the Hammurabi Code ('an eye for an eye'), for example, is perceived by many people in modern societies as barbaric. But this does not change the basic psychological and evolutionary fact that 'tit for tat' (returning payment in kind) is a core feature of evolutionarily stable forms of human cooperation and exchange (see Axelrod and Hamilton, 1981; Yamagishi, 1998). The modern state's penchant for using incarceration as punishment for harm doing does resonate at some level with a basic psychology of tit-for-tat exchanges.

All of these perceptions of justice or fairness are qualified by the fact people typically make social comparisons to similar or proximal others (Festinger, 1954; Wood et al., 1985). Therefore, while the janitor may compare his wage to that of his co-workers or his immediate superior for the work that he does, he does not usually apply equity rules to compare his income and work levels against that of the owner of the business, who may be making hundreds if not thousands of times more money for equal hours. Most psychological research focuses on issues of micro- rather than macro-justice (Brickman et al., 1981); that is, issues involving interpersonal relationships rather than the rules of society. But often crimes are committed by people who share only a glancing relationship with those they have offended against. Hence, restorative justice procedures are likely to work best if the appropriate community can be identified that can mediate between the victim and offender to restore the victim's trust and faith in society and to shame the offender into acknowledging the damage they have done to the victim and apologising in a heartfelt way. These procedures are also likely to be more satisfying from the victim's point of view if the offence committed against them is not too serious (Strang, 2002).

Another interesting feature of equity theory is that people's subjective perceptions of what is fair accommodate or habituate to their situations over time (Greenberg, 1988). People randomly assigned to over-benefited situations at work (for example, a status or pay increase for no reason) initially work harder, but over time return to their baseline work rates without any long-term pangs of conscience. So there may not be absolute standards by which people judge fairness, but rather it is a function of what they become accustomed to. For all forms of justice, including restorative, this means that there is no truly timeless or universal standard for what punishment or compensation fits what offence. Perceptions of justice are not only constructed out of pre-eminent cultural values, but they also depend on the relationship between the people involved in disputes and the nature of the dispute between them.

These findings signal limitations to a simple market metaphor, as it is impossible to assign a single fixed metric of rewards and costs across domains of human interaction involving different activities and resources (Foa and Foa, 1974). Rather, resources tend to be exchanged for similar kinds of resources rather than across all domains (for example, money for goods, but not money for love, see Foa et al., 1993). Different types of resources (for example, information) have different quantitative properties in exchange (for example, information may be given away without depletion, but not money). In effect, to avoid personal feuds between families or individuals, modern states have instituted an impersonal system of punishment that can be applied blindly, irrespective of the relationship between the victim and offender, and converting offences into prison terms or fines. While this impersonal system of crime and punishment may be helpful in keeping order and preventing feuds from developing, it also typically does not provide victims with a feeling of satisfaction with the proceedings. Many people would prefer payment in kind (for example, monetary restitution) where possible (Strang, 2002).

The concept of equity is further restricted by the fact that people in close relationships (most obviously within the family, like spouses or parents and children) do not keep track of rewards and costs or input and outputs as much as people in less intimate, shorter-term relationships (Clark and Mills, 1979). Hence, at least two other justice rules are required to understand perceptions of justice or fairness in social exchange in these types of relationships: equality and need.

Equality has long been understood as a principle of justice that can be used when interpersonal harmony is valued more than productivity or accurate accounting (Deutsch, 1975). Trading off between equality and equity is an important way of balancing organisational efficiency and cohesion (Deutsch, 1985). While the principle of equity in the workplace spurs productivity, it also generates rivalry and a sense of injustice (Leventhal, 1976). Equality builds group cohesion but at the cost of reducing individual incentives to maximise productivity.

At the interpersonal end of the spectrum, intimate long-term relationships have been described as communal (Clark and Mills, 1979). Careful accounting of costs and benefits are not necessary; indeed Kelley (1979) describes various mechanisms used by committed romantic partners to shield their relationship from market forces (that is, more attractive alternative partners) by psychologically devaluing alternatives. Therefore, not only is accurate accounting of rewards and costs not necessary, it may need to be actively avoided by committed partners because maintaining the relationship is more important than short-term costs and benefits. What is fair or just may be considered with the idea of the family in mind rather than from the perspective of the constituent individuals.

In close relationships, it is the emotional side of restorative justice practices that are important, like the apology, and the opportunity for both sides to give voice during, and feel that they have control over, the conflict resolution proceedings. This is especially pertinent in disputes involving spouses. Punishment or payment in kind is usually not required in close relationships, and in some ways restorative justice tries to leverage off the basic human emotions related to close relationships by trying to build remorse for misdeeds on the offender side and forgiveness on the victim side. At their best, procedures such as family group conferencing can act to strengthen relationships or *build community* between, not only a victim and an offender (who might be only slightly connected), but the people making up the community around them. Empathy, something easily felt for people we are close to (Preston and de Waal, 2002), becomes ever more precious when it can connect a wider community of people. John Braithwaite's (1989) concept of reintegrative shaming, where a person is brought before their community to feel the full weight of public opinion on them in a way that does not stigmatise them, but leads them to acknowledge the harm they have done and apologise or make restitution, is very much linked to emotions such as empathy.

Committed social relations at the organisational level also distort pure market considerations in business as well. Toshio Yamagishi and Midori Yamagishi (1994) describe traditional Japanese economic relations as consisting of committed business partners who eschew short-term gains provided by trading with outsiders in favour of reliable social relations within a network of committed others who have little incentive to cheat. Such a strategy reduces transaction costs and incurs 'opportunity costs' (that is, missed opportunities to establish new relationships) that may constrain the global spread of Japanese business.

Another instance where equity cannot serve as a primary rule of distributive justice is in relationships between parents and children. Children in modern societies are largely incapable of functioning equitably in a rewards–costs ratio relationship with their parents. Rationally, in a society where provision for old age is provided for by pensions, no parent would ever raise a child if they subjected this relationship to a cost–benefit analysis! Rather, the typical relationship between parents and children in a post-industrial society is described better by a need rule than an equity rule. The biological needs of children are far greater than those of their parents where their relationship is concerned. Adherence to such a rule may be motivated by a sociobiological drive to maintain the species (see Barkow et al., 1992), but this still deviates from equity or requires a transgenerational conception of equity where every child repays their debt by nurturing their own children rather than directly repaying their parents (Yuki and Yamaguchi, 1996). Family group conferencing in restorative justice touches on these principles as well by involving people around the victim and offender, so that a debt that cannot be repaid by the offender might well be able to be repaid, either emotionally or materially, by the family and friends of the offender and by acknowledgment and support from the community around them.

At the macro-level, modern welfare states provide for the basic needs of their impoverished, elderly or handicapped citizens beyond what a simple accounting for their inputs to society might warrant according to an equity rule. The degree to which society should provide such an unconditional safety net for its citizens has been a topic of continuous and heated debate, most recently spurred by the new conservatism of President Ronald Reagan and Prime Minister Margaret Thatcher (see Halper and Clarke, 2004; King, 1988). The multiple rules for interpreting justice can be seen clearly in the political debates around such issues as social welfare and human rights. Abraham Maslow (1943) notes that as basic needs (for example, safety, security and sustenance) become satisfied, other, higher level, needs become pre-eminent in such a way that the minimum conditions for basic needs become difficult to identify.

Societies can be characterised by the value they give to equality and freedom (including equity issues linked to market freedoms) according to Milton Rokeach's (1976) influential taxonomy differentiating between political systems. Creating a new fusion between social equality and market freedom (that is, equity considerations) in the context of globalisation is the core issue for political science thinking characterised by 'the third way' between capitalism and socialism (see Giddens, 2000).

Culture level differences in macro-level exchange rules can be easily detected in the ways different societies talk about issues and enact legislation. In traditional Asian societies, for instance, close relationships (especially among kin) are regarded as primary, and the metric of exchange is secondary to the maintenance of the relationship, which is lifelong and non-voluntary (Hwang, 1987, 1999). Such justice rules as 'On' govern relationships between parents and children in Japan. 'On' debts are so deep that they can never be repaid (Yuki and Yamaguchi, 1996). Similarly, filial piety (Ho, 1996) is regarded as a basic principle of morality in Chinese societies, as the relationship between parent and child is one of the five cardinal relationships. It is a matter of obligation and a requirement of social standing to provide for one's parents, though in modern times both authoritarian (obedience-based) and benevolent (affect-based) forms of filial piety can be distinguished (Yeh and Bedford, 2004). Recently, Singapore legislated to allow elderly parents to sue their adult children for non-support. In terms of justice issues, traditional East Asian society is clear that children owe their parents a debt that can never be repaid but should be honoured by such actions as lifelong respect and obedience.

## Procedural justice

In addition to evaluating the fairness of outcomes, people also pay attention to the procedures or processes used to determine outcomes. This is probably the most cogent argument for restorative justice. Perhaps the cornerstone of Western civilisation is the ideal that every citizen should have recourse to a legal system that applies the same procedural rules to adjudicate disputes or assign penalties regardless of the status or identity of the people involved (see Rawls, 1971). Accordingly, the key finding of the procedural justice literature is that people will often accept an unfavourable outcome from a third party if they feel that the procedure used to decide the outcome was fair. Sometimes, procedural justice concerns (process) outweigh distributive justice concerns (or outcomes) in determining satisfaction with the judgements of a third party such as the legal system.

Gerald Leventhal (1980) provided a general framework of six procedural justice rules: consistency (in applying the same rules across people), bias suppression, accuracy, ethicality, representativeness (considering everyone's opinions) and correctability. In simulation research using undergraduates, Edith Barrett-Howard and Tom Tyler (1986) found that the first five factors were all rated as important in judging the fairness of allocation decisions across a variety of interpersonal situations. While requiring time and effort to implement, different procedural justice rules are not mutually exclusive, and do not require trading off as the distributive justice rules described previously.

Representation is the most important aspect of the procedural justice rules relevant to restorative justice; the work of E. Allan Lind and Tom Tyler (1988) focused on voice, having a say, as crucial to perceptions of procedural justice. Being included within the debate is crucial to both plaintiff and defendant perceptions of justice; being able to present a point of view and have it heard by officials and by the other parties involved is an important determinant of satisfaction with legal procedures, and this is an area where restorative justice is typically superior to standard court proceedings steeped in formalism and where both victims and offenders face distancing mechanisms.

John Thibaut and Laurens Walker (1975) provided empirical evidence in support of the importance of procedural justice concerns at a time when distributive justice concerns were dominant. They examined satisfaction with adversarial versus inquisitorial systems (used in the United States and France respectively) using a process control model. They theorised and found that people do not want to surrender control over an issue, but if they are unable to resolve a dispute, they will accept a form of proxy control in the form of voice and influence over a third party's conduct of the dispute resolution process rather than control over the outcome itself. Using experimental methods involving mock trials and questionnaires, Thibaut and Walker (1975) found that the adversarial system is preferred to the inquisitorial system (where magistrates hired by the court conduct the investigation rather than lawyers representing the disputants) because it is considered to be objectively fairer, favouring the disadvantaged party and reducing pre-trial bias, and gives the disputants greater voice in the trial process.

Restorative justice processes ideally should involve even greater degrees of participant control over legal proceedings than was allowed for by even Thibaut and Walker. In restorative justice, the parties have direct input into the types of resolutions that are prescribed in order to resolve the conflict; there is much less direction or interference from bureaucratic officials, and, ideally, more input from the community and from the people directly involved in the dispute. Hence, it is no surprise that Strang (2002), in a tightly controlled experimental study using real cases, found greater satisfaction with restorative justice processes and outcomes than with standard court proceedings.

Other research has demonstrated strong procedural justice effects in real world settings where people could be incarcerated (Casper et al., 1988), and where large amounts of money were involved (Lind et al., 1993). It has also extended the work from legal settings to managerial settings like performance appraisal, pay decisions and workplace grievances (see Lind and Tyler, 1988, for an overview; Tyler and Blader, 2000, for a theoretical summary).

According to Tyler et al. (1997), people's evaluations of group authorities, institutions and rules are determined mainly by procedural justice considerations rather than outcomes. This highly optimistic conclusion suggests that attitudes towards authorities are determined by experiences of the fairness of procedures used to adjudicate the situation rather than the outcome itself. Hence, under conditions of scarcity (where not everyone will receive a positive outcome), authorities can retain their legitimacy if they provide even-handed procedures that give voice and input (process control) to their clients. Crime suspects feel more fairly treated if they are allowed to speak about how they should be treated, and victims feel more fairly treated if they can speak about how a criminal should be sentenced.

These basic findings provide the theoretical foundations for a restorative approach to justice in particular, and to the vision of a restorative society more generally. When implemented delicately and fairly, such procedures as involving victims and offenders in face-to-face conferences were judged fairer than a more impersonal day in court (Strang, 2002). Similarly, Gabrielle Maxwell and Allison Morris (2001) report that family group conferences can reduce reoffending when the young person feels involved in the decision making and is not made to feel like a bad person; victims are also more likely to view a court procedure as fair and equitable when they participate in a conference, and this effect is magnified when they also feel they had a role (or were given voice) in the decision making.

In East Asian societies (for example, Leung and Morris, 2001), given the societal focus on maintaining face and harmonious social relations, using informal procedures or conferencing to settle disputes is just as popular, though there may be more complicated issues of face or shame involved. They are less progressive in applying restorative justice principles to criminal law, however (Lo et al., 2006).

Consultation, or giving voice, has now become a by-word of such varied processes as instituting legislative changes or restructuring corporations. However, sometimes such consultation is perceived as mere lip service, where the results of consultation are not taken seriously by authorities, or where the process is under-resourced. When implemented in a genuine and effective manner, appropriate procedures help to confirm the social standing of people involved in the system, repairing the damage done to their standing by any experiences of victimisation, and strengthening identification with the organisation implementing the procedure (Tyler and Blader, 2000). Procedurally just treatment signals to people that they are worthy of respect by authorities and can take pride in their standing within the group. Restorative justice procedures such as group conferences are capable of enhancing these effects.

## Scope of justice and the justice motive

Not all people are included within such boundaries of respect. Justice norms appear to be internalised norms or rules that apply to only particular categories of people and groups within these boundaries (Deutsch, 1985; Opotow, 1994). Justice can be a matter of perspective and protecting one's values (Skitka, 2002, 2003). Justice rules regulate social relations and help the individual to make sense of the world. The need to maintain particular world views is implicated in the process by which people sometimes distort their perceptions to see events as fair, even though they objectively are not fair (Lerner, 1981; Lind, 2000). This approach helps explain why groups harm other groups that seem to be different and why these harm-doings do not seem to evoke feelings of injustice among the perpetrators.

Many people have been refused human or civil rights at one time or another because they haven fallen outside of the society's moral community: for instance, ethnic, religious and sexual minorities. "The social and historical arrangements of power and inequality have tended to mirror decisions about inclusion in and exclusion from the moral community" (Coryn and Borshuk, 2006, p. 586). Over time and place, the border of one's scope of justice is not stable. These borders change as we change while gaining experience – be it experiences of historical change or experiences within one's neighbourhood.

Group membership is one decisive factor that determines whether we care about someone who is treated unfairly or is harmed (Tyler and Blader, 2000). But more than this, the justice rules governing social relations are adjusted according to the demands of the situation. In his seminal synthesis of the literature, Melvin Lerner (1981) argued that the 'justice motive' is an integral part of the social relations involved in achieving different outcomes in different situations. People have a need to maintain a structured interpersonal environment, clearly delineated between people perceived as: 'the same as me' (identity relation); similar to me, or a member of my unit or group; or non-unit, or different from me (one of them, the other). An understanding of these different types of social relations is acquired during childhood, where identity relations typically involve activating need rules and being concerned for the other's welfare, unit relations involve equality rules, and non-unit or different others stimulate concerns about who is getting more or less. These basic templates interact with the goal of the situation, competitive, cooperative or involving dependency.

The final factor is whether the focus is on process or outcome. Different justice rules and social processes are expected to predominate in Lerner's (1981) '3 x 3 x 2' scheme where the three types of social relations interact with the three types of situational goals and two types of focuses (process or outcome) (see Lerner, 1981, p. 30). This typology is among the most sophisticated theoretical schemes for understanding when different justice rules (including the lack of justice) are applied to different situations (see Ross and Miller, 2002a), but because of its complexity has not stimulated much empirical research. Restorative justice practitioners might find some gems of wisdom in it, however, in seeking to identify ideal situations for applying family group conferences and acknowledging other situations where the circumstances are not ideal for restorative practices.

Lerner's other highly influential work on just world beliefs (for example, Lerner et al., 1976) helps to further explain when the scope of justice is limited. According to his theory, people in Protestant cultures acquire a world view where they become invested in believing that people get what they deserve. This is a part of an informal system of social control, and helps people to feel safe themselves. When faced with highly engaging situations where a person is treated in a manifestly unfair manner (and the individual cannot do much about it), people with just world beliefs tend to derogate the victim or tend to avoid helping them in order to maintain their world view. Unlike most of the theories of justice in social psychology, just world beliefs have been measured as an individual difference. According to Carolyn Hafer and James Olson (1993) many recent studies measuring the belief in a just world (BJW) show that the higher the person's BJW scores, the more negative are their reactions to victims of discrimination of nearly all kind.

## Retributive justice

Work on the justice motive and scope of justice signals a critical limitation to the social psychology of justice: it tends to downplay or neglect the role of retribution, punishment or revenge. But as noted by Liu in chapter 2 of this volume, the desire for punishment rather than restoration or equity is primal, emotional, embedded within culture and older than civilisation (see also Hogan and Emler, 1981; Keeley, 1996).

In cases such as rape or murder, people often reject the idea that restoring equity is a just response. There is no suitable metric for equitably restoring the loss of the life of their child to a parent. In this case, the victims demand punishment. Furthermore, to intentionally cause harm to someone and then try to compensate them with money is likely to be treated as morally offensive (Horai and Bartek, 1978). People also tend to reject compensation when they feel that the crime involves immoral behaviour.

Whereas social scientists since Theodor Adorno et al.'s (1950) seminal work on the authoritarian personality have viewed punitiveness as a deviant personality trait, and the prison system as dysfunctional, demands to get 'tougher on crime' are normative in societies at large, including the United States (Ellsworth and Gross, 1994) and New Zealand (Ritchie and Ritchie, 1993, 2002). Tom Tyler and Robert Boeckmann (1997) found that judgements of failing social conditions (for example, the decline of the family or poor socialisation) and social values (for example, authoritarianism or dogmatism) were the primary predictors of support for harsher punishments for crime even more so than concern about crime.

Members of the public tend not to focus on the big picture, where the causes of crime are attributed to the social fabric (for example, poverty or lack of education) rather than to the individual. The money used to build more prisons can come at the cost of having less money for hospitals and schools (Tyler et al., 1997).

## Conclusion

The social psychology of justice paints a rather optimistic view of human beings as highly social, and largely rational beings who accept a need for higher principles of justice to govern their relationships with others. People use different allocation rules to appropriately govern different social relations, and can be satisfied with dispute resolution procedures even when they yield an unfavourable outcome as long as the procedure is viewed as fair.

The limitation of this point of view, as noted by Lerner (2003) and Liu (this volume), is that it neglects the emotional, primal side of human nature that thrives on notions of crime and punishment and views blood as the final measure of satisfaction in retributive justice.

# 16

# Justifying Restorative Justice

*Karen Baehler*

## Introduction

In the same way that Aristotle began his inquiry into the foundations of statecraft by looking at how families and households functioned in the Greek city-state, we can begin this inquiry into the foundations of restorative justice by asking what a restorative model of the modern family would look like. Contemporary ideals of good parenting and family relations suggest a few core features: The model family provides a context of love and mutual support in which family members are allowed to make mistakes and enabled to learn from those mistakes. Family members treat each other with respect and care, and respond with natural empathy to each other's joys and sorrows. Children are given time and space (and social skills) to make their own choices whenever possible, within a framework of basic family rules. These rules are clearly understood by all and enforced consistently and predictably. The only rules that are adopted are those with which all family members are capable of complying. Rules are subject to change when a consensus among members supports change. When children break family rules or make choices that harm others, they are given fair warning before being punished. When punishment is required, the type and severity of the penalty fits the offence. Clear distinctions are always drawn between the person and the behaviour (we do not say 'bad boy' or 'bad girl,' but point out that the child made a bad choice). Punishments never involve withdrawal of love or basic support. The restorative family provides many opportunities for repentance and forgiveness.

Although not everyone will agree with this list, I take it as a rough approximation of some essential characteristics of modern theories of social as well as household justice. Indeed, the household often succeeds in reconciling and even uniting different styles of justice, which, in the hands of academic philosophers, tend to become warring schools. Take, for example, the scholarly debate between Kantian rationalists, on one hand, who emphasise the impartial application of universal rules as the apotheosis of justice, and the more recently emerging 'ethic of care' movement within philosophy, on the other hand, which seeks to nurture a deeper appreciation of the virtues of care, empathy and personal responsibility for others as central to social justice. The restorative household, as sketched above, clearly embraces elements of both schools without apparent contradiction.

This chapter argues that the restorative society movement in its broader form (as documented in this volume) could achieve a similar sort of rapprochement in the realm of ideas and ideological justifications for policy, thereby generating a vision of justice based on the best of multiple traditions. The next section of this chapter quickly introduces key features of the dominant, so-called retributive, approach to justice in Western societies and discusses how restorative practices can operate alongside a retributive system and remedy many of its flaws. The third section briefly introduces both the relatively recent idea of justice as care and the ancient idea of *clementia* or mercy as an essential component of the just society, and shows how the restorative model of justice fits into these formulations as well. In drawing support and justification from both schools of philosophy, the restorative model provides clues about how these schools might be reconciled and, perhaps more importantly, about how the political ideologies associated with these schools might formulate a vision of justice based on the best of both traditions.

## Justice as impartiality and proportionality

Although the restorative model of justice is often presented as a direct competitor to the so-called retributive model (that is, an eye for an eye), a quick tour of the retribution tradition shows that this is not necessarily so. In fact, it may even be argued that restorative practices are needed precisely to enable a just social system of retribution that is analogous to the just household. Restoration (in the form of restitution) and retribution may be seen as two sides of a coin rather than a pair of opposites when the central concept of balance is introduced.

Aristotle provides the classic statement of justice as a balancing act. All justice is a mean, according to Aristotle, and rectificatory or corrective justice, as he calls it, is an intermediate state between the losses suffered by a victim of crime and the gains (material or psychic) enjoyed by the offender. Thus, court-imposed penalties are not judgements about moral character, according to Aristotle, but exercises in balancing accounts (Aristotle, 350 BC/1959, Book V, section 4):

> Now the judge restores equality; it is as though there were a line divided into unequal parts, and he took away that by which the greater segment exceeds the half, and added it to the smaller segment. And when the

whole has been equally divided, then they say they have 'their own' – i.e., when they have got what is equal.

Thus, penalties should be calibrated to equalise gains and losses. Although Aristotle does not go into detail, he acknowledges that some kind of proportionality[1] will need to be invoked when it is either impossible or inappropriate to impose a strictly equivalent penalty. Other passages from Aristotle call for impartiality and consistency in the application of these principles, noting that legal proceedings should consider only the nature of the deed and the extent of its consequences (the benefit and injury), and not the characters of the people involved.

This idea of justice as rebalancing proves to be the most consistent thread connecting notions of justice found in the two millennia before Christ to those prevalent in the two millennia after Christ. The compatibility and longevity of the two central means of rebalancing – restitution and retribution – may, in fact, reflect their common objective of correcting an imbalance caused by a wrongdoer's actions. The relevant imbalance may be understood concretely, in terms of losses borne by a victim and gains enjoyed by an offender, in which case payment of restitution is the logical vehicle for rebalancing. Alternatively, the imbalance may be understood more abstractly, as a breach in the moral and/or cosmic order, in which case some sort of punishment or retribution may be considered the natural response.

Although retribution may be seen as the flipside of restitution, it must be acknowledged that public acts of retribution still involve the disturbing phenomenon of a state intentionally harming its own citizens. Many will argue that such harm is deserved if an offender has been found guilty, but it is harm nonetheless, and so we are left with a nagging sense that somehow the state has stooped to the same degraded level as the criminal. Hegel, with help from his predecessor Kant, addressed this apparent flaw within the principle of retribution, thereby helping to bring the idea of justice as rebalancing into the modern age. He did so by appealing to the moral good of restoring equal rights rather than imposing equal suffering.

In the *Philosophy of Right* Hegel (1821/1967) argued that offenders injure their victims not only directly through the effects of violence or theft and so on, but also indirectly, by essentially negating the victims' rights to security. This amounts to negating the very essence of political community, which depends upon citizens mutually acknowledging each other's status as rights holders. For

---

1   Aristotle equates distributive justice with geometric proportionality, and corrective justice with arithmetic proportionality.

Hegel, as for Kant, such an offence requires an equal and opposite negating of the offender's right to immunity from punishment, in order to nullify the original injury and reaffirm the social contract. Thus, punishment is no longer meant to satisfy angry emotions, perpetuate cycles of harm, or correct an imbalance in the distribution of suffering, but rather to restore the balance of equal rights and equal esteem that makes social and political community viable.

Kant and Hegel anchored their theories of justice on the Kantian maxim that human beings must always be treated as ends rather than means. Fulfilling this maxim requires recognising and respecting both ourselves and others as autonomous moral agents who are the ultimate sources of our own value. With autonomy comes responsibility, and with responsibility comes a Kantian basis for arguing that the retributive view of justice (and only the retributive view) upholds the dignity of wrongdoers by acknowledging their status as autonomous moral agents who can and should be held responsible for their actions. In this way, the Hegelian theorist arrives at the conclusion that appropriate punishments (that is, penalties equivalent to the loss of liberty imposed by the offence) are both justified and required in cases of guilt, because offenders, acting as a rights-holding members of the society, have for all practical purposes consented to their own punishment.

It is difficult to overstate the importance of this consent principle to modern criminal justice theory and practice in liberal states. Some philosophers have argued that the idea of consenting to one's own punishment can be upheld even without referring to the morality or blameworthiness of an offender's actions (Nino, 1991). This is accomplished by positing a tacit contract in which citizens agree to accept the normative consequences (specified punishments) that the law assigns to particular actions (violations of the law). Citizens agree to such a contract on essentially utilitarian, rather than moral, grounds, because they judge that such laws and their enforcement are necessary to protect the community from serious harm. If such a contract can be said to exist, then individuals can be said to have consented to the legal consequences that follow necessarily from their voluntary acts, assuming of course fair (impartial and consistent) processes for determining guilt and punishment. This is why courts seek to determine in each case whether the offence in question was committed voluntarily. Issues of an offender's competence and intentions are of great importance in determining the level of charges that will be brought, in judging guilt, and in fashioning appropriate sentences for those found guilty.

Although proportional retribution is often associated with less civilised worldviews, it has held sway over developed countries' legal systems for many

hundreds of years. Continued support for proportional retribution may be based on its close connection to core liberal principles such as:
- the affirmation of human dignity that comes with holding people accountable and responsible for their deeds;
- the need for protections against biased and arbitrary exercises of power, which points to the value of clear, consistent and impartial guidelines for punishment;
- the postulate that mutual respect for rights is essential to political community, and therefore negation of another's rights demands punishment;
- the recognition that crimes have consequences far beyond their immediate victims, and therefore require public as well as private condemnation;
- the importance of competence and intentionality to justifying punishment; and
- the role of proportionality in determining upper boundaries on allowable punishment.

Despite its connections to these deeply held values, however, the principle of proportional retribution in theory and in practice reveals defects that cannot be ignored. The good news is that restorative justice practices can correct or at least mitigate most of these defects, and in so doing, restore some of the retributive conception's moral standing. Put another way, restorative practices make fair retribution possible.

Defects of the retributive model and the restorative remedies for those defects fall roughly under the following themes.

## *Generalities and particularities*

Aristotle argued that the written law, though essential to justice, is also inherently defective because it must generalise across diverse situations and cannot account for all of the complexities and irregularities found in specific cases. Judges who apply the law too rigidly are therefore likely to miss out on the whole truth. Aristotle's answer to this dilemma was the practice of equity, which he defined as the application of practical reason to the particular features of cases in order to correct errors and fill gaps in the written law.[2] Although Aristotle categorises equity as a species of justice, he also declares that it is better than one kind of justice – "better than the error that arises from the absoluteness of the statement [of the written law]" (Aristotle, 350 BC/1959, Book V, section 10).

---

2 For an excellent discussion of Aristotle on equity, see Nussbaum (1993).

Modern justice systems actively resist the practice of equitable assessment in determinations of guilt and innocence. They do so for a very good reason – because the chief function of formal, impersonal, rule-bound systems is to protect individuals against the arbitrary and unfair exercise of official discretion. Thus, every effort is made to avoid introducing bias into a trial. Once a guilty verdict has been reached, however, equity principles can be used to fashion a sentence that is appropriate to each case. Both aggravating and mitigating factors can be taken into account to adjust the proportionality of a sentence. This is how modern systems strike a balance between the imperatives of impartiality, proportionality and due process, on one hand, and the need to do right by each particular case through equitable assessment, on the other hand.

In the adult courts, restorative justice practices applied at sentencing time work to balance the cold and detached quality of trial court processes with the particularised and personalised processes of restorative conferencing. These conferences provide an additional forum in which to cultivate a deeper understanding of the circumstances and backgrounds of the lives involved in each case – including both the offender and victim as well as their families and communities.

## *Community*

When William the Conqueror announced that crimes were to be treated as offences against the king rather than solely against the victim, he introduced an important, but two-edged feature of modern criminal justice systems. On one hand, the concept of committing an offence 'against the Crown' acknowledges that virtually all crimes have repercussions beyond the injuries done to their victims. One need look no further than the inner city neighbourhoods of most United States metropolitan areas to see the deleterious effects of rampant crime and fear of crime on quality of life for law-abiding people. On the other hand, however, the concept of committing an offence 'against the Crown' turns real experiences into abstractions for virtually everyone involved. Current court practices allow some input from victims, in the form of victim impact statements, and they acknowledge high-level system effects of criminal behaviour (note Hegel's point about criminals grasping more than their fair share of liberty), but they neglect altogether the intermediate effects of crime on victims' and offenders' families and communities.

By contrast, restorative justice practices try to develop a more intimate understanding of what a particular offence means to the many layers of people who are affected by it. Restorative justice conferences aim to generate a sense of connectedness rather than detachment. Although victim and offender are often complete 'strangers' so far as acquaintance is concerned, the restorative justice perspective views them partly as 'neighbours' whose wellbeing is interdependent and linked to the overall health of the communities in which they live.

Restorative justice thus seeks to repair the web of human relationships, understood not simply as the quality of relationships among particular individuals that existed immediately before a particular crime, but in terms of a vision for the interconnected society. By bringing down to earth the abstract idea of a political community founded on mutual respect for individual rights, the restorative justice model aims to develop a richer and more integrated vision of social and political communities and a better understanding of how to nurture the types of social and political capabilities that sustain community. A principle of retribution cannot go this far in envisioning community: it can only acknowledge basic rights and the basic reciprocal social arrangements that follow from them.

### *The missing half of Aristotle*

Aristotle clearly identifies two steps within corrective justice – taking from the one who is in the wrong and giving to the one who has been wronged. Although there are problems associated with calculating amounts to be transferred from offender to victim, due to asymmetry of losses and gains, it is clear that however a penalty is determined, it must not only be removed from the offender but also transferred to the victim. By Aristotle's standards, most present-day criminal systems satisfy only half of what justice requires, for restitution is an uncommon result in criminal proceedings. Although the halfway approach to justice receives support from Hegel, for whom restricting the liberty of offenders is enough to balance society's scorecard, it does not necessarily satisfy a demand for complete rebalancing. This problem reminds me of an essential flaw in the basic idea behind cost–benefit analysis, which says that projects should be approved if the excess of expected benefits over expected costs is great enough so that those who stand to gain from a project *could, in theory,* compensate those who stand to lose from it. The compensation need never take place; it simply needs to be theoretically possible. Since when did the related concepts of restitution and compensation become theoretical abstractions only?

In addition to restoring the larger web of community relationships, restorative justice practices also seek to reintroduce into the criminal justice system a more robust notion of direct restitution between offenders and victims.[3] The idea of restitution – understood not only materially but also in terms of achieving a personal sense of justice – is central to court-referred restorative justice programmes in New Zealand, the stated purpose of which is "to put things right for the people who have been victims of offences" (Department for Courts, 2005).

## Proportionality and practicality

In theory, the principle of proportionality provides an upper boundary on the amount of harm that the state can impose on an offender for a particular offence. Penalties should be commensurate with the wrong that was done, unless aggravating or mitigating features can be identified, in which case lighter or harsher sentences may be justified, but only within defined guidelines. In practice, the proportionality principle can be difficult to interpret, particularly in the contemporary setting where strict equivalence of penalties is no longer tolerated for the most part; for example, we do not punish rapists by having them raped (Finkelstein, 2002).[4] Short of strict equivalence, and in cases where monetisation of harm is impossible or inappropriate, what does proportionality mean? How much prison time is equivalent to the injury inflicted by an act of violence? Or, translated into Hegel's conceptual language, how much loss of liberty is equivalent to the loss of liberty experienced by the victims of these crimes? Answers to these sorts of questions tend to be set by convention rather than clear principle.

Restorative justice conferencing clearly adds value to the conventional system where proportionality is concerned. It does so by introducing a standard for calculating penalties that even Kant might be expected to endorse – the uncoerced agreement of the parties most directly involved. Not all restorative justice conferences try to craft a programme of penalties, and among those that do, not all succeed, but the potential is there for conferences to develop their own understanding of proportional balance and how it might be achieved.

## Conditions for consent

Present-day criminal justice systems tend to place heavy emphasis on the competence and intentions of accused persons when determining guilt and punishment, and this fact can be taken as prima facie evidence that the consent theory of punishment lives on. As discussed above, consent theory posits a

---

[3] It should be noted that the principle of restitution has always been central to civil proceedings.
[4] The exception is of course countries that execute murderers.

social contract in which rights-bearing members of society agree on the laws by which the society will be governed and, therefore, consent to be punished should they themselves be found guilty of breaking those laws. As with nearly all arguments based on a social contract, however, this one quickly encounters the problem of defining the community or society within which the contract, and therefore the assumption of consent, is to be considered binding. Who is to be considered a consenting member and on what grounds?

Because it is the production of social benefits that justifies a political community's existence in the first place, it makes sense to posit a community of citizens who are free and equal (in relevant ways) and who partake of the benefits that flow from social cooperation. But what if these fruits of social cooperation are not distributed evenly? What if opportunities are skewed toward some individuals and groups at the expense of others? If a society is characterised by severe social inequalities, it could be argued that the essential conditions for full membership in that community, and therefore the conditions for assuming universal consent from all members, are not being met. In the absence of consent, retributive punishment may be prohibited. Far more work is needed to describe the background conditions for a fair system of consent-based punishment, but preliminary thinking points to the importance of empowering weaker community members (remembering that both offenders and victims tend to come disproportionately from disadvantaged populations) and fostering tolerance and mutual respect among individuals and groups.

The restorative model of society, broadly understood, seeks to do precisely this across all social sectors – to empower the relevant parties to take positive steps forward in their own lives; to reinforce their identities as members of one or more communities; and to help everyone involved better understand the circumstances of each other's lives. Thus, even the classically liberal, neutral, and minimalist principle of consent, properly understood, cycles us back around to the idea that justice depends at least partly on the quality of human relationships.

## The quality of mercy and the ethic of care

Even if we agree that proportional retribution is potentially just under the proper conditions, a powerful question still remains as to how the repeated exercise of implementing that system – that is, punishing our fellow citizens – shapes the lives and characters of those who do the punishing and those who sponsor it. Is there a hidden moral or psychological cost in achieving fairness in this way?

Philosopher Martha Nussbaum (1993) answers yes to this question, with the help of Seneca the Younger, the first century AD Roman philosopher and dramatist who argued that the practice of retribution, even when publicly sanctioned, has dangerous consequences for the human spirit. According to this view, the practice of retribution hardens people until they eventually take on those qualities that define the criminal personality – detachment from society and indifference to the suffering of others. It causes us to forget our common humanity. Seneca's preferred alternative is *clementia*, a disposition that recognises personal responsibility for wrongdoing but refuses to respond to it with retributive anger, choosing instead a gentler and more humane approach based on the understanding that we are all vulnerable to doing wrong, or in Nussbaum's words (1993, p. 124), that "all human beings are the products of social and natural conditions that are, in certain ways, subversive of justice and love, that need slow, patient resistance". In addition, Nussbaum argues that taking the position of *clementia* changes our focus from judging and punishing the individuals who do wrong to changing the social forces that make goodness so hard to achieve.

The same background assumption that supports Seneca's notion of *clementia* – the idea that we inhabit a world characterised as much by particular human relationships as by abstract universal principles – also figures prominently in a contemporary philosophical tradition, known as the ethic of care. Philosophers and social scientists who belong to this tradition argue that a fully mature understanding of morality and justice requires not only a capacity for impartial application of universal principles (such as proportionality), but also an emphasis on the morality of caring for and being responsible to specific other human beings (Blum, 1988; Gilligan, 1983, 1993; Noddings, 2003).

Emerging initially from feminist studies and the study of gender differences in moral psychological development, the ethic of care has grown into a distinctive philosophical tradition that places human connectedness rather than individual autonomy at the centre of justice. According to this tradition, the model for justice is not necessarily the blindfolded woman holding the scales, but rather the parents, neighbours and friends who respond willingly and sensitively to the perceived needs of those around them. Knowing another person, responding to that person based on personal understanding, and doing so from a stance of love, compassion and empathy (Hoffman, 2000), is a moral act as much as an emotional one, according to the ethic of care. Such acts reflect a different model of justice from the dominant Western model, and one that arises from different 'voices' that are less often heard in modern societies, particularly (but not exclusively) women's voices (Gilligan, 1983).

The restorative conception of justice, understood broadly, seeks to nurture both Gilligan's ethic of care and Nussbaum's/Seneca's gentle and forgiving spirit. Without attenuating responsibility or necessarily substituting for punishment, restorative justice practices provide a setting in which to cultivate the sort of rich, narrative understanding of other lives – and common humanity – that makes empathy and care possible, as well as gentleness of spirit, mercy, and justice, properly understood.

## Conclusion

With the help of thinkers from Aristotle and Seneca to Hegel and Nussbaum, as well as the modern picture of a happy family, it is possible to imagine a truly integrated system of justice that draws from the best of the retributive and restorative traditions, and dismisses the simplistic caricatures of these conceptions that so often find their way into policy debates. Such an integrated system would seek to treat citizens as dignified and responsible moral agents while also nurturing the wider background conditions that sustain their sense of dignity within community, and their capacity for both responsibility and mutual care. Such a system would pursue the larger goal of a well-balanced and flourishing community through the apparently 'unbalanced' preference for particularised rather than generalised judgements, and for sympathetic rather than detached understanding. Such a system would seek constructive responses to offending that are commensurate with the larger social and cultural forces that need to be overcome, rather than devising punishments that are strictly proportional to the original injury. It would seek to repair earlier damage as well as balancing the moral ledger.

Alongside evidence of the power of restorative practices presented in other chapters, this chapter has demonstrated the power of a restorative social model not only to find principled justification in at least two very different schools of philosophy, but also to reveal areas of common ground between these opposing views and the political ideologies often associated with them. In the end, perhaps the main thing in need of reconciliation is our willingness to cooperate across ideological boundaries to build social systems in which the core principles of justice and care strengthen and reinforce each other, rather than competing for political resources and attention.

# Part Five

# Conclusion

# Introduction to Part Five

The journey to belonging is almost inevitably incomplete. Certainly, the stories told in this book are, and so too is restorative theory itself. Many conceptualisations run parallel in the themes developed here. Thus, we have decided not to attempt a conventional conclusion that brings everything together, but rather to present diverse comments that separately and collectively respond to many of the ideas that have been considered.

Central to this book has been a description of the development of restorative justice principles and related practices in New Zealand. Gabrielle Maxwell and James Liu (chapter 17) present their thoughts on how research has demonstrated that many of the initial doubts that most people share when first being exposed to the idea of restorative justice and other restorative initiatives have not been justified by experience. They also discuss some of the reasons it is important to build inclusive rather than exclusive approaches in order to create a cohesive society.

A second critical idea that recurs throughout these pages is that of the nature of justice itself, its fundamental importance for everyone and the extent that it is, in many ways, the benchmark of human goodness. Christopher Marshall (chapter 18) reflects on these ideas in his chapter on the spirit of justice. He also discusses the parallels between restorative justice ideas and the fundamental Christian values that are central to his thinking and to that of many others within our society.

Another important idea underpinning this book has been the idea of a restorative society as a goal for building a new social consensus. Jonathan Boston (chapter 19) picks up this, explores the extent to which it is a promising approach for bringing together may disparate practices, and discusses what needs to happen if we are to build on an idea that is still only implicit in what is currently happening. An essential element in developing successful restorative approaches is to allow innovative experimentation in a bottom-up manner while integrating advances and making corrections as necessary from the top down. Boston sees such a synthesis of grass-root experiences with regulatory practice as central to the continued vitality of the restorative movement.

# 17

# Can a Restorative Approach Heal and Restore?

*Gabrielle Maxwell and James H. Liu*

## Introduction

The rising imprisonment rates, the continual increases in prison security that make conditions less humane for inmates, and the many voices calling for longer sentences and reduced opportunities for reintegration are very much at odds with the reintegrative and restorative options envisaged here. So too are the calls for tougher responses to young people who behave badly in the education system. There is little doubt many people feel afraid and at risk in a world where terrorism is a major international concern and violence seems closer than it did in the past. At the same time, alternatives are being developed in New Zealand and around the world, and much of what is happening here has been ground breaking in offering new options. In this chapter we summarise the central issues that have emerged about the potential of restorative options.

## Can restorative justice be part of the road map for New Zealand's future?

The central issue for this book is whether the restorative values and philosophy underpinning restorative justice options and the development of restorative practice in civil society that have been described in this book provide a road map for the future in New Zealand. Except perhaps in the youth justice system, few examples exist of the type of research that is needed to provide the concrete evidence that can give unequivocal answers: criticisms and questions about the best procedures to follow are not the answer. There is also, at times, a lack of clarity about what does constitute a restorative approach, as well as how best it could be implemented in the range of contexts described here.

On the other hand, most of the practice described here has been developed only since the Children, Young Persons, and Their Families Act 1989 came into force. In the areas of youth justice and adult diversionary practice described in chapters 3–5, there is nevertheless some fairly clear articulation of the principles involved and frameworks that can support practice. In addition, important research has been done around current models, although many questions are still to be asked and answered. Perhaps it is the uncertainty over such broad questions that means much of what has happened has had only limited support from the mainstream. For example in policing and prison practice and rehabilitation, the restorative developments described in chapters 6–8 have had to compete with strong public rhetoric demanding more punitive practice and less tolerance for diversion or low-level responses to criminal offending. Restorative practices in education have met with some success, but are certainly not seen as mainstream, and current policies and practices do relatively little to invite schools to understand and explore these options (see chapters 10 and 11). In the area of responses to civil disputes described in chapter 9, we have seen the development of a multitude of alternative models with little effective critique, empirical research on effectiveness or robust theoretical integration of the key factors important for success. The fundamental rightness of trying to repair harms of the past has been discussed in chapters 12 and 13, but even these initiatives have received considerable criticism from those who see them as unnecessary, inappropriate or limited in meeting restorative objectives for all those affected. Throughout this book it is apparent that even developing a consensus on restorative justice theory and the key characteristics of what can be seen as a restorative process can be problematic. Indeed these questions are still debated fiercely in the international literature (for example, Bazemore and Schiff, 2004; Johnstone and Van Ness, 2007b; McCold, 2000, 2004; Sullivan and Tifft, 2006; Van Ness, 2002).

Equally, if not more difficult, is the question of what are good criteria for a successful outcome of restorative practice; most analysts are forced to rely on relatively simplistic and readily measurable criteria rather than on longer term goals related to the health of citizens and society as a whole. Therefore, many of the big issues are still under debate.

On the other hand, a surprising amount has happened in New Zealand in the past 15–20 years that is exciting and promising. Table 17.1 summarises what has been learnt. New ideas have given currency to old values of caring and the responsibility of society for its citizens. Attacks on 'welfare states' for failing to deliver what was promised have not often led to greater justice or the resolution of inequalities in responses to crime. Nor have they always been balanced by the development of improved strategies for resolving conflict, especially conflict that is bound up with the inevitable inequities within modern society. Ultimately, the more radical among us may believe restorative justice is a poor apology for social justice. However, it does provide an option for at least responding constructively to some of the consequences of disadvantage.

**Figure 17.1:** Conclusions from the New Zealand experience

**Restorative justice**

Restorative practices can be successfully incorporated in a national system of justice but effectiveness depends on how this is done.

- Conferencing is most likely to reduce re-offending and to result in savings when used with medium serious cases – other restorative options can be used in minor cases.
- Effectiveness will be increased if relevant services are provided to prevent reoffending.

Constructive outcomes are when:

- decision making is seen as fair and just;
- victims can be involved in ways not possible in courts;
- victims and offenders report greater satisfaction with outcomes;
- offenders are able to acknowledge their responsibility for doing harm, show genuine remorse, apologise and attempt to repair the harm and develop intentions to change their behaviour; and
- an opportunity exists to discuss and arrange effective and appropriate community service referrals.

**Restorative principles and practices**

In a more humane society restorative approaches to conflict represent a shift in values from:

- denunciation and blame to remorse and apology;
- punishment and exile to healing and repair; and
- exclusion and shaming to forgiveness and reintegration.

**Caveats**

- Restorative practice will inevitably vary in different places and for those of different cultures.
- Effective practice will also have a different face in the different contexts where conflicts occur and need to be resolved.
- We are only at the beginning of the journey and there will be many paths; some will fork, yet many may reconnect ahead.

As noted by critics such as Noreena Heertz (2001), neo-conservatives built an entire blueprint for society as governed by the 'invisible hand' of the free market. What was originally an economic formula for increasing competition and reducing centralised bureaucratic control grew into a programme for a new world order. Restorative justice advocates also have to recognise that at some point, these various and dynamic practices may also require a more powerful set of discourses, languages and, dare we say it, ideology to move restorative practices from their source in justice to society at large. This may help to empower and organise scattered contributors in other domains and engender renewed debate about what is 'the good society' in the context of globalisation and cultural diversity.

At the other extreme, critics of restorative justice have suggested that it is not justice at all because it fails to deter, it cannot meet the needs of victims, and it is impossibly idealistic to think that people could deal with anything but relatively minor matters in participatory processes involving the parties who have offended as well as those who have been offended against (see the critical issues raised in chapter 1). In this respect, at least, this book offers answers. With the right process, those who have harmed others are usually remorseful, and they do attempt to make amends and change their lives – often with considerable success. Nor is restorative justice for only minor matters: on the contrary, with respect to crimes and other disputes, the more serious issues are often best addressed by such strategies. Communities of care can be found to support repair, recovery and reintegration. Consensus can be found even in situations where there are real inequalities of power and resources and major differences in cultures and beliefs. Rights can be protected, victims and the vulnerable can be kept safe; and solutions can be arrived at that are seen as fair by the parties most affected. Furthermore, international reviews, (for example, Hayes and Daly, 2003) show that repeated transgressions are certainly no more likely than when the solutions are arrived at by courts. The rhetoric may seem emotional and distant from the measurable and quantifiable yet perhaps what is needed is more creativity in developing measures of the truly important outcomes of conflict resolution – peace, healing, forgiveness and belonging.

What could also be extremely useful is the continued experimentation with the use of restorative practices in all aspects of society where conflicts need to be resolved. The experience of restorative justice is that a continuous interplay between innovative experimental practices at the grass roots with integration, evaluation and theory-based refinement from central authorities can produce a viable alternative to the traditional system of justice. It is exactly this historical background that characterised the history of the Children, Young Persons, and Their Families Act 1989 in New Zealand (see chapter 3). The challenge before us is to maintain this dynamism in established areas like youth justice while conceptualising it in ways that make the essential elements of restorative justice theory and practice exportable to other segments of society. In many ways the development of restorative justice resonates with the general social science model of action research (initially described by Kurt Lewin (1947); see Bargal (2006) for a review) and community-based participatory research. In this approach, a spiral cycle of planning, action and evaluation is undertaken with input from all parties involved – from top to bottom. Participation and empowerment at the grass roots guided by integrative and responsive central authorities appear to be key to both restorative justice and to effective efforts by community groups, researchers, practitioners and policy makers to make a difference in society.

In the wider society, impatience is expressed with attempts to redress the wrongs of the past; in part because of the enormity of attempting to do so, but also because of a lack of understanding of the way in which the past can cast a long shadow for those who have been the victims, sometimes at second hand, of historical wrongdoing (see Liu, 2005). In civil disputes, cash settlements are often seen as a way to deal with matters when there can be an assessment of financial loss, but perhaps there is less often concern over the emotional consequences (see chapter 15). On the other hand, chapters 12 and 13 indicate that simply recognising what has occurred and acknowledging that it was wrong can go a long way to healing the hurts that are still felt.

## In conclusion

At the end of the day, every society must resolve the problem of how to create cohesion and build the effectiveness of the collective. Inevitably, this means offering support to its members as well as offering them protection against harm. There will always be debate about the point at which it becomes necessary to protect the great majority from the harm that can be caused by the few. However, it is equally important to attempt to rebuild the lives of those who are at risk because of the negative experiences they have had and to enable them to be reintegrated into the group wherever possible. It is often those who have become alienated because of the harm done to them who pose the greatest threat to the rest of society. But more than this, it is a moral imperative that we should respond to others as we wish to be responded to. It is in this way that we can build a society that will best protect both us as individuals and those we care about most.

# 18

# Reflections on the Spirit of Justice

*Christopher D. Marshall*

## Introduction

Over recent years, I have attended several major conferences in New Zealand and overseas on restorative justice. All have been very worthwhile in fostering interdisciplinary discussion and in bringing together academics, practitioners and representatives of different social agencies for dialogue. They have also all been a great source of encouragement for those working at the coalface of restorative justice practice; it is vital to the success and credibility of restorative justice that lines of communication are kept open between practitioners and theorists. But, without taking anything away from previous conferences, I found that the one held at Victoria University in Wellington in 2006 – some of the material from which reappears in this book, along with some new material – was particularly significant in advancing the restorative justice agenda. Its significance lay in its coining the new concept of a 'restorative society'. Rather than focusing narrowly on the role of restorative justice in the criminal justice sphere, conference participants repeatedly raised the question of how restorative values, practices, principles and processes might provide a new paradigm for approaching other major areas of social policy as well. Quite what this might mean in practice is yet to be clarified. But the very fact that people are now asking this kind of question is a further indication that something momentous is taking place, that we may well be, as Professor Jim Ritchie suggested at the conference, on the cusp of a sea-change in the way we think about justice and a just society and the role of the state in the resolution of social conflict.

## A new social movement

In his seminal book *Changing Lenses* Howard Zehr (1990) points out that throughout Western legal history there has always been a combination of centralised, state-administered forms of justice and local forms of community-based justice, with the weight of the balance changing from age to age. In recent centuries the balance has been substantially in favour of the state. But arguably the emergence of restorative justice represents a partial shift of balance back in favour of the community. As it moves now into its second generation, restorative justice can legitimately be thought of as an identifiable social 'movement', an international, grass-roots movement made up of individuals and groups united in their desire to re-empower community-level agencies to deal with criminal offending and other social harms in ways that restore as much wellbeing and wholeness to human relationships as possible. Like all reform movements, it combines idealism with activism, and is impelled forward by a vision of a better society and by the belief that positive change *is* possible.

Although restorative justice first emerged in the criminal justice sphere, it has since been extended into family, educational and employment spheres as well, as is evident in the chapters of this book. Hopefully in coming years the net will be cast even wider. Perhaps we will know that a sea-change really is under way when we have conferences on 'restorative accounting' or 'restorative politics'! This is not an entirely tongue-in-cheek comment, for the way in which politicians and treasury officials calculate the financial feasibility of this or that policy is not an objective science. It reflects a larger worldview or value system that deems some ends to be more worthwhile or morally significant than others. According to prevailing valuations, it is a political or moral imperative to invest hundreds of millions of dollars in building new prisons, despite their manifest failure to do much good, while scrimping and scraping on prevention or rehabilitation programmes. The ambulance (or paddy wagon!) at the bottom of the cliff is considered a more expedient social investment than a fence at the top or a safety net half-way down. The only way to challenge such idiocy is to promote a system in which individual funding decisions are evaluated in terms of the how well they contribute to fostering a larger social order that is committed to restoring people and situations to wholeness when harm occurs. Restorative accounting, in other words, would be number-crunching done in service of a restorative society. Such a change in the way of doing the sums is not unimaginable; the advent of the so-called triple bottom line shows that even accounting practice can be shaped by new moral sensitivities.

## The meaning of justice

One matter that surfaces frequently in discussions about restorative justice or restorative social policy is the meaning of the disputed term 'justice'. Some take a psychological approach to justice, viewing it as a human psychic need (see, for example, Tony Taylor's discussion in chapter 14). Others incline more towards a post-structuralist philosophical or sociological approach, suggesting that justice is an 'empty signifier' whose content is determined by particular, and variable, historical and cultural traditions. Justice in other words is what a social consensus determines it to be. By contrast, there are still those who insist on the essential objectivity of justice. They claim that, notwithstanding its diverse cultural applications, justice has a certain stable content that can be concretised in universal legal norms. Such debates about justice are, of course, almost as old as human society itself. They will always be with us. But perhaps our difficulty in adequately defining justice is itself a sign that restorative justice theory is correct – justice is, finally, about human relationships, and just as human relationships are marked by an irreducible complexity and diversity, so too is justice.

In this respect I personally find it helpful to think of justice, like love, as being a generic or an inclusive concept embracing a wide variety of applications. It is not a technical term with a circumscribed meaning but an umbrella concept with a wide semantic field. I also find it helpful to differentiate between three dimensions of justice. It has a *normative* or public dimension that stands over and above us, and that can be crystallised in legal and moral norms that summon our obedience. It also has an *experiential* or private dimension, something that satisfies our psychological need for resolution, vindication and restitution after a wrong has been done. Thirdly, it has a *visionary* or teleological dimension that points ahead to something greater in the future, that never allows us to rest content with the way things are now, however good they might seem to be, but impels us to reach forward for something better. To date, restorative justice has been most successful in the private or experiential dimension. It has developed practices that aim to leave people feeling more satisfied that their justice needs have been met. What is required now is much more theoretical or philosophical work on the normative dimensions of restorative justice, as well as more occasions for restorative justice advocates to get together to dream about and debate how to create a better, more restorative society in the future.

## Justice and spirituality

Perhaps it is its combination of normative, experiential and visionary qualities that gives justice such a religious or spiritual aura. As the history of human thought shows, there has always been a close correlation between religious belief and judicial practice. It is not surprising then that at all the restorative justice gatherings I have attended over the years, there have been frequent comments made about the *spirituality* of restorative justice, something also evident at several places in the present volume. But, as someone once observed to me, when the topic arises, it is Māori participants who instinctively know how to engage with it, while many Pākehā do not. Wairua is a much more intelligible and tangible (!) reality in Māori discourse than 'spirit' is in everyday Pākehā discourse. Having said that, one of the really interesting phenomena of our day, especially for someone in my academic field, is the way in which the term spirituality has come to be used with such positive connotations in an otherwise stridently secular society. 'Spirituality' is a feel-good word while 'religion' is still dogged with negative connotations. Even those who express deep distrust towards religion sometimes express a yearning for what Taylor described at the 2006 conference as an "unencumbered spirituality"; that is, a spirituality unburdened by religious dogma and morality or by ecclesiastical structures. Yet, whilst spirituality may be increasingly regarded as a good and desirable thing, the meaning of the term spirituality is almost as elusive as the meaning of justice. Like justice, many people may have an intuitive sense of what the term represents but most would be hard pressed to define it in any clear-headed way.

But perhaps definitions are besides the point. Spirituality is primarily a matter of *experience* – the experience of being part of some larger reality or pattern of meaning; the experience of being able to penetrate behind surface appearances to encounter the essence of some thing or some person or some event, to be conscious of the depth-dimension of mundane reality; the experience of joy that comes from loving and being loved; the experience of being interconnected with the rhythms of the universe and the source from which they flow. A moment's thought shows how closely related all this is with justice. Justice too is an experience before it is a concept; it is something we know in our hearts before we know it in our heads. Arguably, one of the key contributions restorative justice theory can make today is to clarify the inherent spirituality involved in doing justice. Indeed if it is true, as I believe it is, that human beings are inherently religious by nature – in the sense of being driven by the desire to find significance and depth and beauty and meaning in human existence by reference to some transcendent or supra-mundane reality – then it is impossible to achieve justice without cognition of its spiritual or even religious dimensions. Certainly, it is impossible to *experience* justice without it satisfying our psychological need for meaning and validation and purpose, which are fundamentally matters of the spirit. The *normative* and *visionary* dimensions of justice are also much more easily understood and articulated with the aid of religious or spiritual categories.

## Justice and language

This, in turn, directs attention to the *language*, and to the adequacy of the language, we often use to describe social goals. One crucial requirement for moving towards a more restorative society will be the development of a fresh language to describe and promote restorative priorities. As someone noted at the 2006 conference, the neo-liberal economic rationalism that has dominated the global order for the past few decades only gained ascendancy after a whole new vocabulary had been consciously devised by right wing ideologues to explain and justify the package of reforms being sought. These ideologues knew that those who claim the right to define the problem thereby acquire the power to determine the solutions. There is a lesson in this for the restorative movement. If we really do believe in restorative solutions, then we need to develop an operating vocabulary that is internally self-consistent, that is evocative of restorative values and goals, and that will resonate with the 'felt needs' of the wider public.

The importance of language may be illustrated by the immensely significant work done in New Zealand by the Waitangi Tribunal, as reviewed in chapter 12 by Maureen Hickey. Not many New Zealanders are aware of how positive, and how hopeful, the achievements of the tribunal have been in addressing in a peaceful or restorative way the dreadful legacy of historical abuses and betrayals of Māori by the Crown. The tribunal has served for years both as a *truth* commission (where stories of injustice have been told and validated) and as a *justice* commission (where recompense has been made, and where, unlike in Australia, powerful and genuine apologies have been offered and received). What is sad, however, is how little the Pākehā community understands of the work of the tribunal and its historical justification, and how little pride we take in the success of our own truth and justice commission, especially when compared to the failed or flawed commissions that have occurred elsewhere in the world. What is also sad is how threadbare is the language used in the public arena to characterise the tribunal's work. By and large we use the language of 'grievance' and 'settlement', not the language of 'truth' or 'justice' or 'apology' or 'forgiveness' or 'reconciliation' or 'healing'. How different the Pākehā community might feel about Treaty matters if it understood more clearly the extent to which the Waitangi Tribunal functions as a truth, justice and reconciliation commission, not just a vehicle for putting tired old grievances to rest. On a similar note, I have sometimes wondered if a sharper distinction between guilt and remorse would help with the buy-in of the wider community. Many Pākehā today insist – rightly I think – they cannot be held responsible for, or feel guilty about, injustices perpetrated by our forebears. But this does not preclude us from feeling a deep sense of remorse or regret that such wrongs were committed against Māori, which in turn should impel us to do all that is necessary to see those wrongs righted, even if we are personally not responsible for them.

Closely related both to the spirituality and language of justice is the need to acknowledge the moral ambiguities always involved in every attempt to achieve justice. In chapter 2, James Liu discusses how any satisfactory account of justice must take into account both the light side and the dark side of human behaviour and must satisfy the needs of both. In his conference presentation on this theme in 2006, Liu commented that if anyone hurt his young daughter he would be "very Old Testament" in his response. All of us can relate to this. Unquestionably, there is a need to reckon with the darker as well as the lighter sides of justice. But our goal should not so much be to *balance* the demands of each as to foster ways in which the darker, or more punitive, aspects of justice can be moderated or restrained or transformed by the lighter, more restorative aspects.

Take prisons as an example. In one sense imprisonment represents the dark work of justice (or what Martin Luther (1483–1546) called the "alien work of love") – the need we feel to impose the pain of long-term isolation as a necessary punishment for criminal offending. Most of us would accept that prisons are a sad necessity, at least in some cases. But it is not enough to defend the existence of prisons by appealing to justice's darker side. Our reliance on them must always be constrained by a commitment to develop restorative alternatives, and what goes on inside prisons must equally be moderated or transformed by restorative values and programmes. The impressive work of Prison Fellowship New Zealand in this respect (see chapter 8 by Kim Workman) is a sterling example of how the darkness of punitive justice can be lightened by programmes based on restorative commitments. As our prison population burgeons to historically and shamefully high levels, there is an urgent need for a public debate in New Zealand on what Canadian writer David Cayley (1998) calls "the expanding prison" – the way in which modern society is becoming increasingly acclimatised to totalitarian modes of social control and the way in which prisons are expanding to colonise more and more areas of social life.

## Restorative justice and retributive justice

This brings me finally to the connection between restorative and retributive approaches to justice, something I have explored in detail elsewhere (Marshall,

2001). It is now commonplace (and not a little politically expedient) for restorative justice proponents to emphasise that there will always be a need for retributive mechanisms, that restorative justice is not an alternative to retributive justice but a complement to it (see Liu's discussion in chapter 2). There is obvious truth here. Restorative justice works best when offenders freely accept their responsibility for doing wrong and seek to rectify it. But not everyone hauled before the court is guilty of wrongdoing, so there will always be the need for a system that can fairly adjudicate in cases of contested guilt, as well as for one that has the power to keep truly dangerous offenders off the streets. Therefore, restorative and retributive approaches to justice are both valid and both necessary; they have a complementary role to play in the justice system. But there is another sense in which both approaches are not really all that different. Both have something profound in common. Both seek to access the same fundamental human justice need, though in different ways. The justice need to which I refer is this – *the need to know that those who have unjustly imposed pain on others do not escape from sharing in the pain they have unleashed*. This unusual claim requires some unpacking.

According to retributivism, when a wrong has been done, justice requires punishment (see chapter 16 by Karen Baehler). The scales must be balanced. Offenders must be made to suffer a commensurate amount of punitive pain (punishment is, by definition, pain delivery) to the harm they have inflicted on the victim. But why is it that *pain* is understood to be the only adequate way to redress serious wrongdoing? Why the instinctive drive to match pain with pain? The reason is because to suffer a wrong is, in essence, to *suffer*, and it is morally unacceptable for someone to inflict avoidable suffering on another person without themselves sharing experientially in the consequences of what they have done. Instinctively we know that justice requires a co-participation in suffering. Since the victim has been made to suffer at the hands of the offender, the offender must now be made to suffer at the hands of the law. Both parties do not suffer in the same way, but at least they both suffer, so that some equity is achieved. If an offender escapes entirely from participation in pain after having needlessly unleashed pain on another, a fundamental injustice results. Hence, our drive to punish.

Now it is true that restorative justice is much less preoccupied with punishment than is retributivism. It is more interested in promoting healing and reconciliation than in measuring appropriate doses of punitive pain for particular crimes. But there remains an important sense in which restorativism still shares the same basic understanding of justice as retributivism – *that justice requires a co-participation in pain*. In the retributive paradigm, the offender's participation in pain is ensured by imposing external penalties on them, such as imprisonment, fines or community service. Such punishments are intended to hurt the criminal, though they usually do little to help the victim. In the restorative approach, the offender's participation in pain is elicited by having them personally confront the suffering of their victim and acting to bring about change, both in the victim's situation and in their own. Arguably the most exquisite pain associated with criminal offending comes, not from incurring secondary penalties, but from facing up to one's culpability for violating another human being and striving to remedy its consequences. The shame and distress entailed for offenders in confronting the personal consequences of their actions, accepting responsibility for them, seeking reconciliation with those whom they have harmed, and working to restore the damage caused should not be underestimated. The suffering entailed is often intense, sufficiently intense to satisfy the victim's need to know that their abuser has not escaped pain in the course of inflicting it. Without that awareness of a co-participation in suffering, their sense of injustice would remain unassuaged.

So then, both restorative and retributive conceptions of justice are united in their recognition that victim and offender must share in a 'fellowship of suffering' if justice is to be achieved. They differ on how such fellowship is most effectively secured, but they agree that a fellowship in pain is needed. Which brings us back to the spirituality of justice, for any spirituality worth its salt must address the problem of human pain and find meaning in human suffering.

## Practical steps

To conclude, let me move from the abstract to the concrete by noting just one or two of the practical steps towards a more restorative society that were mentioned at the 2006 conference, some of which also appear in the present volume. Several chapters testify to the important role of the specialist Youth Court in New Zealand (see chapters 3 and 4 by Gabrielle Maxwell, and Andrew Becroft and Rhonda Thompson respectively). Principal Youth Court Judge Andrew Becroft rightly draws attention to the 'genius' behind our youth justice legislation, yet at the conference he called for more research into how well the Youth Court itself conforms to the restorative principles undergirding the legislation. His point is that it is not enough to encourage restorative commitments from offenders (or victims); the institutional system itself also needs to operate on restorative premises. In line with this, Judge Fred McElrea has frequently argued for the creation of community justice centres to provide a wide range of non-adversarial and restorative justice options to the community. This seems like an eminently sensible proposal worth trialling in a pilot scheme. Recent experimentation within the District Courts (see chapter 5 by Fred McElrea) and new specialist courts, such as the drug court and the family violence court, are themselves a tacit concession that more is needed to combat offending and resolve conflict than a monolithic system for assessing guilt and meting out punishment. Another indication of this is the growing number of pieces of New Zealand legislation that require or refer to mediation and other non-litigious forms of dispute resolution. At the conference, David Hurley called for the creation of a single, independent mediation service to bring greater consistency of practice to what is currently a very fragmented scene.

More examples could be given of small but achievable steps towards the goal of strengthening and extending the values and principles of restorative justice in our collective life. Of course, the concept of justice cannot be wholly reduced to the notion of restoration, and a just society cannot do without a system that honours the best features of retributivism, such as its concern for proportionality, the denunciation of wrongdoing, and the protection of the vulnerable. But to create a genuinely restorative society, retributivism cannot have the final say. Always we must strive for a social order that does not rest content with a narrow conception of justice that focuses solely on the punishment and exclusion of wrongdoers. A restorative society requires a much richer and deeper conception of justice than what often prevails today. It requires a justice inspirited with restorative concerns, a justice that is satisfied only when equal attention is given to the healing of hurts, the reconciliation of enemies, and the eventual reintegration into society of those who offend, as responsible, productive and even respected members of the community.

# 19

# Towards a Restorative Society

*Jonathan Boston*

## Introduction

This book puts forward new and important ideas. In particular, it advances a vision of a 'restorative society' as an organising principle around which to view responses to conflict within society. Such a concept has many positive features, but also presents several difficulties.

This chapter comments briefly on the strengths and weaknesses of the idea of a 'restorative society', identifies some of the lessons and policy issues arising from recent experience with restorative practices in New Zealand, and considers how the ideas and proposals advanced in this volume might be developed further.

## The idea of a 'restorative society': strengths and weaknesses

At the conference held in Wellington in October 2005, it was argued that the notion of a restorative society has several attractive features. At a conceptual level, for instance, it provides an overarching idea or vision that can link the separate, but related, developments in restorative justice and restorative practices that have been occurring in a growing number of policy areas in New Zealand in recent times. Put differently, the idea of a restorative society can take one beyond the relatively narrow confines of criminal justice (and its various associated concepts and policy issues), and provide a meta-level concept that can be applied to a wide range of public issues and policy domains. While it is certainly not as broad or all-encompassing as notions like 'the common good', the 'good society' or 'the good life', it has the potential to supply one of the criteria (or, indeed, a number of criteria) by which to judge whether a society is, in fact, 'good', or at least whether it is on the right path. In other words, a good society, it can be argued, will be one where there is a genuine quest, across the many and varied fields of human endeavour, to restore or rebuild positive relationships and sound social structures, whenever such relationships or structures have been harmed or damaged in some way – whether as a result of human conflict, wilfulness, ignorance or any other cause.

The marks of a restorative society, therefore, will include the widespread use of restorative practices; that is, practices designed to rebuild broken relationships, to bring wholeness and healing, to put right the wrongs of the past and to engender a sense of fairness and justice. Such practices need not be limited to the human or social realm, but might also embrace measures to restore damaged environments and ecosystems. Of course, the application of restorative practices will not always be successful, and there is scope for legitimate debate about the precise nature of such practices, where and when they should be applied, and at what cost. But a good society, it can be argued, will be characterised by the high value it places on the 'restoration' of good things and the effort it expends to achieve such outcomes. Necessarily, such a society will be one that affirms the dignity of all human beings and encourages mutual respect, justice and reconciliation.

On a more pragmatic or practical level, the notion of a restorative society also has several attractions. It provides an additional lens through which social scientists and others can view the world. It has the capacity to bring together many different academic disciplines, research traditions and fields of inquiry, providing a common frame of reference and focus for investigation. It can be applied to a wide range of policy settings and areas of public life, spanning local, national and international arenas. These include such diverse activities as international conflict resolution, the management of workplace relationships, the strengthening of families and the improvement of educational outcomes.

Equally significant, the notion of a restorative society has an inspirational appeal. This is because it resonates with a universal human experience of failure, disorder and brokenness and a universal desire for wholeness, acceptance, forgiveness, healing, reconciliation and peace/shalom. In a similar manner, it resonates with the common human experience of light and darkness, hope and despair, empowerment and bondage, good and evil. It is thus a highly inclusive concept: it embraces the whole of humanity; it is relevant for people throughout time and space; and it has the capacity to transcend and overcome differences based on geography, history, gender, ethnicity, religion, language and culture. All of us have experienced the need for restoration as individuals, as well as in the many groups (and wider associations, communities and nations) of which we are a part. Additionally, the idea of a restorative society links with the major themes of a number of great religious traditions, such as Christianity, Judaism and Islam, with their emphasis on love, compassion, forgiveness and redemption. For all these reasons, the quest for a restorative society has the power to motivate and inspire; it can thus provide the basis for transformative social and political movements.

Against this, like other major themes, concepts and ethical principles – justice, equality, liberty, fraternity, community, sustainability and so on – the idea of a restorative society has certain limitations and drawbacks. What does a restorative society actually mean in practical terms? What would such a society look like? How might it be achieved? How can those who have become detached or alienated from a social group achieve restoration? What are the relevant policy tools and instruments? What are the barriers, constraints and costs?

At another level, there is the problem that 'restoration' implies a return to what used to be, such as a previous state, condition or arrangement. Yet there are some conditions that ought not to be restored. The institution of slavery is a good example; abject poverty is another. Further, returning to a previous state or condition might not be what is wanted or needed by those who are in some way alienated, excluded or disempowered, or who have failed to meet society's standards. Such people may well be seeking something rather different, and indeed much better, from what went before. Hence, 'restoration' may not be enough; in fact, in some situations it might not be appropriate at all. We thus need criteria for deciding the circumstances under which restoration should be cultivated and pursued and when it should not.

This prompts yet further questions. How does the notion of 'restoration' fit with other central human values and concerns – such as freedom, stewardship, distributive justice and sustainability? What priority should be given to the quest for restoration when it conflicts in some way with other values? What moral weight does it carry? And what are the respective roles and responsibilities of the state, community groups and individuals in the quest for a restorative society? After all, while the state can encourage fair play, kindness and forgiveness, it cannot force people to love each other or rebuild broken relationships. To answer questions of this kind would be a major task, but it is certainly a task worth pursuing.

Currently, then, the idea of a restorative society poses many questions. While it has certain strengths and attractions, it is not without weaknesses and limitations. On the one hand, there is something fundamentally appealing about a society that values the restoration of broken relationships, the healing of damaged hearts and minds, the reconciliation of divided communities and the fostering of trust, mutual respect and inclusion. On the other hand, we have but fragments of a philosophy of 'restoration'; we lack a full, integrated, comprehensive theory, one that can bridge different theological and philosophical traditions and provide a rigorous, robust and durable foundation for individual and collective action. Also, as James Liu cogently argues in his contribution to this book (chapter 2), the dark side of human nature poses major ongoing limitations to, and constraints upon, the quest for a restorative society. Restoration is not possible where some prefer to live in darkness or actively force others to do so.

I am reminded here of the work of Reinhold Niebuhr, in particular, his contention that the ideal of love – in the sense of neighbour love or agape – in a world characterised by pride, egoism and self-assertion is an unobtainable ideal. In a memorable phrase, Niebuhr (1963, pp. 62–83) refers to this as an "impossible possibility". For Niebuhr, however, this does not mean we should abandon hope or give up the quest for a better world. Instead, he argues that we need to reject both naive optimism (where love is regarded as a simple possibility) and naive pessimism (where love is seen as irrelevant because it is impossible). Equally, he argues that the ideal of love is relevant to life in this imperfect world (and not merely a hypothetical world or eschatological community), for it provides the benchmark against which all imperfect realisations of agape can and must be measured and judged, both in the private and public spheres of life. Much the same, it seems to me, can be said about the quest for a restorative society: its full expression and realisation is an impossible ideal in a world marred by human evil and folly; yet it is nonetheless something towards which we should aspire, and something that can serve as a source of inspiration and hope.

## Key themes and issues

The contents of this book bear testimony to a great deal of innovative thinking and practice around New Zealand over recent years: there have been many interesting experiments and there is much to celebrate; yet there is also much still to be learned. What is reported here is thus in many respects a 'work in progress'. The findings and analyses demonstrate that there are many opportunities for restorative endeavours, but also many barriers to change, including legal impediments.

Several themes emerge from the many examples that have been described in the preceding chapters. First, in all cases the people responsible for the new initiatives shared a common vision of the possibility of something better. Second, in most cases the changes they have achieved depended not only on effective leadership and interagency cooperation but also on significant buy-in at the grass roots level. Third, innovative restorative practices and developments require adequate resources and support from both the state and local communities. Fourth, successful outcomes have depended more on an 'incrementalist' or 'bottom-up' model than a 'rational' or 'top-down' model. Related to this, the successful models and practices reported here are marked by 'hybridity': they have borrowed heavily from the best of current ideas, theory and practice and have developed through active debate, research and experimentation.

There are policy implications in all this. Developing effective restorative practices depends on the opportunity for trial and error. Accordingly, policy makers must be willing to take risks and experiment (or at least allow experimentation by others, including those they fund). This includes a willingness to accept that mistakes will be made and that some programmes will be less effective than hoped for.

Organisations also need to be willing to use different models and try different solutions in different contexts. In some cases, questions are likely to arise about what is tolerable and justified in a 'secular' state (for example, as highlighted by the development of 'faith-based' units in public prisons). In addressing such issues, it will be important to avoid unnecessary rigidity and conformity, while at the same time ensuring that basic human rights are protected and that any possible harm is minimised.

As developments progress and become better established there will be a need for innovations to be 'institutionalised' through appropriate funding, structures, training and so on. This, of course, may pose additional risks, such as the dead hand of bureaucratisation – new rules, regulations, standardisation and uniformity. There is no simple solution to such risks. In general, however, every effort should be made to provide continuing opportunities for ongoing development and innovation.

Finally, wherever possible, experiments and innovative practices should be properly evaluated. This requires an investment of time, effort and, of course, money. Yet without such evaluation, there is no possibility of evidence-based policy making.

## Where to from here?

In terms of the way ahead, several matters deserve emphasis. To start with, more experiments, more debate and more sharing of experiences are needed if progress is to be made. It is evident to those involved in the debate on restorative justice and restorative practices that much more is happening than is often recognised. The challenge will be to go on hearing the stories, discussing and evaluating what has happened and providing support as we move forward toward the goal of a more restorative society.

Further, there is a need for more attention to be given to the language of discourse, including the way the public debate over a restorative society is framed and conducted. This requires some hard thinking and sound ethical reasoning. In particular, further analysis is needed on how the notion of a restorative society fits within the wider framework of theological and philosophical inquiry. And this needs to be a collective effort – for, by definition, any restorative society will be a community of individuals in relationship with one another, not a grouping of atomised individuals.

# References

Aberle, D. F., A. K. Cohen, A. K. Davis, M. J. Levy Jr, and F. X. Sutton (1949/50) 'The functional prerequisites of a society' *Journal of Ethics* 60, pp. 100–109.

Adair, V., and R. Dixon (2000) *Evaluation of the Restorative Conferencing Pilot Project: Report to the Ministry of Education* Auckland: Auckland UniServices.

Adams, J. S. (1965) 'Inequity in social exchange', in L. Berkowitz (ed.) *Advances in Experimental Social Psychology* vol 2, pp. 267–299, New York: Academic Press.

Adler, P. S., and C. Honeyman (2005) 'Some radical thinking on centrism, politics, and the future of conflict management' *Mediate.com* retrieved from http://www.mediate.com/pfriendly.cfm?id=1776.

Adorno, T. W., E. Frenckel-Brunswick, D. J. Levinson and R. N. Sanford (1950) *The Authoritarian Personality* New York: Harper and Row.

Ali, T. (2003) *The Clash of Fundamentalisms: Crusades, jihads, and modernity* London: Verso.

Allport, G. W. (1960) *Becoming: Basic considerations for a psychology of personality* Terry Lecture Series, New Haven: Yale University Press.

Alter, S. (1999) *Apologising for Serious Wrongdoing: Social, psychological and legal considerations* final report for the Law Commission of Canada, retrieved 1 September 2006 from http://epe.lac-bac.gc.ca/100/200/301/lcc-cdc/apologising_serious_wrong-e/apology.html.

American Psychological Association (2001) 'Tapping your resilience in the wake of terrorism: pointers for practitioners' *APA Online* retrieved 28 November 2001 from http://www.apa.org/practice/practitionerhelp.html.

Anderson, J. (1998a) 'Crown faces $38m Lake Alice "sex, torture" claim' *National Business Review* 18 December, retrieved 2 March 2006 from http://www.grantcameron.co.nz/case_lakealice.php.

Anderson, J. (1998b) 'Health minister 'horrified' by Lake Alice patient–torture allegations' *National Business Review* 18 December, retrieved 2 March 2006 from http://www.grantcameron.co.nz/case_lakealice.php.

Anderson, J. (1999) 'Minister buries his head as Lake Alice suit tops $70m' *National Business Review* 29 January, retrieved 2 March 2006 from http://www.grantcameron.co.nz/case_lakealice.php.

Andrews, D. A. (1994) *An Overview of Treatment Effectiveness: Research and clinical principles* Ottawa: Department of Psychology, Carleton University.

Andrews, D. A., and J. Bonta (1998) *The Psychology of Criminal Conduct* 2nd edition, Cincinnati: Anderson.

Andrews, D. A., C. Dowden and P. Gendreau (1999) 'Psychologically informed treatment and clinically relevant and psychologically informed approaches to reduced re-offending: a meta-analytic study of human service, risk, need, responsivity and other concerns in justice contexts', unpublished, Department of Psychology, Carleton University, Ottawa.

Argyle, M. (2002) *The Psychology of Happiness* 2nd edition, London: Routledge, Kegan Paul.

Aristotle (350 BC/1959) *Nichomachean Ethics* (translated by Sir David Ross), Oxford: Oxford University Press.

Axelrod, R., and W. D. Hamilton (1981) 'The evolution of cooperation' *Science* 211, pp. 1,390–1,397.

Bagshaw, D. (2003) 'Language, power and mediation' *Australian Dispute Resolution Journal* 14 (2), pp. 130–141.

Bargal, D. (2006) 'Personal and intellectual influences leading to Lewin's paradigm of action research: towards the 60th anniversary of Lewin's "Action research and minority problems" (1946)' *Action Research* 4, pp. 367–388.

Barkan, E., and A. Karn (eds.) (2006) *Taking Wrongs Seriously: Apologies and reconciliation* Stanford: Stanford University Press.

Barkow, J., L. Cosmides, and J. Tooby (1992) *The Adapted Mind: Evolutionary psychology and the generation of culture* New York: Oxford University Press.

Barnes, B. E. (1994) 'Conflict resolution across cultures: a Hawaii perspective and a Pacific mediation model' *Mediation Quarterly* 12 (2), pp. 397–404.

Barrett-Howard, E., and T. Tyler (1986) 'Procedural justice as a criterion in allocation decisions' *Journal of Personality and Social Psychology* 50 (2), pp. 296–304.

Bassett, M. (2002) 'Apologies' *The Dominion* 12 June, retrieved 10 March 2006 http://www.michaelbassett.co.nz.

Baylis, C. (1999) 'Reviewing statutory models of mediation/conciliation in New Zealand: three conclusions' *Victoria University of Wellington Law Review* 30 (2), pp. 279–295.

Bazemore, G., L. Nissen and M. Dooley (2000) 'Mobilizing social support and building relationships: broadening correctional and rehabilitative agendas' *Corrections Management Quarterly* 4 (4), pp. 10–21.

Bazemore, G., and M. Shiff (2004) 'Paradigm muddle or paradigm paralysis? The wide and narrow roads to restorative justice reform (or, a little confusion may be a good thing)' *Contemporary Justice Review* 7 (1), pp. 37–57.

Bazemore, G., and L. Walgrave (1999) 'Restorative juvenile justice: in search of fundamentals and an outline for systemic reform', in G. Bazemore and L. Walgrave (eds.) *Restorative Juvenile Justice: Repairing the harm of youth crime* pp. 45–74, Monsey, NY: Criminal Justice Press.

Belich, J. (1986) *The New Zealand Wars* Auckland: Penguin.

Benjamin, R. D. (2002) 'The geo-political factor in negotiation' *Mediate.com* retrieved from http://www.mediate.com/pfriendly.cfm?id=1042.

Best, E. (1952) *The Maori as He Was* 3rd edition, Wellington: R. E. Owen and Government Printer.

Beven, J. P., G. Hall, I. Froyland, B. Steels and D. Goulding (2005) 'Evaluating restorative justice outcomes' *Psychiatry, Psychology and Law* 12 (1), pp. 194–206.

Bhalla, S. S. (2002) *Imagine There's No Country: Poverty, inequality, and growth in the era of globalization.* Washington, DC: Institute for International Economics.

# References

Bishop, R., M. Berryman, T. Cavanagh and L. Teddy (2007) *Te Kotahitanga Phase 3 Whakawhanaungatanga: Establishing a culturally responsive pedagogy of relations in mainstream secondary school* Wellington: Research Division, Ministry of Education.

Bishop, R., M. Berryman, S. Tiakiwai and C. Richardson (2004) *The Experiences of Year 9 and 10 Māori Students in Mainstream Classrooms.* Hamilton and Tauranga: Ministry of Education.

Blum, L. A. (1988) 'Gilligan and Kohlberg: implications for moral theory' *Ethics* 98, pp. 472–491.

Boehm, C. (1999) *Hierarchy in the Forest: The evolution of egalitarian behaviour* Cambridge, MA: Harvard University Press.

Boeree, C. G. (2006) *Abraham Maslow: 1908–1970* biographical note, retrieved from http://www.ship.edu/~cgboeree/maslow.html.

Boulle, L, J. Jones and V. Goldblatt (1998) *Mediation: Principles, process, practice* New Zealand edition, Wellington: Butterworths.

Bowie, K. (2003) *Restorative Justice Rotorua Evaluation June 1999 – June 2001* Rotorua: Mana Social Services Trust.

Braddock, J. (2003) 'Samoans mount protest over restrictive New Zealand immigration law' *World Socialist Web Site* 4 April, retrieved 27 February 2006, http://www.wsws.org/articles/2003/apr2003/samo-a04.shtml.

Braithwaite, J. (1989) *Crime, Shame and Reintegration* Cambridge, Cambridge University Press.

Brickman, P., R. Folger, E. Goode and Y. Schul (1981) 'Microjustice and macrojustice', in M. P. Lerner and S. C. Lerner (eds.) *The Justice Motive in Social Behavior: Adapting to times of scarcity and change* pp. 173–202, New York: Plenum.

Bridgeman, D. (2003) 'Lake Alice victims battle court over differential payouts' *National Business Review* 11 April, retrieved 10 March 2006 from http://www.grantcameron.co.nz/case_lakealice.php.

Brooks, R. L. (1999a) 'The age of apology', in R. L. Brooks (ed.) *When Sorry Isn't Enough: The controversy over apologies and reparations for human injustice* chapter 1, Critical American Series, New York: New York University Press.

Brooks, R. L. (1999b) *When Sorry Isn't Enough: The controversy over apologies and reparations for human injustice* Critical American Series, New York: New York University Press.

Brown, B. J., and F. W. M. McElrea (1993) *The Youth Court in New Zealand: A new model of justice* Auckland: Legal Research Foundation.

Buckley, S., and G. M. Maxwell (2007) *Respectful Schools: Restorative practices in education: A summary report* Wellington: Office of the Children's Commissioner and Institute of Policy Studies, Victoria University of Wellington.

Burns, P. (2006) 'Justice, torture, and restoration', in A. J. W. Taylor (ed.) *Justice as a Basic Human Need* chapter 12, New York: Nova Science.

Cabinet Policy Committee (2002) *Minute of Decision: New Zealand Administration of Samoa in the First Half of the Twentieth Century* POL Min (02) 12/1, 22 May, Wellington: New Zealand Government.

Cahill, F. (2006) 'Crossing the road from home to secondary school: a conversation with Samoan parents' *Waikato Journal of Education* 12, pp. 57–72.

Carruthers, D. (2004) 'Can courts and judges tackle social problems: problem-solving courts, the new approach', paper presented at the University of Portsmouth, 23 March.

Carruthers, D. (no date) 'Restoring youth justice', unpublished paper held by the Principal Youth Court Judge's office.

Carter, C. (Minister of Ethnic Affairs) (2004) 'Funding for recognition of Chinese heritage announced' *New Zealand Government* 11 February, retrieved 25 August 2005 from http://www.beehive.govt.nz/ViewDocument.aspx?DocumentID=18896.

Casper, J. D., T. Tyler and B. Fisher (1988) 'Procedural justice in felony cases' *Law and Society Review* 22 (3), pp. 483–508.

Cayley, D. (1998) *The Expanding Prison: The crisis in crime and punishment and the search for alternatives* Toronto: Anansi Press.

Clark, H. (Prime Minister) (2001) 'Settlement for former Lake Alice patients' *New Zealand Government* 7 October, retrieved 25 August 2005 from http://www.beehive.govt.nz/ViewDocument.aspx?DocumentID=11995.

Clark, H. (Prime Minister) (2002a) 'Address to Cape Town University: contemporary New Zealand: a nation in transition' *New Zealand Government* 6 September, retrieved 25 August 2005 from http://www.beehive.govt.nz/ViewDocument.aspx?DocumentID=14853.

Clark, H. (Prime Minister) (2002b) 'Address to Chinese New Year celebration' *Office of Ethnic Affairs* 12 February, retrieved 25 August 2005 from http://www.ethnicaffairs.govt.nz/oeawebsite.nsf/wpg_URL/Advisory-Services-Consultations-Prime-Ministers-Speech-To-Chinese-Community?OpenDocument.

Clark, H. (Prime Minister) (H. Clark) (2002c) 'Helen Clark apology to Samoa' (full text) *New Zealand Herald* 4 June, retrieved 10 March 2006, http://www.preventgenocide.org/prevent/news-monitor/2002june.htm.

Clark, H. (Prime Minister) (2002d) *New Zealand Administration of Samoa in the First Half of the Twentieth Century* paper to the Cabinet Policy Committee, Pol (02) 127, 20 May, Wellington: New Zealand Government.

Clark, H., and G. Hawkins (Prime Minister and Minister of Ethnic Affairs) (2001) *Early Chinese Settlers* paper to the Cabinet Policy Committee, POL (01) 323, 6 November, Wellington: New Zealand Government.

Clark, M. S., and J. Mills (1979) 'Interpersonal attraction in exchange and communal relationships' *Journal of Personality and Social Psychology* 37, pp. 2–24.

Clemmer, D. (1963) *The Prison Community* New York: Rinehart and Co.

Cloke, K. (2001) *Mediating Dangerously: The frontiers of conflict resolution* San Francisco: Jossey-Bass.

# References

Coate, R. A., and J. A. Rosati (eds.) (1988) *The Power of Human Needs* Boulder, COL: Lynne Rienner.

Collins, S. (2001) 'Terrible legacy of Lake Alice' *New Zealand Herald* 27 October, retrieved 10 March 2006 from http://www.nzherald.co.nz/section/story.cfm?c_id=1&objectid=224779.

Confidential Forum for Former In-patients of Psychiatric Hospitals (2005) *Appointments Confirmed for Forum for Former Psychiatric In-patients* media release, 11 April.

Confidential Forum for Former In-patients of Psychiatric Hospitals (2007) *Te Āiotanga: Report of the Confidential Forum for Former In-patients of Psychiatric Hospitals* Wellington: New Zealand Government.

Consedine, J. (1999) *Restorative Justice: Healing the effects of crime* Lyttleton: Ploughshare Publications.

Cooper, S. (interviewee) (2004) Transcript of Radio New Zealand interview *Nine to Noon* 7 November.

Coryn, C. L. S., and C. Borshuk (2006) 'The scope of justice for Muslim Americans: moral exclusion in the aftermath of 9/11' *The Qualitative Report* 11 (3), pp. 586–604.

Crime and Justice Research Centre, Victoria University of Wellington, and S. Triggs (2005) *New Zealand Court-Referred Restorative Justice Pilot: Evaluation* Wellington: Ministry of Justice.

Cullen, F. T. (1994) 'Social support as an organizing concept for criminology. presidential address to Academy of Criminal Justice Sciences' *Justice Quarterly* 11, pp. 527–559.

Daly, K. (2001) 'Conferencing in Australia and New Zealand: variations, research findings and prospects', in A. Morris and G. M. Maxwell (eds.) *Restorative Justice for Juveniles: Conferencing, mediation and circles* chapter 4, Oxford: Hart Publishing.

Dauenhauer, B. (2002) 'Paul Ricoeur', in E. N. Zalta (ed.) *The Stanford Encyclopedia of Philosophy* winter edition, retrieved from http://plato.stanford.edu/archives/win2002/entries/ricoeur.

Department for Courts (2005) *Restorative Justice: Information on court-referred restorative justice* Wellington: Department for Courts, retrieved November 2005 from http://www.justice.govt.nz/pubs/courts/restorative_justice.pdf.

Department of Justice (1986) *Te Whainga i te Tika: In search of justice* report of the Advisory Committee on Legal Services, Wellington: Department of Justice.

Department of Social Welfare (social work staff at the Lower Hutt District Office) (1989) *Whakapakari Whanau: Family decision-making* Wellington: Maori Unit, Department of Social Welfare.

Deutsch, M. (1975) 'Equity, equality, and need: what determines which value will be used as the basis of distributive justice?' *Journal of Social Issues* 31 (3), pp. 137–149.

Deutsch, M. (1985) *Distributive Justice: A social psychological perspective* New Have, CT: Yale University Press.

Deutsch, M. (2002) 'Social psychology's contributions to the study of conflict resolution' *Negotiation Journal* 18 (4), pp. 307–320.

Doolan, M. P. (1988) *From Welfare to Justice: Towards new social work practice with young offenders: An overseas study tour report* Wellington: Department of Social Welfare.

Doolan, M. P. (2003) 'Restorative practices and family empowerment: both/and or either/or?' *Family Rights Newsletter* p. 3.

Dowden, C., and D. A. Andrews (1999) 'What works in young offender treatment: a meta-analysis', *Forum on Corrections Research*, Department of Psychology, Carleton University, Ottawa.

Drewery, W. (2004) 'Conferencing in schools: punishment, restorative justice, and the productive importance of the process of conversation' *Journal of Community and Applied Social Psychology* 14, pp. 332–344.

Drewery, W. (2005) 'Why we should watch what we say: position calls, everyday speech, and the production of relational subjectivity' *Theory and Psychology* 15 (3), pp. 305–324.

Dugatkin, L. (2004) *Principles of Animal Behaviour* New York: W. W. Norton.

Dugatkin L. (2005) 'Kiss and make up' *New Scientist* (7 May), p. 35.

Eaton, J., and F. W. M. McElrea (2003) *Sentencing: The new dimensions* Wellington: New Zealand Law Society.

Eccleston, L., and T. Ward (2006) 'Criminal justice and good lives', in A. J. W. Taylor (ed.) *Justice as a Basic Human Need* chapter 5, New York: Nova Science.

Ellsworth, P., and S. R. Gross (1994) 'Hardening of the attitudes: America's views on the death penalty' *Journal of Social Issues* 50 (2), pp. 19–52.

Enright, R. D., and J. North (eds.) (1998) *Exploring Forgiveness* Madison: University of Wisconsin Press.

Epstein, J. (2005) 'Native American wisdom: lessons learned from mediation' *Mediate.com* retrieved from http://www.mediate.com/pfriendly.cfm?id=1715.

Ergenzinger Jr, E. R. (2002) 'Conversations with Phineas Gage: a neuroscientific approach to negotiation strategy' *Mediate.com* retrieved from http://www.mediate.com/articles/ergenzinger.cfm.

Evans, I., T. Yamaguchi, J. Raskauskas and S. Harvey (2007) *Fairness, Forgiveness and Families* Blue Skies Report 17/07, Wellington: Families Commission.

Farrington, D. P. (1994) 'Human development and criminal careers', in M. Maguire, R. Morgan and R. Reiner (eds.) *The Oxford Handbook of Criminology* Oxford: Clarendon Press.

Fergusson, D. M., L. Horwood and M. Lynskey (1994) 'The childhoods of multiple problem adolescents: a 15-year longitudinal study' *Journal of Child Psychology and Psychiatry and Allied Disciplines* 35 (6), pp. 1,123–1,140.

Festinger, L. A. (1954) 'A theory of social comparison processes' *Human Relations* 7, pp. 117–140.

Field, M (2002) 'Mixed reactions in Samoa to New Zealand's apology' *Pacific Magazine* 1 August, retrieved 18 January 2006 from http://www.pacificislands.cc/pm82002/pmdefault.php?urlarticleid=0030.

# References

Finkelstein, C. (2002) 'Death and retribution' *Criminal Justice Ethics* 21 (2), pp. 12–22.

Firebaugh, G. (2003) *The New Geography of Global Income Inequality* Cambridge, MA: Harvard University Press.

Fischer, R., and L. Skitka (2006) 'Social aspects of justice', in A. J. W. Taylor (ed.) *Justice as a Basic Human Need* chapter 8, New York: Nova Science.

Fisk, M. (ed.) (1993) *Justice* Atlantic Highlands NJ: Humanities.

Fiske, A. P. (1992) 'The four elementary forms of sociality: framework for a unified theory of social relations' *Psychological Review* 99 (4), pp. 689–723.

Fitzgerald, C. P. (1964) *The Birth of Communist China* Victoria, Australia: Penguin Books.

Fleming, D. (1999) 'A suspension by any other name? Changes to school discipline in New Zealand' *YouthLaw Tino Rangatiratanga Taitamariki* retrieved 29 June 2006 from http://www.youthlaw.co.nz/default.aspx?_z=86.

Foa, U. G., J. Converse, K. Y. Tornbloom and E. B. Foa (eds.) (1993) *Resource Theory: Explorations and applications* San Diego: Academic Press.

Foa, U. G., and E. B. Foa (1974) *Societal Structures of the Mind* Springfield, IL: Charles C. Thomas.

Folger, R. A., and J. P. Bush (1994) *The Promise of Mediation* San Francisco: Jossey-Bass.

Fox, D. R. (1999) 'Psycholegal scholarship's contribution to false consciousness about injustice' *University of Illinois at Springfield*, retrieved from http://www.uis.edu?~fox/papers/injustice.html.

Giddens, A. (2000) *The Third Way and Its Critics* Cambridge, UK: Polity Press.

Gillespie, V. (1979) *Religious Conversion and Personal Identity* Birmingham: Religious Education Press.

Gilligan, C. (1983) 'Do the social sciences have an adequate theory of moral development?', in N. Haan, R. Bellah, P. Rabinow and W. Sullivan (eds.) *Social Science as Moral Inquiry* New York: Columbia University Press.

Gilligan, C. (1993) *In a Different Voice* 2nd edition, Cambridge, MA: Harvard University Press.

Goddard, T. G. (1993) 'Mediation: past endeavours, future trends' *Employment Law Bulletin* 4, pp. 47–51.

Goldberg, S. B., E. D. Green and F. E. A. Sander (1985) 'Hybrid processes' *Dispute Resolution* pp. 246–271, Boston, MA: Little, Brown and Co.

Goodyer, H. (2003) 'Rethinking justice in New Zealand: a critical assessment of restorative justice' *Canterbury Law Review* 9, pp. 179–199.

Gordon, E. E. (2000) 'Attorneys' negotiation strategies in mediation: business as usual?' *Mediation Quarterly* 17 (4), pp. 377–390.

Government Administration Committee (2004) *Report of the Government Administration Committee: Petition 2002/44 of Dr George Paterson Barton Vaitoa Sa and 100,000 others* presented 20 May, Wellington: New Zealand House of Representatives, retrieved 10 March 2006 from http://www.parliament.nz/NR/rdonlyres/1C699BFB-B56A-46E7-8C14-7E889D8C96C8/14400/DBSCH_SCR_2759_2286.pdf.

Graham, D. (1997) *Trick or Treaty?* Wellington: Institute of Policy Studies, Victoria University of Wellington.

Greenberg, J. (1988) 'Equity and workplace status: a field experiment' *Journal of Applied Psychology* 73, pp. 606–613.

Gregory, R. J. (2001) 'The spirit and substance of community psychology: reflections' *Journal of Community Psychology* 29 (4), pp. 473–485.

Hafer, C. L., and J. M. Olson (1993) 'Beliefs in a just world and reactions to personal deprivation' *Journal of Personality* 57, pp. 799–823s.

Haines, K. (1998) 'Some principled objections to a restorative justice approach to working with juvenile offenders', in L Walgrave (ed.) *Restorative Justice for Juveniles: Potentialities, risks and problems* a selection of papers from the international conference of the International Network for Research on Restorative Justice for Juveniles, Leuven, 12–14 May 1997, pp. 93–113, Belgium: Leuven University Press.

Hall, D. (1996) 'Restorative justice: a Maori perspective', submission to the Ministry of Justice on behalf of the New Zealand Maori Council.

Halper, S. A., and J. Clarke (2004) *America Alone: The neo-conservatives and the global order* New York: Cambridge University Press.

Harris, N. (1999) 'Can state and civil institutions shame?', paper presented at *Restorative Justice and Civil Society* 16–18 September, Canberra.

Harrison, T. R. (2003) 'Victims, targets, protectors and destroyers: using disputant accounts to develop a grounded taxonomy of disputant orientations' (2003) *Conflict Resolution Quarterly* 20 (3), pp. 307–329.

Harvey, L. (2005) 'The hearing and settlement process' *Waitangi Tribunal Conference 2004* pp. 89–109, Wellington: New Zealand Law Society.

Hayden, A. (2001) *Restorative Conferencing Manual of Aotearoa New Zealand* Wellington: Department for Courts.

Hayes, H., and K. Daly (2003) 'Youth justice conferencing and reoffending' *Justice Quarterly* 20 (4), pp. 725–764.

Hedeen, T. (2004) 'The evolution and evaluation of community mediation: limited research suggests unlimited progress' *Conflict Resolution Quarterly* 22 (1–2), pp. 101–133.

Heertz, N. (2001) *The Silent Takeover: Global capitalism and the death of democracy* New York: The Free Press.

Hegel, G. W. F. (1821/1967) *Philosophy of Right* (translated by T. M. Knox), Oxford: Oxford University Press.

Helmich, R. G., and R. L. Petersen (eds.) (2001) *Forgiveness and Reconciliation* Pennsylvania: Templeton Foundation Press.

Hensler, D. R. (2002) 'Suppose it's not true: Challenging mediation ideology' *Journal of Dispute Resolution* pp. 81–99.

Henwood, C. (1997) 'The Children, Young Persons and Their Families Act 1989: the New Zealand situation 1997: a judicial perspective', unpublished.

Henwood, C. (2004) 'Golden rules for inter-agency meetings', unpublished, available from the Office of the Principal Youth Court Judge.

# References

Hewitt, G., and R. Pritchard (1992) 'Healing grievances model', unpublished.

Hickey, M. (2006) 'Negotiating history: Crown apologies in New Zealand's historical Treaty of Waitangi settlements *Public History Review* 13, pp. 108–124.

Higginbotham, P. E. (2004) 'The disappearing trial and why we should care' *Rand Review* retrieved from http:/www.rand.org/publications/randreview/issues/summer2004/28.html.

Hill, C. (1972) *The World Turned Upside Down: Radical ideas during the English revolution* Harmondsworth: Penguin.

Ho, D. Y. F. (1996) 'Filial piety and its psychological consequences', in M. H. Bond (ed.) *Handbook of Chinese Psychology* pp. 155–165, Hong Kong: Oxford University Press.

Hobsbawm, E. (1994) *Age of Extremes* New York: Penguin.

Hoffman, M. L. (2000) *Empathy and Moral Development: Implications for caring and justice* Cambridge: Cambridge University Press.

Hogan, R., and N. P. Emler (1981) 'Retributive justice', in M. P. Lerner and S. C. Lerner (eds.) *The Justice Motive in Social Behaviour: Adapting to times of scarcity and change* pp. 125–143, New York: Plenum.

Holt C. R., and J. B. DeVore (2005) 'Gender, culture, organizational role and styles of conflict resolution: a meta-analysis' *Conflict911.com* retrieved from http://conflict911.com/resources/conflict_research_and_academic_papers.

Horai, J., and M. Bartek (1978) 'Recommended punishment as a function of injurious intent, actual harm done, and intended consequences' *Personality and Social Psychology Bulletin* 4 (4), pp. 575–578.

Hoskins, M. L., and J. M. Stoltz (2003) 'Balancing on words: human change processes in mediation' *Conflict Resolution Quarterly* 20 (3), pp. 331–349.

Howard-Hassmann, R. E. (2006) *Political Apologies and Reparations* http://political-apologies.wlu.ca.

Howard League for Penal Reform (1999) *The Imprisonment of Maori* fact sheet 8, retrieved from http://www.howardleague.co.nz/factsheets/8.pdf.

Howden-Chapman, P., and M. Tobias (2000) *Social Inequalities in Health: New Zealand 1999* Wellington: Ministry of Health.

Hughes, D., H. Lauder, T. Robinson, I. Simiyu, S. Watson et al. (1999) *Do Schools Make a Difference? Hierarchical linear modelling of school certificate results in 23 schools: The Smithfield Project, phase three: Eighth report to the Ministry of Education* Wellington: Ministry of Education.

Human Rights Commission (2004) *Human Rights in New Zealand Today: Ngā Tika Tangata o te Motu* Auckland: Human Rights Commission.

Hunter, A. J. (1985) 'Private, parochial and public social orders: the problem of crime and incivility in urban communities', in G. D. Suttles and M. N. Zald (eds.) *The Challenge of Social Control: Citizenship and institution building in modern society* Norwood, NJ: Aldex.

Hurley, D. (2002) 'I'm sorry – but I won't apologise: practical aspects of apologies in mediation', address to the New Zealand Institute for Dispute Resolution, July.

Hwang, K. K. (1987) 'Face and favor: the Chinese power game' *American Journal of Sociology* 92 (4), pp. 944–974.

Hwang, K. K. (1999) 'Filial piety and loyalty: two types of social identification in Confucianism' *Asian Journal of Social Psychology* 2, pp. 129–149.

Indiana University (2005) 'Lisa B. Bingham' *Media Relations* retrieved from http://newsinfo.iu.edu/sb/page/normal/274.html.

Jackson, M. (1988) *The Maori and the Criminal Justice System: A new perspective: He Whaipaanga Hou Part 2* Wellington: Department of Justice.

Johnson, A. W., and T. Earle (2000) *The Evolution of Human Societies* 2nd edition, Stanford, CA: Stanford University Press.

Johnson, B. R., and D. B. Larson (2003) *The InnerChange Freedom Initiative: A preliminary evaluation of a faith based prison program* Pennsylvania: Center for Research on Religion and Urban Civil Society, University of Pennsylvania.

Johnstone, G., and D. Van Ness (2007a) 'Introduction', in G. Johnstone and D. Van Ness (eds.) *Handbook of Restorative Justice* Cullhompton, Devon: Willan.

Johnstone, G., and D. Van Ness (eds.) (2007b) *Handbook of Restorative Justice* Cullhompton, Devon: Willan.

Jones, W., and S. H. Hughes (2003) 'Complexity, conflict resolution, and how the mind works' *Conflict Resolution Quarterly* 20 (4), pp. 485–494.

Jose, P. (2006) 'From Darwin to Piaget: the development and acquisition of moral beliefs', in A. J. W. Taylor (ed.) *Justice as a Basic Human Need* chapter 4, New York: Nova Science.

Joseph, R. (2001) *Denial, Acknowledgement and Peace Building through Reconciliatory Justice* Te Mātāhauariki Research Institute working paper, Hamilton: University of Waikato, retrieved 30 April 2006 from http://lianz.waikato.ac.nz/papers/rob/denial.pdf.

Keelan, T. J. (2004) 'Ka pū te ruha, ka hao te rangatahi: a model of human development in Aotearoa', in W. Drewery and L. Bird (eds.) *Human Development in Aotearoa* 2nd edition, pp. 43–47, Sydney: McGraw-Hill.

Keeley, L. W. (1996) *War before Civilization* Oxford: Oxford University Press.

Kelley, H. H. (1979) *Personal Relationships: Their structures and processes* Hillsdale, NJ: Lawrence Erlbaum Associates.

Kelley, H. H., and J. Thibaut (1978) *Interpersonal Relations: A theory of interdependence* New York: Wiley.

Kelley, T., and J. Littman (2001) *The Art of Innovation: Lessons in creativity from IDEO, America's leading design firm* New York: Doubleday.

Kelsey, J. (1995) *The New Zealand Experiment* Auckland: Auckland University Press.

Kim, S. (1999) 'Review of *When Sorry Isn't Enough: The controversy over apologies and reparations for human injustice* by Roy L. Brooks (editor)' *Law and Politics Book Review* 9 (12), pp. 558–562, retrieved 1 June 2007 from http://www.bsos.umd.edu/gvpt/lpbr/subpages/reviews/brooks2.html.

# References

King, A. (Minister of Health) (2001) 'Former Lake Alice patients to receive Crown aid' *New Zealand Government* 8 October, retrieved 25 August from http://www.beehive.govt.nz/ViewDocument.aspx?DocumentID=12066.

King, D. S. (1988) 'New Right ideology, welfare state form, and citizenship: a comment on conservative capitalism' *Comparative Studies in Society and History* 30 (4), pp. 792–799.

Kolb, D. M., and J. Williams (2000) *The Shadow Negotiation: How women can master the hidden agendas that determine bargaining success* New York: Simon and Schuster.

Kubler-Ross, E. (1997) *The Wheel of Life: A memoir of living and dying* New York: Scribner.

Kurtines, W. N., and J. L. Gewirtz (eds.) (1991) *Handbook of Moral Behaviour* New Jersey: Lawrence Erlbaum.

Ladley, A. (2005) 'The treaty and democratic government' *Policy Quarterly* 1 (1), pp. 21–27.

Ladley, A. (2006) 'The human condition as evidenced in the International Bill of Rights', in A. J. W. Taylor (ed.) *Justice as a Basic Human Need* chapter 13, New York: Nova Science.

Lange, D. (2005) *My Life* Auckland: Penguin/Viking.

Laub, J., and R. J. Sampson (2001) 'Understanding desistance from crime', in M. Tonry and N. Morris (eds.) *Crime and Justice* pp. 1–70, Chicago, Ill: University of Chicago.

Lazare, A. (2004) *On Apology* New York: Oxford University Press.

Lazarus, L. (2005) 'A conversation with Professor Leonard Riskin about mindfulness, dispute resolution and mindfulness resources for mediators' *Mediate.com* retrieved from http://www.mediate.com/pfriendly.cfm?id=1695.

Lederach, J. P. (2005) Conflict management in other countries: partiality as beneficial for mediator' *Mediate.com* retrieved from http://www.mediate.com.

LeResche, D. (ed.) (1993) 'Special edition: Native American perspectives in peacemaking' *Mediation Quarterly* 10 (4).

Lerner, M. J. (1980) *The Belief in a Just World: A fundamental delusion* New York: Plenum.

Lerner, M. J. (1981) 'The justice motive in human relations: some thoughts about what we know and what we need to know about justice', in M. J. Lerner and S. C. Lerner (eds.) *The Justice Motive in Social Behavior: Adapting to times of scarcity and change* pp. 11–35, New York: Plenum.

Lerner, M. J. (2003) 'The justice motive: where social psychologists found it, how they lost it, and why they may not find it again' *Personality and Social Psychology Review* 7 (4), pp. 388–399.

Lerner, M. J., D. T. Miller and J. G. Holmes (1976) 'Deserving and the emergence of forms of justice', in L. Berkowitz (ed.) *Advances in Experimental Social Psychology* vol. 9, pp. 133–162, New York: Academic.

Leung, K. (1988) 'Some determinants of conflict avoidance' *Journal of Cross-cultural Psychology* 19 (1), pp. 125–136.

Leung, K., and M. W. Morris (2001) 'Justice through the lens of culture and ethnicity', in J. Sanders and V. Hamilton (eds.) *Handbook of Justice Research in Law* pp. 343–378, New York: Kluwer.

Leventhal, G. S. (1976) 'The distribution of rewards and resources in groups and organizations' *Advances in Experimental Social Psychology* 9, pp. 91–131.

Leventhal, G. S. (1980) 'What should be done with equity theory? New approaches to the study of fairness in social relationships', in K. J. Gergen, M. S. Greenling and R. H. Willis (eds.) *Social Exchange: Advances in theory and research* pp. 27–55, New York: Plenum.

Levine, M., A. Eagle, S. Tuiavi'i and C. Roseveare (1998) *Creative Youth Justice Practice* Wellington: Social Policy Agency and Children, Young Persons and their Family Service.

Levine, M., and Wyn, H. (1991 *Evaluation of Orders of the Youth Court: Interim statistical report on orders made November 1989 to December 1990* Wellington: Department of Social Welfare.

Lewin, K. (1947) 'Frontiers in group dynamics, I' *Human Relations* 1 (1), pp. 2–38.

Lind, E. A. (2000) 'Social justice', in A. E Kazdin (ed.) *Encyclopedia of Psychology* vol. 7, pp. 346–347, Washington, DC: American Psychological Association.

Lind, E. A., C. T. Kulik, M. Ambrose and M. V. de Vera Park (1993) 'Individual and corporate dispute resolution: using procedural fairness as a decision heuristic' *Administrative Science Quarterly* 38, pp. 224–251.

Lind, E. A., and T. Tyler (1988) *The Social Psychology of Procedural Justice* New York: Plenum.

Lipsey, M., and J. Derzon (1998) 'Predictors of violent or serious delinquency in adolescence and early adulthood', in R. Loeber and D. Farrington (eds.) *Serious and Violent Juvenile Offenders: Risk factors and successful interventions* Thousand Oaks, CA: Sage.

Lipsky, D. B., and A. C. Avgar (2004) 'Commentary: Research on employment dispute resolution: towards a new paradigm' *Conflict Resolution Quarterly* 22 (1), pp. 175–189.

Liu, J. H. (2005) 'History and identity: a system of checks and balances for Aotearoa/New Zealand', in J. H. Liu, T. McCreanor, T. McIntosh and T. Teaiwa (eds.) *New Zealand Identities: Departures and destinations* pp. 69–87, Wellington: Victoria University Press.

Liu, J. H., and S. H Liu (2003) 'The role of the social psychologist in the "benevolent authority" and "plurality of powers" systems of historical affordance for authority', in K. S. Yang, K. K. Hwang, P. B. Pedersen and I. Daibo (eds.) *Progress in Asian Social Psychology: Conceptual and empirical contributions* pp. 43–66, Westport, CT; Praeger.

Lo, W., G. M. Maxwell and D. S. W. Wong (2006) 'Diversion from Youth Courts in five Asia Pacific jurisdictions' *International Journal of Offender Therapy and Comparative Criminology* 50, pp. 5–20.

Luke, G., and B. Lind (2002) 'Reducing juvenile crime: Conferencing versus court' *Crime and Justice Bulletin* 69.

# References

Luna, E. (2000) 'Reason and emotion in restorative justice', lecture, New Zealand Institute for Dispute Resolution, Victoria University of Wellington, 5 July, retrieved from http://www.scoop.co.nz/archive/scoop/stories/51/19/200007051755.74daa57b.html.

Lundin, R. W. (1996) *Theories and Systems of Psychology* 5th edition, Lexington, MA: Heath & Co.

Macfarlane, A. H. (2000) 'The value of Maori ecologies in special education', in D. Fraser, R. Moltzen and K. Ryba (eds.) *Learners with Special Needs* 2nd edition, Palmerston North: Dunmore Press.

MacRae, A., and H. Zehr (2004) *The Little Book of Family Group Conferences: New Zealand style* Intercourse, PA: Good Books.

Marmot, M. (2005) 'Social determinants of health inequalities' *The Lancet* 365, pp. 1,099–1,104.

Marshall, C. D. (2001) *Beyond Retribution: A new testament vision for justice, crime and punishment* Grand Rapids, Mich.: Eerdmans.

Marshall, C. D. (2006) 'The meaning of justice: insights from the biblical tradition', in A. J. W. Taylor (ed.) *Justice as a Basic Human Need* chapter 3, New York: Nova Science.

Marshall, J., and D. Marshall (1997) *Discipline and Punishment in New Zealand Education* Palmerston North: Dunmore Press.

Maruna, S. (2001) *Making Good: How ex-convicts reform and rebuild their lives* Washington, DC: American Psychological Association.

Maslow, A. H. (1943) 'A theory of human motivation' *Psychological Review* 50, pp. 370–396.

Maslow, A. H. (1954/1970) *Motivation and Personality* New York: Harper & Row.

Maslow, A. H. (1968/1999) *Toward a Psychology of Being* 3rd edition, Canada: John Wiley & Sons.

Maxwell, G. M. (2004a) 'Achieving effective outcomes in youth justice' *Social Work Now* (December), pp. 17–23.

Maxwell, G. M. (2004b) 'Youth justice: a research perspective' *Social Work Now* (August), pp. 4–10.

Maxwell, G.M. (2005) 'Achieving effective outcomes in youth justice: implications of new research for principles, policy and practice', in E. Elliot and R.M. Gordon (eds.) *New Directions in Restorative Justice: Issues, practice, evaluation* chapter 3, Cullompton, Devon: Willan.

Maxwell, G. M., and H. Hayes (2006) 'Restorative justice: developments in the Pacific region: a comprehensive survey' *Contemporary Justice Review* 9 (2), pp. 127–154.

Maxwell, G. M., and H. Hayes (2007) 'Pacific', in G. Johnstone and D. Van Ness (eds.) *Handbook of Restorative Justice* section F in chapter 24, pp. 519–529, Cullompton, Devon: Willan.

Maxwell, G. M., V. Kingi, J. Robertson, A. Morris and C Cunningham (2004a) *Achieving Effective Outcomes in Youth Justice: Final report* Wellington: Ministry of Social Development.

Maxwell, G. M., and A. Morris (1993) *Families Victims and Culture: Youth justice in New Zealand* Wellington: Social Policy Agency and Institute of Criminology, Victoria University of Wellington.

Maxwell, G. M., and A. Morris (1996) 'Research on family group conferences with young offenders in New Zealand', in J. Hudson, A. Morris, G. M. Maxwell and B. Galaway (eds.) (1996) *Family Group Conferences: Perspectives on policy and practice* pp. 108–110, Annandale: Federation Press.

Maxwell, G. M., and A. Morris (1999a) *Community Panel Adult Pre-trial Diversion* Wellington: Crime Prevention Unit, in association with Institute of Criminology, Victoria University of Wellington.

Maxwell, G. M., and A. Morris (1999b) *Understanding Reoffending* Wellington: Institute of Criminology, Victoria University of Wellington.

Maxwell, G. M., and A. Morris (2001) 'Family group conferences and reoffending', in A. Morris and G. Maxwell (eds.) *Restorative Justice for Juveniles* Oxford: A. Hart.

Maxwell, G. M., and A. Morris (2002a) 'Restorative justice and reconviction' *Contemporary Justice Review* 5, pp. 133–146.

Maxwell, G. M., and A. Morris (2002b) 'The role of shame, guilt and remorse in restorative processes for young people' in E. G. M. Weitekamp and H. Kerner (eds.) *Restorative Justice: Theoretical foundations* chapter 13, Cullompton, Devon: Willan.

Maxwell, G. M., and A. Morris (2006) 'Meeting human needs: the potential of restorative justice', in A. J. W. Taylor (ed.) *Justice as a Basic Human Need* chapter 7, New York: Nova Science.

Maxwell, G. M., A. Morris and P. Shepherd (1997) *Being a Youth Advocate: An analysis of their role and responsibilities* Wellington: Institute of Criminology.

Maxwell, G. M., A. Morris and T. Anderson (1999) *Community Panel Adult Pre-Trial Diversion: Supplementary evaluation* Wellington: Crime Prevention Unit, Department of Prime Minister and Cabinet, and Institute of Criminology, Victoria University of Wellington.

Maxwell, G. M., and J. Paulin (2004) *The Impact of Police Responses to Young Offenders with a Particular Focus on Diversion* report to New Zealand Police, Wellington: Crime and Justice Research Centre, Victoria University of Wellington.

Maxwell, G. M., J. Robertson and T. Anderson (2002) *Police Youth Diversion: Final report* Wellington: Crime and Justice Research Centre, Victoria University of Wellington.

Maxwell, G. M., J. Robertson, V. Kingi, A. Morris, and C. Cunningham (2004b) *Achieving Effective Outcomes in Youth Justice: An overview of findings* Wellington: Ministry of Social Development.

McCold, P. (2000) 'Toward a mid-range theory of restorative criminal justice: a reply to the Maximalist model' *Contemporary Justice Review* 3 (4), pp. 357–414.

McCold, P. (2004) 'Paradigm muddle: the threat to restorative justice posed by the merger with community justice' *Contemporary Justice Review* 7 (1), pp. 13–35.

McElrea, F. W. M. (1994a) 'The intent of the Children, Young Persons, and Their Families Act 1989: restorative justice?' *Youth Law Review* (July/August/September), retrieved from http://www.restorativejustice.org/resources/docs/mcElrea18.

# References

McElrea, F. W. M. (1994b) 'Restorative justice: The New Zealand Youth Court: a model for development in other courts' *Journal of Judicial Administration* 4 (1), pp. 33–54.

McElrea, F. W. M. (2001) 'Restoring justice', address to Organisation of Commonwealth Caribbean Bar Associations' fourth conference *Law Forum 2001* Nassau, Bahamas, 24–26 May.

McElrea, F. W. M. (2002) 'Restorative Justice: a New Zealand perspective', conference paper for *Modernising Criminal Justice: New World Challenges* London, 16–20 June, retrieved 4 April 2004 from http://www.library.napier.govt.nz/mcelrea/restorative_justice_nz_perspective.htm.

McElrea, F. W. M. (2006) 'Restorative justice: a New Zealand perspective', in D. J. Cornwall *Criminal Punishment and Restorative Justice* pp. 119–134, Winchester: Waterside Press.

Mead, H. M. (2003) 'Speech on the Occasion of the Signing of the Ngati Awa Deed of Settlement with the Crown at Parliament Buildings, Wellington, on Thursday 27th March' *Ngati Awa* retrieved 30 April 2006 from http://www.ngatiawa.iwi.nz/documents/settlement/NADSS_27thMar.pdf.

Menkel-Meadows, C. (1995) 'The many ways of mediation: the transformation of traditions, ideologies, paradigms, and practices' *Negotiation Journal* 11 (3), pp. 217–242.

Menkel-Meadows, C. (2001) 'Book review: Negotiating with lawyers, men, and things: the contextual approach still matters' *Negotiation Journal* 17 (3), pp. 257–293.

Metge, J. (1986) *In and Out of Touch: Whakamaa in cross-cultural context* Wellington: Victoria University Press.

Metge, J. (2001) *Korero Tahi: Talking together* Auckland: AUP.

Miller, S. (1996) *Shame in Context* Hillsdale: Analytic Press.

Ministerial Advisory Committee on a Maori Perspective (1988) *Puao-Te-Ata-Tu (Day Break)* Wellington: Department of Social Welfare.

Ministerial Taskforce on Youth Offending (2002) *Youth Offending Strategy: Preventing and reducing offending and re-offending by children and young people: Te Haonga* Wellington: Ministry of Justice and Ministry of Social Development.

Ministry of Education (1999) *Guidance for Principals and Boards of Trustees on Stand-Downs, Suspensions, Exclusions, and Expulsions* Wellington, Ministry of Education.

Ministry of Education (2005) *Report on Stand-Downs, Suspensions, Exclusions and Expulsions 2004* retrieved 5 October 2005 from http://www.minedu.govt.nz/index.cfm?layout=document&documentid=10412&indexid=5611&indexparentid=1072.

Ministry of Education (2006a) *Educate: Ministry of Education statement of intent 2006–2011* Wellington: Ministry of Education.

Ministry of Education (2006b) *How the Decile is Calculated* http://www.minedu.govt.nz/index.cfm?layout=document&documentid=7697&data=l.

Ministry of Education (2006c) *Te Kotahitanga* retrieved 27 May 2007 from http://www.minedu.govt.nz/index.cfm?layout=document&documentid=8771&data=l&goto=00.

Ministry of Education (2007a) *A Report on New Zealand Student Engagement 2006* Wellington: Ministry of Education, retrieved 19 June 2007 from http://www.educationcounts.edcentre.govt.nz/themes/downloads/student-engagement-2006.pdf.

Ministry of Education (2007b) *Stand-Downs and Suspensions from School* Wellington: Ministry of Education, retrieved 27 May 2007 from http://educationcounts.edcentre.govt.nz/indicators/downloads/simu5-Suspensions.pdf.

Ministry of Education (2007c) *Statement of Intent 2007–2012* Wellington: Ministry of Education, retrieved 28 May 2007 from http://www.minedu.govt.nz/web/downloadable/dl11939_v1/ministry-of-education-soi-2007-2012.pdf.

Ministry of Social Development (2004) *The Social Report: Indicators of social wellbeing in New Zealand* Wellington: Ministry of Social Development.

Mnookin, R. H., S. R. Peppet and A. S. Tulumello (2000) *Beyond Winning: Negotiating to create value in deals and disputes* Cambridge Mass.: Bellknap Press of Harvard University Press.

Monk, G., J. Winslade, K. Crocket and D. Epston (eds.) (1997) *Narrative Therapy in Practice: The archaeology of hope* San Francisco: Jossey-Bass.

Moore, C (1996) *The Mediation Process: Practical strategies for resolving conflict* San Francisco: Jossey-Bass.

Morris, A., and G. M. Maxwell (2001) 'Restorative conferencing', in G. Bazemore and M. Schiff (eds.) *Restorative Community Justice: Repairing harm and transforming communities* pp. 173–197, Cincinnati, OH: Anderson.

Morris, A., and G. M. Maxwell (2003) 'Demystifying family group conferences' *New Zealand Law Journal* (April), pp. 94–95.

Morris, A., and G. M. Maxwell (eds.) (1999) *Youth Justice in Focus* proceedings of Australasian conference, Wellington, 27–30 October 1998, Wellington: Institute of Criminology, Victoria University of Wellington.

Morris, A., G. M. Maxwell and P. Shepherd (1997) *Being a Youth Advocate: An analysis of their roles and responsibilities* Wellington: Institute of Criminology.

Morris, A., and W. Young (1987) *Juvenile Justice in New Zealand: Policy and practice* study series 1, Wellington: Institute of Criminology, Victoria University of Wellington.

Morris, A., and W. Young (2000) 'Reforming criminal justice: the potential of restorative justice', in H. Strang and J. Braithwaite (eds.) *Restorative Justice: From philosophy to practice* chapter 2, Aldershot: Ashgate.

Moxon, J. (no date) 'The restorative chat', Massey High School, New Zealand.

Murphy, N. (2003) *The Poll Tax in New Zealand: A research paper* Wellington: Office of Ethnic Affairs.

NAACP Legal Defense and Educational Fund (no date) *Dismantling the School-to-Prison Pipeline* retrieved 29 June 2007 from http://www.naacpldf.org/content/pdf/pipeline/Dismantling_the_School_to_Prison_Pipeline.pdf.

# References

Nader, L. (1969) *Law in Culture and Society* California: University of California Press.

New Zealand Law Commission (2004) *Delivering Justice for All: A vision for New Zealand courts and tribunals* NZLC R85, Wellington: New Zealand Law Commission.

Niebuhr, R. (1963) *An Interpretation of Christian Ethics* San Francisco: Harper & Row.

Nino, C. S. (1991) 'The duty to punish past abuses of human rights put into context: the case of Argentina' *Yale Law Journal* 100 (2,619), pp. 2,547–2,615.

Noddings, N. (2003) *Caring: A feminist approach to ethics and moral education* 2nd edition, Berkeley: University of California Press.

Nussbaum, M. C. (1993) 'Equity and mercy' *Philosophy and Public Affairs* 22 (2), pp. 83–125.

O'Donohue, W. (1989) 'The (even) bolder model' *American Psychologist* 44 (12), pp. 1,460–1,468.

Office of Ethnic Affairs (2003) *Analysis Summary* retrieved 25 August 2005 from http://www.ethnicaffairs.govt.nz/oeawebsite.nsf.

Office of Treaty Settlements (1994) *Crown Proposals for the Settlement of Treaty of Waitangi Claims: Summary* Wellington: Office of Treaty Settlements.

Office of Treaty Settlements (1995) *Report of Submissions: Crown proposals for the Treaty of Waitangi claims* Wellington: Office of Treaty Settlements.

Office of Treaty Settlements (1999) *Healing the Past, Building a Future: A guide to Treaty of Waitangi claims and direct negotiations with the Crown – Ka Tika ā Muri, Ka Tika ā Mua: He tohutohu whakamārama i ngā whakatau kerēme e pā ana ki Te Tiriti ō Waitangi me ngā whakaritenga ki te Karauna* Wellington: Office of Treaty Settlements.

Office of Treaty Settlements (2002) *Healing the Past, Building a Future: A guide to Treaty of Waitangi claims and negotiations with the Crown – Ka Tika ā Muri, Ka Tika ā Mua: He tohutohu whakamārama i ngā whakataunga kerēme e pā ana ki te Tiriti o Waitangi me ngā whakaritenga ki te Karauna* 2nd edition, Wellington: Office of Treaty Settlements.

O'Regan, T. (2001) 'Old myths and new politics: some contemporary uses of traditional history', in J. Binney (ed.) *The Shaping of History: Essays from the New Zealand Journal of History* pp. 19–23, Wellington: Bridget Williams Books.

Oliver, W. H. (1993) 'Getting facts on your side: Waikato Raupatu Claims Settlement Act 1995' *New Zealand Books* 5 (5), p. 15.

Olthoff, T. (2000) 'Shame, guilt, anti-social behaviour and juvenile justice: a psychological perspective', paper presented at *Punishing Children* 8 and 9 June, Utrecht.

Opotow, S. (1994) 'Predicting protection: scope of justice and the natural world' *Journal of Social Issues* 50 (3), pp. 49–63.

Oruvwuje, P. R., and A. J. W. Taylor (2006) 'Mental health consumers, social justice and the historical antecedents of oppression', in A. J. W. Taylor (ed.) *Justice as a Basic Human Need* chapter 9, New York: Nova Science.

Page N., and C. Czuba (1999) 'Empowerment: what is it?' *Journal of Extension* 37 (5), retrieved 3 September 2006 from http://www.joe.org/joe/1999october/comm1.html.

Peacemakers Trust (no date) *Pathways toward Reconciliation: Research and education*, http://www.peacemakers.ca/research/Reconciliation.

Phillips, V. (1995) 'Mediation: the influence of style and gender on disputants' perceptions of justice' *New Zealand Journal of Industrial Relations* 21 (3), pp. 297–311.

Porter, L. W., G. A. Bigley and R. M. Steers (eds.) (2003) *Motivation and Work Behaviour* 7th edition, New York: McGraw-Hill.

Preston, S. D., and F. B. M. de Waal (2002) 'Empathy: its ultimate and proximate bases' *Behavioral and Brain Sciences* 25 (1), pp. 1–72.

Pringle, K. L. (1996) 'Aboriginal mediation: one step towards re-empowerment' *Australian Dispute Resolution Journal* 7 (4), pp. 253–270.

Public Health Advisory Committee (2004) *The Health of People and Communities: A way forward: Public policy and economic determinants of health* Wellington: Public Health Advisory Committee.

Putnam, R. (2000) *Bowling Alone: The collapse and revival of American community* New York: Simon & Schuster.

Rappaport, J. (1981) 'In praise of paradox: a social policy of empowerment over prevention' *American Journal of Community Psychology* 9 (1), pp. 1–25.

Rappaport, J. (1984) 'Studies in empowerment: introduction to the issue' *Prevention in Human Services* 3, pp. 1–7.

Rawls, J. (1971) *A Theory of Justice* Cambridge, Mass: Belknap Press of Harvard University Press/Oxford: Oxford University Press.

Rawls, J. (1993) 'Justice as fairness: political not metaphysical', in M. Fisk (ed.) *Justice* chapter 4, New Jersey: Humanities.

Redfern, M. (2005) 'A place for the courts in the dispute resolution *Australian Dispute Resolution Journal* 16, pp. 79–84.

Renouf, J., A. Lagzdins and J. Angus (1989) *Children, Young Persons, and Their Families Act 1989: The process of policy development* Wellington: Ministry of Social Welfare.

Restorative Practices Development Team (2004) *Restorative Practices in Schools: A resource* Hamilton: School of Education, University of Waikato.

Riskin, L. L., and Westbrook, J. E. (1988) *Dispute Resolution and Lawyers* American Casebook Series, Missouri: West Group.

Ritchie, J. (2005) 'Te ao po – te ao marama: New Zealand character: the light and the dark', paper presented at *Towards a Restorative Society* 10 and 11 October, Wellington.

Ritchie, J., and J. Ritchie (1993) *Violence in New Zealand* Wellington: Huia.

Ritchie, J., and J. Ritchie (2002) 'The rainbow path to overcoming violence', in P. Garside (ed.) *Overcoming Violence in Aotearoa New Zealand* pp. 8–17, Wellington: Philip Garside.

Robertson, B. (2003) 'Editorial' *New Zealand Law Journal* (May), p. 141.

Rokeach, M. (1976) *Beliefs, Attitudes and Values: A theory of organization and change* San Francisco: Jossey-Bass.

Ross, M., and D. T. Miller (2002a) *Justice and Empathy* New York: Cambridge University Press.

# References

Ross, M., and D. T. Miller (eds.) (2002b) *The Justice Motive in Everyday Life* Cambridge, UK: Cambridge University Press.

Rothfield, J. (2004) 'Is it really just about the money?' *Australian Dispute Resolution Journal* 15, pp. 188–193.

Royal Commission on Social Policy (1988a) *The April Report* Wellington: Government Printer.

Royal Commission on Social Policy (1988b) *Towards a Just and Fair Society* Wellington: Government Printer.

Ruhl, J. B. (1997) 'Thinking of mediation as a complex adaptive system' *Brigham Young University Law Review* retrieved from http:/www.findarticles.com/p/articles/mi_qa3736/is_199701/ai_n8741985.

Rutter, M. (1979) *Fifteen Thousand Hours: Secondary schools and their effects on children* London: Open Books.

Sampson, R., and J. Wilson (1995) 'Toward a theory of race', in J. Hagan and R. D. Peterson (eds.) *Crime and Urban Inequality* pp. 37–45, Stanford, CA: Stanford University Press.

Satyanand, A. (interviewee) (2006) Transcript of Radio New Zealand interview *Morning Report* 6–7 am, 14 February.

Schmid, D. J. (2003) 'Restorative justice: a new paradigm for criminal justice policy' *Victoria University of Wellington Law Review* 34, pp. 91–133, retrieved 17 September 2005 from http://www.austlii.edu.au/au/journals/VUWLRev/2003/4.html.

Schneider, C. D. (2000) 'What it means to be sorry: the power of apology' *Mediation Quarterly* 17 (3), pp. 265–280.

Schreier, L. S. (2002) 'Emotional intelligence and mediation training' *Conflict Resolution Quarterly* 20 (1), pp. 99–119.

Scott, M. (2004) 'Collaborative law: a new role of lawyers' *Australian Dispute Resolution Journal* 15 (3), pp. 207–216.

Senge, P. M., C. O. Scharmer, J. Jaworski and B. S. Flowers (2004) *Presence: Human purpose and the field of the future* Cambridge, MA: Society for Organizational Learning.

Serventy, N. (2002) 'NLP for mediators: understanding and influencing yourself and others' *Australian Dispute Resolution Journal* 13 (4), pp. 201–209.

Shearhouse, S. (2003) 'Reader response: Emotional intelligence and mediation training' *Conflict Resolution Quarterly* 20 (4), pp. 501–504.

Sherman L., D. Gottfredson, D. Mackenzie, J. Eck, P. Reuter et al. (1997) *Preventing Crime: What works, what doesn't, what's promising* Baltimore: Department of Criminology and Criminal Justice, University of Maryland.

Sherman, L. W., H. Strang and D. Woods (2000) *Recidivism Patterns in Canberra Reintegrative Shaming Experiment (RISE)* Canberra: Centre for Restorative Justice, Research School of Social Sciences, Institute of Advanced Studies, Australian National University.

Shields, M. (1979) 'Social indicator development in New Zealand', in C. D. Cant, D. Hill and M. Watson (eds.) *Social Indicators for Development Planning in New Zealand* pp. 15–35, Wellington: National Commission for UNESCO and New Zealand Social Development Council.

Shy, Y. (2006) 'Restorative justice jurisprudence in New Zealand (1998–2005)', postgraduate research paper submitted for degree of Juris Doctor at Northeastern University School of Law, Massachusetts.

Skiba, R., and R. Peterson (1999) 'The dark side of zero tolerance: can punishment lead to safe schools?' *Phi Delta Kappa International* retrieved 20 January 2006 from http://www.pdkintl.org/kappan/kski9901.htm.

Skiba, R., A. Simmons, L. Staudinger, M. Rausch, G. Dow et al. (2003) *Consistent Removal: Contributions of school discipline to the school–prison pipeline* Indiana: Indiana Education Policy Centre, Indiana University, School to Prison Pipeline Conference Harvard Civil Rights Project.

Skitka, L. J. (2002) 'Do the means always justify the ends, or do the ends sometimes justify the means? A value protection model of justice reasoning' *Personality and Social Psychological Bulletin* 28, pp. 588–597.

Skitka, L. J. (2003) 'Of different minds: An accessible identity model of justice reasoning' *Personality and Social Psychology Review* 7 (4), pp. 286–297.

Sluka, J. A. (2006) 'On common ground: justice and survival', in A. J. W. Taylor (ed.) *Justice as a Basic Human Need* chapter 11, New York: Nova Science.

Smith, L., and F. Cram (1998) *An Evaluation of the Community Panel Diversion Pilot Programme* Auckland: Auckland UniServices.

Smith, M. (2005) 'Restorative justice is a human right: a transformative discourse within UN paradigms', paper presented to Eleventh United Nations Congress on Crime Prevention and Criminal Justice, Bangkok (private circulation).

Spiller, P. (1999) *Dispute Resolution in New Zealand* Auckland: Oxford University Press.

Stahura, B. (2001) 'Law that heals' *Renaissance Lawyer Society* retrieved from http://www.renaissancelawyer.com/law_that_heals.htm.

Stern, V. (2004) 'Are prisoners enemies or citizens? What is the responsibility of the state?' *Justice Reflections* 6.

Stouffer, S. A., E. A. Suchman, L. C. DeVinney, S. A. Star and R. M. Williams Jr (1949) 'Adjustment during army life' *The American soldier* vol 1, Princeton, NJ: Princeton University Press.

Stowers, P. (2005) 'Cultural differences from an anecdotal perspective', unpublished training paper to Wellington Mediation Team, Department of Labour.

Strang, H. (2002) *Repair or Revenge: Victims and restorative justice* Oxford: Clarendon.

Sullivan, D., and L. Tifft (2006) *Handbook of Restorative Justice* London: Routledge.

Sullivan, M. (1989) *Getting Paid: Youth, crime and work in the inner city* Ithaca, NY: Cornell University Press.

Summerfield, D. (2000) 'Conflict and health: war and mental health: a brief overview' *British Medical Journal* 321, pp. 232–235.

# References

Tangaere, A. R. (1997) 'Māori development learning theory', in P. Te Whaiti, M. McCarthy and A. Durie (eds.) *Mai I Rangiatea: Māori well-being and development* pp. 46–59, Wellington: Auckland University Press.

Tangney, J. (1991) 'Moral affect: the good, the bad and the ugly' *Journal of Personality and Social Psychology* 61 (4), pp. 598–607.

Tangney, J. P., and R. L. Dearing (2002) *Shame and Guilt* New York: Guilford Press.

Taylor, A. J. W. (2003) 'Bringing complex terrorism and corporate malfeasance into a classification schema for disasters' *Australian Journal of Emergency Management* 18 (1), pp. 27–34.

Taylor, A. J. W. (2006) 'Dovetailing justice into a framework of needs', in A. J. W. Taylor (ed.) *Justice as a Basic Human Need* chapter 14, New York: Nova Science.

Taylor, S. E., and J. D. Brown (1988) 'Illusion and well-being: a social psychological perspective on mental health' *Psychological Bulletin* 103 (2), pp. 193–210.

Te Rūnanga o Ngāi Tahu (no date) 'The apology', *Te Rūnanga o Ngāi Tahu* (condensed but updated version of Te Karaka Special Edition Crown Settlement Offer, which was a consultation document sent out from the Ngāi Tahu Negotiating Group in November 1998), retrieved 30 April 2006 from http://www.ngaitahu.iwi.nz/About%20Ngai%20Tahu/The%20Settlement/The%20Crowns%20Settlement%20Offer/The%20Apology.

Thibaut, J., and L. Walker (1975) *Procedural Justice* Hillsdale, NJ: Lawrence Erlbaum.

Tolman, C. W. (2006) 'Agency and the need for justice', in A. J. W. Taylor (ed.) *Justice as a Basic Human Need* chapter 2, New York: Nova Science.

'Treaty of Waitangi' (2002–05) *Political Policy Online* retrieved 21 November 2005 from http://www.policy.net.nz/tw.shtml.

Trépanier, J. (1998) 'Restorative justice: a question of legitimacy', in L Walgrave (ed.) *Restorative Justice for Juveniles: Potentialities, risks and problems* a selection of papers from the international conference of the International Network for Research on Restorative Justice for Juveniles, Leuven, 12–14 May 1997, pp. 55-73, Belgium: Leuven University Press,.

Triggs, S. (2005) *New Zealand Court-Referred Restorative Justice Pilot: Two year follow-up of reoffending* Wellington: Ministry of Justice.

Truth and Reconciliation Commission (2003) *Truth and Reconciliation Commission of South Africa Report* retrieved from http://www.info.gov.za/otherdocs/2003/trc.

Tyler, T., and S. Blader (2000) *Cooperation in Groups: Procedural justice, social identity, and behavioural engagement* Philadelphia: Psychology Press.

Tyler, T., and R. Boeckmann (1997) 'Three strikes and you are out, but why? The psychology of public support for punishing rule breakers' *Law & Society Review* 31 (2), pp. 237–266.

Tyler, T., R. Boeckmann, H. J. Smith and Y. J. Huo (1997) *Social Justice in a Diverse Society* Denver, CO: Westview.

United Nations (2005) *In Larger Freedom: Towards development, security, and human rights for all: Report of the Secretary-General* A/59/2005. New York: United Nations.

Ury, W. L. (1995) 'Conflict resolution among the bushmen: lessons in dispute systems design' *Negotiation Journal* 11 (4), pp. 379–389.

Van der Kolk, B. (1994) 'The body keeps the score: memory and the evolving psychobiology of posttraumatic stress' *Harvard Review of Psychiatry* 5 (1), pp. 253–265.

Van Gramberg, B. (2003) 'ADR and workplace justice: just settlement?' *Australian Dispute Resolution Journal* 14, pp. 233–242.

Van Ness, D. (2002) 'The shape of things to come: a framework for thinking about a restorative justice system', in E. Weitekamp and H. Jurgen-Kerner (eds.) *Restorative Justice Theoretical Foundations* chapter 1, Cullhompton, Devon: Willan.

Van Ness, D., and K. H. Strong (1997) *Restoring Justice* Cincinnati, OH: Anderson.

Varnham, S. (2005) *Seeing Things Differently: Restorative justice and school discipline* Wellington: Massey University.

'Virtues' (no date) *7 Deadly Sins* retrieved 6 May 2004 from http://www.deadly.sins.com/virtues.html.

Wade, J. (2005) 'Mapping the deceptive dance of hard bargainers: what are the possible roles of mediators when supervising the dances of deception, delusion, and decision-making?' *Bond University Email Newsletter* 19, retrieved from http:/epublications.bond.edu.au/drcn/19.

Waitangi Tribunal (2006) *The Kaipara Report* Wellington: Legislation Direct.

Waldron, J. (2002) 'Redressing historic injustice' *University of Toronto Law Journal* 52 (1), pp. 135–160.

Waldron, J. (2003) 'The supercession thesis: the process and legacy of settlement', paper prepared for conference on Israeli settlements and related cases, Minerva Center for Human Rights, Tel Aviv University, Israel, June.

Walgrave, L. (ed.) (1998) *Restorative Justice for Juveniles: Potentialities, risks and problems* a selection of papers from the international conference of the International Network for Research on Restorative Justice for Juveniles, Leuven, 12–14 May 1997, Belgium: Leuven University Press.

Walker, P. (2005) 'Alternative dispute resolution clauses in legislation', unpublished draft.

Walster, E., G. W. Walster and E. Berscheid (1978) *Equity: Theory and research* Boston: Allyn & Bacon.

Ward, A. (2001) 'History and historians before the Waitangi Tribunal: some reflections on the Ngai Tahu claim', in J. Binney (ed.) *The Shaping of History: Essays from the New Zealand Journal of History* pp. 114–128, Wellington: Bridget Williams Books.

Ward, C., S. Bochner and A. Furnham (2001) *The Psychology of Culture Shock* 2nd edition, London: Routledge.

Ward, G. (2002) 'Apology to Samoa surprises New Zealand' *BBC News World Edition* 4 June, retrieved 18 January 2006 from http://news.bbc.co.uk/2/hi/asia-pacific/2025041.stm.

Ward, T., and M. Brown (2004) 'The good lives model and conceptual issues', in *Offender Rehabilitation, Psychology, Crime* 10 (3), pp. 243–257.

# References

Ward, T., and S. Maruna (2007) *Rehabilitation* London: Routledge, Kegan Paul.

Watt, E. (2003) 'A history of youth justice in New Zealand', paper commissioned by Principal Youth Court Judge Andrew Becroft.

Weiss, R. P. (1998) 'Conclusion: imprisonment at the Millennium 2000: its variety, and patterns throughout the world', in R. P. Weiss and N. South (eds.) *Comparing Prison Systems: Towards a comparative and international penology* chapter 14, Australia: Gordon and Breach.

Wethey, E. (2002) 'The politics of apology: issues arising from state apologies to indigenous peoples for historical injustices in Australasia and North America', unpublished master's thesis, University of Cambridge.

Wexler, D. (2006) 'Therapeutic jurisprudence', in A. J. W. Taylor (ed.) *Justice as a Basic Human Need* chapter 6, New York: Nova Science.

White, M., and D. Epston (1992) *Narrative Means to Therapeutic Ends* New York: Norton.

Williams, K. (2004) 'Maori and Pacific youth and the judiciary', keynote speech at *Ngakia Kia Puawai: New Zealand Police Conference* Auckland, 11 and 12 November.

Wilson, M. (interviewee) (2004) Transcript of Radio New Zealand interview *Nine to Noon* 7 November.

Wood, J. V., S. E. Taylor and R. R. Lichtman (1985) 'Social comparison in adjustment to breast cancer' *Journal of Personality and Social Psychology* 49 (5), pp. 1,169–1,183.

World Commission on the Social Dimension of Globalization (2004) *A Fair Globalization: Creating opportunities for all* Geneva: International Labour Office.

Wright, M. (1998) 'Victim/offender conferencing: the need for safeguards', in L Walgrave (ed.) *Restorative Justice for Juveniles: Potentialities, risks and problems* a selection of papers from the international conference of the International Network for Research on Restorative Justice for Juveniles, Leuven, 12–14 May 1997, pp. 75-91, Belgium: Leuven University Press.

Yamagishi, T. (1998) *Trust: The evolutionary game of mind and society* Tokyo: Tokyo University Press.

Yamagishi, T., and M. Yamagishi (1994) 'Trust and commitment in the United States and Japan' *Motivation and emotion* 18 (2), pp. 129–166.

Yeh, K. H., and O. Bedford (2004) 'A test of the Dual Filial Piety model' *Asian Journal of Social Psychology* 6 (3), pp. 215–228.

Yergin, D., and J. Stanislaw (1998) *The Commanding Heights: The battle for the world economy* Touchstone: New York.

Young, I. M. (1990) *Justice and the Politics of Difference* Princeton, NJ: Princeton University Press.

Young, M. A. (2001) *The Community Crisis Response Team Training Manual* 2nd edition, revised, Washington, DC: National Organization for Victim Assistance.

Young, P. M. (2000) 'Mediation and the power of apology: the case of the missing snowman' *Missouri Lawyers Weekly* (April).

Young, S. (2002) 'The Chinese Canadians' fight for redress for their Head Tax and Exclusion Act' *Chinese in New Zealand* retrieved 25 August 2005 from http://www.stevenyoung.co.nz/chinesevoice/polltax/Canadareport.htm.

Young, S. (2005) 'The New Zealand experience', presented at *Head Tax and Exclusion Act Redress Consultation Conference* 3–5 May, Canada, retrieved 25 August 2005 from http://www.stevenyoung.co.nz/chinesevoice/polltax/Canadaspeech.htm.

Yuki, M., and S. Yamaguchi (1996) 'Long-term equity within a group: an application of the seniority norm in Japan', in H. Grad, A. Blanco and J. Georgas (eds.) *Key Issues in Cross-Cultural Psychology: Selected papers from the Twelfth International Congress of the International Association for Cross-Cultural Psychology* pp. 288–297, Lisse, The Netherlands: Swets and Zeitlinger.

Zamble, E., and V. Quinsey (1997) *The Criminal Recidivism Process* Cambridge: Cambridge University Press.

Zaoui, A. (2005) 'The roots of religious extremism and our response', public lecture in religious studies programme, Victoria University of Wellington, 7 July.

Zehr, H. (1990) *Changing Lenses: A new focus for crime and justice* Scottsdale, PA: Herald Press.

Zehr, H. (1994) 'Justice that heals: the vision' *Stimulus* 2 (1), pp. 5–11.

Zehr, H. (1995) 'Rethinking criminal justice: restorative justice', reprinted in F. W. M. McElrea (ed.) *Re-thinking Criminal Justice* vol 1, p. 211, Auckland: Legal Research Foundation.

Zehr, H. (2002) 'Journey to belonging', in G. Weitekamp and H. Kerner (eds.) *Restorative Justice: Theoretical foundations* chapter 2, Cullhompton, Devon: Willan.

Zehr, H. (2004) 'Commentary: Restorative justice: beyond victim-offender mediation' *Conflict Resolution Quarterly* 22 (1–2), pp. 305–315.